WO

IN LATIN AMERICA

AND THE CARIBBEAN

WOMEN'S ACTIVISM IN LATIN AMERICA AND THE CARIBBEAN

Engendering Social Justice,

Democratizing Citizenship

EDITED BY

ELIZABETH MAIER AND

NATHALIE LEBON

FOREWORD BY

SONIA E. ALVAREZ

RUTGERS UNIVERSITY PRESS

New Brunswick, New Jersey, and London

EL COLEGIO DE LA FRONTERA NORTE A. C.

Tijuana, Mexico

Library of Congress Cataloging-in-Publication Data

Women's activism in Latin America and the Caribbean : engendering social justice, democratizing citizenship / edited by Elizabeth Maier and Nathalie Lebon ; foreword by Sonia E. Alvarez.

    p.   cm.

Includes bibliographical references and index.

ISBN 978-0-8135-4728-2 (hbk. : alk. paper) — ISBN 978-0-8135-4729-9 (pbk. : alk. paper)

1. Women in politics—Latin America. 2. Women in politics—Caribbean Area. 3. Feminism—Latin America. 4. Feminism—Caribbean Area. 5. Women— Latin America—Social conditions. 6. Women—Caribbean Area—Social conditions. I. Maier, Elizabeth. II. Lebon, Nathalie.

HQ1236.5.L37W665 2010

320.98082—dc22

2009020399

A British Cataloging-in-Publication record for this book is available from the British Library.

Chapters 1, 5, 6, 7, 11, 16, and 19 originally appeared in Spanish in *De lo privado a lo público: 30 años de lucha ciudadana de las mujeres en América Latina*, edited by Nathalie Lebon and Elizabeth Maier and published by Siglo Veintiuno in collaboration with the Latin American Studies Association and the United Nations Development Fund for Women, 2006. Translated into English and published here with permission.

Visit our Web site: http://rutgerspress.rutgers.edu

Manufactured in the United States of America

For Benita Galeana, and all the other women leaders
who came before and cleared the way for us.
For our parents, who shared their dreams.
For Leila, Roman, Adèle, Mathilde, and Samuel . . .
our hopeful next generation.

Contents

**Part IV   Broadening the Circle of Women's Activism:
             New Meanings from Intersecting Oppressions**

Part V   Shaping Public Policy with a Gender Perspective

Foreword

SONIA E. ALVAREZ

This exceptional collection is the fruit of the very processes it analyzes: the growth
and vitality of Latin American and Caribbean feminist organizing and scholarship
over the course of the past four decades and the concomitant configuration of
vibrant, multifaceted feminist academic and activist fields spanning the Americas
and beyond. While privileging the voices of feminists from South and Central
America in translation, this book is the product of ongoing transnational, transdis-
ciplinary conversations among feminists working to bridge North and South, politics and culture, the academy and the movement. Indeed, *Women's Activism in Latin
America and the Caribbean* grows out of the always lively and productive debates
enacted in an arena that has done much to facilitate transnational processes of feminist translation across the Americas: the Gender and Feminist Studies Section of
the Latin American Studies Association (LASA), a space that has fostered a diverse
and expansive network of scholars and activist-intellectuals engaged in sustained
dialogue across geopolitical, disciplinary and other borders.[1]

This first truly comprehensive anthology on Latin American women's movements and politics features essays by consecrated founding mothers of the field and
newer voices alike. Taken together, they offer a richly detailed and analytically
discerning overview of feminist cultural and political interventions in the Latin
American and Caribbean region. Unprecedented in breadth and depth, the collection provides a vivid, multidimensional picture of the heterogeneous arenas,
actions, and actors found today among the wide-ranging expressions of feminist
and women's movement organizing across the region, while affording unparalleled
insight into trends in evidence in a number of countries. The editors' incisive
introductory essays and those in the opening section on globalization, women's
work, and female-headed households, moreover, offer an overview of the complex
socioeconomic, political, and cultural context in which women's struggles for
citizenship and social justice have unfolded over the past four decades.

Perhaps the most noteworthy of the region-wide trends documented in the
chapters that follow is the pronounced visibility and expressive expansion of what
the editors and contributors variously refer to as third-wave feminism, complex-
identity feminisms, or the feminism of shifting identities. The very women whom
the hegemonic feminism of the so-called second wave viewed as "others"—poor
and working-class women, Afro-descendant and indigenous women, and lesbians—
have translated and radically transformed some of its core tenets and fashioned
other feminisms, *"feminismos con apellidos"* (Ríos et al. 2003) that are deeply

entwined, and sometimes contentiously entangled, with national and global struggles against all forms of inequality and for social, sexual, and racial justice.

As is in the case of the United States, moreover, the wave metaphor is rendered problematic by the narratives collected here, as black women, lesbians, and those "othered" are shown to have been on the frontlines of feminist organizing for decades, even when they often enacted their feminisms in autonomous or mixed movement spaces. These diverse feminisms—together with young women from all social groups and classes who proclaim themselves *feministas jóvenes*, with agendas distinct from earlier generations—have produced effervescent movement currents that proffer trenchant critiques of enduring inequalities *among women*, as well as between women and men of diverse racial and social groups, thereby expanding the scope and reach of feminist messages and revitalizing women's cultural and policy interventions across the region.

To be sure, one clear outcome of these profound and productive critiques of hegemonic feminism has been what we might call the sidestreaming of feminist politics—a second trend amply in evidence in the essays assembled in *Women's Activism in Latin America and the Caribbean*. "Trickling up, down, and sideways," as in Fiona Macaulay's apt depiction of Brazil's "multinodal women's movement" and "gender-policy community," feminism in many, if not most, countries in the region today not only has been "mainstreamed" so that it extends vertically across different levels of government, traverses much of the party spectrum, and engages with a variety of national and international policy arenas; feminism also spreads horizontally into a wide array of class and racial-ethnic communities and social and cultural spaces, including parallel social movement publics.

An emergent and internally heterogeneous *pueblo feminista*—to borrow Graciela Di Marco's evocative characterization of the "popular feminism" embraced by Argentinean *piqueteras* (picketers), women workers in recovered factories, and mothers who organize against police brutality—is brought from the margins to the center of feminist analysis in this anthology and is a marked presence in the stories here told.[2] Racial, ethnic, sexual, generational, and class differences color and variegate that pueblo's distinctive feminist politics, bringing diversity to the forefront of women's organizing.

Yet while diversity may be embraced by today's enduring, if now more scattered, feminist hegemonies, much remains to be done to challenge inequalities, redress power imbalances, and dismantle racial, class, and generational privilege and heteronormativity in politics and society and *within* the region's women's movements, as a number of the authors assembled here make painfully clear (see also Grewal and Kaplan 1994). Whereas some activists lament the dispersion and disarticulation of feminist and women's movements consequent to the decentering and pluralization of movement fields, Ana Lorena Carrillo and Norma Stoltz Chinchilla admonish against the all-too-common tendency to conflate diversity with dispersion. In the place of facile platitudes that recognize and even celebrate diversity, we need concerted political efforts by *all* feminists to put redistributive teeth into now fashionable discourses on multiculturalism—such as promoting positive discrimination and other public policies to reduce racial, class, and other inequalities.[3]

The "upward, downward, and sideways" dispersion of feminist interventions into a multiplicity of spaces and places, moreover, must be understood as at least part of what accounts for the region's feminisms' not-insignificant success in the policy and cultural realms. And the chapters make abundantly clear that feminist and women's movements have exercised considerable influence in key democratizing conjunctures: from Central American national liberation struggles and ensuing peace accords, to the transition process in Brazil and the Southern Cone, to contemporary constitutional refoundations in the Andean region.

Nonetheless, the more widespread *diffusion* and potential "massification" of feminist discourses, such as their mainstreaming into the state and policy arenas, always runs a risk of being politically *defused*—a dilemma that will continue to animate feminist debate and confound our practices.[4] Indeed, the trials and tribulations of what has been variously dubbed "institutionalized" or "state" feminism since the 1990s signal a third overarching trend covered by these collected essays. From the embattled local women's machineries of Mexico, discussed by María Luisa Tarrés, many of which have been purposefully colonized by explicitly antifeminist conservative currents, to the tergiversation of feminist understandings of violence against women evident in Costa Rican legislation, poignantly critiqued by Montserrat Sagot, many chapters attest to the fact that despite some significant policy gains the institutional terrain since the 1990s has been a slippery, when not treacherous, one for most of the region's feminisms. Several also document policy retrenchments and political backlashes that have emerged over the past decade— including the consolidation of antichoice forces in some countries.

But a fourth trend culled from the pages of this volume concerns the new challenges and opportunities that the current turn toward the Left and Center-Left and the resurgence of the National-Popular (or according to some, the rise of neopopulism) pose for feminist and women's movements in the region. If chapters by Karen Kampwirth, Morena Herrera, and Ana Lorena Carrillo and Norma Stoltz Chinchilla on the Central American liberation struggles make clear that feminism and the Left have proven strange bedfellows historically, they also show conclusively that revolutionary struggles of the 1970s and 1980s provided fertile terrain for the development of feminisms in a variety of often unrecognized ways. Several essays explore the extent to which what some have called the "Pink Tide" that has swept much of the region since the late 1990s—spanning more or less intense shades of leftist "red" governments from Venezuela to Paraguay to Brazil to Chile and backed, as in the cases of Bolivia and Ecuador, by previously marginalized ethno-racial majorities—might similarly offer fresh opportunities for feminist interventions in institutional and extrainstitutional political arenas, perhaps especially generating further space for other feminisms to flourish.[5]

Finally, *Women's Activism in Latin America and the Caribbean* highlights the manifold ways in which transnational processes—such as the periodic regional Encuentros Feministas de América Latina y el Caribe (Latin American and

Caribbean Feminist Encuentros), the string of United Nations conferences of the 1990s and their follow-up processes, feminist engagements with the anti- or alter-globalization movements and the World Social Forums, and other translocal feminist practices—have also markedly expanded the spaces for feminist and women's movement activism and influence over the past two decades. The coconstitutive dynamics of local, national, regional, and global feminisms are amply in evidence in the chapters that follow.

In sum, this invaluable collection is brimming with compelling conceptual innovations, fresh empirical insights, and provocative political analysis, setting new parameters for future studies of feminist and other social movements in politics in Latin America and the Caribbean. It is certain to become required reading for specialists and students of feminist studies, Latin American studies, comparative politics and sociology, cultural studies, critical race studies, and development studies, as well as for feminist activists and policy advocates worldwide.

NOTES

1. For more on the history of the Gender and Feminist Studies Section, see the preface of this volume.

2. Di Marco (forthcoming) develops a provocative analysis of the notion of "pueblo feminista" in her essay "Social Movement Demands, beyond Civil Society."

3. On neoliberal multiculturalism, see especially Hale (2002) and Hale and Millamán (2006).

4. Reed (2005) develops the tension between diffusion and defusion of social movement discourses.

5. On feminism, LGBTI movements, and the Pink Tide, see Friedman (2007).

REFERENCES

Davis, Kathy. 2007. *The making of "Our bodies, our selves": How feminism travels across borders.* Durham, NC: Duke University Press.

Di Marco, Graciela. Forthcoming. Social movement demands, beyond civil society? In *Interrogating the civil society agenda: Social movements, civic participation, and democratic innovation,* ed. Sonia E. Alvarez, Gianpaolo Baiocchi, Agustin Laó-Montes, Jeff Rubin, and Millie Thayer.

Friedman, Elisabeth Jay. 2007. Introd. to How pink is the "Pink Tide"? *NACLA Report on the Americas* 40 (2): 16.

Grewal, Inderpal, and Caren Kaplan. 1994. *Scattered hegemonies: Postmodernity and transnational feminist practices.* Minneapolis: University of Minnesota Press.

Hale, Charles R. 2002. Does multiculturalism menace? Governance, cultural rights and the politics of identity in Guatemala. *Journal of Latin American Studies* 34 (3): 485–524.

Hale, Charles R., and Rosamel Millamán. 2006. Cultural agency and political struggle in the era of the indio permitido. In *Cultural agency in the Americas,* ed. Doris Sommer, 281–304. Durham, NC: Duke University Press.

Reed, Thomas V. 2005. *The art of protest: Culture and activism from the civil rights movement to the streets of Seattle.* Minneapolis: University of Minnesota Press.

Ríos Tobar, Marcela, Lorena Godoy Catalán, and Elizabeth Guerrero Caviedes. 2003. *¿Un nuevo silencio feminista? La transformación de un movimiento social en el Chile postdictadura.* Santiago: Centro de Estudios de la Mujer, Cuarto Propio.

Preface

This book results ultimately from the kind of reflection impelled by an intense stage of cultural and social reorganization and renovation. It is the second volume in an effort to take stock of the significance of nearly forty years of women's agency and activism for democracy and citizenship in Latin America and the Caribbean. Indeed, it closely follows an initial anthology in Spanish, cosponsored by the United Nations Development Fund for Women (UNIFEM) and the Latin America Studies Association (LASA), and was published in 2006 to celebrate the thirtieth anniversary of the first International Women's Year. LASA's Gender and Feminist Studies Section, on the initiative of its then president, Elizabeth Maier, decided to take on this challenge to identify the lessons from these decades of women's activism useful today as Latin American and Caribbean women increasingly participate in international to local political scenes and shape public policy. UNIFEM funded a Gender and Feminist Studies Section conference, and the book that ensued was presented in many countries of Latin America and the Caribbean on and around March 8, 2006, as a symbolic closing gesture for those transformative three decades for women's rights and citizenship and for the growing consciousness of gender equity. That first volume was very well received in the region by feminist academics and activists, politicians, functionaries, and the general public. It quickly entered its second edition.

This new volume in English is geared toward bridging cultural realities and targeting a worldwide audience not always familiar with the region, with the intention of being accessible to a wide range of readers without sacrificing its academic rigor. Most of the chapters have been significantly revised and updated to reflect new developments. This version includes two new chapters—one on Afro-Brazilian women's movements and the other on the socioeconomic context of neoliberal globalization—and both the introduction and conclusion have been rewritten to reflect the change in audience and the new material covered.

We think of this book as a tribute to the women who have been active on a broad spectrum of political and cultural fronts throughout Latin America and the Caribbean, working toward social justice and a more inclusive citizenship over these almost four decades since the beginning of second-wave feminism in the region. The book reflects the diversity of geographic, national, socioeconomic, political, linguistic, and cultural environments in which women maneuver. Understanding the dialectical relationship between women and their multiple environments and social locations, and respecting the diversity of opinions that emerge from it (while reserving the right to not assume all the positions expressed), has been one of our main goals.

It was important to us that the first volume be published in Spanish, as we wanted it to be of use for the advancement of gender studies in the region. However, this volume in English is equally crucial because it offers readers from the continental North an opportunity to become familiar with the voices and analytical perspectives of distinguished feminist thinkers and actors from the South, precisely in a post-9/11 moment of global connectivity that facilitates, but also requires, a deeper understanding among peoples. Our other contributors, generally referential North American Latin Americanists and Caribbeanists, including two past presidents of the Latin American Studies Association, are no less distinguished. Together, they are a mix of prominent academics, many of whom have been closely involved in women's movements in Latin America and the Caribbean, as well as activists, who are not generally involved in scholarly work but whose analyses are more than pertinent.

Collaborative work takes a place of choice in feminist writing, and this is no less true of this volume, in which several of the pieces are coauthored, often by women of different national origins, to ensure a more inclusive perspective. The very compiling of the volume has also been a significant collaborative effort between two feminist academics whose perspectives and interests have been differentially informed by distinct generations, countries of origin, geographic areas of expertise, professional formations, and locations in unequal regions of the world. This kaleidoscope of difference provided an enriching and wonderful learning experience for us.

We would like to take a moment to reflect on the pioneering role of the Gender and Feminist Studies Section of LASA in promoting and stimulating the study of women in Latin America since its inception as early as 1972 as the Women's Caucus of Latin Americanists, which became in 1982 the Task Force on Women in Latin American Studies. Reflecting its feminist ideology and methodology, this task force was the first and only one within LASA to elect its own coordinators and to always include women from Latin America and the Caribbean in executive positions (Poggio and Schmukler 2004, 7).

We would like to thank Adi Hovav, our editor at Rutgers University Press, for her support; the Spanish-language publishing company Siglo Veintiuno, for relinquishing all rights to the English volume; and UNIFEM—especially Marieke Velzeboer-Salcedo of UNIFEM–New York—for smoothing out copyrights issues for some of the chapters. Thanks also to Gettysburg College for funding for translations, copyediting, formatting, and indexing, as well as to the Colegio de la Frontera Norte for administrative and institutional support.

Certainly, most of our thanks go to each of the contributors, who have worked diligently under difficult conditions due to the challenges posed by translation and, for some, by the unfamiliar requirements of the publishing process in the United States. We are especially indebted to Helen Safa, Karen Kampwirth, Fiona Macaulay, and Blanca Torres for thorough editing on specific chapters, and to Peter Cousins, Jillian Shaumbaugh, Graciela Di Marco, and Sonia E. Alvarez for their contribution to revisions. Juan Manuel Avalos, Patricia Torres, Areli Veloz at the

Colegio de la Frontera Norte, and Katie Gramlich at Gettysburg College spent countless hours formatting chapters. We are also grateful to Joyce Sprague at Gettysburg College for her help with financial matters. Finally, coediting twenty-one texts, most of them translations from Spanish, has been a mighty feat. It required arduous work that taught us new lessons on the challenging, but necessary, precision of intercultural communication. While one of us had a more extensive role in the Spanish edition, the other assumed that role in the English one. The order of authorship in this volume is reversed to reflect that effort.

Elizabeth Maier and Nathalie Lebon

REFERENCES

Poggio, Sara, and Beatriz Schmukler. 2004. Introd. to *Género, sexualidad e identidad en América Latina*. Mexico City: LASA / Instituto Nacional de las Mujeres.

List of Abbreviations

AFM	Articulación Feminista Marcosur (MarcoSur Feminist Organization)
AMB	Articulação de Mulheres Brasileiras (Network of Brazilian Women)
AMNB	Articulação de Organizações de Mulheres Negras Brasileiras (Network of Black Brazilian Women's Organizations), Brazil
AMNLAE	Asociación de Mujeres Nicaragüenses Luisa Amanda Espinoza (Luisa Amanda Espinoza Association of Nicaraguan Women), Nicaragua
AMPRONAC	Asociación de Mujeres ante la Problemática Nacional (Association of Women Confronting National Problems), Nicaragua
ANC	Asamblea Nacional Constituyente (National Constituent Assembly), Venezuela
ANCIFEM	Asociación Nacional Cívica Femenina (National Female Civic Association), Mexico
ANDRYSAS	Asociación Nacional de Regidoras, Síndicas y Alcaldesas Salvadoreñas (National Association of Women City Council Members, Prosecutors, and Mayors), El Salvador
ANIMU	Asociación Nicaragüense de la Mujer (Nicaraguan Women's Association), Nicaragua
ANPROVIDA	Asociación Nicaragüense Pro Vida (Nicaraguan Pro-Life Association), Nicaragua
ASC	Asamblea de la Sociedad Civil (Assembly of Civil Society), Guatemala
ATC	Asociación de Trabajadores del Campo (Association of Rural Workers), Nicaragua
Bureau du TAG	Bureau des Techniques d'Administration, d'Animation, et de Gestion (Office of Administration, Animation, and Management), Haiti
CAFTA	Central American Free Trade Agreement
CDD	Católicas por el Derecho a Decidir (Catholics for the Right to Decide), Latin America
CEDAW	Convención sobre la Eliminación de todas las Formas de Discriminación contra Mujeres (Convention on the Elimination of All Forms of Discrimination against Women), Latin America
CEFEMINA	Centro Feminista de Información y Acción (Feminist Center for Information and Action), Costa Rica

CEM-UCV	Centro de Estudios de la Mujer de la Universidad Central de Venezuela (Women's Studies Center of the Central University of Venezuela), Venezuela
CEPAD	Consejo de Iglesias Pro-Alianza Denominacional (Council of the Ecumenical Alliance of Churches), Nicaragua
CEPAL/ECLAC	Comisión Económica para América Latina y el Caribe/Economic Commission for Latin America
CERIGUA	Centro de Reportes Informativos sobre Guatemala (Center for Informative Reports on Guatemala), Guatemala
CFC	Catholics for Choice (United States)
CFEMEA	Centro Feminista de Estudos e Assessoria (Feminist Research and Advisory Center), Brazil
CFFC	Catholics for a Free Choice (United States)
CFP	Círculos Femeninos Populares (Popular Women's Circles), Venezuela
CFWY	Comité sobre Familia, Mujer y Juventud (Committee on Family, Women, and Youth), Venezuela
CIPAF	Centro de Investigación para la Acción Femenina (Research Center for Female Action), Dominican Republic
CLHARI	Comité de Lesbianas y Homosexuales en Apoyo a Rosario Ibarra (Lesbian and Gay Support Committee for Rosario Ibarra), Mexico
CNDM	Conselho Nacional dos Direitos da Mulher (National Council for Women's Rights), Brazil
CNZFE	Consejo Nacional de Zonas Francas de Exportación (National Council of Free Trade Zones), Dominican Republic
COAMUGUA	Coordinadora de Agrupaciones de Mujeres de Guatemala (Coordinating Committee of Women's Groups of Guatemala), Guatemala
CONAIE	Confederación de Nacionalidades Indígenas del Ecuador (Confederation of Indigenous Nationalities of Ecuador), Ecuador
CONAMU	Consejo Nacional de la Mujer (National Women's Council), Venezuela, Ecuador
CONAP	Coordination Nationale de Plaidoyer pour les Droits des Femmes (National Coordinating Committee of Advocacy for Women's Rights), Haiti
CONAVIGUA	Coordinadora Nacional de Viudas de Guatemala (National Coordinating Committee of Guatemalan Widows), Guatemala
CONG	Coordinadora de Organizaciones No Gubernamentales de Mujeres (Coordinator of Women's Nongovernmental Organizations), Venezuela
CONMIE	Consejo Nacional de Mujeres Indígenas (National Indigenous Women's Council), Ecuador

CUC	Comité de Unidad Campesina (Committee of Peasant Unity), Guatemala
DHS	Informe Demográfico y de Salud (Demographic and Health Survey), Dominican Republic
Las Dignas	Asociación de Mujeres por la Dignidad y la Vida (Women's Association for Dignity and Life), El Salvador
ECLAC/CEPAL	Economic Commission for Latin America/Comisión Económica para América Latina y el Caribe
ERA	Empresas Recuperadas y Autogestionadas (Recovered and Self-Managed Enterprises), Argentina
FEVA	Federación Venezolana de Abogadas (Venezuelan Federation of Women Lawyers), Venezuela
FMLN	Frente de Liberación Nacional Farabundo Martí (Farabundo Martí National Liberation Front), El Salvador
FNCR	Frente Nacional contra la Represión (National Front against Repression), Mexico
FSLN	Frente Sandinista de Liberación Nacional (Sandinista Front for National Liberation), Nicaragua
GGM	Grupo Guatemalteco de Mujeres (Guatemalan Women's Group), Guatemala
IMO	Instituto de la Mujer Oaxaqueña (Oaxacan Women's Institute), Mexico
INAMUJER	Instituto Nacional de la Mujer (National Institute for Women), Venezuela
INIM	Instituto Nicaragüense de la Mujer (National Women's Institute), Nicaragua
INMUJERES	Instituto Nacional de la Mujer (National Women's Institute), Mexico
LASA	Latin American Studies Association
LFAS	Ligue Féminine d'Action Sociale (Feminine League of Social Action), Haiti
LGTTB	Lesbian, gay, transgendered, transvestite, and bisexual
MEAMUJER	Ministerio de Estado para los Asuntos de la Mujer (Ministry of State for Women's Affairs), Venezuela
MNU	Movimento Negro Unificado (United Black Movement), Brazil
MRS	Movimiento de Renovación Sandinista (Sandinista Renewal Movement), Nicaragua
MVR	Movimiento Quinta República (Fifth Republic Movement), Venezuela
PAISM	Programa de Assistência Integral à Saúde da Mulher (Women's Comprehensive Health Care Program), Brazil
PAN	Partido de Acción Nacional (National Action Party), Mexico
PLC	Partido Liberal Constitucionalista (Liberal Constitutionalist Party), Nicaragua

PMDB	Partido do Movimento Democrático Brasileiro (Party of the Brazilian Democratic Movement), Brazil
PPDL	Programa de Participación Política y Desarrollo Local (Program for Political Participation and Local Development), El Salvador
PRD	Partido de la Revolución Democrática (Democratic Revolution Party), Mexico
PRI	Partido Revolucionario Institucional (Institutional Revolutionary Party), Mexico
PROEQUIDAD	Programa Nacional de Igualdad de Oportunidades y no Discriminación contra la Mujer (National Equal Opportunity and Nondiscrimination Program for Women), Mexico
PRONAL	Proyecto Nacional (National Project), Nicaragua
PRT	Partido Revolucionario de los Trabajadores (Revolutionary Workers Party), Mexico
PSDB	Partido da Social Democracia Brasileira (Party of Brazilian Social Democracy), Brazil
PSUV	Partido Socialista Unido de Venezuela (United Venezuelan Socialist Party), Venezuela
PT	Partido dos Trabalhadores (Workers' Party), Brazil
RedeSaúde	Rede Nacional Feminista de Saúde, Direitos Sexuais e Direitos Reprodutivos (Feminist Network on Health, Sexual Rights, and Reproductive Rights), Brazil
RN	Resistencia Nacional (National Resistance), El Salvador
SEPPIR	Secretaria Especial de Políticas de Promoção da Igualdade Racial (Special Secretariat for the Promotion of Policies on Racial Equality), Brazil
SPM	Secretaria Especial de Políticas para as Mulheres (Special Secretariat for Policies on Women), Brazil
UNIFEM	United Nations Development Fund for Women
UNRISD	Instituto de Investigación de las Naciones Unidas para el Desarrollo Social (United Nations Research Institute for Social Development), Mexico
URNG	Unidad Revolucionaria Nacional Guatemalteca (Guatemalan National Revolutionary Unity), Guatemala
WMW	World March of Women
WSF	World Social Forum, Foro Social Mundial

PART I

SETTING THE STAGE

Introduction

WOMEN BUILDING PLURAL
DEMOCRACY IN LATIN AMERICA
AND THE CARIBBEAN

NATHALIE LEBON

The past four decades have witnessed the rapid and profound transformation of women's roles and gender ideologies in Latin America and the Caribbean, much of which has revolved around women taking their destinies into their own hands, individually and collectively. The resurgence of feminism and women's activism in the region since the seventies has been hard to ignore: women have been active on a broad spectrum of political and cultural fronts, working for social justice and for a more inclusive citizenship with attention to gender power differentials.

Over these four decades, the political and economic context has changed radically, transforming, often dramatically, the realities of women and men but also shifting opportunities and challenges for activism. As the region moved from the oligarchic, dictatorial regimes and state-led industrialization of the seventies and eighties to the consolidated formal democracies and neoliberal market-driven globalized economies of today, the focus and strategies of women's individual and collective action had to change. Given that the claims of social movements generally include some measure of both redistribution (of resources across segments of society) and recognition (of group identity and rights), emphasis in the relation between the two shifted back and forth with these evolving political opportunities and economic contexts (Fraser 1997; Richards 2004). The first involves greater attention to the class-inflected gender needs of working-class and poor women. Heretofore neglected social actors, such as Afro-Latina, lesbian, indigenous, working-class, poor, and trade union women, are gaining presence and voice in the heterogeneous social field that encompasses women's movements in the region today. The international and transnational environment has also changed, and women are learning to navigate the various levels of policy making for social action, from the local to the international.

This volume reflects the breadth and variety of contemporary feminist scholarship and reflection in and on Latin America and the Caribbean. It brings together political scientists, anthropologists, sociologists, historians, cultural critics, lawyers, and activists, each distilling the lessons to be learned from these forty years of agency and activism in a challenging and moving context.

At this juncture, we hope that this book finds its place in the lineage of feminist writings that have been providing the kind of "impertinent knowledge" Peruvian activist Virginia Vargas refers to: knowledge that opens windows on how to constructively shake the established order, of which gender-equity policy making has become a part (this volume). In other words, this book seeks to glean from a wealth of past and contemporary experiences what we need to keep our critical lens on to make the best of the current phase of the institutionalization of feminist organizing.

These writings also attempt to capture—although this is surely a tall order—the diversity of women's experiences and organizing in the broad and varied terrains that comprise Latin America and the Caribbean, whether as a result of geographic or national contexts or of women's positioning in their societies' social structures because of race, class, gender, sexuality, generation, or religion. All generalizations in this introduction must be tempered by an awareness of this diversity. Still, this introductory essay hopes to capture the main themes and concerns that run through our authors' analyses, as well as offer the background necessary to understand the essays that follow.

Latin America and the Caribbean are characterized by their geographic, ethnic, socioeconomic, and cultural diversity. Yet the countries of the region share important features, such as four hundred years of colonization and an economic history epitomized by distorted land distribution, subordination to the needs of (former) colonizing countries, and the presence of enduring economic and political oligarchies. These factors go a long way to explain the region's sad distinction of having the most unequal income distribution in the world today: a small but growing middle class is squeezed between a large low-income, poor, and indigent majority and a tiny but extremely wealthy and politically powerful elite. Continuing asymmetrical political and economical power relations with the United States and the rest of the Global North also contributes to the scenario that impacts women's daily lives today, both in small, extremely poor countries such as Haiti and in large, industrialized countries such as Argentina, Mexico, or Brazil, which export manufactured goods and advanced technology.

We strove to include the non-Spanish-speaking countries in this anthology in the spirit of the Encuentros Feministas de América Latina y el Caribe (Latin American and Caribbean Feminist Encuentros). Since 1981 and about every three years after, feminists throughout the region have been meeting in broad-based, massively attended, loosely themed gatherings to offer a plethora of workshops, exhibits, activities, plenary sessions, and maybe most importantly, possibilities for free exchange and dialogue: the Encuentro, a word with no good English translation (Sternbach et al. 1992; Alvarez et al. 2003). Encuentros have welcomed activists from French- and English-speaking islands, a process not free of considerable tension, as racial relations dovetail with language differences (Alvarez et al. 2003).

Women's Agency and Collective Action in Latin America and the Caribbean: Learning from the Global South

Over ten years after the publication of Amrita Basu's landmark collection, *The Challenge of Local Feminisms*, it is worth reconsidering her statement that the vast Western literature on women's movements "ignores women's movements in the postcolonial world, considers women's movements products of modernization or development, and assumes a sameness in the forms of women's oppressions and women's movements cross-nationally" (1995, 1). Indeed, women's collective action and agency in Latin America and the Caribbean, as in most of the rest of the Global South, were long ignored, neglected, or misinterpreted by Western scholars and feminists. Women often fell prey to ubiquitous representations as passive victims of poverty and sexism and desperately in need of help. The strong colonial legacy of these images can not be denied (Mohanty 1986; Narayan 1997): Latin American "insurmountable machismo" is a case in point! Even the early work of North American and European Latin Americanist feminists until the early eighties tended to focus on the need for socioeconomic development rather than on women's rights and collective action.

Since the seventies, however, a rich literature by feminist scholars from Latin America and the Caribbean, and later from elsewhere, developed exponentially, in keeping with the growth of women's organizing. In fact it is so vast that it is dangerous to venture any generalizations, given the multiplicity of national knowledge productions and the various disciplinary perspectives involved. As in the case of scholarship on social movements generally, academic discussions have usually trailed the debates in and among feminist and women's movements themselves.

The vibrancy and effectiveness of women's movements in the Global South have been hard to miss. Yet the recognition of how much Western feminism can learn from them has been slow. Latin American and Caribbean feminisms, along with Indian feminisms, are arguably among the most diverse and mass-based worldwide. Their theoretical production is equally remarkable, although generally unknown in the Global North, in part due to the cost and difficulty of translation but mostly as a result of the politics of knowledge production, which tend to reproduce international differentials in resources and determine who gets published where. For this reason we chose to provide ample space in this anthology to native speakers in translation.

Debates among academics over the nature of these movements, and in particular over which qualify as feminist, have taken many shapes through the years. In the Latin American context, a distinction has often been drawn between feminism and the larger women's movement: feminism referring to women explicitly and consciously organizing to fight the oppression and subordination of women, and the women's movement referring more inclusively to women organized to defend their interests, often as women but not always. This distinction resurfaces in the much-used concepts of strategic gender interests and practical gender needs, originally formulated by Maxine Molyneux (1986). Examples of strategic gender interests that feminists have organized around are equal pay for equal work, domestic violence, and the right to legal abortion. Practical gender needs have been understood as those concerns women experience as a result of their gendered roles and duties (generally as mothers and wives) often in their daily life, such as the need for child care or access to fuel and clean water to feed their families.

Most scholars agree that this dichotomy has outgrown its usefulness and recognize that it is often difficult to disentangle the strategic from the practical: for example, child care needs, as most others, reflect both a practical daily need for working mothers but also a failure on the part of society to recognize the value of women's reproductive labor (hence it challenges women's subordination). Also, what seems practical to some may be strategic to others. Often what is seen as practical are the needs faced by working-class women, while what is defined as strategic are the concerns of middle-class white or mestiza heterosexual women. Indeed, in Latin America as elsewhere, the general tendency has been to equate feminism with the white or mestiza, educated, urban, middle-class manifestation of women's struggle against subordination. Finally, no organization is homogenous enough for all women to share the same motivations.[1] Ultimately, these distinctions led to the divisive question of "who is feminist enough."

More recently, scholars have acknowledged that nation, race, class, and sexuality shape women's experience of gender oppression and the ways and spaces women chose to resist and organize for change (Ferree and Tripp 2006; Naples and Desai 2002; Ricciutelli et al. 2004). We are still striving to work out these biases, as is clear from many of the essays in this book.

Four Decades of Latin American and Caribbean Women's Movements

Although Basu argues that in global terms "regional similarities are most evident in Latin America, where women's movements are closely connected to democratization movements against authoritarian states" (1995, 4), the following outline of the main developments of women's struggles necessarily overgeneralizes and homogenizes. The economic and political systems, political culture, and gender relations of each national context are related to its historical, ethnic, and class makeup, making for a distinct set of characteristics. What follows is a broad-stroke sketch in advance of the finely drawn analyses offered by the chapters, outlining the political and economic context that has shaped progressive women's activism.

Origins in Inhospitable Times

A multiplicity of strong and visible women's movements developed in the 1970s as a response to the economic policies and political repression of the authoritarian, bureaucratic, or military dictatorial regimes of various stripes in places in the Southern Cone, some Andean countries, and many Caribbean islands since the sixties. In Central America, protracted civil wars resulting from efforts to unseat corrupt oligarchic regimes lasted until the early 1990s.[2] While many were puzzled by the emergence of feminist and women's movements in the face of such repressive regimes, feminist theorists brought to our attention the contradictions between state discourse and state actions: while military authoritarian regimes extolled the virtues of nurturing motherhood and women's vital role in the care of their families and, indeed, their nations, they disappeared loved family members. Their economic policies, first favoring industrial investments to "grow the pie before sharing it," inordinately profited the wealthy and later were derailed by the international economic crisis resulting from the 1973 and 1979 oil shocks.[3] Ordinary family budgets shrank, making it increasingly difficult for mothers and wives to fulfill their idealized roles (Chuchryk 1989; Alvarez 1990; Stephen 1997; Safa 1990). Two types of women organizing appeared as a result of these challenges: women's human rights groups, such as the Argentinean Madres y Abuelas de la Plaza de Mayo (Mothers and Grandmothers of May Plaza), and poor women's neighborhood organizations, originally focused on basic needs such as housing and food.

Another contradiction was key to igniting women's understanding of subordination. As they joined opposition organizations, at first often as underground groups and later as legitimate political parties, women—moved by their discourse extolling equality and freedom for all—could not fail but notice that their own roles were often limited to serving coffee and cleaning up meeting rooms and that principles of equality did not carry over in the home or the workplace. Indeed, in large measure women's movements were born out of the opposition sectors to military dictatorships. Experiences with socialist egalitarian economic models in Cuba (after 1959) and Nicaragua (after 1979) promoted women's activism by raising often unrealistic expectations about the capacity of revolutionary states to eradicate sexism. Although we cannot disregard right-wing women's organizing (González and Kampwirth 2001), this volume is focused on women struggling to expand political, social, and economic citizenship.

Parallel developments occurred in black movements, indigenous movements, and urban and rural trade unions, where women started to raise questions about unequal power relations between women and men. The common narrative about feminism's origins has often tended to emphasize the role of middle-class consciousness-raising groups of women of mostly European or mixed descent, those later called *feministas históricas* or historic feminists.[4] We now know that black, working-class, indigenous, and lesbian feminisms were present as early as—and not a by-product of—what came to be seen as hegemonic feminism. They were organized on their own terms, often in mixed organizations.[5] One difference is that the first self-proclaimed autonomous feminist organizations were those of middle-class women of mostly European or mixed descent.

The United Nations International Women's Year (1975) and its conference in Mexico City (itself in part a result of women's activism) provided legitimacy to women's claims and in many countries prodded further organizing. By the late seventies and early eighties, a number of politically engaged women who had lived in exile in Italy, France, and other Latin American countries during the height of the repressive regimes were returning, bringing back their experiences with feminist organizing to reinforce already existing groups. Nonetheless, there are considerable subregional differences, most obviously in terms of timing: movements began earlier in the larger, more industrialized nations of the Southern Cone or Mexico than in Central America, for example.

Weathering the Transition to Formal Democracy and the "Lost Decade"

In many countries, women constituted the majority of participants in urban popular movements organizing for decent housing, basic sanitation, and health care, among others, which were at their height during the 1980s, also dubbed the "lost decade" of Latin American development. As rural populations flooded to the cities, economic chaos resulted from the deepening world crisis and the regimes' inability to repay an exponentially growing external and internal debt.[6] Most countries found themselves dependent on the dictates of international financial institutions, such as the International Monetary Fund and the World Bank, to open their economies to world trade and restrict their spending to refinance their loans. Unable to compete with cheaper imported international products, numerous national industries shut their doors, leaving many in urban areas unemployed. Structural Adjustment Programs mandated states to cut food subsidies, health and education budgets, and overall safety nets for the population, leaving families to struggle for survival. Assembly plants (maquiladoras) in export-processing zones mushroomed, first along the U.S.-Mexican border, where multinational companies pay no taxes, can hire cheap labor—mostly women—and have free rein in terms of environmental and labor regulations. These turned out to be particularly lethal places for women, as they proved fertile ground for femicide.[7]

These economic hardships generated urban popular organizing and contributed to the success of democracy in the sense that in many countries, military dictators were forced to or chose to return to their barracks by the middle of the decade. Women contributed considerably to the return of formal democracy, often being among the first to publicly protest (Maier; Di Marco, ch. 5, both in this volume). The 1980s were thus a decade of transition as newly established, formally democratic regimes found their way (this process did not take place until the 1990s in Central America). However, the resurgence of party politics, as opposition forces returned to the legal political arena, marginalized women and split feminists along party lines. Debates raged as activists disagreed, often bitterly, about which strategy was most appropriate: working within or without the party system. This debate opposed *políticas* (women involved in party politics) to *feministas* (in favor of autonomous feminist organizing without allegiance to party politics). Many políticas argued that they engaged in double militancy, working to advance both women's interests and their party's interests. Related to these tensions was the debate over what came to be known as "the General and the Specific." Some activists believed that focusing on class inequalities (the general) and bringing about economic and social justice was imperative and would in time lead to the eradication of women's oppression (the specific). For most of those who claimed the feminist label, the struggle against women's subordination should not be considered specific or secondary but equally important. In time and in the face of the contradictions experienced by women in socialist regimes, most came to understand that gender issues cannot be subordinated to class issues and, more recently, to recognize how strongly class inequalities also shape women's experience of gender subordination.

During this transition period, women, especially in areas where armed conflicts occurred, won the right to be heard to varying degrees as a result of their participation in opposition forces to the repressive regimes. The relative fluidity of this period of institution building also allowed organized women greater influence on the sphere of politics. Women used this space to influence their national constitutional processes, to set in place national women's machineries (national-level state institutions for women's rights) and to experiment with innovative models, such as special police stations in Brazil to address violence against women (Nelson 1996) or electoral quotas for party candidates.

At the beginning of the decade, the movement was visible and strong. It started networking at the regional level with the first Encuentro in 1981. By mid-decade the first wave of nongovernmental organizations (NGOs) or professionalized feminist organizations (with paid staffs) began to appear. Most shared roots in social movements and a strong commitment not only to local and grassroots work but also to class-related gender issues.

Toward the end of the 1980s some observers began to lament the lack of movement activities (in Brazil for example). Popular movements no longer had the capacity to mobilize large segments of the population into the streets for protest now that channels of communication with the state were reopened. Middle-class consciousness-raising circles, long considered the hallmark of early feminist organizing, were on the wane. But as Lynn Stephen notes (1997), observers see what they want to see. What they failed to see was the budding of new forms of feminist activism in unexpected places as it interacted with the state through various forms of advocacy and research. They also missed the greater visibility and formal organizing of Afro-Latin, rural, lesbian, and popular feminisms—and later indigenous feminism and autonomous groups claiming their respective identities—activism with unexpected actors.

The 1990s: NGOs, Institutionalization, and Internationalization

At the national level, the 1990s meant the return of politics as usual. Institutions regained stability. Much flexibility and wiggle room were lost for new ideas while traditional political actors regained control over national institutions. During the so-called consolidation phase, women had to retreat in most national political settings. However, the seeds of institutionalization had been planted and started to bear fruit, as well as bring challenges.

While the region's economies recovered somewhat in the 1990s, it also became clear that they were more vulnerable to global economic shocks due to their openness to global markets. Argentina's economy, for example, collapsed in 1999 as a result of instability in Asia, Russia, and Brazil. Globalization and neoliberal policies accelerated the bifurcation in the distribution of income and generated discontent and poverty in many places throughout the 1980s and 1990s, although it has also opened opportunities for others. The Chiapas uprising in 1994, for example, can be traced to the long-lasting oppression of indigenous peoples in Mexico but was also precipitated by the impending North American Free Trade Agreement (NAFTA).

The dominance of neoliberal ideology, launched from Washington, was strengthened by the collapse of the Soviet Union in the late 1980s. Latin American states have always had limited means to devote to redistributive social policy. However, social policy is now generally guided by principles of personal responsibility for pulling oneself up by one's bootstraps and rolling back the state, while leaving market forces, for profit, and nonprofit organizations to provide services. Limited social programs target specific populations instead of warranting universal access to services for all those who need them. Besides the dire consequences for large segments of the population (and women in particular, as detailed in the pages of this book), since the mid-1980s these policies have contributed to the disarticulation of social movements' demands. Redistribution demands made by low-income popular movements were resisted, as demands based on recognition of group identity and rights gained ground (Richards 2004).

In this context, focusing on legal reforms for women's rights (generally recognition-based claims) appealed to many middle-class feminist activists, especially as new openings for action in this direction presented themselves at the international level. The end of the cold war facilitated the attention of global governance institutions to issues beyond security in the eighties and nineties. The United Nations promoted discussions around these topics through world conferences, bringing together state representatives in the official forum and civil society in a "parallel forum," the most notable of which were on the environment (Rio de Janeiro 1992); human rights (Vienna in 1993); population and development (Cairo in 1994); social development (Copenhagen in 1995); racism, xenophobia, and other forms of intolerance (Durban in 2001); and, of course, women's issues (Mexico City for the International Women's Year 1975, Copenhagen in 1980, Nairobi in 1985, Beijing in 1995). This political moment has facilitated a greater focus on a discourse of rights and the construction of citizenship internationally, which reverberated at the national level—often in an effort on the part of states to appear to stay abreast of these international trends—as well as in civil society (Vargas, this volume).

The strength and vitality of the Latin American women's movement was demonstrated vividly by the size and impact of its contingent of activists at these United Nations conferences. They contributed to redefining women's rights as human rights—making it clear that rape and domestic violence are human rights violations, for example, and pushing the limits of reproductive and sexual rights. This heightened international participation was not without conflict and tension, as several essays explore in this book.

Against this backdrop of weakening popular movements, feminist organizations focused their energy on the increasing opportunities for advocacy, research, and lobbying at the national and international levels, for which funding was now available from international donor agencies, which actually sought to encourage this move. As this "technical-professional" face of NGOs (Alvarez 1999) and concomitant professionalization grew, it contributed to a distancing from community-based women's groups and increased differential access to resources (not only in monetary terms but also in terms of time and information) and power in the women's movements, which increased tensions between their various segments (Lebon 1996). This trend was intensified by the involvement at the international level, which took activists literally farther away from local needs and realities. Organizing at the grassroots level is certainly not inherently participatory, democratic, and inclusive and therefore should not be romanticized. Nonetheless, issues of representativity and accountability are key issues that are complicated by the politics of race, class, sexual orientation, gender, and other axes of identity and inequality (Naples and Desai 2002).

New Millennium, New Trends

As fundamentalisms of all stripes—economic, political, and religious—have gained ground worldwide, notably in the United States, stimulating the radicalism of the religious right in the region (see Kampwirth; Tarrés, both in this volume), feminists have strengthened their responses: Catholics for the Right to Decide in Latin America continues to battle religious fundamentalism and largely contributed to the legalization of abortion in Mexico City in 2007 (Navarro and Mejía, this volume). The Tu Boca (Your Mouth) campaign by the feminist NGO network Articulación Feminista Marcosur (MarcoSur Feminist Organization) promoted the notion that speaking out is essential to defeat fundamentalism at its core.

After almost two decades of an entrenched neoliberal agenda, people have made their discontent heard nationally through the polls, which no doubt contributed to what some have dubbed the Pink Tide, as well as internationally through transnational social movements. The Pink Tide refers to a series of electoral victories by center-left to left parties and/or coalitions in Venezuela (Chavez in 1998), Brazil (Lula da Silva in 2002), Argentina (Néstor Kirchner in 2003 and Cristina Fernández de Kirchner in 2007), Uruguay (Vázquez Rosas in 2004), Bolivia (Morales in 2005), Ecuador (Correa in 2006), Chile (Michele Bachelet in 2006), and Paraguay (Lugo in 2008). Some may add Nicaragua (Ortega in 2006). The notion of a Pink Tide may be misleading because, in reality, much differentiates these regimes. Remarkably two of them are headed by women. Yet, how pink the Pink Tide has been, in other words, to what extent have these governments been beneficial to women and sexual minorities in particular and to the marginalized and the poor in general, remains to be seen (Friedman 2007). Each has its own characteristics; some have been characterized as neopopulist rather than as truly engaged in a meaningful redistribution of national resources and wealth, others as blatantly opportunistic, as in Nicaragua. Their social policies have been tied down by the dictates of the international economy. In some cases though, as in Brazil, redistributive policies have started to begin to slightly impact income distribution inequality.[8] On the other hand, electoral alliances have led to antifeminist policies, such as the ban on therapeutic abortion in Nicaragua under the second Ortega administration (see Kampwirth, this volume).

The region finally experienced several consecutive years of sustained growth rates in per capita Gross Domestic Product in the new millennium (an increase of 3.5 percent in 2005) (ECLAC 2006, 55). This growth contributed to "significant progress" since 2004 in reducing poverty and indigence after two decades of rising trends (58). However, we should not lose sight of the fact that it took the region twenty-five years to reduce poverty back to 1980 levels (from 40.5 percent in 1980, up to 44 percent in 2002, and back down to 39.8 percent in 2005) and that the absolute number of people living in poverty has increased considerably (from 136 million in 1980, up to 221 million in 2002, and back down to 209 million in 2005) (59). ECLAC expresses similar caution about progress made in terms of the reduction of inequalities in income distribution, as stated in its *Social Panorama of Latin America and the Caribbean*: "Although Latin America is still a highly inequitable region, the deteriorating trend in income distribution evident at the start of this decade, at least, seems to have been halted" (84).

Internationally, globalization has intensified the movement of people, information, and ideas, as well as of consumer culture. This connectivity, as most strikingly manifested by the Internet, has been crucial to the alter-globalization—as opposed to the antiglobalization—movement. Alter-globalization is a worldwide confluence of social movements working to promote a more people- and ecofriendly form of globalization. Its vitality in Latin America and the Caribbean may be a sign of the impact of the globalized economy on their people, including the women. Regional spaces, such as the international socialist-feminist World March of Women network (WMW) (Dufour and Giraud 2007) and especially the World Social Forum (WSF), which since 2001 has brought together a broad spectrum of social movements, have become a crucial part of this mobilization. In other words, this period of intense change that has undermined and unsettled institutions and systems of power has provided openings: new political forces and new alliances have emerged and new technologies are available for new strategies. Ultimately, a global civil society is being created (Naples and Desai 2002; Vargas, this volume). These two American initiatives (the WSF was born in Brazil and the WMW in Canada) have contributed to redrawing power relations among women's movement segments within national contexts, gathering renewed strength for a thoroughly class-informed, popular feminism and bringing back redistribution claims on the feminist agenda.

Under these new circumstances, rural women's movements, domestic workers' movements, trade union feminism, and popular feminism, along with black women's and indigenous women's movements (these categories are not mutually exclusive, as most indigenous women live in rural areas and women of color are overrepresented among the working and poor classes) have become especially dynamic segments of the larger women's movement. Yet much work remains to be done for a full acknowledgement of *privilege* on the part of middle- and upper-class women of mostly European or mixed descent, both in society and in movement-wide forums.

It may be no surprise that this strengthening is occurring at the same time as professionalized feminist and women's organizations are contending with seriously reduced international support. There has never been a great deal of funding for women's issues, but Latin America and the Caribbean are no longer considered a priority for aid agencies, as they must now compete with Africa and Eastern Europe. States in the region certainly do not have the capacity to step in, even if they had the political will—which they often do not (Shepard 2007). As they have done in the past, women's movements are coming up with new ways to respond to, and take advantage of, the current set of conditions they are faced with. The chapters that follow brilliantly exemplify their flexibility and inventiveness.

The Chapters in This Book

There are many ways that the readings in this book could be organized. We have chosen to arrange them into five sections beyond our introductory chapters. The first group of authors sets the stage by examining the effects of the changing political and socioeconomic context over the last four decades on the lives of women, their work, and their families in our neoliberal and globalized world. The next two sections present narratives of national and regional movement histories, successes, and challenges: the second of the two highlights how "feminism's others articulate other feminisms" (Alvarez et al. 2003, 572). The fourth section focuses on more pointed analyses of institutional design and the national context of women's machineries and gender-equity policy formulation and implementation. The last section critically examines experiences of women's organizing at the local as well as the regional and international levels.

Status of Women: How Far Have We Come?

Women's sense of self and their participation in family, society, and polity have changed dramatically since the seventies. Regionally, women's literacy and educational achievements have greatly improved. In many cases girls now enjoy more years of education than their male peers. The region now compares relatively favorably with the rest of the Global South: the ratio of the female youth literacy rate to the male youth literacy rate is equal to or above one hundred in all but seven countries (Elson and Keklik 2002, 22). In all but three countries do we now find higher enrollments of girls than boys in secondary education, a pattern very similar to that of the Global North (14).

However, expected consequences in terms of a reduced gender wage gap did not pan out, as demonstrated by Alice Colón and Sara Poggio. Progress has been uneven when taking ethnicity, race, and national contexts into consideration, as it takes political will and resources to provide basic education. In Haiti, for example, girls still trail boys in school enrollment by almost 9 percent, according to longtime activist Myriam Merlet.

One essential transformation has been the dramatic increase in women's labor force participation, including in professional, technical, and clerical fields, where women in 2005 exceeded men in numbers. Working-class and rural women and in particular indigenous and Afro-Latin women have long been active in the productive sphere for sheer survival and/or as a result of the gender roles in their ethnic community, but changes in paid employment have been nothing short of dramatic. Women now represent 40 percent of the economically active population (Colón and Poggio, this volume). South and Central America experienced the largest increase worldwide in this regard between 1980 and 1997 (Chen et al. 2005, 37).

The positive impact of paid employment for women on their ability to make decisions in all spheres of life is clear in the Cuban case, analyzed by economist Marta Núñez Sarmiento. Having more independence, women are empowered to negotiate and readjust male-female relations in the workplace, as well as in the home. Anthropologist Helen Safa's examination of female-headed households in the Spanish-speaking Caribbean concludes that, with more options available, women increasingly resist marriages that are not fulfilling materially or emotionally, explaining in part the rise in the numbers of female-headed households.

Despite these gains, the sexist nature of gender relations persists. We no longer believe that *machismo* and *marianismo*, that is, men's belief in the inherent superiority of males expressed through dominance, especially toward women, and women's long-suffering and sacrificial journey to moral superiority at the hands of insufferable male partners, ever held that much sway in men's and women's minds (Navarro 2002). Nevertheless, our contributing authors demonstrate again and again the devaluation of all things feminine, in ways that ring close to home, be it through the humiliation of boys who behave like girls, the reluctance of men to do "women's work," or ubiquitous violence against women. Occupational segregation, which results sometimes in real ghettos, and a stubborn wage gap are further examples (Colón and Poggio, this volume). The difficulties faced by women of color, poor women, lesbians, and transsexuals in each of these instances are exacerbated by the intersection of these various axes of identity and inequality. Ironically, ideologies that devalue women's labor often hurt everyone. Safa, as well as Colón and Poggio, demonstrate this by showing that the sexist ideology that justifies paying women less is generously padding the profit margins of corporations. This ultimately punishes all workers, since a supply of lower-paid women puts downward pressure on overall wages.

Moreover, the positive effects of paid employment for women have been considerably eroded by the conditions under which they have been integrated into the labor market. Cólon and Poggio show how, with labor regulations reduced to a minimum, the macroeconomic policies meant to integrate Latin American and Caribbean economies to the global economy have afforded employers the best of working-class women's capacities as cheap labor power for manufacturing and services, while these women have been increasingly ghettoized in these insecure, low-paid jobs with few benefits. This is also true in other parts of the developing world (Elson and Keklik 2002; Chen et al. 2005).

Overall, national economies, including Cuba's during the "special period" following the fall of the Soviet Union, have leaned on the survival strategies devised by women to see to the needs of their families (Cólon and Poggio; Núñez Sarmiento, both in this volume). On the other hand, Safa's piece highlights the difficulties faced by men who, no longer able to fulfill their role as breadwinners due to reduced employment opportunities, often prefer to leave their families behind.

The Many Faces of Women's Struggles for Citizenship

Many of our chapters allow us to follow the varied beginnings, accomplishments, and contemporary trends and challenges facing women's movements in various national contexts. An important theme throughout these stories is the quest for visibility.

Women have had to gain recognition for themselves as activists and for their issues and concerns within progressive political movements, be they guerilla movements in Central America (Herrera; Carrillo and Chinchilla), labor unions, indigenous movements (Prieto et al.) and black movements (Caldwell), urban popular movements (Maier), and in the most recent forms of workers' movements in Argentina (Di Marco, ch. 9). They benefited from the ideological and organizational ferment of other political movements, as sociologist Elizabeth Maier illustrates in her account of early women's struggles, but also had to fight the sexism of these movements. The example of Nicaragua is revealing in this sense: Karen Kampwirth discusses the catalyzing character of the Sandinista Revolution for feminism in the country, as the women involved gained organizational skills and learned models to challenge traditional authority. Ultimately though, the ability of women's associations to challenge sexual inequality within the party was limited.

Making public the issues traditionally restricted to the domestic sphere has been a major focus of feminist work, as illustrated by sociologist Montserrat Sagot's account of Costa Rican activists' efforts to put domestic violence on the public agenda. Vargas argues that the impossibility faced by feminists to interact with the then authoritarian states pushed them early on to reinterpret reality by "politicizing the private." Focusing on societal norms and cultural patterns, they made previously private issues visible but *"de costas al estado"* (with their backs to the state). However, sociologist Graciela Di Marco points out that not all of women's collective action can be categorized in this way. The militant motherhood of the Argentinean Madres and Abuelas de la Plaza de Mayo, for example, was geared toward the state (ch. 5). As a matter of fact, this group was among the first to confront the military regime. Similarly, the struggles of popular women described by Maier and by Di Marco (ch. 9) around issues such as housing and work have all addressed demands to public authorities. Yet, in many ways, they too politicized private matters by stressing the social rather than individual nature of their concerns. One could argue that these movements used the "prescribed," nurturing roles of motherhood to make demands on the state, while the others challenged the prevailing sexist ideology related to control over women's bodies and sexualities. The distinction between the two is neither simple nor linear though, as discussed earlier.

Finally, our authors tell of the quest for visibility of the concerns and priorities of women from the working classes (Di Marco, ch. 9; Maier), of indigenous women (Prieto et al.; Carrillo and Chinchilla), of black women (Caldwell) and of lesbians (Mogrovejo) within and outside of women's movements. In her discussion of the Latin American lesbian movement, lawyer and sociologist Norma Mogrovejo refers to this period as both "the moment of universality," in which women focus on equal rights, and as "difference feminism," which claims women's difference from men and the importance of establishing new values and a new symbolic order. Both of these conceptions, however, make it difficult to articulate differences among women. The chapters mentioned earlier reveal to what extent feminism in the region has become a feminism of shifting identities. They shed light, some in a more optimistic tone than others, on the ground gained over these past forty years by the notion that other facets of a woman's identity interlock with gender in her everyday experience, in her interactions with others, and in how she is perceived and dealt with by institutions. They also highlight how much more ground needs to be gained. Also apparent from these chapters is the fact that sexism, racism, and other forms of oppression all function on the same principle: a socially constructed norm of the exclusion of those who differ. Vargas suggests that the body provides a useful point of connection between social movements focusing on these various struggles: be it women's controlled bodies, the discriminated, racialized bodies central to antiracist struggles, or the overworked or malnourished bodies that are the focus of alter-globalization movements. This point is well illustrated by Mogrovejo when she shows the importance for feminism of transgendered people's struggle in bringing to light the constructed nature of gender and how the body of "women" has been colonized by patriarchal/heterosexual norms.

Working across class boundaries was the first challenge acknowledged by middle-class feminists, given most of their origins in left-leaning political parties and the very reality of class in their national environments. As Maier argues, this process remains incomplete, although it contributed to the beginnings of popular feminism. Di Marco's inspiring story of women's involvement in mixed workers' movements in response to neoliberal economic policies in Argentina since the nineties illustrates the strengthening of popular feminism and its appropriation of demands that had long been those of middle-class women, such as the legalization of abortion (ch. 9). Interestingly, fundamentalist forces have not failed to note the political importance of this development and have hardened their stance against women's reproductive rights.

Anthropologists Kia Caldwell and Mercedes Prieto and her colleagues tell parallel stories of the development of women of color feminisms, given the reality of racism and its denial in the region. The clear lack of connections of middle-class mestiza women activists with indigenous women in the context of Ecuador led indigenous women to find closer allies in the indigenous movement, although they are increasingly becoming critical of gender inequity within indigenous communities and within the movement. Caldwell analyzes the dynamics of racism and sexism in the development of Afro-Brazilian pro-women organizing and traces the participation of Afro-Brazilian activists from their early presence in the black movement and a variety of other political and cultural organizations, including feminist organizations, to the strong, broad-based networks of autonomous black feminist organizations of today. She underscores their contribution to our understanding of the intersectionality of oppression and a redefinition of citizenship.

Several authors consider that being able to work across differences is crucial to the future of inclusive citizenship. Ana Lorena Carrillo and Norma Stoltz Chinchilla's account of feminisms in Guatemala shows a budding coming together across class and ethnic lines for a more inclusive citizenship in a pluralist and multiethnic nation. Di Marco (ch. 9) suggests that we "build new ways of relating that ensure mutual respect and acknowledgement" to facilitate the confluence of the women's movement and feminism. Very cogently she argues that such work is essential to expand the circle of those who press for a feminist agenda, while also broadening the nature of our demands. Our challenge is indeed to find out how to deal with diversity, not only in a celebratory mode but in a way in which we truly address power hierarchies among women.

Organizational Issues

Concerns with the centralization of power, representativity, and hierarchical forms of organization have been present—some would say central—to feminist movements since their inception. As Maier notes, "hierarchy was rejected as a mode of operation, being considered a means of patriarchal reproduction," while experimentation with participatory models of decision making was favored. Such concerns are echoed in a number of other chapters and in Nicaraguan feminists' recent preference for flexible, less hierarchical networks, as opposed to coordinating committees.

Movements' preferred strategies are influenced by, but also impact, their organizational features. Both movement strategies and organizational forms changed considerably over the years as the political scenario around them changed. Many chapters, starting with the testimonies of the Madres and Abuelas of Argentina (Di Marco, ch. 5), attest to the sheer power of consciousness raising, going to the streets, and organizing broad-based movements to push for democratic change or gender equity. Besides the new opportunities of regime democratization, the very nature of processes of NGOization and professionalization, which started depending on the national context in the mid- to late eighties (Carrillo and Chinchilla; Di Marco, ch. 9; Herrera), also reinforced the movement away from the streets and toward legal reform and public policy.

Although many NGOs originated in women's movements, Di Marco (ch. 9) corroborates other accounts that a number of organizations emerged without a feminist orientation and offer services, on a limited scale, for which the state should be responsible on the basis of the economic and social rights of its citizens. Others have shown that feminist organizations are also at times sucked into this process (Alvarez 1999). Moreover, competition for resources among movement organizations and concerns for organizational survival have now appeared, which undermine the possibilities for building a strong movement, as noted by Carrillo and Chinchilla.

Institutionalization and Gender Politics: Feminism Inside and Outside the State

Autonomy from mainstream state and international institutions, including political parties and donor agencies, has been defended, more fiercely by some than others, since the movement's inception. But with a democratizing environment during these last four decades, feminist understandings of, and approaches to, the state have changed. As almost all the chapters in section four attest, the state is not a monolith but instead a collection of decision-making nodes not always in concordance with one another, which we can use to our benefit. Still, institutionalization has not been without challenges.

STRUCTURE AND POLITICAL CONTEXT

Feminist sociologist María Luisa Tarrés and political scientist Fiona Macaulay argue, in line with much of the literature on the topic, that to push the gender-equity agenda forward, we need to take into consideration the structural features of a particular state, as well as the political conjuncture. In her analysis of the Mexican Institutos de la Mujer (Women's Institutes), Tarrés demonstrates that when it comes to women's machineries, the context in which they operate is at least as important in explaining their success or failure as institutional design in itself.

The furthest advances in terms of institutional design come from countries with progressive administrations and strong women's movements, such as Brazil and Venezuela. One is the inclusion of a gender perspective in the budgeting process. Governments seem to possibly be ready to put their money where their mouths are! This has been done by the state government of Oaxaca in Mexico (Tarrés, this volume) and at the federal level in Brazil since 2003, though not without difficulties. Venezuela's new constitution also boasts nonsexist language and benefits from a gender perspective. Another exciting new trend is the mainstreaming of the gender-equity perspective throughout the executive branch. This means that a central women's machinery is no longer solely responsible for implementing gender policies; instead, such efforts are coordinated throughout the various departments.

INSTITUTIONALIZATION: HOW MUCH AND AT WHAT COST?

Research by Macaulay and by Tarrés illustrates how some institutionalized women's machineries are better able to withstand changes in ruling parties than others. They do better in Brazil, where the party system is weak and often opportunistic. Both essays demonstrate how much an independent budget and staff is necessary. However, in general, party politics still very much affect such agencies.

Macaulay's discussion of women's councils at the various levels of government in Brazil highlights the benefits, such as broadening and invigorating debate, of the institutionalization of representation and input by civil society. But how much should such "gender units" be involved in guiding and/or stimulating the organizing efforts of civil society? Cathy Rakowski and Gioconda Espina, in the case of Venezuela, illustrate the trade-offs when leadership switches from civil society to the legislative assembly, as well as the negative consequences of a women's machinery's attempt to take the lead in organizing civil society in a context of deep politicization and ideological division.

Most of our authors are aware of other perils of institutionalization. Several address the issue of what Morena Herrera calls the depoliticization of gender. Tarrés refers to it as the "neutral and technocratic tone" of the gender perspective adopted in policy circles, a perspective that no longer requires a reorganization of power relations between men and women and that allows new, postfeminist actors to appropriate the discourse on gender. The best concrete example is offered by Sagot's discussion of Costa Rica's legislation on violence against women: gender-neutral language in the final legal text ignores the fact that women bear the brunt of violence as a result of gender power differentials. In the end, this legislation takes an assistentialist focus instead of granting women their rights "as citizens with a right to . . . integrity, justice and to live without violence." It assumes women as passive beneficiaries of good will rather than deserving of these rights. Mogrovejo, an *autónoma*—as feminists who prefer to work outside formal power structures choose to identify themselves—writes a critique, enlightened by a lesbian perspective, adding that this gender perspective continues to define women in relation to men. Institutionalization and its focus on legal rights are also faulted for the obvious lack of implementation of the laws on the books. Herrera's answer to this problem is the need to rebuild a movement able to push for this implementation.

Implicit or explicit in these authors' analyses is thus the notion that our efforts should not be limited to a focus on public policy. Herrera reminds us that the public sphere *is* the general space of debate and discourse so vital to democracy. Influencing changes in discourse and cultural norms is thus essential to gender equity. Through the media or the political arena, it is possible to debate the contradictions in state or hegemonic rhetoric, such as the Costa Rican state's discourse on "peace abroad" and lack of commitment to "peace in the home."

On the other hand, both Mogrovejo and Herrera make a point of mentioning the problems of a position exclusively outside of the national and international institutional framework, such as the one advocated by those sectors of the movement who identify themselves as *autónomas*. Despite all that an emphasis on autonomy can bring to the movement, Mogrovejo identifies a tendency to the creation of ghettos (even within the movement) and fundamentalism, as well as a certain arrogance and intolerance on the part of these sectors, which make it difficult for them to work with others and build a strong movement.

Most authors in this volume agree that a two-pronged strategy of feminist activism both from within and outside the state and other institutions, such as international organizations, is warranted to move a gender-equity agenda forward. Giving up on participating in policy making would be tantamount, as Herrera argues, to disregarding the fact that "the public sphere [is] one of full human realization from which women have been excluded only because of their gender."

Going one step further than the two-pronged inside/out strategy, many authors press for the need for spaces for dialogue and interaction. Indeed, the book gives numerous examples of coalitions, mutual support between políticas, autonomous women's organizations, and women in government structures. It provides several examples of collaboration of feminists across party lines (see, for example, Kampwirth, Merlet, Carrillo and Chinchilla, and Herrera). Rakowski and Espina's analysis of coalitions in Venezuela since the 1970s identify some contributing ingredients: "The coalitions formed later were opportunistic; women took advantage of them to create new political opportunities or to mobilize to confront a perceived threat." They were voluntary, used consensus decision making, focused on legal reform and public policy, and "often used international accords to pressure lawmakers." Despite the deep and growing antagonism between Chavez supporters and others in the Venezuelan women's movement, the successful experiences of the seventies and eighties and the long-time feminist networks existing across political divides contributed to successful collaboration on specific issues. Yet, such broad coalitions carry the serious disadvantage that those feminist demands perceived as the most radical, such as abortion and lesbian rights, might be left out, as in the case of the Minimum Agenda presented to political parties by Nicaragua's cross-partisan, cross-class Coalición Nacional de Mujeres (National Women's Coalition).

Organizing at the Local, National, Regional, and International Levels

Women activists have become increasingly savvy about navigating the various levels of institutional policy-making arenas and making the most of regional and international civil society forums. Our authors point at the advantages and trade-offs involved.

THE INSTITUTIONAL SPHERE AND THE POLITICS OF SCALE

Margaret Keck and Kathryn Sikkink (1998) have demonstrated the efficacy of what they call the boomerang effect: when policy advances at the international level are brought back by activists to the national level. More recently, scholars have begun to pay attention to moves in different directions, as activists take advantage of strength at one scale to influence an outcome at another (Vargas, this volume; Blackwell 2006).

Our authors demonstrate that the benefits of international institutional work are not limited to policy making but also lead to increased gender consciousness and provide greater legitimacy to feminist discourse and ideas in larger society. In Costa Rica, for example, the feminist discourse around violence against women gained greater legitimacy through the international reformulation of the concept of human rights to include women's rights.

A number of chapters also attest to the catalyzing effect of United Nations conferences on women's organizing. The annual national Encuentros in Argentina started in 1986, after some participants went to Nairobi in 1985. Numerous issue-specific networks were formed after initial contact at such conferences. The latest and most exciting example of such connection was how the preparatory process for Santiago +5 conference in 2005—the regional meeting for the follow-up on the Durban conference on racism—brought together indigenous and Afro-descendant women. Such a catalyzing effect is not automatic though: Mexican activists with concerns about movement autonomy in 1975 decided not to participate in the International Women's Year (Lau 2006). In the end, participation in these various international arenas have brought women to the WSF, one of the most exciting poles of alternative thinking about our political and social world, with some of the highest levels of experience at international networking and organizing (Vargas, this volume).

The national preparation processes related to the United Nations conferences also clearly contributed to the institutionalization of the gender perspective, through the establishment of national gender-equity machineries, such as in Venezuela as early as 1975, or more recently in Mexico, as the government attempted to ensure implementation of the Beijing Platform of Action. Also note that in Venezuela, the women's machinery's call for support for the elaboration of their official report for the Nairobi conference in 1985 led to the first large-scale coalition of women's organizations in civil society, highlighting how institutional arena and civil society organizing influence each other.

On the other hand, in a trend that many have found less positive, United Nations activities also led to the professionalization of the movements through the legitimacy and funding they made available for gender-focused work. These activities have also influenced the kind of work and the issues feminist organizations focus on. In her critique, Herrera does not deny the importance of participation, apprenticeship, and skill learning from these processes that focus on legal rights but argues that the lack of political will to change social norms makes their implementation difficult. Indeed, she cogently argues that, in the face of the crisis of the state and the lack of implementation of gender-positive legislations, it is essential to focus our energies at the municipal level, the closest to our day-to-day lives.

CIVIL SOCIETY

As this book goes to press, feminists throughout Latin America and the Caribbean are preparing to meet for the eleventh regional Encuentro, to be held in Mexico in March 2009. According to Vargas, these large-scale regional meetings have played a crucial role in the development of feminisms. The chapters on Central America attest to the push that the Taxco Encuentro (1987), for example, provided for feminist activism by inspiring consciousness raising (Guatemala), the creation of independent feminist organizations (Nicaragua) and help for feminists to move forward to a propositive stance toward the central government (El Salvador). Interestingly, the Encuentros have been a place not only for all women to come together but also where differences among women were often ignored but also later discussed and negotiated: Mogrovejo tells this story for lesbian feminists.

Other civil society forums have played similar roles for women organizing on axes in addition to gender: indigenous women have benefited from greater negotiating power with donor agencies, alliances with sectors of the indigenous movement, and strengthening of their organizing at the national level through the Encuentros Continentales de Mujeres Indígenas (Continental Encuentros of Indigenous Women) (Prieto et. al, this volume, Palomo Sánchez 2006).

Conclusion

Throughout this book, again and again, the authors bring to our attention the need for working across differences and for alliances and coalitions. It seems appropriate then, in conclusion, to highlight the importance of pluralism for democracy, what Teivo Teivainen refers to as demodiversity (*demodiversidad*), or the "peaceful or conflictive existence of different models and practices of democracy in a given social field" (quoted in Vargas, this volume). We have reasons to be hopeful that this is the direction in which we are traveling, both among women's movements and between women's movements and other movements for social justice.

Indeed, acknowledgement of this necessity among women's movements is apparent in the description by its organizers of the tenth Encuentro, held in Brazil in 2005:

> [Participants] are autonomous feminists or linked to organizations, networks, coalitions, or universities; they are indigenous, black, young, lesbian, sex workers, rural and urban working-class feminists, etc. The X Encuentro wishes to provide a space for dialogue, debate, conflict, controversy, and coalition building for the region's various lineages of feminist thinking, which it brings together. (Tenth Encuentro Organizing Committee e-mail, October 10, 2005)

Although the organizers did not anticipate that the demands for inclusion that most shook up the meeting and divided the participants that year would be male-to-female transsexuals (Pizarro 2005; Tinoco 2005; De Cicco 2005), once again the Encuentro gave strength to and articulated the voice of the most recently formally organized sector in the movement and served as a platform from where the boundaries of inclusion are negotiated and pushed further outward.

Finally, the efforts of feminists to keep interacting with democratizing forces outside of feminism within the World Social Forum, fighting for gender equity and for a gendered analysis of the realities of our times, bring another source of hope. Such efforts seem to be one of our best chances to ensure respect for the fundamental social and economic rights that affect both men and women, but the violation of which relegates women to the very bottom of the social hierarchy, as is vividly illustrated in the Haitian case by Myriam Merlet.

ACKNOWLEDGMENTS

I would like to thank Liz Maier, Scott Hill, Jane Jaquette, and especially Jean Potuchek for their insightful comments on earlier drafts of this chapter.

NOTES

1. For a more in-depth discussion, see Stephen (1997).

2. Armed violence in this region was fueled by U.S. involvement after the successful takeover of Nicaragua by the Sandinistas in 1979. The Sandinistas, or Frente Sandinista de Liberación Nacional (Sandinista Front for National Liberation), are a leftist political party, named after Augusto César Sandino, leader of a revolt against the U.S. military presence in Nicaragua in the 1930s. For more, see Kampwirth (this volume).

3. Oil prices rose sharply on both occasions due to the concerted efforts of oil-producing countries. For various reasons, this financial bounty did not translate in the hoped-for improvement of living conditions for the few oil-producing Latin American countries, such as Mexico and Venezuela.

4. National identity discourse and pride focused on mestizaje (race mixing) or "racial democracy" have contributed to downplaying racial inequality in most of the region until the new millennium (Lebon 2007; Safa 2005).

5. See Thompson (2002) on this argument for the U.S. narrative.

6. The inability to pay was largely due to out-of-control international interest rates on the loans international banks had been more than happy to provide during the fat cow years of the previous decades to build infrastructure and industry.

7. The term *femicide* has been used to describe the murders of (young and poor) women in Ciudad Juárez, Mexico (more than 400 murdered since 1993) and in Guatemala (2,500 since 2001, including 600 in 2006), where simply being a woman largely explains the killing.

8. One-third of the recent improvement in Brazil's still highly inequitable income distribution—the second highest in the region—can be attributed to the government's income transfer policies (ECLAC 2006, 92).

REFERENCES

Alvarez, Sonia E. 1990. *Engendering democracy in Brazil: Women's movements in transition politics.* Princeton, NJ: Princeton University Press.

———. 1999. Advocating feminism: The Latin American feminist NGO "boom." *International Journal of Politics* 1 (2): 181–209.

Alvarez, Sonia E., Elisabeth Friedman, Ericka Beckman, Maylei Blackwell, Norma S. Chinchilla, Nathalie Lebon, Marysa Navarro, and Marcela Ríos Tobar. 2003. Encountering Latin American and Caribbean feminisms. *Signs* 28 (2): 537–580.

Basu, Amrita, ed. 1995. *The challenge of local feminisms: Women's movements in global perspective.* Boulder, CO: Westview.

Blackwell, Maylei. 2006. Weaving in the spaces: Indigenous organizing and the politics of scale in Mexico. In *Dissident women: Gender and cultural politics in Chiapas,* ed. Shannon Speed, R. Aída Hernández Castillo, and Lynn M. Stephen, 115–154. Austin: Texas University Press.

Chen, Martha, Joann Vanek, Francie Lund, and James Heintz, with Renana Jhabvala and Christine Bonner. 2005. *Progress of the world's women 2005:* Women, work and poverty. New York: UNIFEM.

Chuchryk, Patricia. 1989. Feminist anti-authoritarian politics: The role of women's organizations in the Chilean transition to democracy. In *The women's movement in Latin America: Feminism and the transition to democracy,* ed. Jane Jaquette, 149–184. Boston: Hyman.

De Cicco, Gabriela. 2005. Décimo Encuentro Feminista de América Latina y el Caribe: Una entrevista a Marusia López Cruz. WHRNet. Association for Women's Rights in Development. www.whrnet.org/docs/entrevista-lopez-0511.html (accessed July 3, 2008).

Dufour, Pascale, and Isabelle Giraud. 2007. Globalization and political change in the women's movement: The politics of scale and political empowerment in the World March of Women. *Social Science Quarterly* 88 (5): 1152–1173.

ECLAC. 2006. *Social panorama of Latin America and the Caribbean.* Santiago: ECLAC.

Elson, Diane, and Hanke Keklik. 2002. *Gender equality and the millennium development goals.* Vol. 2 of *Progress of the world's women 2002.* New York: UNIFEM.

Ferree, Marx Myra, and Aili Mari Tripp, eds. 2006. *Global feminism: Transnational women's activism, organizing, and human rights.* New York: New York University Press.

Fraser, Nancy. 1997. *Justice interruptus: Critical reflections on the "postsocialist" condition.* New York: Routledge.

Friedman, Elizabeth J. 2007. Introd. to How pink is the "Pink Tide": Feminist and LGBT activists challenge the left. *NACLA Report on the Americas* 40 (2): 16.

González, Victoria, and Karen Kampwirth, eds. 2001. *Radical women in Latin America: Left and right.* University Park: Penn State University Press.

Keck, Margaret E., and Kathryn Sikkink. 1998. *Activists beyond borders: Advocacy networks in international politics.* Ithaca, NY: Cornell University Press.

Lau, Ana J. 2006. El feminismo mexicano: Balance y perspectivas. In *De lo privado a lo público: 30 años de lucha ciudadana de las mujeres en América Latina,* ed. Nathalie Lebon and Elizabeth Maier, 181–194. Mexico City: Siglo Veintiuno.

Lebon, Nathalie. 1996. Professionalization of women's health groups in São Paulo: The troublesome road towards organizational diversity. *Organization* 3 (4): 588–609.

———. 2007. Beyond confronting the myth of racial democracy: The role of Afro-Brazilian women scholars and activists. *Latin American Perspectives* 34 (6): 52–76.

Mohanty, Chandra T. 1986. Under Western eyes: Feminist scholarship and colonial discourses. In *Third world women and the politics of feminism,* ed. Chandra Mohanty, Ann Russo, and Lourdes Torres, 51–81. Bloomington: Indiana University Press.

Molyneux, Maxine. 1986. Mobilization without emancipation? Women's interests, state and revolution. In *Transition and development: Problems of third world socialism,* ed. Richard Fagen, Carmen Diana Deere, and José Luis Coraggio, 280–302. New York: Monthly Review.

Naples, Nancy, and Manisha Desai, eds. 2002. *Women's activism and globalization: Linking local struggles and transnational politics.* New York: Routledge.

Narayan, Uma. 1997. *Dislocating cultures: Identities, traditions, and third-world feminism.* New York: Routledge.

Navarro, Marysa. 2002. Against marianismo. In *Gender's place: Feminist anthropologies of Latin America,* ed. Rosario Montoya, Lessie Jo Frazier, and Janise Hurtig, 257–272. New York: Palgrave Macmillan.

Nelson, Sara. 1996. Constructing and negotiating gender in women's police stations in Brazil. *Latin American Perspectives* 23 (1): 131–154.

Palomo Sánchez, Nellys. 2006. Las mujeres indígenas: Surgimiento de una identidad colectiva insurgente. In *De lo privado a lo publico: 30 años de lucha ciudadana de las mujeres en América Latina,* ed. Nathalie Lebon and Elizabeth Maier, 236–248. Mexico City: Siglo Veintiuno.

Pizarro, Ana María. 2005. Décimo Encuentro Feminista de América Latina y el Caribe: Feminismo y Democracia. *América Latina en Movimiento,* October 12. http://alainet.org/active/9458&lang=es (accessed July 3, 2008).

Ricciutelli, Luciana, Angela Miles, and Margaret H. McFadden, eds. 2004. *Feminist politics, activism, and vision: Local and global challenges.* Toronto: Inanna.

Richards, Patricia. 2004. *Pobladoras, indígenas, and the state: Conflicts over women's rights in Chile.* New Brunswick, NJ: Rutgers University Press.

Safa, Helen I. 1990. Women's social movements in Latin America. *Gender and Society* 4 (3): 354–369.

———. 2005. Challenging mestizaje: A gender perspective on indigenous and afrodescendant movements in Latin America. *Critique of Anthropology* 25 (3): 307–330.

Shepard, Bonnie. 2007. Patterns of northern donor support: Implications for sexual and reproductive rights advocacy NGOs in Latin America. Paper presented at the Twenty-seventh International Congress of the Latin American Studies Association, Montreal, Canada, September 5–8.

Stephen, Lynn. 1997. *Women and social movements in Latin America: Power from below.* Austin: University of Texas Press.

Sternbach, Nancy S., Marysa Navarro-Aranguren, Patricia Chuchryk, and Sonia E. Alvarez. 1992. Feminism in Latin America: From Bogotá to San Bernardo. *Signs* 17 (2): 393–434.

Thompson, Becky. 2002. Multiracial feminism: Recasting the chronology of second wave feminism. *Feminist Studies* 28 (2): 337–360.

Tinoco, Chuy. 2005. Encuentro Feminista de América Latina y el Caribe: El movimiento feminista ya nada tiene que ver con el feminismo. www.creatividadfeminista.org/articulos/2005/fem_encuentro%20chuy.html (accessed July 2, 2008).

1

Accommodating the Private into the Public Domain

EXPERIENCES AND LEGACIES OF THE PAST FOUR DECADES

ELIZABETH MAIER

One of the most distinctive characteristics of Latin America over the past four decades has been the increasing visibility of women as collective actors in the public domain of politics, clearly contributing to the gradual forging of a regional culture of rights. Whether propelled onto the political arena from the tensions of gender inequality that historically have shaped the lives of over half of the population, or having emerged from the dense national narratives of dictatorial repression in the Southern Cone and the insurgent uprisings that polarized Central America during the seventies and eighties, or having coalesced around the material wants of the great majority of the population, women's organized presence on national sociopolitical scenes has fashioned new representations of the feminine in the collective imaginary of the region. In the case of Mothers' and Grandmothers' committees for the disappeared, for example, these new representations resignified traditional gender roles of mother and homemaker, while renegotiating power relationships between partners and within the family. Through multiple expressions of sociopolitical participation, Latin American and Caribbean women have achieved a more complete citizenship, while also promoting the democratization of family, society, and nation.

In this chapter, I will revisit some of the female collective actors who mobilized during those early years of Latin America's second-wave feminist movement, with the intention of exploring their objectives, modes of organization, strategies, and the intensity of their mission.[1] Highlighting the dialectics between structure, identity, agency, and strategy (Alvarez et al. 1998, 318), my aim is to review the multiple ways in which feminist and nonfeminist women's agency of this period has facilitated the gradual deconstruction of gender inequality. I propose to do so in the spirit of not only rekindling the memory of these notable figures of contemporary Latin American history, their passion for the cause, and their impact on the moment but also reflecting on their value for the current phase of feminist shaping of public policy. What can women's strategies and methodologies of previous decades offer to the contemporary, institutional ways of conceiving gender politics and honing gender policies?

The Joy of Beginning

Since the first International Women's Year focused attention on the subaltern condition of the world's women in 1975, Latin America and the Caribbean discovered new female, symbolic representations on its political stage. Educated, middle-class feminists, female guerrilla fighters, activist Mothers, and militant urban homemakers from class-oriented, grassroots organizations injected seemingly private grievances, needs, and demands into the public arena.[2] While feminists underscored the deconstruction of the sociocultural production of body-identity, rejecting sexual, socioeconomic, and political restrictions that disciplined a subordinate and docile female body, other women anchored their participation to the traditional roles that historically reproduced patriarchal gender orders. Still others migrated to the habitually masculine terrain of war and arms. The mobilization of tens of thousands of women in these public expressions of new femininities created synergies that decentered the customary Latin American female image from its marianist discourse of abnegation, obedience, devotion, surrender, dependence, and shame (Vuola 1993, 12). Their objectives and the ways in which they transgressed typical gender roles, their motivation (and destination) in leaving the private sphere, and the strategies chosen varied according to structural conditions, cultural patterns, and political realities. Particularly relevant was the scope of democracy in each country. In democratic countries with solid industrial development, feminism rooted itself in reduced sectors of a growing middle class as a cultural-identity movement, dedicated to achieving gender equality through the modification of structural and legal impediments, and the renovation of women's symbolic representations in the collective imaginary.[3] For some, the feminism that sprang up in Latin America at the beginning of the seventies was an exotic and luxurious import, far removed from the needs and interests of the majority of women of a region with almost half its population living in poverty. For others, especially left-wing organizations, feminism's exogenous birth certificate stoked a postcolonial, anti-imperialistic distrust of the foreign, while suggesting a threat to the unity of their class-based, strategic objectives. These and other factors linked to the radical nature of the renegotiation of social power inherent to feminism staked new frontiers in the dispute for sociocultural meaning that the suffragist movement had initiated decades before in the majority of these countries.[4]

Feminist effervescence during the early years of the second wave was intensely experiential, largely unaware of the historical and economic factors that gave rise to the movement. There was little awareness of how industrial development and the consequent reorganization of class and gender relations during the first half of the twentieth century had consolidated a small but dynamic sector of middle-class women ready to broaden their horizons and ignite their opportunities. Though in reduced numbers compared to highly industrialized countries, these well-educated Latin American women enjoyed economic well-being and autonomy, lived freedom-oriented lifestyles, and were anxious to transgress and transform the sociocultural discourses that informed economic, social, and political practices of gender subordination and discrimination. While modern feminist organization, mobilization, and theorization surfaced initially in the advanced industrial nations, it quickly spread throughout the Latin American and Caribbean region. A feminist critical mass coalesced in many countries, negotiating its place on the national scene within the structural, political, and cultural specificities of each country. Its international scope has characterized second-wave feminism as the first globalized social movement of late modernity.

While World War II reconfigured the social geography of gender in the developed countries and women replaced absent soldiers in the national economy, in Latin America the phase of industrialization known as import substitution transformed the industrial base and expanded the state apparatus of most nations, increasing opportunities for stable, well-paid urban employment with labor benefits for a small but growing sector of privileged employees. Starting in the forties, rural-urban migration overflowed into the cities, satisfying the demand for labor in factories, government offices, and the private service sector. A minority urban middle-class was consolidated, creating a demand for luxury goods, specialized services, and quality higher education, resulting in more skilled employment for a growing sector of women. The advent of a consolidated urban middle class reshaped customary, rural gender norms that traditionally excluded women from educational opportunities, professional training, and economic autonomy. This restructuring of class geography paved the way for one of the most transcendent cultural readjustments of twentieth-century Latin America: the gradual establishment of conditions for full women's citizenship through increasing recognition of the need to transform pervasive gender inequality.[5]

"The personal is political" was the emblematic motto of the feminist second wave. It refers to the traditional division of society into two universes, public and private, considered to be separate and independent dominions. Gradually, through collective reflection and analysis, second-wave Latin American and Caribbean feminists discovered the mechanisms by which the personal and intimate had been tattooed on the cultural representations of the feminine. Woman, private and intimate, had been symbolically fused in a world of hierarchical and sublimated human relations, apparently loving, complementary, and harmonic. Early second-wave exploration of female identity also revealed the lack of social valorization of the private sphere and concluded that women had been excluded from public power because they lacked a collective voice that compellingly expressed their gendered perspective of life and validated their needs and proposals (Ardener 1986, 36). They also found that in the masculine collective imaginary of the region, their bodies had been symbolically fragmented into binary identities of sexuality or reproduction, erotica or maternity, which limited their individual and collective development. They identified the category of patriarchy as the prime theoretical instrument for the production of new cultural meaning, given its ability to inform understanding of the myriad forms of gender oppression and exclusion.

Thus, the idea of the "personal is political" represented a truly radical proposal that rendered visible the sexual division of society into private and public spheres, pinpointed its historical and social nature, and unveiled its negative impact on women's lives. At the same time, the notion of the personal as political highlighted the intimate dialectic between the two spheres, while emphasizing the need to socially value both dimensions equally. Thus, the feminist motto induced an experiential exploration of the multiple linkages between women's everyday lives, their subordinate gender position, and the mechanics of power within contemporary Latin American patriarchal systems, patterned on the dynamics of the urban middle classes. Furthermore, the affirmation that the "personal is political" in the passionate public protests of the seventies and the influential feminist publications and media coverage of the era credited the subjective dimension as the command center for the reproduction of gender identities.[6]

Consciousness-raising groups brought together small numbers of women to explore their gender condition, embodying a methodology of collective scrutiny, interlocution, and accountability among peers. Through sharing personal histories; examining their socialization as children and adolescents; revising school and work experiences as women; exploring likes and dislikes, friendships, loves, and sexual adventures; or reflecting on past social and political participation, a common acknowledgement of the social nature of their gender identity was revealed. Gradually, the political economy of the power relationship implicit in the gender binary was laid bare, until then veiled by the essentialist discourses of sexual identities. This methodology of collective contemplation unraveled customary beliefs, interrogating the social mechanisms that sustained women's subordination and identifying concrete areas and forms of discrimination that required attention and intervention.

In a sense, these groups functioned as autonomous territories ruled by principles of similarity and equality. Hierarchy, considered a means of patriarchal reproduction, was rejected as a mode of operation, and horizontal forms of organization and decision making were encouraged. Concerns over power and representation were founding considerations of feminists in Latin America and the Caribbean. Early strategy proposed substituting "power over" with "power among," or what was called "power to," promoting a direct form of democracy where each individual exclusively represented her own person. However, second-wave feminists often tended to essentialize patriarchal power, conceiving that one sole model of patriarchy applied to all social classes, cultures, and historical times. Michel Foucault's demonstration that power is found in the day-to-day playing out of all social relationships and in the network of resistances created by subordinate actors (1977, 112–125) was not initially understood by Latin American feminists, but rather it was thought that gender trumped all other social exercises of power. In that sense, early second-wave feminism replaced the productive determinism of economic materialism, omnipresent in Latin American social sciences at the time, with a gender determinism that positioned the social relations of reproduction at the center of all historical and social interpretation.[7]

The initial feeling of victimization that accompanied the discovery of the mechanics of gender oppression acted as a factor of identity cohesion that propelled and consolidated this new sociopolitical actor. However, while increasing comprehension of gender discrimination also sensitized feminists to the social exclusion of other collective actors, the reductionism of their interpretation of gender as the hegemonic model of all social relations hampered the process of identification with women belonging to other expressions of social marginality and failed to recognize how compounded dimensions of exclusion nuance the experience of gender. However, within just a few years, the questioning of binary metanarratives at the end of the cold war, together with new theorization on complex identities, lessons learned from women's diversified sociopolitical participation in Latin America, and the impact of total immersion in the era of structural and cultural globalization, all contributed to the renovation of feminist perspectives.[8]

Autonomy and the Constitution of Collective Subjects

Autonomy was always strategic for foundational Latin American feminism: autonomy from the state, political parties, social organizations, and from male domination itself. Latin American and Caribbean governments' frequent use of a patronage system to control social organizations and political parties, along with their co-optation of leaders, close ties to national oligarchies, and the presumed corruption of a significant part of the political class, had historically defined the state as an untrustworthy adversary for most social movements. Moreover, feminist characterization of the state as patriarchal made it a threatening institution for women who were barely initiating a process of self-recognition as subjects of their own lives, agents of social transformation, and sociopolitical power players. They had just begun to realize that political parties and other social movements had forged their strategies in the andocentric paradigm that historically had muted the voice of women's experience and needs. In preparation for honing that voice and making it heard, autonomy became the keystone of an initial strategy of empowerment.[9] It fenced off a symbolic space where feminists could construct collective self-esteem, validate "the right to have rights" (Arendt 1973, quoted in Jelin 1997, 67) as the essence of subjectivity and modernity, discover areas and expressions of exclusion, inhabit new representations of the feminine, and access the abilities to successfully transit the public sphere in conditions of equality.

These early second-wave feminists elaborated powerful countercultural discourses that progressively revised and resignified theoretical concepts so essential to the interpretation of social life: history, power, politics, the private and public, democracy, equality, human rights, and, of course, citizenship. At first, the feminist movement focused its efforts on raising awareness of gender inequality. They centered their prime demands on the reappropriation of the female body, stressing sexuality, reproduction, the right to abortion, and an end to gender-based violence, while also highlighting the need for socioeconomic conditions of greater equality.[10] These demands signified a symbolic earthquake for mainstream Catholic culture, which was based on a feminine binary of the *good woman*, an obedient, demure, maternal keeper of the hearth, and the *bad woman*, an independent, uninhibited, public, sensual being: a paradigm that informs a litany of gender prohibitions, restrictions, permissions, and privileges.

This gender rebellion was fully enjoyed by the *historic* feminists of the seventies. It was a time of sisterhood based on similarity, without the tensions that set in with recognition of difference. The political strength of identity cohesion, the illusion of utopia, and the clarity of the tension between us and male others converged in the definition of the movement's central objective, the deconstruction of patriarchy and the devaluation of its cultural expressions and representations. This essentialist phase of Latin American and Caribbean feminisms was characterized by its radicalism, energy, and transgression, and its focus on the relationship between the private and the public domains. As such, feminism situated women's rights not just in the area of gender relations but also in the reconsideration of what is public and what is private (Jelin 1997, 69).

Political conditions in each country, the quality of life, and specific needs of diverse social classes and subordinate cultural groups informed distinct modes of women's participation. The articulation of premodern, modern, and postmodern socioeconomic contexts (Vargas 2002) and significant racial-ethnic-cultural heterogeneity determined that the interests and priorities of women were not homogeneous, as feminists had initially thought. Thus, parallel to the emergence of feminism in certain nations, women with different objectives occupied the public squares and collective imaginations of countries with dictatorships or authoritarian governments, revealing through the diversity of their demands and strategies the complexity of the female condition in Latin America.

The Mothers

In Latin American dictatorships of the sixties, seventies, and eighties, state brutality—as Homi Bhabha (1994, 6) calls extensive and indiscriminate repression—prohibition of alternative sociopolitical agency, and the edification of traditional gender values, roles, and representations as a personal demonstration of patriotism, all influenced feminist prioritization of the antidictatorial struggle. The repressive experience under authoritarian military regimes made it clear that the right to life and the liberty of opinion and association were an indispensable precondition to begin the struggle for women's rights and citizenship (see Pitanguy 1998). It is in this sense that Maxine Molyneux asserts, "The subject of women's rights, indeed of rights in general, could not be detached from the broader question of the quality and character of democratic rule" (2002, 8).

The discourse of dictatorship situated the trinity of mother-family-home as the cornerstone of a conservative political-religious-social control that collided head-on with feminist philosophy. This authoritarian discourse on women's place in society also interrogated the activity of the Madres de Plaza de Mayo (Mothers of May Plaza), a new political actor that, in the name of traditional motherhood, emerged from the horrors of repression to publicly demand the devolution of their sons and daughters. Their children were victims of the emblematic tactic of state terrorism, the forced disappearance of persons, which characterized all the undeclared, dirty wars of Latin America. As collective expressions of maternal pain and tenacity, Mothers' committees erupted onto the political scenes of countries with military—or civilian—authoritarian regimes, unexpectedly, inadvertently, and progressively uncovering how the application of a military strategy of national security took a toll of between 90,000 and 120,000 disappeared persons in the region.[11] Driven by the mandates of traditional maternity—which their highly public and political actions inadvertently transgressed—these women left the comfort of their homes, taking their pain to the streets, police stations, military camps, and public squares to confront these patriarchal, authoritarian governments with the symbolism of their personas and their nonnegotiable demand: "You took them alive; we want them back alive." In Buenos Aires every Thursday the Argentinean Mothers risked their lives marching around the Plaza de Mayo, with white scarves on their heads and a photo of their son or daughter over their heart (Maier 2001, 56). In San Salvador the members of Comadres tracked down clandestine cemeteries with the desperate hope of finding the remains of their loved ones and documenting the terrifying state in which they had been buried (Schirmer 1993, 38). In Mexico City the Mothers of the Comité Eureka crucified themselves one Mother's Day, tying themselves to enormous crosses that they erected in front of the National Palace, in a symbolic conversion that expressed the pain of the Mother as one with that of her son or daughter crucified by disappearance (Maier 2001, 192).

In the sinister national scenarios of terror, torture, and death, the Mothers of the disappeared symbolically spoke as equals with the authoritarian fathers of the nation, interrogating them with their presence as though the women were archetypical figures of a Greek tragedy, who, in subtle and surprising ways, blurred traditional gender schemes with the force of their empowerment. They appeared to somehow be protected by an intense, primordial maternal power, still alive in the depths of the collective masculine unconscious, which left both patriarchs and feminists uncomfortable, although for totally different reasons. For the authoritarian regimes, the transgression of the privacy of traditional maternity threatened the reproduction of sociopolitical control, while some feminists questioned the gender implications of this public and political participation in the name of traditional motherhood, arguing that it only reinforced customary female roles and subordination in the family (Jelin 1997, 2).[12] Although feminists viewed the Mothers with admiration and solidarity for being the first women's organizations to take a political role and the first public expressions of opposition to state authoritarianism in Latin America, the Mothers' committees nonetheless represented a challenge for feminism, with their emphasis on the centrality of maternity in the cultural construction of femininity. Situated on the interstices between traditionalism and transgression, the members of this collective expression of militant motherhood experienced important personal transformations as a result of their participation. As the president of the Committee of the Madres de la Plaza de Mayo asserts "To me, the Mothers are women who have broken with many aspects of this system we live in. First, because we went into the streets to confront the dictatorship and we were capable of doing things that the men couldn't do" (Fisher 1989, 157).

The Mothers' committees in Latin America were differentiated by factors such as the extension of the theater of national conflict, the degree and type of repression, the alliances that each committee established with other opposition movements, participation in national and international networks of solidarity, the margins for legal political activity, and the cultural characteristics of each country (Macleod 1985). While the committees in Argentina, Uruguay, Colombia, and Mexico evolved spontaneously and autonomously, in countries like El Salvador, Chile, and Brazil they were championed by the Catholic Church. What they all shared, however, was a valiant, tenacious, public, collective, and activist motherhood that gradually progressed from their initial demand for the return of their loved ones to their later advocacy for human rights and the return to constitutional legality. Finally, they became a sort of collective guardian of historic memory and social ethics, with their uncompromising insistence on identifying and punishing those responsible for these perverse national narratives as a necessary preamble to the establishment of an informed democracy.

The Mothers' committees sowed the seed for the Latin American human rights movement, training their members as the first regional forensic experts and specializing in methodical practices of investigation, documentation, and denunciation of massive human rights abuses. They expressed concern not only for the fate of their own children but also for the children of all other mothers in the same situation, thus redefining the individual nature of maternity (Maier 2001, 45) while collectivizing the practice of citizenship (Schirmer 1993, 48). Through their sit-ins, protests, and hunger strikes, the Mothers mothered in the streets in an upside-down world that had violently torn them from the privacy of their homes to fulfill their maternal obligations in parks, squares, governmental offices, and international organizations. Doing so, they unintentionally incarnated the feminist motto "the personal is political" and symbolically resignified motherhood as a collective, public, and political practice, while imbuing the notion of citizenship with a new, intimate reference.

Even when their sociopolitical participation outside the home did not correspond to what Molyneux (1985) has termed "women's strategic interests," referring to gender-based struggles, the amount of time and commitment employed in their activism and—in certain cases—their personal experiences of official repression led to gender consciousness for many Mothers. Being away from home frequently caused tensions with their husbands and children, and in many cases, those tensions led to a new understanding of the sociocultural influences on the sexual division of society. In other cases, the effects of political rape—employed officially as a weapon of war against them—were transformed in time from silent shame into consciousness about gender violence against women. That was the experience of the Comadres of El Salvador after the war, when they were finally able to face and process the meaning of this form of official repression that had marked so many of their bodies with the stamp of this historical gender torture. Examining those experiences through a gender perspective in times of peace led to the further exploration of the problem of domestic violence in their lives and to the formulation of other gender-centered projects (Schirmer 1993; Stephen 1994).

Although they based their agency on traditional motherhood, the Mothers went beyond the limits of customary maternal identity, positioning themselves as primary political actors during and after the authoritarian period. Paradoxically, their political participation in the name of motherhood created conditions in which they could see many of the discriminatory facets of gender and identify new possibilities for renegotiation and transformation. This is one of the lessons that Latin America offers to international feminism: the diversity of contexts and agencies not based on gender that ultimately allows women to recognize the profound injustices of their gender condition.

"Popular" Feminism: The Gender-Class Perspective

The takeoff of industrial development in the forties brought with it the progressive rural-urban migration of peasant families, who arrived in the cities of Latin America with nothing more than hopes for a better life as the centerpiece of a new strategy for family survival. They settled on the peripheries of the cities, where they appropriated uninhabited, undeveloped plots without infrastructure. Through hard work, they broke ground; cleared underbrush; collected scrap; pieced together rudimentary, fragile homes; and began the long process of environmentally, socially, and legally colonizing these spatial configurations that would soon come to be known as the symbol of Latin American poverty. With each passing decade of incessant immigration, these marginal settlements multiplied and became more demographically concentrated, creating extensive urban ghetto areas with countless structural and day-to-day necessities to resolve. The multiple and complex bureaucratic procedures dealing with these problems were resolved more effectively through collective intermediation. Thus, in the sixties and seventies, neighborhood organizations sprang up in response to the clamor for better living conditions.

Although housewives accounted for approximately 85 percent of total membership, the leaders were always men, frequently running these organizations in an authoritarian, hierarchical, paternalistic, and caudillo-like fashion, while gradually satisfying needs for basic infrastructure and services. Lack of infrastructure—electricity, water, sewage—was always hardest on women, extending and intensifying their domestic workday. They joined these neighborhood organizations as a strategy to ease the demands of their precarious living conditions, as the ones in charge of daily and generational family reproduction within the traditional sexual division of labor. Wanting a better life, they organized, had periodical meetings, mobilized, and negotiated, pressuring government agencies to attain more favorable structural conditions for their family and domestic work. Their husbands usually consented to their participation, even though it took place in the public arena, because they considered resolving daily household problems to be "women's work."

As such, women's *popular*-sector activism embraced a class-based perspective that informed their negotiations with the state.[13] At the same time, their activism was informed by the gender implications of their traditional role as caretaker of household and family. Molyneux (1985) calls this amalgam of working-class women's needs and demands practical interests, referring to demands that emerge from women's traditional gender roles without consciousness—initially, at least—of their own subordinate social condition. Years of organizational and reflective dialectics have called into question the rigidity of Molyneux's distinction between women's practical and strategic interests. It's now understood that gender consciousness is produced in multiple contexts and through a variety of practices. Thus, as in the case of the Mothers of the disappeared, women's community activism also promoted awareness of gender hierarchy, as well as of the sociocultural nature of the gender division of labor, and so this became a valuable place to identify the mechanics of gender oppression in everyday working-class lives.

The negative impact of the foreign-debt crisis that became apparent in many countries at the end of the seventies and the corrosive consequences of neoliberal economic policies of state constriction and privatization during the eighties reduced the quality of life even more for growing segments of Latin American and Caribbean society (Stephen 1994, 114). The weight of the crisis was especially borne by women. Researchers have shown how Latin American and Caribbean women have subsidized neoliberal globalization, pointing to the intensification and extension of domestic and family labor since the beginning of the application of free-market measures, in compensation for the elimination of government subsidies and programs. They have also noted an increase in female-headed households stemming from male unemployment, migration, and abandonment, as well as women's growing participation in the formal and informal workforce; increased feminization of the most insecure, volatile, and exploited labor markets; and the subsequent feminization of poverty. Women have been overburdened with double and triple workdays that have been exhausting and overwhelming, rather than liberating. The 1980s witnessed increased poverty in Latin America, and grassroots neighborhood organizations became mechanisms of self-defense, as well as collective survival strategies.

During the decade of the eighties, small groups of feminists, originally from the left of the political spectrum, formed the first associations dedicated to addressing the specific needs of women from the most vulnerable strata of urban society. Committed to social justice and convinced that the secret to a mass women's movement in Latin America lay in the intersection of gender and class, *popular feminists* saw the women of the neighborhood organizations through the lens of gender-consciousness solidarity and with prospects of growing the movement.[14] One of the most important differences between the feminism of highly industrialized countries and that of developing countries was the relative importance of the middle class. While industrialized feminisms were rooted in a majority middle class and constituted a robust mass movement, feminisms of developing countries emerged from a minority middle class, without possibility of major growth unless based on an interclass movement.

Thus, popular feminists decided to accompany low-income women in their fight for better living conditions, hoping to discover how the confluence of gender and class would reorganize feminist demands. They were particularly interested in the connection between gender and economic and social rights, emphasizing the right to a decent quality of life, equal pay for equal work, recognition of the social value of housework and family care, health care (especially reproductive and sexual health care), the right to participate in and lead social organizations, and the right to education and training. The Women's Decade, from 1975 to 1985, and the signing of the Convention on the Elimination of All Forms of Discrimination against Women (CEDAW) in 1979 were ultimately invaluable resources, although in the first years of popular feminism, their impact was barely noticeable. Rather, this initial stage of the feminist alliance with women from grassroots organizations was built on the premise of solidarity among women and on the belief—on the part of feminists—that all true social transformation had to be based on the deconstruction of masculine dominance and gender hierarchy. The enthusiasm of feeling part of a more radical and holistic utopia served as the driving force in the search for communication across class lines. At the same time, it promoted the exploration of a gender-class linkage that resulted in new political agendas, which, based on the needs and interests of low-income women, helped create a new Latin American culture of rights (Molyneux 2002, 1–10).

Specific programs for low-income populations and women's role within them varied according to the country, the size and strength of grassroots movements, their aptitude for negotiating with the state, the type of projects agreed on, and their modes of administration. In Peru, for example, the state promoted the Programa del Vaso de Leche (Glass of Milk Program) in working-class neighborhoods, with the instrumental participation of neighborhood women's organizations. In Mexico, on the other hand, the leadership of neighborhood organizations administrated the distribution of *tortibonos* (tortilla stamps) sponsored by a state program of social welfare, as well as allocating plots of land—and after the 1985 earthquake, houses—negotiated with the government.

In all cases the methodologies used by popular feminists rested on the shared identification, systematization, analysis, and comprehension of women's personal experiences as the source of collective knowledge about the meaning of gender, which then served as the reference for the development of political agendas based on a gender-class perspective. Through weekly get-togethers, workshops, forums, and conferences, these methodologies prompted processes of self-discovery, self-esteem, entitlement, and a fuller understanding of the mechanics of gender in daily life. They also facilitated the cathartic examination of painful gender-based experiences that many women had deeply buried until then, letting shame dictate a feminine language of silence that had served as a means of reproducing gender subordination. For the first time for many of them, gender violence and sexual abuse could be named, recounted, shared, and understood not only as instances of personal pain but also as social power that harms the health and well-being of women, and hinders their freedom.

At the same time, attendance at feminist public events and marches swelled with the participation of working-class women. Indeed, in many countries the intersection of gender and class had impelled a massive presence of women in search of multiple forms of social justice. Their demands were frequently linked to the structural needs of community activists, and they especially worried about unemployment, rising prices, the lack of stable and well-paid jobs, unequal pay for equal work, and the dearth of quality child-care centers and collective kitchens for working women and their families. In countries such as Brazil, Peru, Costa Rica, Nicaragua, and Mexico, they also demanded the elimination of violence—public and private—against women; individual and family health care coverage, with particular emphasis on reproductive and sexual health; and more male responsibility in parenting. Thus, informed by class experiences that reformulated the original agenda of founding middle-class feminists, working-class women contributed to expanding the liberal notion of democracy by including economic, social, and family practices as references.

The lessons of popular feminism have been veiled by the profound transformational implications of the watershed events of the 1990s: the debilitating effects on social movements from the abrupt economic, social, political, and cultural reorganization brought about by neoliberal globalization; the radical changes inherent in the inauguration of the information age, as Manuel Castells (2000, 4) calls it; and the geopolitical reconfiguration imposed by the collapse of socialism. The establishment of democracy in all Latin American countries was, at the same time, an expression of the will of the people; a condition of the new, stabilizing phase of free-market economics; and a result of increasing regional, economic integration. It constituted a new arena of political action and set new rules of the game, giving many feminists the opportunity to initiate a novel form of social protagonism within institutionalized politics. Concurrently, the convergence of economic restructuring and the loss of the traditional capitalist and socialist ideological referents that constructed modern social subjects (Touraine 1997, 45) debilitated grassroots organizations in many Latin American and Caribbean countries. Given that the state had been reduced in its function and orphaned of its charge of social responsibility, the methodology of mass mobilization, political pressure, and negotiation no longer achieved the same results as before. The lack of ideological referents and the shift of feminist agency toward the complex terrain of formal democracy and public policy left popular feminisms with shrinking economic resources. As international funding priorities changed, the grassroots subject of social change of the twentieth century was suddenly replaced at the beginning of the 1990s by a better-trained and more professionalized subject of social transformation: civil society organized in NGOs. Many of the 1980s popular feminist groups followed this road of professionalization, fully committed to the new strategy that Sonia Alvarez (1998) has defined as "the NGOization of the movement."

A more encompassing evaluation of popular feminist activism, and its implications for this new stage of feminist agency, was muted by the impassioned and conflictive debate over the new institutional approach that the majority of Latin American feminist supported.[15] The accelerated events of our cybertechnological phase of globalization and the enormous challenges of learning the institutional ropes for feminist bureaucrats, advisers, and politicians appear to have blurred the political importance of nurturing an alliance with a growing critical mass of women from majority sectors, who had increasingly become gender conscious and had begun to dispute the cultural meanings of patriarchal hegemony in their everyday lives.

Conclusion

The Latin American and Caribbean socioeconomic contexts of the 1970s and 1980s, in which the social actors reviewed in this chapter emerged and flourished, were transformed rapidly and profoundly in the nineties because of four macrotendencies: neoliberal globalization, the cybernetic revolution, the demise of the socialist bloc, and the (re)establishment of democracy as the political model of the region. This transformation brought with it new landscapes for political intervention and new forms of agency that forged new sociopolitical feminist actors, who institutionalized the promotion of gender equity on a national, regional, and local level. The experiences, strategies, and methodologies of the initial phase of women's consciousness raising on the injustices of gender nourished an evolving process of social visibility and participation, along with the recognition of women's subordinate social position. Added to the resignification of traditional gender roles implicit in the sociopolitical activism of mothers and homemakers and to the reorganization of the Latin American collective imagination to include new symbolic representations of womanhood, a propitious environment progressively came into being in which women's concerns could be transformed into public policy and laws. The intersection of social struggles for women's needs, interests, subjectivities, entitlements, and rights progressively informed more complex gender-equity strategies in all the countries of the region.

However, rooted in the many discontinuities of the Latin American and Caribbean social fabric as a result of the intense economic, technological, cultural, and political changes of the nineties (Guzmán 2002), the roadmap for the advancement of women's rights also experienced fractures. Symbolic barriers now exist in the collective feminist imaginary that divide strategies of the recent past from the present, marking a general tendency to ignore the importance of women's pre-institutional experiences. What lessons could women's and feminists' agency from the Women's Decade offer to the actual institutional mode of promoting gender politics? In my opinion, past contributions to contemporary strategies of *mainstreaming* are to be found in three basic levels of knowledge—the conceptual, the political, and the methodological—contributing to an interpretation of the gender perspective that is rooted in its original radical, all-encompassing, holistic meaning.

In that sense, the category patriarchy that characterized early second-wave feminism encloses historical and hierarchical dimensions that inspired the construction of gender as a concept and defined its relational content. While the concept of patriarchy may lack historical and cultural specificity, recognizing the reality of a male-centered and male-privileged social order is essential for understanding the social condition of women. The present disuse of the term in institutional gender discourses leads to a multiplicity of imprecise definitions behind gender politics on local and national levels in Latin America and the Caribbean. "It just means men and women," responded a Mexican congressperson to a young woman who asked her to define gender. Redeploying patriarchy as an analytical-political category infuses the gender perspective with the notion of the power that arranges all androcentric social orders and, at the same time, helps the understanding of the mechanics of women's marginalization from full economic, social, and cultural benefits.

On the other hand, the category of gender-class that popular feminism fashioned underscores the need to overlap two or more dimensions of identity to effectively respond to the needs and interests of the vast majority of low-income, racially and ethnically diverse Caribbean and Latin American women. Mainstreaming gender in public policy is an excellent vehicle for intersecting subaltern identity axes. The premise of the indivisibility of human rights—defended by the Mothers' committees—also offers a matrix for weaving an integral approach that views economic, social, and cultural rights from a gender perspective. Presently, the gender-class outlook opens possibilities of strategically reimagining a new working-class, feminist critical mass that integrates the viewpoint and priorities of diverse female collective actors positioned in local and national political arenas.

The methodologies of small group consciousness raising and of popular education, used during the sensitizing phases of liberal and popular feminisms, should be revived again to explore women's shared knowledge regarding their actual needs, interests, demands, entitlements, and rights. Funding could make it possible to apply a proven methodology to the urgent examination of the impact of globalization on the lives and identities of women of the region, detecting measures to address their situation while garnishing the political will to support necessary changes. Equally, the adaptation of the second-wave practices of autonomy, self-representation, and accountability to current globalized conditions provides a mechanism to make the inner workings of institutional gender politics more transparent, while building bridges between civil society and feminist bureaucrats and politicians. Public officials would have direct input to give voice to the concerns of women from popular sectors at the same time as this popular-feminist critical mass would defend gender policies, which is all the more important in the face of the current aggressively antifeminist posture of religious fundamentalisms.

Finally, the main lesson that these female collective actors bring to the gender-equity challenges of present-day Latin America is that many forms of activism can have an effect on the reformulation of the symbolic representations of women in the collective imaginary of their cultures, emphasizing the multiple paths to achieving a gender consciousness that empowers women to believe in their right to have rights. This is a lesson that fully applies to today's gender-equity challenges—highlighting the need for policies to finance projects that bring together distinct expressions of women's rights activism in local, national, and regional autonomous caucuses—to mutually recognize, listen to, and negotiate with each other, while informing and defending gender-oriented public policy that also responds to different women's specific interests. That is how women will actively continue to enrich the notion of citizenship and democracy in Latin American and Caribbean societies.

NOTES

1. My emphasis on these particular representations of recent Latin American history is not in any way meant to lessen the influence of other female collective actors on the process of transforming gender. Rather, I chose these examples of women's collective agency to illustrate the ways in which private and public realms have intersected in women's activism.

2. In contrast to first-wave feminism's struggle for the basic right of citizens to vote, second-wave feminism refers to the period from the midsixties and on, in which women's growing consciousness of gender oppression and discrimination informed the determination to achieve equitable social, economic, and cultural conditions.

3. Touraine distinguishes cultural movements from social ones, asserting that the former develops collective actions to transform representations of a subject by emphasizing the acquisition of cultural rights that protect this social actor and dispute, sometimes in a conflictive way, hegemonic cultural significance (1997, 112).

4. Alvarez and others correctly point out that social movements are complex, multidimensional processes that involve the production of alternative sociocultural meanings, the constitution of new collective identities, and the struggle for material conditions (1998, 319).

5. I do not wish to ignore the influence of *industrialized feminisms* in the fomenting of Latin American feminisms but rather assert the importance of the relationship between context, identity, and agency in the constitution of sociocultural actors in particular places and moments. Thus, I am stressing that the existence of a sector of women, receptive to and in need of the meanings proposed by feminist discourse, corresponds to the specific conditions of each country.

6. It is important to stress the extraordinary symbolic influence of second-wave Latin American feminists, especially in the media, universities, and the political arena. The extension, depth, and velocity of the progressive penetration of the feminist discourse into all areas of sociocultural production of meaning, on one hand, and the virulent reaction it produced in the most conservative sectors of national societies, in particular the Catholic Church, were totally disproportionate to the small number of activists at the time. From the beginning of the second wave, the feminist discourse circulated as a genuine challenge to the hegemonic interpretation of reality. This dispute over cultural meaning not only referred to women's rights and citizenship in process of evolution but also framed contemporary contentions about the very paradigm of modernity, enriching the meaning of liberty, social justice, citizenship, and the idea of the individual.

7. In contrast to liberal feminism's exclusive focus on patriarchal social relations and the need for a "women's liberation," Latin American and Caribbean socialist feminists posed a more complex interpretation of gender discrimination, calling for "women's emancipation" from the synergy of patriarchy and capitalism, as a mutually reinforcing dialectic of subordination. Understanding the differential impact of the intersection of gender and class and identifying examples of that linkage in working-class women's everyday lives constituted a first step in fomenting a more nuanced comprehension of gender in the region (De Barbieri and de Oliveira 1986; Tarrés 1998; Randall 1981; Maier 1985; Molyneux 1985; Stephen 1994; Lagarde 1990).

8. For more on the theorization on complex identities, see Foucault (1977), Butler (1990), Bhabha (1994), and Mouffe (1999); for greater detail on women's diversified participation, see Stephen (1994), Schirmer (1993), and Vargas (2002); for the impact of total immersion in the era of globalization, see Castells (2000), Giddens (2003), and Soja (2000).

9. The term *empowerment* came into use without a precise reference. Due to its growing popularity and imprecision, Trotner and Smith suggest that the concept has become "contentious and controversial" (2004, 5). In this article, I refer to the United Nations' definition, which states empowerment to be "women's feeling of self-value; their right to have and decide on options; their right to have the power to control their lives, within as well as outside the home; and their capacity to influence the direction of social change to create a more just national and international social and economic order" (Trotner and Smith 2004, 12).

10. The value of the workforce marked a fundamental difference between feminisms of industrialized countries and those of Latin America. With a cheap and abundant workforce, middle-class employment of domestic workers postponed renegotiation of the sexual division of labor between men and women. A substantial part of the second workday was left to these less privileged women, thus avoiding more radical questioning of sexual roles within middle-class families.

11. These statistics reflect figures of Amnesty International (1982) and the Federación de Familiares de Desaparecidos (Federation of Relatives of Disappeared Persons) (FEDEFAM 1982), respectively.

12. A theoretical debate contingent on the Mothers' committees created two distinct tendencies within Latin American feminist praxis. The maternalists, an offshoot of cultural feminism, sustained that the nurturing and altruism associated with the experience of maternity informs a new and superior political ethic that is evident in women's political participation (Ruddick 1989). In contrast, antimaternalists argued that those cultural characteristics associated with maternity, such as the altruism of being a "body for others," (Bassaglia and Kanoussi 1983; Lagarde 1990) sustain women's subordination. This contention questioned the significance of the Mothers' transgression of the traditional geographies of the sexual division of society to engage in politics in the name of motherhood (Jelin 1997; Lamas 1987).

13. Sojo (1985) defines the term *popular* as including the multiple representations that constitute the Latin American working class.

14. Popular feminism refers to a gender-perspective interpretation of low-income women's needs, interests, and demands. During the 1980s middle-class feminists worked with women from popular organizations to specify the components of a gender-class perspective. At that time popular feminism evoked two distinct images: one referring to middle-class feminists linked to these grassroots movements and the other referring to the women from those movements who participated in gender-oriented activities. Over the years the impact of changing gender representations and discourses on women's gender awareness has resulted in more women in grassroots movements with gender consciousness and demands. This has redefined popular feminism as exclusively referring to the gender rights–based vision and agency of those women activists.

15. The significance of women's grassroots militancy was addressed by authors such as Schmukler, when she asserted that the public agency of Argentinean women in the name of their traditional roles ultimately brought about family democratization (1994). On the other hand, Barrig argues that the participation of the Peruvian women in community kitchens of working-class neighborhoods, or in the Programa del Vaso de Leche, served as a means of reproducing women's traditional roles, rather than signifying real change in gender content or renegotiation (1994, 151–173). However, the paradigmatic shift of the nineties unsettled a sense of feminist continuity, leaving popular feminism without a comprehensive analysis that could have informed a methodology of integration with the current institutional strategy. Along with a study of its achievements and shortcomings, it is necessary to understand the dynamics of autonomy and empowerment within structural situations in which women are not able to be economically independent. A precise analysis of the differential power relations among women resulting from class, ethnicity, and race, among other factors, is needed, as well as the identification of ways to render these relations visible, deal with them, and go beyond.

REFERENCES

Alvarez, Sonia E. 1998. Latin American feminisms "go global": Trends of the 1990s and challenges for the new millennium. In *Cultures of politics / politics of cultures: Revisioning Latin American social movements*, ed. Sonia Alvarez, Evelina Dagnino, and Arturo Escobar, 293–324. Boulder, CO: Westview.

Alvarez, Sonia, Evelina Dagnino, and Arturo Escobar, eds. 1998. The cultural and the political in Latin American social movements. In *Cultures of politics / politics of cultures: Revisioning Latin*

American social movements, ed. Sonia Alvarez, Evelina Dagnino, and Arturo Escobar, 1–32. Boulder, CO: Westview.

Amnesty International USA. 1982. What is a disappearance? In *Disappearances. A workbook.* New York: Amnesty International.

Ardener, Shirley. 1986. The representation of women. In *Visibility and power: Essays on women in society and development*, ed. Leela Dube, Eleanor Leacock, and Shirley Ardener. Delhi: Oxford University Press.

Arendt, Hannah. 1973. *The origins of totalitarianism.* New York: Harcourt, Brace, and World.

Barrig, Maruja. 1994. The difficult equilibrium between bread and roses: Women's organizations and democracy. In *The women's movements in Latin America: Participation and democracy*, ed. Jane Jaquette, 151–176. Boulder, CO: Westview.

Bassaglia, Franca O., and Dora Kanoussi. 1983. *Mujer, locura y sociedad.* Puebla, Mexico: Universidad de Puebla.

Bhabha, Homi. 1994. *The location of culture.* New York: Routledge.

Butler, Judith. 1990. *Gender trouble: Feminism and the subversion of identity.* New York: Routledge.

Castells, Manuel. 2000. *La era de la información: Economía, sociedad y cultura.* Madrid: Alianza.

De Barbieri, Teresita, and Orlandina de Oliveira. 1986. Nuevos sujetos sociales: La presencia de las mujeres en América Latina. *Nueva Antropología* 8 (30): 5–29.

De Beauvoir, Simone. 1981. *La experiencia vivida.* Vol. 2 of *El segundo sexo.* Buenos Aires: Siglo Veinte.

FEDEFAM. 1982. *Convención sobre Desaparecimiento Forzado.* Lima, Perú: FEDEFAM.

Fisher, Jo. 1989. *The mothers of the disappeared.* Boston: South End.

Foucault, Michel. 1977. *Historia de la sexualidad I: La voluntad de saber.* 15th ed. Mexico City: Siglo Veintiuno.

Giddens, Anthony. 2003. *Runaway world: How globalization is reshaping our lives.* New York: Routledge.

Gúzman, Virginia. 2002. *Las condiciones de género en un mundo global.* Serie Mujer y Desarrollo. Santiago: CEPAL.

Jelin, Elizabeth. 1997. Engendering human rights. In *Gender politics in Latin America*, ed. Elizabeth Dore, 65–83. New York: Monthly Review.

Lagarde, Marcela. 1990. *Cautiverio de las mujeres: Madresposas, monjas, putas y locas.* Mexico City: UNAM.

Lamas, Martha. 1987. Maternidad y política. In *Jornadas feministas*, ed. Grupo de Mujeres en Acción Social, 159–177. Mexico City: EMAS.

Macleod, Morna. 1985. *Ciencia y tecnología para Guatemala.* Cuadernos 12. Mexico City: CITGUA.

Maier, Elizabeth. 1985. *Las Sandinistas.* Mexico City: Cultura Popular.

———. 2001. *Las madres de desaparecidos: ¿Un nuevo mito materno en América Latina?* Mexico City: COLEF-UAM La Jornada.

Molyneux, Maxine. 1985. Mobilization without emancipation? Women's interests, state and revolution. In *Transition and development: Problems of third world socialism*, ed. Richard Fagen, Carmen Diana Deere, and José Luis Coraggio. New York: Monthly Review.

———. 2002. The local, the regional and the global: Transforming the politics of rights. In *Gender and the politics of rights and democracy in Latin America*, ed. Maxine Molyneux and Nikki Craske, 1–31 Basingstoke, NY: Palgrave.

Mouffe, Chantal. 1999. *El retorno de lo político.* Barcelona: Paidós.

Pitanguy, Jacqueline. 1998. The women's movement and public policy in Brazil. In *Women's movements and public policy in Europe, Latin America, and the Caribbean*, ed. Geertje Nijeholt, Virginia Vargas, and Saskia Wieringa, 97–109. New York: Garland.

Randall, Margaret. 1981. *Sandino's daughters*. Vancouver: New Star Books.

Ruddick, Sara. 1989. *Maternal thinking: Toward a politics of peace*. Boston: Beacon.

Schirmer, Jennifer. 1993. The seeking of truth and the gendering of consciousness. In *Viva: Women and popular protest in Latin America*, ed. Sara Radcliffe and Sallie Westwood. 30–64. New York: Routledge.

Schmukler, Beatriz. 1994. *Maternidad y ciudadanía femenina, en repensar y politizar la maternidad*. Mexico City: GEM.

Schmuckler, Beatriz, and María Elena Valenzuela. 1998. Women in transition to democracy. In *Women in the third world: An encyclopedia of contemporary issues*, ed. Nelly Stromquist. 69–75. New York: Garland.

Soja, Edward W. 2000. Cosmopolis: The globalization of cityspace. In *Postmetropolis: Critical studies of cities and regions*, ed. Edward W. Soja, 189–232. Los Angeles: Blackwell.

Sojo, Ana. 1985. *Mujer y política: Ensayo sobre el feminismo y sujeto popular*. San José, Costa Rica: Departamento Ecuménico de Investigaciones.

Stephen, Lynn. 1994. The politics of urban survival. In *The women's movement in Latin America*, ed. Jane Jaquette, 111–148. Boulder, CO: Westview.

Tarrés, María Luisa. 1998. *Género y cultura en América Latina: Cultura y participación política*. Mexico City: COLMEX.

Touraine, Alan. 1997. *¿Podremos vivir juntos? La discusión pendiente: El destino del hombre en la aldea global*. Buenos Aires: Fondo de Cultura Económica.

Trotner, Jenifer L., and Peter H. Smith. 2004. Introd. to Empowering women: Agency, structure, and comparative perspective. In *Promises of empowerment: Women in Asia and Latina America*, ed. Peter H. Smith, Jenifer L. Trutner, and Christine Hünefeldt, 1–30. Lanham, MD: Rowman and Littlefield.

Vargas, Virginia. 2002. The struggle of Latin American feminisms for rights and autonomy. In *Gender and the politics of rights and democracy in Latin America*, ed. Máxime Molyneux and Nikki Craske, 199–217. Basingstoke, NY: Palgrave.

Vuola, Elina. 1993. La Virgen María como ideal femenino, su crítica feminista y nuevas interpretaciones. *Pasos*, no. 45:11–20.

PART II

WOMEN, WORK, AND FAMILIES
The Structural Context of Globalization

2 Women's Work and Neoliberal Globalization

IMPLICATIONS FOR GENDER EQUITY

ALICE COLÓN

SARA POGGIO

Even after thirty years of active women's movements and advances in gender equity, we are still far from full citizenship for women in Latin America. We need not detail the impressive increase in women's education, their declining fertility, or their growing social, economic, and political participation, all of which have changed their lives over the past decades. However, these years also saw changes in the world capitalist order, impelling policies of neoliberal globalization that transformed Latin American social, economic, and political structures and intensified poverty and inequality throughout the region. It is increasingly evident that without social and economic equity enabling the exercise of rights, the viability of citizenship is undermined for a majority of people, and particularly for women in the region.

Since the 1980s, external debt crises and subsequent structural adjustment policies have led to declining real earnings, massive unemployment, privatization, and cuts in social services and target programs, all of which forced poor households to engage in multiple strategies for subsistence, depending most heavily on women's contributions and intensified work (Arriagada 1998; González de la Rocha 2001). Since the 1990s measures of industrial restructuring geared to opening Latin American economies to international trade has virtually institutionalized precarious work (Mazza 2004; Benería 2006; González de la Rocha 2001). Women became even more central to such economic and globalizing trends as their increasing economic activity became part of growing precarious labor (Arriagada 1998; Mazza 2004).

It is impossible in this chapter to go into a detailed account of every country, subregion, or particular ethnic and racial group. We concentrate on the broad trends generally accompanying neoliberal policies and economic globalization in Latin America, including the Spanish-speaking Caribbean. We also discuss the economic, social, and political impact for women and men in the region and see how the exclusionary effects of these policies have hindered women's social and political advances.

Industrial Restructuring and Precarious Labor

With the retrenchment of state benefits and limits to employment in the public sector since the 1980s, neoliberal policies have made the private economic sphere and the labor market more central for subsistence and social inclusion (Mazza 2004). Economic security and social inclusion have to increasingly be attained through private, familial resources rather than from governmental or social organizations. The same structural trends that made remunerated labor more important, however, pushed employers to seek greater flexibility in their use of workers as a means to become more competitive in a globalizing economy. With the weakening of both workers' bargaining position and the states' capacity to regulate employment conditions, it became easier to fire workers and to impose more precarious labor conditions. Through legal regulations and established practices, the new labor regime has been characterized by the increase of insecure, unstable, low-paid jobs, which do not provide the rights, guarantees, and benefits that were considered the standard working conditions of formal employment (Leiva 2000; León 2000).

It is in this context that women have become a growing proportion of the region's labor force. Working-age women's participation increased from 34.5 to 39.3 percent between 1995 and 2005; only in Argentina, Mexico, and Costa Rica was it consistently lower than 50 percent in urban areas throughout this period (CEPAL 2006, 2007). Male labor force participation, on the other hand, remained at nearly 72 percent, declining or remaining relatively stagnant in most countries since the 1990s (Montaño 2007a, 2007b; CEPAL 2006, 2007). With male employment declining and female participation growing, women exceeded 40 percent of the economically active population by 2005.

Health, education, and other social services were the sectors that increasingly incorporated higher-educated women into the Latin American and Caribbean modernization process throughout the twentieth century (Colón and Reddock 2004). Incorporation into global markets included the expansion of commercial and producer services—activities servicing economic production such as finance, accounting, scientific research, specialized design, and other business support—that provided further professional, technical, and office jobs. The proportion of women working in professional and technical occupations and in clerical and related services surpassed that of men in practically all countries in 2005 (CEPAL 2006, 2007). Nonetheless, women still remain concentrated in the less economically valued educational, health, and social service professions, as well as in lower-level administrative office and commercial positions, while men take greater hold of higher-status scientific, technical, administrative, and managerial jobs (CEPAL 2006; Giacometti 2005, 2007; León 2000; INMUJERES 2005).

It is thus ironic that until 2002 we found the widest earnings gap precisely between the higher-educated men and women, despite the fact that the pattern seemed to be changing in close to half of the Latin American countries by mid-decade (CEPAL 2007; Colón Warren 2003; Montaño 2007a, 2007b). Moreover, in practically all countries, women tended to be more concentrated than men in the public sector, threatening women's economic opportunities as government jobs declined throughout the region during the period between 1990 and 2005 (CEPAL 2007; Arriagada 1998). Nonetheless, the closing of the earnings gap between higher-educated men and women since 2002 in most countries suggests some advancement in gender equity in these social sectors (CEPAL 2007; Montaño 2007a, 2007b).

Poor Latin American women have also been main participants in the globalizing labor market. If continuing groups of women entered the labor force impelled by aspirations of personal and social fulfillment, many were also propelled by economic pressure, particularly as they faced men's declining employment and earnings (INMUJERES 2005). While higher-educated women continued to have higher levels of economic activity than lower-educated women, it was the latter group who tended to accelerate more in their labor force participation since the 1990s. It was these poor women who moved into an increasingly precarious labor market (Arriagada 1998; Mazza 2004; Montaño 2007a, 2007b; CEPAL 2007; Bravo 2004; Espinosa 2005a, 2005b; Giacometti 2005, 2007; Lara 2006a; Sanz 2007).

To the old categories of precarious labor—traditional agriculture, paid domestic work, and unskilled self-employment—neoliberal trends added new precarious jobs characterized by their low productivity, low quality, and low pay and associated with invisible pauperization (Leiva 2000). Such work is usually done in smaller enterprises, through self-employment or in the informal economy, subcontracted to what appear as independent producers or to those in jobs without formal contracts. This work is also increasingly found in the flexible, part-time, short-term work arrangements that have become part of the formal sector. Further undermining workers' security, these jobs tend to offer less access to social welfare and security, which in the region have been particularly tied to formal, stable employment (Arriagada 1998; Leiva 2000; León 2000; Montaño 2007a, 2007b).

Of the traditional precarious job spheres, live-in domestic service has tended to decline in most countries. Yet poor women still provide this service in higher-status homes, in many instances under conditions akin to servitude. The proportion of paid domestic workers actually increased in Argentina, Brazil, and Mexico from 1990 to 2005 (CEPAL 2007; Montaño 2007a, 2007b). They represented between 10 percent of economically active women in urban areas in Venezuela to more than 20 percent in Paraguay; in countries such as Puerto Rico, they remain hidden from official statistics as part of an unregistered informal economy (CEPAL 2006; Colón Warren 2003). Although domestic workers' mobilization has won some improvement in their rights and working conditions, they still lack legal protection in terms of hours worked and social benefits recognized to other workers and remain vulnerable to arbitrary firings (Montaño 2007a, 2007b).

Agriculture, considered more precarious than urban labor, still employs over one-fourth of women in poorer Andean countries and Paraguay (CEPAL 2006). The proportion in agriculture is probably underregistered in other countries, particularly those with large indigenous populations that share a tradition of female agricultural work. The presence of women appears more important as global markets threaten and degrade subsistence agriculture, and women have become de facto heads of household as men migrate in search of economic alternatives (Bravo and Zapata 2005; Calla 2007; Correia and Van Bronkhorst 2000; Giacometti 2006; Hopenhayn and Bello 2001; Lara 2006b).

Although they represent a smaller proportion of agricultural workers in other countries, women have also become a major labor supply for nontraditional agricultural exports of the region's global trade. Catering to the year-long demand for fresh produce in the North, numerous producers from Mexico to Chile provide fruit, vegetables, and flowers (Barrientos 1999; Gideon 1999; Friedemann-Sánchez 2006; Montaño 2004). Although there is evidence of some changes in Colombia (Friedemann-Sánchez 2006), women in nontraditional agricultural production have been concentrated in the lower-paid, lower-status posts, particularly in processing and packing, where they may face intense long hours of seasonal work without legal contracts and under unhealthy working conditions during long periods of unemployment (Barrientos 1999; Gideon 1999). Making use of women's flexible labor, the smaller producers have adjusted employment to the fluctuations in consumer demand and to the particular risks of agriculture, including weather conditions affecting crops. Larger export companies and retail importers in core countries are spared the risks, while remaining in economic control through the marketing of products (Barrientos 1999).

Economic integration with the U.S. markets through mechanisms such as free trade zones, the North America Free Trade Agreement, and the Caribbean Basin Initiative have also promoted, since the 1980s, the further expansion of existing maquiladoras (export-oriented assembly line factories) throughout Mexico, the Caribbean, and Central America. The expansion has favored female economic activity so much that the industry has come to employ one-fifth or more economically active women in most of these countries (CEPAL 2006; Alvarenga Jule 2001; Safa 1995). Export production provides not only traditional goods such as textiles and clothing but also more modern electronics, professional instruments, automobile and mechanical parts, software, and even data processing (Colón Warren 2003; Gideon 1999; Freeman 2000; Fussel 2000). Maquiladoras may offer greater stability than self-employment to women lacking higher education, but these jobs remain lower paying, require more intense work than other jobs, and are sometimes oppressive in terms of rights and working conditions. No contract, no extra pay for night work, and restrictions to effective unionization are but some of the conditions objected to by maquiladora workers (Alvarenga Jule 2001; Benería 2006; Fussel 2000; Safa 1995). Low pay and intense labor are found even among data processing work, which, although "modern" in style and emulating office employment, subjects workers to the same pressure as factory assembly lines (Freeman 2000).

Moreover, economic trends have restrained the long-term tendency of women's employment. Women's participation based on labor-intensive manufacturing has not been irreversible but is bound by the same setbacks, fluctuations, and tendencies to reduce labor costs that characterize capitalist production in general (Colón Warren 2003). Since the 1970s, as workers gained bargaining power and higher wages in countries such as Puerto Rico, Jamaica, and Mexico, enterprises have moved to lower-paid areas within the same nation or to other countries of the region or beyond, as seen in the recent industrial expansion into China. Industries have continued moving and displacing workers even when they have not faced rising salary levels (Báez 1998; Colón and Reddock 2004; Fussel 2000). The slowdown in labor-intensive manufacturing may explain the decline in economic participation among poorly educated Salvadoran women, and why, in Honduras and Puerto Rico, women represented a lower proportion of the economically active population in 2004 than in the previous decade (CEPAL 2006; Montaño 2007a, 2007b).

Women's employment opportunities may also be affected by competition from male workers. Under the pressure of declining or stagnant male employment, and as some groups of women become less available or more demanding, men have also been incorporated into the most diverse factory production. Such jobs become redefined in gender terms so that they are no longer typified as "female" but maintain their "feminine" low pay and insecure working conditions (Freeman 2000; Safa 2002). In the same vein, the touted move toward more technologically advanced or capital intensive industries as a strategy of development, observed, for example, in Mexico or Puerto Rico, has limited poor women's working opportunities to the extent that industries tend to employ not only fewer workers but a greater proportion of men and higher-skilled labor (Colón and Reddock 2004; Fleck 2001).

Women's growing economic activity is thus facing a declining or stagnant labor market and increasing levels of open unemployment for those actively seeking jobs in the formal sector (Mazza 2004). While the modern formal sectors may be considered relatively competitive in terms of global trade, they have been unable to absorb the available labor supply that presently includes a growing proportion of women (Bravo 2005; Giacometti 2005). Even when a move toward economic recovery in all but the poorest countries, such as Paraguay and Bolivia, contributed to a decline in unemployment after 2002, in 2005 unemployment was still similar or higher than in 1990 in a great majority of countries. It remained in the double digits in the Southern Cone countries, Brazil, Colombia, Panama, and Venezuela (CEPAL 2006, 2007; Montaño 2007a, 2007b). Unemployment levels remained higher for women in all countries but Mexico, El Salvador, and Nicaragua, ranging from 3 percent in Mexico to 16 percent in Colombia (CEPAL 2006).

Open unemployment remains but the tip of the iceberg in terms of the lack of adequate jobs. The pressure of joblessness has furthered the acceptance of precarious employment and underemployment, already common in Mexico, Central America, and the Caribbean (Mazza 2004). Beyond the aforementioned agricultural and manufacturing sectors, this has meant the growth of low-level services, including small-scale commerce and personal services, as well as an expanding tourist industry, promoted as an alternative for the region's faltering economies (Freeman 2000; Montaño 2004; Colón and Reddock 2004). Trends of restructuring in the diverse economic sectors have included not only reorganizing and reducing the larger enterprises but pushing for further flexibility of labor relations. Such flexibility allows for the adjustment of employment levels to fluctuations in product demand, while avoiding the payment of higher benefits provided to more stable workers (Alvarenga Jule 2001; Leiva 2000; León 2000). This has included practices of irregular employment—part-time and, most often, temporary work—as well as the subcontracting of small enterprises or independent and home-based producers, who are really disguised salaried workers but do not receive the benefits of formal employment (Gideon 1999; Leiva 2000; Mazza 2004; Ministerio de Desarrollo Social Panama 2007).

A study of twelve countries in the region shows the proportion of formally employed women with indefinite contracts declined from 19 percent to 13 percent between 2002 and 2005, or a reduction in one-fifth of the long-term, stable jobs (Montaño 2007b). Labor displacement meant a move to lower-quality jobs, even in countries with better indices of recovery, such as Chile and Brazil (León 2000). The loss of jobs and the immersion in precarious sectors probably explains why the proportion of working women with earnings below poverty levels has been higher than the proportion of men in practically all countries (Mazza 2004; CEPAL 2007).

In a resurgence of forms of work that were presumed to have disappeared with capitalist development, a high proportion of both men and women, including employers and salaried workers of microenterprises, were found working in low-productivity sectors in both paid domestic work and in unskilled self-employment. These sectors continued to expand in a majority of countries after 1990, becoming the occupation of up to 40–50 percent of women by 2005 in more economically advanced South American countries, Panama, Costa Rica, and the Dominican Republic, and around two-thirds or more in poorer Andean and Central American countries (CEPAL 2007; Montaño 2007b). Following a historical pattern, only in the Dominican Republic and in Venezuela did we find a higher proportion of employed men than of employed women working in such low productivity jobs (CEPAL 2007; Machinea et al. 2005; Montaño 2007b).

As salaried employment declined, unskilled self-employment and the informal sector remained as survival mechanisms for the working poor population (Mazza 2004; Bravo 2005; Bravo and Zapata 2005; INMUJERES 2005; Lara 2006a; Ministerio de Desarrollo Social, Panama Republic 2007; Sanz 2007). Self-employment has increased in most countries since the 1990s, ranging from about 20 percent of occupied women in Argentina, Chile, and Panama to more than 50 percent in Bolivia and Peru in 2005 (CEPAL 2006, 2007). The proportion of men who were self-employed among employed men in 2005, on the other hand, ranged from around 20 percent in Mexico and Costa Rica to nearly 60 percent in Nicaragua. The proportion of self-employed men surpassed the proportion of self-employed women only in Nicaragua, the Southern Cone, Brazil, and the Dominican Republic (CEPAL 2006). The expansion of such work underscores the sluggishness of the formal economy in generating adequate jobs and the resulting pressures and vulnerability experienced by working women and men.

In addition to the pressures of gender inequality, indigenous and Afro-descendant women suffer from ethnic and racial exclusions that keep them proportionately indigent and less educated, holding the most precarious jobs. Indigenous and Afro-descendant women appear disadvantaged in terms of literacy, school attendance, and educational levels compared to white men and women. In some cases, this disadvantage holds even when compared to indigenous and Afro-descendant men (Calla 2007; Duryea and Genoni 2004; Montaño 2004). Ethnic and racial differences in overall economic activity may be less pronounced, so Afro-descendant women surpass white and mestiza women in labor force participation (Safa 2005) and indigenous women surpass white women's participation in some Andean countries (Calla 2007; Duryea and Genoni 2004). Afro-descendant and indigenous women, however, tend to be most concentrated in low-paying and informal jobs, not only in agriculture but also in menial services, small-scale commerce, domestic service, and street vending in the informal sector (Mazza 2004; Montaño 2004; Montaño 2007a; Sanz 2007; Giacometti 2007). The disadvantage in the labor market reinforces their poverty and inequality so that, for example, in Guatemala 24 percent of indigenous women were indigent, compared to 6.5 percent of mestiza and white women, and in Brazil 22 percent of Afro-descendant women were indigent compared to 8 percent of white women (Montaño 2007b).

Migration and Transnational Aspects of Precarious Labor

With intensified global economic, cultural, and political linkages, and constraining job opportunities in their home countries, women have also become a substantial part of the migrant workers who are the counterpart of mobile capital (Sassen 1988) and a majority of Latin American migrants in practically all countries of the region. Women's migration is defined not only by their gendered and familial responsibilities at home but by the gendered labor demand at places of destination. A sector of migrant women have responded to the demand for higher-skilled workers, such as nurses from the Caribbean employed in the United States, leaving their home countries with an unmet need for their labor (ECLAC et al. 2004). The vast majority of migrant workers from Latin America and the Caribbean are, nonetheless, constituted by poorer women. Their low pay has allowed for the persistence of restructured manufacturing industries in the United States, which offer meager earnings and poor working conditions. Women have also catered to the need for personal and other menial services in hotels, restaurants, offices, and other buildings required by the higher- and middle-status populations in North American and European cities (Montaño 2004; Sassen 1988).

Most often, poor migrant women are employed in paid domestic services, providing traditionally female household or care work no longer done by employed middle- and upper-class women (Benería 2006). In what has become a transnational chain of care work, Mexican, Central American, and Dominican women care for the children and the aged in the United States and European countries, particularly in Spain, while their family members or other poor women do the same for the migrants' families in their home countries (in Mexico, the Dominican Republic, etc.). The transnational chain is also being reproduced within the region as, for example, Paraguayan women provide domestic service for Argentinean women, Nicaraguans for Costa Ricans, or Dominicans for Puerto Ricans (Montaño 2007a, 2007b). Along with those involved in domestic services, precariousness and vulnerability is perhaps most evident among migrant women entangled in what has become a diverse and complex transnational trade of sexual services (Montaño 2007a, 2007b; Colón and Reddock 2004).

Implications for Social and Gender Equity

It has been widely acknowledged that women have carried the heaviest brunt of neoliberally inspired economic and social policies. Through personal and collective survival measures—including adjustments in consumption, the exchange of goods and services, and networking with family and community members—they have made up for the lost social services and declining earnings that have accompanied structural adjustment and economic restructuring. In addition to adjustments within households, women have engaged in "collective survival strategies," such as communal kitchens, informal child-care groups, "self-built" housing projects, community or village banks, microenterprises, and consumer groups (Craske 1999). If at first these were only extensions of individual responses as the economic situation worsened, women's organizations have become politicized, engaging in strikes and demonstrations and making demands on the state for programs that would support their domestic responsibilities. Programs developed in Peru, Ecuador, Argentina, and elsewhere, have recognized the contribution of women's work, assigning funds directly to women responsible for ensuring their children's health and education or caring for other dependents (Montaño 2007a, 2007b; Ministerio de Desarrollo Social, Panama Republic 2007; INMUJERES 2005; Hays-Mitchell 2002; Giacometti 2005).

While such autonomous projects or government programs have offered women some economic respite and the possibility of providing for their families and children's immediate needs, they also afford more than economic advantages. Women have gained a sense of the worth of their ascribed social functions and their potential capabilities, a heightened political identity, and an assessment of their organizational skills, all of which led them to resist neoliberal reforms (Craske 1999; Hays-Mitchell 2002). Neighborhood organizations became spaces in which women contested sexism and power in gender relations, enabling some changes in their status in the family and their engagement in feminist actions (Di Marco 2006). Nonetheless, such programs and organizations still tend to make the family, and particularly women, responsible for the intensified domestic and caring work that accompanies the prevailing economic policies (Hays-Mitchell 2002; Montaño 2007a, 2007b).

Women's increasing employment has also been central in paving the way for Latin American economies' incorporation into global markets. As the labor demand for export-led production and other economic sectors expanded, women's flexible work and lower earnings provided employers with additional workers at lower costs (Arriagada 1998; Mazza 2004). Women's earnings also "made ends meet" within families and in some cases helped them live beyond the level of poverty or indigence, allowing for the adjustment to conditions of unemployment and underemployment imposed by neoliberal policies.

This increase in women's economic activity has implied a redefinition of female status and roles, with possibilities for advancement in gender equity. Studies have found that if women maintain control of their earnings, they may command greater recognition in the household and enhance their mobility and participation in decision making in the family, weakening some of the most open patterns of male authoritarianism (García and de Oliveira 2007; Safa 1995). Still, what possible advancement women may obtain from having control over their own earnings must be considered in relation to the prevailing conditions of poverty and socio-economic inequality pervasive in the region. If highly educated women have shown some improvement in their social and economic conditions, for a much larger group of women, the flexibilization of the labor market has meant precarious work, insecurity, and overt or hidden poverty. Strategies of family survival based on increasing the number of members in the labor force, mainly women, were premised on conditions of great vulnerability. Given their lack of skills and the labor conditions, women are pressured to accept any available job in the formal or informal sectors.

Official documents suggest that since 2002 there has been some alleviation of the most abject conditions of indigence in most countries of the region, which could be related to the increase in additional earners and multiple earning activities within households. Nonetheless, if the increase of newly remunerated members at least replaced the income lost by unemployed men, the alternative of precarious work generally did not improve the quality of life of families. Even when at one point they may not appear as poor, the unstable earnings impose greater levels of risk and indebtedness, affecting consumption patterns. Families must intensify their work and engage in additional survival strategies as they spread out resources over periods when there are fewer or no earners (Benería 2006). In the most developed countries of the continent, even middle classes have had to face unprecedented unemployment and underemployment.

As Lourdes Benería (2006) notes, precarious work entails the intensified vulner-ability of an economically disadvantaged population, whose earnings may at one point appear to place them above official poverty levels, but which provide no secu-rity for the future. For working-class sectors, lacking access to regular earnings hin-ders other support and subsistence strategies. As suggested by Mercedes González de la Rocha (2001), the move from the resources of poverty to the poverty of resources entails not only a lack of adequate employment and intensified work but also the loss of social exchange and self-help.

For women particularly, the precarious labor regime includes not only a drain on material resources but an increasing "poverty of time," as they need to engage in more intense work with longer hours, including both paid and unpaid labor (Gideon 1999; Montaño 2007a, 2007b; Benería 2006). This undermining of energy, time, and regular earnings has been found to affect poor women's consumption patterns and their capacity to maintain the health, nutrition, and social cohesion of their families, resulting in conditions that test the limits of their social inclusion and well-being (Montaño 2007b; Gideon 1999; González de la Rocha 2001). To the extent that poor women are more likely to be in precarious jobs, earn less, and tend to suffer more interruptions to their paid work to fulfill their domestic responsibil-ities, they face a cumulative chain of disadvantages and discrimination throughout their life, which leads to the lack of pensions, economic destitution, and insecurity in their old age (Giacometti 2005; Montaño 2007a, 2007b; Machinea et al. 2005).

Resources are also drained as prevailing socioeconomic conditions tend to fragment family and community networks, straining their possibilities of social support. Among other processes, stagnant male employment and women's access to their own earnings may pose a challenge to stable marital unions if changes in traditional gender roles are not accepted. This may become a factor in the increasing divorce and separation rates, as well as in cases of domestic violence (Safa 1995; Colón and Reddock 2004). Male migration, demographic factors, or simply the increase of unemployed men help account for the multiplication of women heads of households among the lower-income families in most of the countries of Latin America.

The number of female-headed households is growing, not only among lower-status sectors nor are they necessarily the most poor or destitute, particularly if women garner greater control of resources and receive support from other family members (Lara 2006a; Espinosa 2005b; Safa 2002, this volume). Sara Poggio (2003), however, has pointed out that the democratization of relations in extended families is more apparent when there is no spouse living in the household than when unemployed men are present. A great proportion of poor female heads of family, on the other hand, are in one-parent homes, not part of extended families with whom to share economic burdens (Montaño 2007b). Women may in fact be left with greater responsibilities and with less support from other family members or from the state.

Conclusion

The previous discussion underscores a number of conclusions regarding alternatives to problems within the prevailing economic policies. Democracy and gender equity are contingent on the conditions of social, economic, and cultural equity that provide for the satisfaction of people's needs and of the social inclusion of women of diverse classes, races, ethnicities, and other categories. Even though education is extremely necessary in the development of women's capacities and resources, it is not the only condition for gender equity. It is important that women have the opportunity to achieve the highest occupational levels and decision-making positions, breaking down stereotypes that define power and scientific and mechanical capacities as masculine traits. An equitable valuation and remuneration of the personal, social, humanistic, and educational services and job spheres in which women have been concentrated is also necessary.

Most importantly, ensuring decent working conditions and access to social services should become a priority to enable equity among the majority of poor women. This should include not only increasing the productivity and commercial capacity of what are presently precarious job spheres but also providing more adequate and secure earnings and provisions to what are now irregular workers. Extending more universal conditions of social welfare and security should also promote both gender and social equity. Policies and programs promoting gender equity will not be complete, however, without redistributing domestic responsibilities between men and women and providing them with the institutional support for the harmonization of their productive and reproductive work. Only then will women be able to engage more equitably in the market and public sphere, without the poverty of time intensified under conditions of social and economic precariousness (Montaño 2007a, 2007b; Benería 2006; Gideon 1999). Struggles of the most diverse groups of women—domestic, maquiladora, home-based, community, and enterprise workers, along with the feminist and other nongovernmental organizations supporting them—have already achieved some positive advances throughout the region (Alvarenga Jule 2001; Arriagada 1998; Carr et al. 2000; Friedemann-Sánchez 2006; Hays-Mitchell 2002). It is a call for our continuing mobilization!

REFERENCES

Alvarenga Jule, Ligia Elizabeth. 2001. *La situación económica-laboral de la maquila en El Salvador: Un análisis de género*. Santiago: CEPAL.

Arriagada, Irma. 1998. *The urban labour market in Latin America: The myth and the reality*. Santiago: United Nations.

Báez, Clara. 1998. Participación laboral y migración de las mujeres dominicanas en un mundo global. In *Las mujeres del Caribe en el umbral del 2000*, 45–56. Madrid: Dirección General de la Mujer, Comunidad de Madrid.

Barrientos, Stephanie. 1999. La mano de obra femenina y las exportaciones globales: Mujeres en las agroindustrias chilenas. In *Globalización y género*, ed. Paloma de Villota, 297–318. Madrid: Síntesis.

Benería, Lourdes. 2006. Trabajo productivo / reproductivo, pobreza y políticas de conciliación. *Nómadas* 24:8–21.

Bravo, Rosa. 2004. *Las metas del milenio y la igualdad de género: El caso de Perú*. Santiago: CEPAL / UNIFEM.

———. 2005. *Las metas del milenio y la igualdad de género: El caso de la República Bolivariana de Venezuela*. Santiago: CEPAL / UNIFEM.

Bravo, Rosa, and Daniela Zapata. 2005. *Las metas del milenio y la igualdad de género: El caso de Bolivia*. Santiago: CEPAL / UNIFEM.

Calla, Ricardo. 2007. *La mujer indígena en Bolivia, Brasil, Ecuador, Guatemala y Panamá: Un panorama de base a partir de la ronda de censos de 2000*. Santiago: CEPAL .

Carr, Marilyn, Martha Alter Chen, and Jane Tate. 2000. Globalization and home-based workers. *Feminist Economics* 6 (3): 123–142.

CEPAL. 2006. *Anuario estadístico de América Latina y el Caribe: Estadísticas sociales*. Santiago: División de Estadísticas y Proyecciones Económicas, CEPAL.

———. 2007. *Panorama social de América Latina 2006*. Santiago: CEPAL / UNFPA.

Colón Warren, Alice. 2003. Empleo y reserva laboral entre las mujeres en Puerto Rico. In *Género, sociedad y cultura*, ed. Loida Martínez and Maribel Tamargo, 224–246. San Juan, Puerto Rico: Gaviota.

Colón Warren, Alice, and Rhoda Reddock. 2004. The changing status of women in the contemporary Caribbean. In *The Caribbean in the twentieth century*. Vol. 5 of *General history of the Caribbean*, ed. Bridget Brereton, 465–505. Paris: UNESCO / London: Macmillan Caribbean.

Correia, María, and Bernice Van Bronkhorst. 2000. Ecuador gender review: Issues and recommendations. A World Bank Country Study, Report 20830, June. Washington, DC: World Bank.

Craske, N. 1999. *Women and politics in Latin America*. New Brunswick, NJ: Rutgers University Press.

Di Marco, Graciela. 2006. Movimientos sociales y democratización en Argentina. In *De lo privado a lo público: 30 años de lucha ciudadana de las mujeres en América Latina*, ed. Nathalie Lebon and Elizabeth Maier, 249–270. Mexico City: Siglo Veintiuno.

Duryea, Suzanne, and María Eugenia Genoni. 2004. Origen étnico, raza y género en los mercados de trabajo de América Latina. In *Inclusión social y desarrollo económico en América Latina*, ed. Mayra Buvinic, Jaqueline Mazza, and Juliana Pungiluppi, with Ruthanne Deusch, 265–279. Washington, DC: Banco Interamericano de Desarrollo.

ECLAC, CDCC, CIDA, UNIFEM, and CARICOM. 2004. Report of the ECLAC/CDCC Fourth Caribbean Ministerial Conference on Women: Review and Appraisal of the Beijing Platform for Action. Kingstown, St. Vincent, and Grenadines, February 12–13.

Espinosa, Isolda. 2005a. *Las metas del milenio y la igualdad de género: El caso de Guatemala.* Santiago: CEPAL / UNIFEM.

———. 2005b. *Las metas del milenio y la igualdad de género: El caso de Nicaragua.* Santiago: CEPAL / UNIFEM.

Fleck, Susan. 2001. A gender perspective on maquila employment and wages in Mexico. In *The economics of gender in Mexico: Work, family, state, and markets*, ed. Elizabeth Katz and María C. Correia, 133–173. Washington, DC: World Bank.

Freeman, Carla. 2000. *High tech and high heels in the global economy: Women, work and pink-collar identities in the Caribbean.* Durham, NC: Duke University Press.

Friedemann-Sánchez, Greta. 2006. Assets in intrahousehold bargaining among women workers in Colombia's cut-flower industry. *Feminist Economics* 12 (1–2): 247–269.

Fussel, Elizabeth. 2000. Making labor flexible: The recomposition of Tijuana's maquila female labor force. *Feminist Economics* 6 (3): 59–81.

García, Brígida, and Orlandina de Oliveira. 2007. Trabajo extradoméstico y relaciones de género: Una nueva mirada. In *Género, familias y trabajo: Rupturas y continuidades*, comp. María Alicia Gutiérrez, 49–88. Buenos Aires: CLACSO.

Giacometti, Claudia. 2005. *Las metas del milenio y la igualdad de género: El caso de Argentina.* Santiago: CEPAL / UNIFEM.

———. 2006. *Las metas del milenio y la igualdad de género: El caso de Paraguay.* Santiago: CEPAL.

———. 2007. *Las metas del milenio y la igualdad de género: El caso de Uruguay.* Santiago: CEPAL.

Gideon, Jasmine. 1999. Looking at economies as gendered structures: An application to Central America. *Feminist Economics* 5 (1): 1–28.

González de la Rocha, Mercedes. 2001. From the resources of poverty to the poverty of resources? *Latin American Perspectives* 28 (4): 72–100.

Hays-Mitchell, Maureen. 2002. Resisting austerity: A gendered perspective on neo-liberal restructuring in Peru. *Gender and Development* 10 (3): 71–81.

Hopenhayn, Martín, and Álvaro Bello. 2001. *Discriminación étnico-racial y xenophobia en América Latina y el Caribe.* Santiago: CEPAL.

INMUJERES. 2005. *Las metas del milenio y la igualdad de género: El caso de México.* Santiago: CEPAL.

Lara, Silvia. 2006a. *Las metas del milenio y la igualdad de género: El caso de Colombia.* Santiago: CEPAL.

———. 2006b. *Las metas del milenio y la igualdad de género: El caso de Ecuador.* Santiago: CEPAL.

Leiva, Sandra. 2000. *El trabajo a tiempo parcial en Chile: ¿Constituye empleo precario? Reflexiones desde la perspectiva de género.* Santiago: CEPAL.

León, Francisco. 2000. *Mujeres y trabajo en las reformas estructurales latinoamericanas durante las décadas de 1980 y 1990.* Santiago: CEPAL.

Machinea, José L., Alicia Bárcena, and Arturo León, eds. 2005. Autonomía de las mujeres e igualdad de género. Chap. 4 in *Objetivos de desarrollo del Milenio: Una mirada desde América Latina y el Caribe.* Santiago: CEPAL.

Mazza, Jacqueline. 2004. Inclusión social, mercados de trabajo y capital humano en América Latina. In *Inclusión social y desarrollo económico en América Latina,* ed. Mayra Buvinic, Jaqueline Mazza, and Juliana Pungiluppi, with Ruthanne Deusch, 191–214. Washington, DC: Banco Interamericano de Desarrollo.

Ministerio de Desarrollo Social, Panama Republic. 2007. Informe de país. Paper presented at the Tenth Women's Regional Conference of Latin America and the Caribbean, CEPAL, Quito, August 6–9.

Montaño, Sonia, coord. 2004. Caminos hacia la equidad de género en América Latina y el Caribe. Document for the Ninth Women's Regional Conference of Latin America and the Caribbean, CEPAL, Mexico City, June 10–12.

———, coord. 2007a. El aporte de las mujeres a la igualdad en América Latina y el Caribe. Document for the Tenth Women's Regional Conference of Latin America and the Caribbean, CEPAL, Quito, August 6–9.

———, coord. 2007b. *Objetivos de desarrollo del milenio: Informe 2006; Una mirada a la igualdad entre los sexos y la autonomía de la mujer en América Latina y el Caribe.* Santiago: CEPAL.

Poggio, Sara. 2003. Transiciones familiares en la República Mexicana. In *Las políticas de familia en México y la transformación de las relaciones sociales,* ed. Beatriz Schmuckler and Rosario Campos. Mexico City: Instituto Nacional de la Mujer, UNDP.

Safa, Helen I. 1995. *The myth of the male breadwinner: Women and industrialization in the Caribbean.* Boulder, CO: Westview.

———. 2002. Questioning globalization: Gender and export processing in the Dominican Republic. *Journal of Developing Societies* 18 (2–3): 11–31.

———. 2005. Challenging mestizaje: A gender perspective on indigenous and Afrodescendent movements in Latin America. *Critique of Anthropology* 25 (3): 280–330.

Sanz, Mariana. 2007. *Los desafíos del milenio ante la igualdad de género.* Santiago: CEPAL / UNIFEM.

Sassen, Saskia. 1988. *The mobility of labor and capital: A study in international investment and labor flows.* Cambridge: Cambridge University Press.

3

Female-Headed Households and Poverty in Latin America

A COMPARISON OF CUBA, PUERTO RICO, AND THE DOMINICAN REPUBLIC

HELEN SAFA

Female household headship has long been associated with poverty. Women's lower salaries, coupled with other forms of gender discrimination in the labor market, and the lack of a stable male breadwinner imply that households headed by females have lower incomes. But Sylvia Chant (1997) and others have questioned this automatic assumption, claiming that female heads are not always "the poorest of the poor." In Latin America during the 1990s the percentage of urban female headship increased overall and, while indigent households represented the largest proportion of female headships, the increase was not confined to this sector (ECLAC 2004, 23).

In this chapter, I analyze the way in which globalization has accentuated the poverty of female heads by examining data from three countries in the Hispanic Caribbean—Cuba, Puerto Rico, and the Dominican Republic—in all of which female headship has increased during the 1990s. Part of this increase can be attributed to the rapid gains in female labor force participation in each of these countries, which coincides with a decline or stagnation in male labor force participation. In my book *The Myth of the Male Breadwinner: Women and Industrialization in the Caribbean*, which compares these three countries, I show that as real wages and male employment deteriorates, women step in to bolster the household economy and have now become principal contributors to the household in each country. The massive increase in married women's labor force participation is also decisive because it threatens the partner's role as provider, a role that traditionally formed the basis of his authority in the household. When married women have to substitute for men as principal breadwinners, family conflict and marital breakdown often ensue, contributing to the rising percentage of female heads of household in each of the Caribbean countries studied. This pattern is clearly not confined to the Caribbean, but may help explain the increase in female-headed households worldwide (Chant 1997). Amy Bellone Hite and Jocelyn Viterna (2005) have shown that in Latin America as a whole, due to economic restructuring, increased female labor force participation rates have been accompanied by declines in male rates.

But the impact of economic restructuring and globalization on female heads may differ in each country, depending on demographic differences among female heads of household and the resources available to them, which range from jobs to state benefits to remittances. Female heads are found at different socioeconomic levels and also vary in marital status, including those never married, divorced, separated, or widowed.[1] In the Caribbean there is a high proportion of consensual unions, which are less stable than legal marriages and therefore increase the likelihood of single motherhood. Most of these single mothers have never married, although some are separated and divorced.

These single mothers rely mostly on their own employment for survival, but in developing countries like Cuba and the Dominican Republic they are traditionally embedded in extended families who offer economic and emotional support. This often leads to an undercount of female heads, who are instead embedded as subheads in the extended households of their parents, as we see in the Dominican Republic. However, in Puerto Rico, state policy encourages the breakup of extended families, and there is a higher percentage of widows, due to the aging of the Puerto Rican population. As a result, Puerto Rican female heads are more likely to live alone without the presence of extended families. The state support available to female heads also enables this independence and is much higher in Puerto Rico than in the Dominican Republic or Cuba, where remittances from relatives living abroad play a larger role. All three countries have experienced large-scale emigration, chiefly to the United States. Migration started in Puerto Rico as early as the 1940s, so remittances are no longer as important.

This chapter will compare the status of female-headed households in Cuba, Puerto Rico, and the Dominican Republic by examining the importance of each of the factors affecting vulnerability to poverty, namely differences in marital status and household composition, employment, and other sources of income like state support and remittances. I argue that female heads are more vulnerable to poverty if (1) they live alone with young children and do not have the support of extended family, (2) they receive little or no financial support or social services from the state, and/or (3) they have inadequate alternative sources of income, whether from jobs or remittances. I cannot correlate these factors with accurate income data, but focus more on the strategies that female heads use to maximize resources from these different sources. My focus is on female factory workers, from which my original sample in the 1980s was drawn, and which in each country contains a considerable segment of female household heads. I have not done systematic field research since then, except in the Dominican Republic, where I conducted another study on female employment and family structure in a free trade zone in 1997 (Safa 2002). I also consult national-level statistics to see how continued economic restructuring in the 1990s affects the status of female-headed households in each country.

Both the amount and kind of female headship varies by country. Women in Cuba now head over one-third of the households, while in the Dominican Republic and Puerto Rico they constitute about 27 percent. Widows constitute one-third of female heads of household in Puerto Rico, while single mothers are the most frequent form of female head in Cuba and the Dominican Republic. Caribbean women are resisting marriage and remarriage because the "marriage market" of eligible men who could fulfill the role of male breadwinner has shrunk. Male emigration contributes to the formation of female-headed households, while remittances have become an important source of income for those left behind. There is also an increasing percentage of female heads among professional women in the Caribbean, resulting largely from rising divorce rates in each of these countries. However, these professional women are less vulnerable to poverty than the low-income factory workers focused on here.

Despite these differences, all three countries share a similar historical and cultural background as Spanish colonies that came under strong U.S. economic control in the early twentieth century. Cuba broke this control with its 1959 revolution, which established a socialist state. Puerto Rico remains a U.S. colony, but Puerto Ricans are U.S. citizens, which makes them eligible for many federal benefits. The Dominican Republic also remains under U.S. tutelage, but was able to establish a democratically elected government after the overthrow of the dictator Trujillo in 1965. All three economies focused on sugar cultivation, which helps account for the relatively large Afro-descendant population, many of whom were brought as slaves in the colonial period. But with the decline in sugar production, Puerto Rico, the Dominican Republic, and even Cuba are now more geared toward tourism and export processing.

The Economic Crisis in the Caribbean in the 1990s

Neoliberal reforms in Latin America in the 1990s encouraged the informalization of the labor market, the weakening of unions, and the growth of cheap labor. In 2003, according to the Economic Commission for Latin America (ECLAC), 220 million or 43 percent of Latin Americans lived in poverty, a high social cost that has made increasing numbers question the efficacy of market reform (Hershberg 2003). Globalization and neoliberal reform hit the small economies of the Caribbean even harder than the rest of the region. They had long been dependent on foreign investment and exports to sustain their economies, but as globalization opened up new markets for investment, particularly in China, they became less competitive and more dependent on cheap labor. Meanwhile, neoliberal reform was driving up the cost of living and reducing the value of real wages even more.

No country illustrates these effects of globalization better than the Dominican Republic. It abandoned sugar as a primary export commodity in the mid-eighties and sought foreign exchange through export manufacturing and tourism but became even more dependent on the vagaries of the world market. As the value of the Dominican peso dropped along with high inflation at the end of the 1990s, the cost of living increased and the female share of the labor force increased to 38 percent in 2000. Since 1980 the rate of female labor force participation has grown at a higher rate than that of men, reflecting the need for additional wage earners in the household (Báez 2000, 45, table 2.2). Women continue to be the predominant labor force in the free trade zones, but by 2004 this percentage had declined to about 52 percent (CIPAF 2005).

Dominican free trade zones continued to prosper through the 1990s, spurred on by generous financial incentives and cheap labor, and employed two hundred thousand people by the end of 2001. But declines started in 2005–2006, both in the number of workers and volume of exports, especially in the apparel industry (CNZFE 2006). The Dominican free trade zones are under increasing pressure from international competition, especially China. Special quotas for clothing imports to the United States were terminated with the end of the Multifiber Agreement in 2005. Textiles and clothing were integrated into the World Trade Organization, and China entered as a full competitor. Clothing and textiles still constitute about 35 percent of all production in the free trade zones, despite efforts at diversification toward high value-added products. The inclusion of the Dominican Republic in the Central American Free Trade Agreement (CAFTA-DR) in 2007 may somewhat reduce this competition. But as the economy worsened in 2004, remittances grew substantially, reaching 2.7 billion, including 1.6 billion from emigrants living in the United States (Columbia University 2004).

Puerto Rico has totally lost its comparative advantage over neighboring countries as a site for light manufacturing, and Operation Bootstrap, the government's ambitious industrialization program conceived in the 1950s as the engine of growth, has became obsolete. The apparel industry, once the principal employer of women in Puerto Rico, has virtually ground to a halt. As educational levels rose, women shifted into white-collar and professional employment and the service sector, and government employment became the most important source of job creation. Male labor force participation rates declined from 54 percent in 1980 to 49 percent in 2000, while the female rate rose to 35 percent and then from 1990 to 2000 also began to decline (Colón Warren 2006). Despite growing unemployment and withdrawal from the labor force, especially by men, poverty rates declined to about 49.3 percent in 1990 (Dietz 2003, 164). James Dietz attributes this to the important role that federal transfer payments have played in the Puerto Rican economy. Since the late 1970s federal transfers, including earned transfers such as social security and Medicare and means-tested transfers like welfare and food stamps, have approximated 20 percent of personal income and have become a major source of support for the Puerto Rican economy (2003, 162–163), including female-headed households.

Of the three countries discussed here, Cuba suffered the greatest economic crisis in the 1990s, due to the breakup of the socialist bloc and the elimination of trade and aid from the former Soviet Union. The 1990s in Cuba has become known as the Special Period, the worst peacetime economic crisis in its history. Between 1989 and 1993 the GDP declined 35 percent, as exports and imports collapsed and nutritional levels declined drastically. During the 1990s, as the Cuban state shifted priorities, a dual economy evolved, with a dynamic or emergent sector based largely on tourism and a traditional sector including most agriculture and manufacturing (Monreal 2001, 10). As Cuba legalized the U.S. dollar (later changing to the euro and the convertible peso), a dual currency system emerged, benefiting those with access to dollars through tourism, remittances, and self-employment in the informal sector. In 1997 it was estimated that 50 percent of the population had access to dollars through remittances or various work incentives (Espina 2001, 34). The result has been growing inequality and the erosion of the social contract, which guaranteed everyone a minimum standard of living (2001).

The Special Period has hit the Afro-Cuban population particularly hard, because they have less access to dollars through remittances (since the émigré population is largely white) and through the new tourist economy, which favors white employees. Shortcomings in public services and particularly the low wage rate in the formal state sector forced the Cuban population to develop survival techniques, in which women played a critical role. However, the state also maintained a high level of social expenditure, particularly through a universal free education and health care system. These expenditures rose to 32 percent of the GDP in 1998, nearly double the average in Latin America (Uriarte 2002, 36). The at-risk urban population rose from 6.3 percent in 1986 to 14.7 percent in 1995 (Martínez Reinosa and Castro Flores 2004, 52), which includes many female-headed households.

In all three countries, then, the economic crisis of the 1990s resulted in an increase in female-headed households, amid growing poverty and inequality. However, a high level of public expenditure in both Puerto Rico and Cuba ameliorate this inequality, while increasing remittances play a major role in the Dominican Republic. Remittances also increased in Cuba with the advent of the Special Period, but aggravated this inequality, as we shall see.

The Special Period in Cuba

Any analysis of Cuban family structure must not only take account of the dramatic changes ushered in by the Special Period in the 1990s but also examine the longer-term changes brought about by the revolutionary Cuban government's commitment to gender equality. The Cuban state tried to promote women's equality through incorporating them into the labor force, raising educational levels, increasing job opportunities, and providing generous maternity leaves and free day care. Female labor force participation increased rapidly, reaching 40.6 percent in 1993 (Catasús 1999, 5), and also changed qualitatively. As a result of higher educational levels, in 1995 women held two-thirds of technical and professional jobs, a change that began in the 1970s (Catasús 1999, 3, table 1). But the Cuban state did not expect women's increased economic autonomy to contribute to marital instability. On the contrary, the sharing of rights and responsibilities spelled out in the Cuban family code was designed to stabilize the conjugal bond by reinforcing more egalitarian marital relations (cf. Benglesdorf 1997). However, the percentage of households headed by women has grown at an alarming rate, from 14 percent in 1953 to 28.1 percent in 1981, to 36 percent in 1995 (Catasús 1999). What are the factors producing this increase?

Historically, female-headed households predominated among low income, Afro-Cuban households and were often attributed, in Cuba and elsewhere, to the deleterious effects of slavery on the conjugal bond. However, the revolutionary commitment to the promotion of gender equity and other factors appears to have contributed toward a striking convergence of marital patterns along racial lines since 1959. Consensual unions have increased among the white population, while more blacks are getting married (De la Fuente 1995, 147). The rate of female heads of household continues to be somewhat higher among blacks, who have higher rates of marital dissolution. But a comparison of white, black, and mulatto heads of household shows a striking similarity in educational and occupational levels and labor force participation (Catasús 1999, 9, table 2), again demonstrating remarkable racial convergence. This also demonstrates the educational and occupational achievements of Afro-Cuban women under the revolution, including those who are female heads.

I would attribute this racial convergence in marital patterns and the increase in female-headed households to the Cuban Revolution's commitment to the reduction of class and racial barriers, which weakened the legitimacy of the old dual marriage system whereby legal marriage was confined to the white elite (Martínez-Alier 1974). Prerevolutionary racial differences in fertility and mortality began to converge in the early years of the revolution and by 1981 had virtually been eliminated. Educational and occupational racial differences were also leveled, and by 1981 the proportion of blacks and mulattoes employed as professionals (one-fifth of the labor force) was virtually identical to that of whites (De la Fuente 1998, 2–3). Interracial unions also grew, as mulattoes coupled with whites and blacks, but there were few white-black unions (Rodríguez 2006).

Another factor influencing the increase in female heads is the rising rate of consensual unions, from 58.70 consensual unions per 100 marriages in 1970 to 60.00 in 1981 to 81.70 in 1987 (Catasús 1996, 92–93). Much of this increase is due to the younger generation under twenty-five, particularly among mulattas. This increase in consensual unions among the young helps explain why age at first union and first pregnancy also declined since 1959, despite free access to birth control, abortion, and sex education programs. Legalized abortions have increased dramatically. The birthrate continues to fall and is now below replacement levels. Divorce also increased from 0.06 per thousand in 1960 to 3.50 in 1990 (Catasús 1996, 94).

Certain features unique to Cuba may also have contributed to the increase in female headship. Socialist Cuba was among the first Latin American countries to grant women in consensual unions and their children equal legal recognition as women in legal marriage, further debilitating the validity of legal marriage. The provision of free health care and education as well as increasing educational and occupational opportunities for women made it easier for them to have children on their own and greatly weakened dependence on a male breadwinner, despite full employment for men prior to the Special Period. One of our Cuban respondents from the mid-eighties, a woman textile worker who raised three small children on her own, commented, "Ahora actualmente, cualquiera mujer, para mí, cualquiera mujer cría un hijo sola, porque hay mucho trabajo, hay más facilidades para la mujer" [Now any woman, for me any woman can raise a child alone, because there is a lot of work, there are more facilities for women (Safa 1995, 139). In 1995, 47 percent of all women heading their households were employed (Núñez Sarmiento 2001, 61).

The extended family is essential to the survival of these Cuban female-headed households, especially among the young. The proportion of extended families in Cuba is generally high, due in part to a housing shortage, but is higher still among female-headed households. In the study of Cuban women textile workers we conducted in the 1980s, over half of the female-headed households consisted of three generations. Adolescent mothers often live with their parents, which helps them to engage in paid employment but also keeps them in a subordinate position in the household (Safa 1995).

The Cuban state has made a great effort to maintain a high level of social expenditures, despite the severe economic pressures brought on by the Special Period. Social expenditures increased in the decade of the 1990s from 3.816 to 4.705 million pesos and also increased as a proportion of the GDP (Uriarte 2002, 35). Special programs have been started targeting the most vulnerable groups, including single mothers, departing somewhat from the socialist policy of universality. However, increased expenditures could not make up for the reduced buying power of the peso and the decrease in allocation to convertible currency (U.S. dollars), which severely limit the importation of crucial items such as medicines, building materials, and school supplies, especially paper (36).

Given the cutback in support services from the state, the extended family has become even more essential. One of the extended families we interviewed in 1986 had twenty-six members, consisting of Rosa, the grandmother, and her five married children and their children. The family had been given a house by the government with a relatively large patio, in which each of the children has built an independent residence for themselves out of a communal fund. They continue to live together and now number about thirty-six, since Rosa has fifteen grandchildren and two great-grandchildren. Rosa is over sixty and no longer works but receives a small pension and earns some money sewing clothes at home for sale in a retail store. The textile factory in which most of the family worked has now been reduced to a skeleton staff of one shift. Initially, many of the factory workers were employed in agriculture, but now many are self-employed. Families like Rosa's continue to grow some of their own food, as well as chickens and other livestock, although these are now severely limited in urban areas by government regulation.

Generational differences are apparent between older women like Rosa and her daughter Ximena, now in her forties. Rosa had a total of twelve children; Ximena has two. Rosa undertook formal employment only after the revolution, while her daughters have worked since they completed school. All eight siblings completed high school, and one became a teacher. Ximena left her first compañero (a man much her senior) when he would not allow her to work or be active in the community. She became legally married to her second partner of twenty years only after they joined a nearby Pentecostal church during the Special Period.

Women's economic autonomy was threatened in the Special Period. Female labor force participation fell to 31.5 percent by 1995 (Catasús 1999, 3), indicating that women were having a harder time holding down a full-time job as the crisis deepened. Some professional college-educated women abandoned careers as teachers, doctors, and scientists in the state sector to work in higher-paid, less-skilled jobs in tourism (Toro-Morn et al. 2002, 51). Transportation problems mounted and women spent more time finding and preparing food and attending to other household chores. Men's labor force participation also declined, more precipitously than that of women. But in 1997 unemployment was more than twice as high for women as for men (10.1 percent vs. 4.4 percent) (Uriarte 2002, 28). Unemployment grew as employees were discharged from the state sector (45 percent of discharged workers were women in 1997–1999) or withdrew because the purchasing power of the state salary in pesos had steeply declined (Echevarría 2004, 74).

In a study of 334 Cuban households in 2000 (Blue 2004), 85 percent agreed that having a professional job no longer guarantees Cubans a good standard of living. Racial inequality grew during the Special Period, with only 10 percent of blacks in the highest-income category, compared to 58 percent of whites and 31 percent of mulattoes. These differences are due to differential access to the dollar economy, such as earning supplements in dollars and through self-employment. Remittances greatly accentuated these income differences, by pushing many more white than black households into the highest income bracket. Remittances doubled the average household earnings, and 60 percent of the recipients were in Havana (Eckstein 2004, 342). White households had many more family members living abroad and twice as many white as black households receive remittances (Blue 2004). Thus, the racial and territorial difference associated with the receipt of remittances accentuated inequality rather than reducing it.

Women Workers in the Free Trade Zones of the Dominican Republic

No state support for female-headed households exists in the Dominican Republic, yet the percentage has increased from 21.7 percent in 1981 to 29.1 percent in 1991 (Duarte and Tejada 1995, 47), declining again to 26.8 percent in 1996 (Báez 2000, 33, table 1.2). Female heads have a higher labor force participation rate than married or even single women, and this rate has increased rapidly for all women since 1960, standing at 37.6 percent in 2000 (Báez 2000, 45, table 2.1). Here again the extended family plays a critical role, and women working in the free trade zones frequently leave their children with their parents in the rural area (Safa 1995). Women facing an emergency like illness, unemployment, or marital breakup seem to have no difficulty moving back with their parent(s) or other relatives, despite very crowded living conditions.

Mothers and daughters are especially flexible at exchanging roles and reflect the strength of the mother-daughter tie in most Dominican families. Dominica, at forty-seven, has been in three consensual unions and "raised her children [while] working in the factories." At her age, it would be difficult to find a factory job, so she stays home and watches her daughter's two preschool children, while her daughter works in the zone and also attends school every night until ten. Her daughter says she is lucky to have her mother's support, but Dominica claims, "I take care of her children and she studies at night. She is already in the second year of high school. If she really achieves something, then I also gain. I have to sit and take care of her children so that she can get ahead."

The household composition of female heads of household, whether living alone or in extended families, plays a fundamental role in determining the standard of living of these households, regardless of the absence of a male breadwinner. An analysis of the 1991 national-level Informe Demográfico y de Salud (Demographic and Health Survey) by the Instituto de Estudios de Población y Desarrollo (Population and Development Studies Institute) in the Dominican Republic found that although female heads of household earn less than male heads and have a much higher rate of unemployment, the average household incomes are nearly equal (Duarte and Tejada 1995, 80–81; Safa 2002). Apparently female heads of household are able to raise their income through the contributions of other family members, particularly subheads, because over half (53 percent) of households headed by women are extended, compared to only 35 percent of male-headed households. Extended households in the Dominican Republic represented 40 percent of all households surveyed in 1991 and are even more prevalent in urban than in rural areas.

Analysis of the survey in the Dominican Republic shows that nearly three-fourths of these subheads living in extended families are young daughters of the head of household and over half have only one child. Many of these young, single mothers living as subheads go undetected in the census because they are counted as part of the extended family in which they live. Households with subheads are found in even greater proportion among middle- and high-income groups than among the poor (Duarte and Tejada 1995, 90). This suggests that the incorporation of subheads or other additional wage earners is a strategy used not just by the poor but also by the middle class to combat the economic crisis and the high cost of living.

Initially men rejected employment in the free trade zones as "women's work," but since 1980 the percentage of men employed nationally in the free trade zones has more than doubled, reaching 49 percent in 2006 (CNZFE 2006, graph 13). Part of this increase can be explained through diversification toward higher value-added products, a strategy used in the Dominican Republic to upgrade the apparel industry in a trend that has also been noted globally (United Nations 1999, 10). Men are employed in plants producing trousers and coats, which they have redefined as "men's work." But acceptance is also due to the deterioration in male employment, which left men few alternatives. The new labor code issued in 1992 assured working women three month's maternity leave at half pay. Some see obviating maternity leave as a factor in increased male employment in the free trade zones, which shows how difficult it is to improve women's working conditions.

Older men who have a particularly difficult time finding employment are very resentful of the independence that paid employment has conferred on women working in the free trade zones. They stereotype females who work in the free trade zones as flirts and spendthrifts who contribute little to the household economy (Safa 2002). Women clearly reject this stereotype and claim that they are working to support their children. One young woman worker argues that it was more difficult for women when the sugar mill was in operation because men "worked and earned money for the home and did what they pleased, but now the woman works, she maintains herself, she dresses herself, it cannot be the same" (Safa 2002, 18). As a result of improved economic autonomy, women increasingly take the initiative in breaking relationships that are unsatisfactory, whereas previously female heads of household were often the result of male abandonment. My ethnographic research among Dominican workers in the free trade zones shows that female heads of household often resist marriage or remarriage and prefer to support themselves if they cannot find a good provider (Safa 2002).

As emigration has increased, the volume of remittances has grown enormously, more than doubling from 1997 to 2.4 billion in 2003. However, it is unclear how this applies to women working in the free trade zones. We found that women receiving remittances from their husbands were often forbidden from working in the free trade zones, to maintain stricter control over their behavior (McClenaghan 1997; Safa 2002).

Studies done on Dominican remittance patterns reveal the matrifocal extended nature of the Dominican family. In a large sample comparing households receiving remittances in four Latin American countries, Dominicans show the highest proportion of extended and single-parent households, while the Dominican recipient population of three-generation households doubles that of Mexico (Sana and Massey 2005, 518). In an earlier 1991 comparative study focusing on Santo Domingo, women in female-headed and older households were shown to receive remittances more than other family members and were often not working (Itzigsohn 1995, 640–645). In the latter sample, remittances constituted nearly 40 percent of household income, boosting incomes in all strata from the urban poor to professionals.

I would argue that remittances are taking the place of low and inadequate state support for the urban poor. There is no targeted public support for female-headed households, while general public health, education, and other public services are poorly funded. The percentage of public social expenditures continues to be one of the lowest in Latin America, averaging 5.4 percent of the Dominican GDP from 1994–1996 (CIPAF 2005). The government has failed to enforce the new labor code issued in 1992, which was to sanction collective bargaining rights in the free trade zones. As a result, few collective bargaining agreements in the free trade zones have been signed and implemented, so workers rights are still being violated (U.S. Department of Labor 2002). Men are preferred in technical and managerial positions and receive higher salaries (Safa 2002). Although the Dominican Republic recently entered a new free trade pact with the United States through CAFTA-DR, the Dominican government is still worried about competition from cheaper wages elsewhere and is therefore reluctant to enforce workers rights. Female-headed households are thus forced to rely heavily on the extended family and remittances from abroad.

The End of Operation Bootstrap in Puerto Rico

In Puerto Rico, the decline in export manufacturing is far more severe. Although Puerto Rico started early and served as a model of export growth for much of the Caribbean (and other parts of the world), decline began as other countries offered even cheaper wages and more lucrative tax incentives. U.S. government policies such as the Caribbean Basin Initiative in the 1980s and NAFTA in the 1990s favored export manufacturing in other countries in the region, which accelerated this trend (Safa 1995).

A 2002 study of displaced garment workers in Puerto Rico found that since 1997, the number of garment workers island-wide declined from 21,818 to 9,739 (Colón et al. 2008). In addition, one-fourth of all garment workers were over fifty, a demographic trend that was already apparent in 1980 when we collected data on our original sample of women workers in Puerto Rico. Few new younger workers were hired, and many of the older women workers had been working in the same plant for twenty to thirty years. The older female heads revealed that when they were younger and raising children on their own, most lived with or relied on the help of extended family members, usually female kin. Like Dominican women, two-thirds of the female heads of household in our Puerto Rican sample say they would prefer not to remarry (Safa 1995, 83).

Today in Puerto Rico, the percentage of three-generation families has dropped sharply, and the ethos of the residential income-pooling extended household has been sharply reduced. Even the displaced older garment workers report receiving only minimal aid from children and other kin (Colón et al. 2008). Nationally, 29 percent of female heads live alone, much higher than in Cuba or the Dominican Republic. This partly reflects the high percentage of widows (30 percent), who in Cuba and the Dominican Republic normally would live with extended families. Nuclearization is also the result of public policy, which through public housing, social security, and other social programs stressed the U.S. middle-class nuclear family as the ideal (Safa 2001, 99).

Federal transfer payments made it easier for widows and other female heads to live separately. In 2000, 35 percent of female heads were receiving public welfare, and 48 percent of these were living below the poverty line (Colón Warren 2006, 16). In all, 61 percent of female heads of households in 2000 were living below the poverty rate, which can be explained by their dependence on government assistance, low female labor force participation rates, and the absence of support from extended families. Nationally, only 16 percent of Puerto Rican female-headed households have more than one person employed, compared to 39 percent among married couples (Colón Warren 2006). Colón and others (2008) note that 65 percent of garment workers earned under ten thousand dollars annually, and 40 percent are female heads.

Dependence on public welfare may have dampened formal employment among female heads, but encouraging them to live alone also makes it harder for mothers of young children to work outside the home (cf. Burgos and Colberg 1990).

The labor force participation rate of Puerto Rican female heads of household is much lower than in Cuba or the Dominican Republic. Only 35 percent of Puerto Rican female heads of household were employed in 2000 and 42 percent had no one employed in the household (Colón Warren 2006, 85). Again, this may be explained partially by the large percentage of elderly widows living on social security or other pension payments. Unemployment is also high, but it is higher for men than for women in Puerto Rico.

Clearly, Puerto Rican female heads of household differ in certain important respects from the profile of Cuban and Dominican female heads outlined earlier. The percentage of Puerto Rican female heads of household reached 31 percent in 2006 (American Community Survey 2006, table B11001) but many more of these are widows than in the other islands. The percentage of single mothers may be lower due to the decline in consensual unions, which have largely disappeared, now numbering only 5 percent. The decline in consensual unions is a deliberate result of state policy, which as early as 1898, when Puerto Rico was occupied by the United States, promoted a new civil code to make civil marriage more accessible in an effort to cut down on the 50 percent of the population living in consensual unions (Findlay 1999). The promotion of legal marriage was defined as part of the U.S. "civilizing mission" and was later reinforced by privileging couples in legal unions in terms of access to federal transfer payments such as social security, veteran benefits, and payments to family dependents of Puerto Ricans enrolled in the U.S. military. However, eliminating consensual unions has not brought about marital stability, because the divorce rate is so high. Nationally, 57 percent of female heads of household are divorced, much higher than in Cuba or the Dominican Republic (Colón Warren 2006, table 1) and even higher than the United States. The marriage rate has also declined.

Structural factors such as rapid urbanization and migration also help explain the nuclearization of the Puerto Rican family. Migration to the United States started in the 1940s, reached its peak in the 1950s, and now over half of the Puerto Rican population lives in the United States. Remittances seem to have declined in importance because of the free flow of people and money to the United States and the frequency of travel.

In place of remittances, federal transfer payments have assumed more importance as a long-term survival strategy and on the island go primarily to families (such as female heads) where the head of household is unemployed. Half of the displaced garment workers in 2002 received government aid (Colón et al. 2008), to which they are entitled because of plant closings. In 2006 the percentage of Puerto Rican families where the householder did not work in the past year stood at 52 percent, rising to 56 percent among female heads (American Community Survey 2006, table S1702), many of whom are dependent on federal transfer payments. In 1995, 71 percent of all Puerto Rican transfer payments were earned benefits such as Medicare and social security (Dietz 2003, 161), which again reflects the aging of the Puerto Rican population.

Conclusion

Globalization and economic restructuring has contributed to the increase in female-headed households in Cuba, Puerto Rico, and the Dominican Republic by further weakening the role of the male as breadwinner. Male employment has deteriorated or stagnated in each of these countries, while female employment and participation rates have increased. Women have become increasingly resistant to marriage, because it offers them neither economic nor, apparently, emotional support.

A small class of professional women in the Caribbean have benefited from the changes economic restructuring has helped produce. They have taken advantage of increased educational opportunities in Cuba, Puerto Rico, and the Dominican Republic and are surpassing men in university education and professional employment. The high rate of divorce among professional women in all three countries would suggest that female educational and occupational advancement alone will not stem the increase in female-headed households, although it may make them less poor.

This analysis reinforces the importance of household composition in alleviating the poverty of female heads. This is particularly true in Cuba and the Dominican Republic, where young, single mothers rely primarily on extended families for both emotional and financial support. Extended families become less important as a household form in Puerto Rico as the percentage of widows grows and female-headed households receive more government aid.

But the three countries studied here differ not only demographically but also in terms of state policy. The Dominican state never provided adequate public services to its citizens (Safa and Antrobus 1992), and structural adjustment only aggravated this tendency. The state relies on remittances and the extended family to provide the primary source of aid for the urban poor, including female heads.

The Cuban state has had to reduce the number of public employees (including women) and its wages no longer provide an adequate standard of living, forcing many employees to leave or supplement their state jobs in the nonstate sector. But the state strives to maintain universal access to public health and education, while the increasing importance of remittances threatens to undermine the high level of racial and class equality that Cuba had achieved. Women's autonomy is also jeopardized, but I doubt that Cuban women will revert to dependence on a male breadwinner. Female heads are likely to continue to depend on the extended family and on access to dollars through self-employment, the tourism sector, and remittances when they are available. The role of remittances in the formation and support of female-headed households certainly bears further investigation.

Puerto Rico provides the strongest level of state financial support specifically directed to female-headed households, thanks to massive federal aid. The high percentage of widows in Puerto Rico who are entitled to social security and other transfer payments partially explains this high level of support. But the way in which this support is administered also contributes to a low labor force participation rate and to the breakup of extended families, making them more dependent on the state for survival. Remittances also appear to have declined in importance.

However, the public support that Puerto Rican female heads of household enjoy does not appear to have contributed significantly to an increase in their number. The increase has been much higher in the Dominican Republic and especially Cuba, where specific public support for female-headed households is minimal or nonexistent. This suggests that the common assumption in the United States, that public welfare has increased the percentage of female-headed households, is greatly exaggerated. Rather than eliminating public support for female-headed households, as some critics demand, I would suggest modifying this policy to facilitate rather than deter household extension. My Caribbean data shows that female-headed households are better off economically (and psychologically) if women share household expenses with relatives who provide additional sources of income or child care, rather than being on their own. This implies moving away from the nuclear family model upon which much public policy in the United States (and elsewhere) is now based.

NOTE

1. Widows are not included in my category of single mothers, since most are older and no longer raising children.

REFERENCES

American Community Survey. 2006. Puerto Rican community survey. U.S. Census. http://factfinder.census.gov.

Báez, Clara. 2000. *Estadísticas para la planificación social con perspectiva de género*. Santo Domingo: Secretaría de la Mujer, UNDP, UNPF.

Benglesdorf, Carollee. 1997. (Re) Considering Cuban women in a time of troubles. In *Daughters of Caliban: Caribbean women in the twentieth century*, ed. Consuelo L. Springfield, 229–258. Bloomington: Indiana University Press.

Blue, Sara. 2004. State policy, economic crisis, gender and family ties: Determinants of family remittances to Cuba. *Economic Geography* 80 (1): 63–83.

Burgos, Nilsa, and Eileen Colberg. 1990. *Mujeres solteras con jefatura de familia: Características en el hogar y el trabajo*. Río Piedras, Puerto Rico: CERES, Centro de Investigaciones Sociales, University of Puerto Rico.

Catasús, Sonia. 1996. The sociodemographic and reproductive characteristics of Cuban women. *Latin American Perspectives* 23 (1): 87–98.

———. 1999. Género, patrones reproductivos y jefatura de núcleo familiar por color de la piel en Cuba. Paper presented at the Red de Estudios de Poblacion ALFAPOP, Center of Demographic Studies, Bellaterra, Spain, February 8–12.

Chant, Sylvia. 1997. *Women-headed households: Diversity and dynamics in the developing world*. New York: St. Martin's Press.

CIPAF (Centro de Investigación y Promoción para la Acción Femenina; Center of Research and Development for Women's Action). 2005. *Continuous improvement in the Central American workplace project*. Washington, DC: United States Agency for International Development.

CNZFE. 2006. *Informe estadístico del sector de zonas francas*. Santo Domingo: CNZFE.

Colón, Alice, María Maité Mulero, Luis Santiago, and Nilsa Burgos. 2008. *Estirando el piso: Acciones de ajuste y relaciones de género ante el cierre de fábricas en Puerto Rico*. Puerto Rico: Centro de Investigaciones Sociales, University of Puerto Rico.

Colón Warren, Alice. 2006. Incremento en las mujeres jefas de familia y feminización de la pobreza en Puerto Rico. *Plerus* 23–24:78–96.

Columbia University. 2004. *Remittances and the Dominican Republic*. New York: Columbia University. www.earthinstitute.columbia.edu (accessed July 12, 2006).

De la Fuente, Alejandro. 1995. Race and inequality in Cuba, 1899–1981. *Journal of Contemporary History*, no. 30:31–167.

———. 1998. Recreating racism: Race and discrimination in Cuba's "Special Period." Cuba Briefing Paper 18. Caribbean Project, Center for Latin American Studies, Georgetown University, Washington, DC.

Dietz, James L. 2003. *Puerto Rico: Negotiating development and change*. Boulder, CO: Rienner.

Duarte, Isis, and Ramón Tejada. 1995. *Los hogares dominicanos: El mito de la familia nuclear y los tipos de jefaturas del hogar*. Santo Domingo: Instituto de Estudios de Población y Desarrollo.

Echevarría, León Dayma. 2004. Mujer, empleo, y dirección en Cuba: Algo más que estadísticas. In *Crisis, cambios económicos y subjetividad de las cubanas*, 71–89. Havana: Varela.

Eckstein, Susan. 2004. Transnational networks and norms, remittances, and the transformation of Cuba. In *The Cuban economy at the start of the twenty-first century*, ed. Jorge Dominguez, Omar E. Pérez Villanueva, and Lorena Barbería, 319–352. Cambridge: Harvard Univerrsity Press.

ECLAC. 2004. *Understanding poverty from a gender perspective*. Santiago: Women and Development Unit, ECLAC. Espina, Mayra. 2001. The effects of the reform on Cuba's social structure: An overview. In *Cuba in the 1990s: Economy, politics and society*. Special issue, *Socialism and Democracy* 15 (1): 23–40.

Findlay, Eileen J. 1999. *Imposing decency: The politics of sexuality and race in Puerto Rico, 1870–1920*. Durham, NC: Duke University Press.

Hershberg, Eric. 2003. Latin America at the crossroads. *NACLA* 37 (3): 20–23.

Hite, Amy Bellone, and Jocelyn S. Viterna. 2005. Gendering class in Latin America: How women effect and experience change in the class structure. *Latin American Research Review* 40 (2): 50–82.

Itzigsohn, Jose. 1995. Migrant remittances, labor markets, and household strategies: A comparative analysis of low-income household strategies in the Caribbean Basin. *Social Forces* 74 (2): 633–655.

Martínez-Alier, Verena. 1974. *Marriage, class and colour in nineteenth-century Cuba*. London: Cambridge University Press.

Martínez Reinosa, Milagros Elena, and Ma. Margarita Castro Flores. 2004. La crisis, la reforma y el cambio social en Cuba. In *Crisis, cambios económicos y subjetividad de las cubanas*. Havana: Varela. 47–62.

McClenaghan, Sharon. 1997. Women, work and empowerment: Romanticizing the reality. In *Gender politics in Latin America*, ed. Elizabeth Dore, 19–35. New York: Monthly Review.

Monreal, Pedro. 2001. Cuba: The challenge of being global and socialist . . . at the same time. In *Cuba in the 1990s: Economy, politics and society*. Special issue, *Socialism and Democracy* 15 (1): 5–22.

Núñez Sarmiento, Marta. 2001. Cuban strategies for women's employment in the 1990s: A case study of professional women. In *Cuba in the 1990s: Economy, politics and society*. Special issue, *Socialism and Democracy* 15 (1): 41–65.

Rodríguez, Pablo. 2006. La inter- y la intrarracialidad en las estructuras familiares. In *Las relaciones raciales en Cuba: Aportes empíricos y nuevas interpretaciones*, ed. Kalid Argyriadis. Documento IDYMOV, no. 10. Xalapa, Mexico: CIESAS-Golfo.

Safa, Helen I. 1995. *The myth of the male breadwinner: Women and industrialization in the Caribbean*. Boulder, CO: Westview.

———. 2001. Changing forms of U.S. hegemony in Puerto Rico: The impact of the family and sexuality. *Itinerario: European Journal of Overseas History* 25 (3–4): 90–111.

———. 2002. Questioning globalization: Gender and export processing in the Dominican Republic. *Journal of Developing Societies* 18 (2–3): 11–31.

Safa, Helen I., and Peggy Antrobus. 1992. Women and the economic crisis in the Caribbean. In *Unequal burden: Economic crisis, persistent poverty and gender inequality*, ed. Lourdes Beneria and Shelley Feldman, 49–82. Boulder, CO: Westview.

Sana, Mariano, and Douglass Massey. 2005. Household composition, family remittances, migration and community context: Migrant remittances in four countries. *Social Science Quarterly* 86 (2): 509–528.

Toro-Morn, Maura, Anne Roschelle, and Elisa Facio. 2002. Gender, work and family in Cuba: The challenges of the Special Period. *Journal of Developing Societies* 18 (2–3): 32–58.

United Nations. 1999. *1999 world survey on the role of women in development: Globalizations, gender and work*. UN document A/54/227. New York: Division for the Advancement of Women, Department of Economics and Social Affairs.

Uriarte, Miren. 2002. *Cuba: Social policy at the crossroads*. Boston: Oxfam America.

U.S. Department of Labor. 2002. *Foreign labor trends: Dominican Republic*. Washington, DC: Bureau of International Labor Affairs, Office of Foreign Relations.

4

A "Top-Down"–"Bottom-Up" Model

FOUR DECADES OF WOMEN'S
EMPLOYMENT AND GENDER IDEOLOGY
IN CUBA

MARTA NÚÑEZ SARMIENTO

Since 1959 the Cuban cultural identity nationwide has been enriched by the new needs and values generated in women's and men's gender ideology. This essay argues that the feminization of the Cuban workforce, especially among professionals, has contributed to a change in what it means to be a woman and a man in my country.[1] The processes linked to the increasing participation of Cuban women in the labor force are similar in many respects to those taking place in other countries of the region, including the United States and Canada. Nevertheless, there are notable differences that singularize the Cuban phenomenon, which I describe in this chapter.

Two hypotheses guide my reflections. First, the Cuban programs to promote women's participation in society have operated at two interrelated levels, that of the general policies promoted "from the top" and that of the reactions to these policies due to specific needs "from the bottom" (which have modified the policies constantly). The dynamics of women's employment have resulted from a highly intertwined process nurtured by different experiences and ideas for four decades and conditioned by Cuban economic, political, and ideological structures in its recent history. According to the second hypothesis, the feminization of labor has contradictorily impacted the gender identities of all members of society, not only the identity of women, with evident trends toward nondiscrimination. Women have been the engines of these transformations.

Gender Transformations in Cuban Society:
A "Top-Down"–"Bottom-Up" Model

Women's participation in Cuban society has been part of the comprehensive social justice programs started in the early sixties to eliminate all sorts of discrimination. Since the beginning, criticisms of these programs have aimed to reinterpret the realities that the programs wished to transform, claiming the programs were either obsolete or unable to grasp people's lived reality. This critical consciousness has been present since 1959, stemming from the highest echelons of the political hierarchies—scholars, intellectuals, and artists—and from the everyday experiences of men and women. Critical thought and its concerns have been constrained by patriarchal trends persistent in Cuba, as well as by dogmatic positions.

I have labeled the program to promote women's incorporation to the labor force as a "top-down"–"bottom-up" model. Conceived and in operation at the higher political levels, the program includes social policies, legal frameworks, economic measures, and new cultural patterns that have been systematically modified as they have been implemented in day-to-day women's and men's lives. This critical flexibility, developed through multiple participation, is one of the program's successes.

It is difficult to separate the "above" actions from those that operate at the "bottom," for the way in which the model functions makes it difficult to distinguish any well-defined structure within it that could be labeled as belonging to a certain level. Nevertheless, in considering how these two levels operate, I have selected certain topics concerning women's employment and the gender ideology linked to it and have analyzed the interactions between measures dictated from above and the reactions that they provoked from the bottom.

There were many economic, political, and ideological conditions that characterized the Special Period in Cuba during the nineties and impacted women's employment and gender ideology. This crisis affected Cuban society as a whole and was the result of severe economic shortages due to the disappearance of the Eastern European socialist bloc centered around the Soviet Union. These countries accounted for 85 percent of all Cuban foreign economic relations. The reinforcement of the blockade by the U.S. government against Cuba, with the Torricelli law (1992) and the Helms-Burton amendment (1996), were also influential.

Throughout these years the Cuban economy plummeted, and the quality of life of the population experienced a sudden and enormous decrease. The extent of the damages can be shown through the following example. For thirty years Cuba purchased 12 million tons of oil annually from the Soviet Union on preferential terms, based on a trade treaty that benefited both countries. The breakup of the Soviet Union in 1991 ended this treaty and Cuba started buying oil on the world market. That year, and the following, Cuba was able to purchase only around 4 million tons of oil and the economy nearly collapsed.

Readjustments were introduced simultaneously in various spheres of society. Overcoming the crisis has been a very slow process, lasting from 1995 to the present. One date proves the political importance in Cuba of women's participation in society. On March 8, 1990, International Women's Day—a day of mobilization for women throughout the world—Fidel Castro announced the beginning of the Special Period. Fifteen years later, on March 8, 2005, the Cuban president declared that Cuba was starting to come out of the Special Period. Why did Fidel select this date to communicate such politically relevant events? In 1990 he knew that he could count on Cuban women to discover the survival strategies that helped the country withstand the years of crisis and readjustment that awaited all Cubans, years that were aggravated by the fall of the socialist bloc, the strengthening of the U.S. blockade, and the impossibility of concluding the Cuban process of rectification of mistakes and negative trends initiated in 1984. In 2005 he wanted to proclaim what the Cuban population had been already sensing, the recuperation from the crisis was on its way.

Various legal actions and public policies have been generated from above during the last forty-eight years, which have clearly impacted women's employment and gender identities. The maternity law of 1974, part of the labor code, regulates maternity leave for women workers. The family code of 1975 requires divorced or separated parents to pay a food allowance to their children. Day care centers were established in 1961 for children ages forty-five days to five years old, and school lunchrooms at primary schools were added to benefit working mothers' children. Universally free education from preprimary to graduate studies has been available since 1961, along with the right for students to apply for stipends to pay for room and board. University and technical education graduates are required to be employed by the state for two years to fulfill social service. All workers have the right to a month of paid vacation every year. There are also a number of public health services offered to the population that have promoted healthy habits, including family planning, Pap exams and breast cancer tests, vaccinations, and free access to all levels of public health care, from the family doctor to hospitals and specialized institutions.

These measures have been modified to adjust to shifting circumstances and the influence of cultural patterns. The maternity law was changed to face the difficulties brought on by the Special Period. Originally each pregnant woman had the right to three months of paid leave to look after her newborn, and her job was secured for her. In 1993 the maternity-leave period was extended to six months and, in subsequent years, to one year. Since 2000 both parents have the right to paid maternity or paternity leave. However, from 2000 to 2009 only two dozen fathers in all of Cuba have used this right.

Two articles in the family code were added that encourage both partners to share household chores. They are read in all marriage ceremonies, but no one has used them in arguing for divorce. The family code articles are perceived differently by women and men according to their ages. In a recent study I asked professional men and women how they had benefited from them. Those who were over thirty-five years of age at the time of the interview and who had experienced the upward mobility that favored the lowest income groups in Cuba from the early 1960s to the end of the eighties were very aware of what these changes meant to them. Interviewees younger than thirty-five years scarcely commented on these measures because they took them for granted.

Positive and Negative Facts on Women's Employment

The proportion of women in the nation's labor force rose steadily from 13 percent in 1959 (Núñez Sarmiento 1988, 13) to 38 percent in 1989 (ONE 1997, 116), the threshold of the Special Period. From 1989 to 2002 this upward trend decreased, reaching a plateau in which women's employment indexes swayed and even slightly decreased in relation to 1989. Since 2003 the proportion of women in the total labor force has started to increase again.

Beginning in 1977, women represented more than half of the professionals and technical workers in the Cuban labor force. This trend continued during the Special Period. In 2007 women accounted for 66 percent in this category of workers, while men represented only 34 percent (ONE 2006, table 6.9). From 1978 on, women in the labor force had higher educational levels than working men; in 2006, 18.5 percent of all working women had graduated from the university, while only 11.1 percent of all working men were university graduates, and 55.7 percent of all working women were high school graduates in comparison with 44.4 percent of men in the work-force (ONE 2006, table 6.7).

Women are employed in all sectors of the economy, including traditional and nontraditional ones. In 2006, 60 percent of all faculty members at Cuban universities were women, as well as 50 percent of all scientists, 52 percent of physicians, and 51 percent of lawyers. These facts show advances in women's employment, but inequalities still persist in terms of enormous physical and psychological burdens.

During the nineties, women adapted to new forms of employment. In the first part of the Special Period, almost all Cuban workers belonged to the public sector. As a result of the economic restructuring initiated around 1995 that expanded the private sector in Cuba, women's participation in this sector increased from 15 percent in 1989 to 22.9 percent in 1997. In this same year, women represented 34.3 percent of workers in joint ventures and mercantile agencies. The distribution of working women by occupation in 1989 and 1997 confirms the trend of job relocation. According to the Ministry of Labor, 89 percent of all female workers were employed in the public sector in 1989, while by 1997 only 81.3 percent belonged to this sector.

The adaptation of women to the restructuring of the economy in the midst of the crisis years has a positive outcome in the sense that women gained flexibility in the Cuban job market. But further studies have to be done to determine if these women accepted less qualified jobs and to see if new and future discriminatory signs exist in the private sectors, especially among the self-employed workers, in joint ventures where workers benefit indirectly from hard currency, and in the agricultural cooperative sector.

Surveys regularly conducted by the National Office of Statistics show that Cuban women workers carry the burden of the second shift. They spend thirty-six hours a week doing house chores, while male workers declare that they spend twelve hours a week performing these activities. Cuban women are judges, professors, scientists, physicians, and blue-collar workers, but they are also the ones who iron, cook, and clean the homes. Men dedicate their time to shopping, paying the bills, and putting the garbage out (ONE 1999, 148). Of the multiple reasons that explain why this gender discriminatory division of house chores persists, two have to do with material scarcities in Cuba while the third relates to patriarchal cultural patterns.

Cuba has an enormous housing deficit that causes up to three or four genera-tions to live under one roof, with several female figures in each household who distribute household chores among themselves. Under the influence of patriar-chal ideology, the mothers, grandmothers, and aunts do not assign household duties to the younger male members of the family because they consider that it erodes their virility. For the last fifty years, food, soap and detergent have been extremely scarce and therefore have been rationed. Women have learned to econ-omize these few resources better than men. A woman interviewed said, "At home men waste the scarce things we have and mess up everything when they perform household chores. That is why I prefer to do them myself, even if I take up the whole burden."

The "victims" (women) should not be blamed for their own victimization; as explained in Marxist and feminist theory, both at the societal and at the individual level it is very difficult to change ideologies that support social discrimination, far more difficult than changing those sustained by political ideologies. The oppressed tend to incorporate into their behaviors the ruling classes' ideological representa-tions. For centuries patriarchal ideology has sustained power patterns in all socio-economic formations, a sociological process that can be compared with racist forms of domination. Even in societies where the economic structures and the political institutions based on old cultural patterns have been radically transformed do patriarchal ideologies survive and prevail in the minds of the population. These phenomena have been widely treated by social scientists in developed and devel-oping countries. Among the Marxist classics, I point out Antonio Gramsci's thesis of hegemony and culture, Inessa Armand's works on women's subordination, and Alexandra Kollontai's materials on women's political participation. Feminist U.S. authors Helen Safa, Sherryl Lutjens, and Carmen Diana Deere, Brazilian writers Mary Garcia Castro, and Cuban authors Mayda Alvarez, Nara Araújo, and Luisa Campuzano have recently referred to this.

The fact that only 30 percent of all leadership positions in the Cuban workforce are held by women is another discriminatory characteristic of women's employ-ment (ONE 2006, table 6.9). This proportion has been approximately the same since 1992, although women account for 60 percent of all professional and technical workers and should be the appropriate source for managers.

Why Women Stayed in the Workforce during the Special Period

At the beginning of the crisis in 1990, women workers benefited from public poli-cies that promoted their participation in society. They had lived through decades of sustained economic growth and higher levels of human development. At the initial stages of the crisis, human development and, in particular, quality of life in Cuba was higher than in any other developing country.

Several arguments explain why Cuban women stayed in the labor force during the years of crisis and readjustments in the nineties and are continuing to stay now. One-third of all women workers head their households and are the main breadwin-ners of their families. When we add to them the number of women who remarry, who bring their children from a previous marriage to this new union, and who consider themselves responsible for their children's maintenance, then the proportion of women breadwinners increases.

Cuban development strategy promotes high technology and efficiency, and a skilled workforce is needed. Women represent almost two-thirds of all professional and technical workers and are therefore essential to accomplishing this goal. Because Cuban women workers have been increasingly active in the labor force for the last thirty-five to forty years, at present many younger ones represent a second generation of working women in their families. Real and present maternal references of what it means to be a paid worker could explain the second generation's willingness to stay in the labor force.

During the years of crisis and readjustment, the legal and public policy frameworks that favored the incorporation and permanence of women in the labor force accommodated the new conditions. For example, in 1997 the Council of State passed the National Plan of Action, following the agreements of the Fourth United Nations World Conference on Women, held in Beijing in 1995. The Cuban Plan of Action summarized in ninety articles the political will of the state to continue promoting women's equality. These articles are mandatory for all public institutions and progress is controlled through workshops organized by the Federation of Cuban Women.

Community-based activities center on the everyday lives of Cubans. In several case studies, women acknowledged that during the crisis years they switched to jobs near their homes because of the lack of transportation; they also asked for their neighbors' help and worked out survival strategies in their neighborhoods. They started seeing their family doctors and nearby polyclinics instead of going to distant hospitals.

In the sixties, seventies, and eighties, Cubans in the whole country, not only the capital, benefited from an upward social mobility that improved education, health, nutrition, and social security levels. The gains were much more equitable than those prevailing in other developing countries. The mobility had a positive outcome, in the sense that it helped to create certain reserves in working women for confronting the crisis. But it also had a downside, because these same women deeply understood how much they had lost with the sudden decrease in the living standards of the population.

Official actions and ideas against women's discrimination did not stop in the nineties. Women played a visible and essential role in assuring the survival of their families and of the country's economy, and this elevated their self-esteem. The crisis also unveiled not only persistent inequalities among women and men but also women's potential, strengths, and capacities to overcome the crisis at the individual, family, community, and national levels. Women stepped out of this crisis with renewed strength, as was forecast by U.S. scholar Collette Harris (1995) and by Cuban professor and essay writer Luisa Campuzano (1996).

These women had to build their strategies while living in a patriarchal society, where they carried the burden of the second shift while men dominated managerial positions. The high rate of divorce and separation increased the number of female-headed households, making working women the main breadwinners.

Decision Making and Leadership Positions

During the last half-century, women's growing capacity for decision making has been one of the most important changes in terms of gender ideology, due largely to women's increased employment. Of course, this does not mean that Cuban women lacked the ability to solve their problems before the revolution or before women's massive incorporation into the labor force.

Working women have trained themselves to simultaneously perform several tasks at their jobs and at home. This ability is based on their high educational levels, their lives in a society that has been fundamentally transformed, and the fact that they have been subject to these changes in greater terms than men. In-depth studies are needed to help us understand how working women, whether professionals or not, have constructed a decision-making know-how for all spheres of their lives, including in the working world, from their traditional roles in the household. There are generational differences, as the younger women tend to expect and persuade men in their families to perform domestic activities.

In exercising decision-making abilities, women not only develop a sense of empowerment as human beings but also confirm their right to behave independently, a basic civil right that Cuban women did not exercise fully after 1959. Nevertheless, the social category of women as managers needs to be redefined, both through assigning women to such positions and strengthening this category in the social imaginary to promote women's willingness to occupy managerial positions.

Decision making is the ability to evaluate scenarios, point out their main problems, explain what causes them, and propose solutions. It also includes the ability to judge gains and losses in each situation and, according to the information at hand, to determine which actions are needed to reach the goals. I exclude from this definition the concept of formal leadership that includes decision making and other institutional aspects. Nevertheless, both concepts of formal leadership and decision making are related to empowerment, which is relevant to gender ideology.

In my research on women and employment in Cuba over the last twenty-five years, I have shown that changes in gender ideology have generated decision-making abilities in working women in all spheres of their everyday lives. Since 2001, in more recent studies where I included professional men and women, I noted different answers according to gender.

At the time of the interviews, the majority of the men in these case studies were occupying a managerial post or had occupied one in the past. All of them were willing to perform leading responsibilities at their jobs. On the other hand, only one-fifth of the women interviewed had been managers before or were willing to do so. As stated earlier, in 2006 only 29 percent of all Cuban managers were women. Out of the total of women workers, only 6 percent were managers. This percentage, consistent for the last fifteen years, is proportionately low, considering that women are the majority among professional and technical workers and should be considered the natural source for managers. In 2006 men filled 70 percent of all managerial positions, while their participation among professional and technical workers hardly rose (ONE 2006, table 6.9).

The men in my sample who have held managerial positions or who desired to become managers considered that they were qualified for these responsibilities or were capable of being trained for such. They were seeking these positions. Women in the sample explained why they did not want to become managers. Almost all of them admitted that they were not sufficiently trained; others answered that it would take too much of their time, paying very little. Others considered that it would be an extra burden for the second shift. Some said that they preferred to continue upgrading their professional knowledge instead of being trained as managers. All of them believed that they are already decision makers at their jobs. It is a mistake to interpret these answers as a lack of self-confidence. Rather, what frequently happens is that they know what they want to achieve in their fields of employment and becoming managers is considered an obstacle to their projects or goals. Although the decision to avoid managerial and leadership positions to comply with professional and life purposes is realistic according to these women's present conditions, at the national level it means that women cannot contribute a gendered perspective to the Cuban managerial field and employment leadership.

The few women in the sample who were managers at the time of my study or who had occupied managerial positions in the past declared that they had not looked for these responsibilities but had been assigned to them. Some of the women had been union leaders at the grassroots level. They acknowledged that their coworkers respected their authority and felt that they were capable of solving problems. Although they were not completely satisfied performing managerial posts, they had exercised them responsibly. The majority of the Cuban women who are capable of becoming managers or employment leaders do not want to seem to reflect the limitations of their own process of gender ideology. However, all conditions also have to be present at the social level to accomplish this goal.

Professional women, who are the natural source for managers or leaders in the job sphere, were first perceived in the Cuban job market as a stable category at the threshold of the Special Period. During the crisis years all women workers, not only professionals, had to stay employed to keep their salaries, regardless of whether or not they had a stable partner. As the value of the Cuban peso decreased, they were compelled to find a second job to contribute to their household incomes. At that point, and even at the present, if they assumed a managerial position it would have been difficult to work for the needed additional income. When managerial posts can fulfill the material needs of those that perform them, then more women will be interested in them.

Cuban managerial culture has been designed by men and for men, and this has to be changed to convince women to become managers. The presence of six women ministers in fundamental ministries today proves that such change is possible. Professional women comply with the requisites to perform managerial positions. They are present in all sectors of the economy and have represented the majority of professional and technical workers for the last thirty years. Their educational levels are high, they perform complex tasks simultaneously, and they are already decision makers at their jobs and in their homes. Their lists of past employment are relatively long, beginning from the grassroots level, so they are familiar with their job environment. When all the necessary conditions to promote women to managerial posts flourish in Cuba, the process will be irreversible. Women managers have started at the basic levels of employment and have risen with constant feedback and learning through job experience, so they are familiar with all the complexities of the jobs they will direct.

Women's access to managerial positions cannot be postponed until the patriarchal cultural patterns in Cuba are completely transformed. Women's promotion to managerial posts has to contribute to these changes. This is what happened with the incorporation and permanence of women in the labor force in the sixties and seventies, widely explained by the Communist Party and the Federation of Cuban Women; they did not wait for perfect conditions in the jobs or in society.

Gender Ideology at the Workplace

Gender ideology has changed more among Cuban women than men, including the new attitudes women have assumed in society. Paradoxically, though, they reproduce the macho patterns in Cuban gender ideology in bringing up their children. What follows summarizes what professional Cuban women and men reported to me during the in-depth interviews included in the case studies I conducted from 2001 to 2006.

In terms of gender ideology linked to employment, both women and men identify complexities at their job, but women are less afraid than men to acknowledge that they do not know certain aspects of their work environments. Women confessed insecurities at their jobs and men never did. Such statements could be interpreted as supporting the notion that women are incapable of decision making and lack self confidence if they weren't clarified by women's assertions in the interviews, as well as by the data concerning women and employment in Cuba. Women declared their willingness to upgrade their job expertise. In fact, their professional training is higher than men's. For example, they had more PhD's and Master's degrees than men in the sample, completed more graduate and foreign-language programs than men, and participated in more scientific events than men did.

Women and men in my case studies considered that women in the workforce had altered men's attitudes at their jobs. Still, women detailed more precisely than men what they meant by those changes. Men simply pointed out these new attitudes without any further explanation and used socially accepted slogans. On the other hand, professional women believe that they incorporated new ways of approaching their tasks in the long and medium range. They are capable of linking general objectives with actions necessary to accomplish them. They said that they dedicate more time than men to figuring out their job planning and that they reject improvisations and simple solutions more than fellow male workers do. One of the women said in her interview, "That is why women are capable of making utopias come true."

Working women use traditional feminine traits to convince their colleagues at work. They are "delicate," "affectionate," and "charming." They like to hear others' opinions and tend to approach fellow workers, men and women, to exchange personal experiences. Women develop several tasks at the same time and consider themselves "indispensable." Women interviewees believed that the reaccommodation of men and women at their jobs should be obtained through negotiation rather than confrontation. They consider themselves key factors in these negotiations.

Women in my studies believed that they had indirectly influenced the new attitudes of many of their working men. Men who are married to or live with working women sometimes do household chores and this transforms certain attitudes at their jobs. For example, fathers who take their kids to day care or to school have to wake up very early to arrive on time at work. Some men buy food and other household goods in shops near their work.

Women have richer perspectives on how employment has influenced their attitudes toward labor. The difference can possibly be explained by the fact that they entered the Cuban job market more recently than men did, in the midst of a process that was broadly transforming attitudes beyond job behavior. For example, compared to their mothers, these working women have fewer children and are involved in more marital or consensual relationships. Their educational levels are also higher than their mothers'. Many of these professional women head their households and govern their own everyday lives. The rich, new, and unfinished experiences that these women have lived through in relatively short periods may have enriched their ability to reflect on themselves and guide themselves in unfamiliar spaces.

Men did not openly blame women for the problems they confronted at work, at home, and in their intimate relations, but they are concerned with the many changes influencing women. Only two of all the men I interviewed considered that those who accuse women of being "extremely liberated" are "backward" and "camouflaged *machistas*." Another two said that such awkward sentiments have to do more with professional competitiveness than with gender differences. Men tend to disguise their apprehensions about women workers, mainly professional ones that compete with them, because they would be criticized by the prevailing antidiscrimination norms in public spaces.

Women said that, at least in Cuba, men react paradoxically toward working women because they feel both attracted to and threatened by them. They are afraid of competing with them when "designing work projects and carrying on their duties in bed." They believe that men are attracted to these challenges because they promote in them the desire to hunt this "difficult prey." If they "trap" them, their macho ego would grow. Women in the study pointed out that this "hunting" process also takes place at work. Men there are compelled to demonstrate that they are better trained than their female colleagues and they have to impose their leadership to assure their official power.

Two-thirds of the interviewed women admitted that men feel threatened by women at their jobs for the following reasons: (1) professional women have higher educational levels than men; (2) professional women who are not managers spend more time upgrading their skills and acquiring knowledge, which could lead to conflicts between them and the managing men who dedicate more time to bureaucratic tasks; (3) accustomed to fitting in tasks at their jobs and at home, professional women are better trained than men to organize their work schedules; (4) women could snatch managerial jobs away from men; (5) annual evaluations at the workplace show that women perform more activities than men; (6) Working women depend less on men; and (7) men depend on women's contribution to the family income.

These ideas reflect how paradoxical the gender patterns of the labor market are. Their contradictory origins transcend the labor sphere and must be found in the broader cultural patterns conditioning gender identities in Cuba. To understand changing gender ideology, I selected some of the cultural gender patterns valid in Cuba today, which were also present in society during the upbringing of the men and women in my studies. I asked the interviewees to comment on the cultural gender patterns that influenced them during their childhood, adolescence, and time at their university. They commented on the prevalent sexist patterns they experienced during their childhood.

Regarding the tradition of dressing girls in pink and boys in blue, all men considered this correct because pink is "delicate," "feminine," and "sweet," and boys who wear pink are considered "sissies." Women's evaluations were more flexible. All of the women said that this is a tradition, and parents decide whether or not to use it with their children. Girls have the advantage of being able to dress in either pink or in blue, mainly with the use of jeans. But boys are not permitted to dress in pink.

Considering how differently boys and girls play, even the youngest of the interviewees answered that their parents made them play with children of their same sex. The gender division of games is evident at home. Boys play ball outdoors or practice whatever sport is popular at the moment. Girls play with dolls or "play school" inside their homes or on the porches. On the sidewalks they play hopscotch, jacks, or jump rope.

Day cares, the state institutions for preschool children of working mothers, persuade Cuban boys and girls to exchange gender roles in their games. But gender divisions persist when they play without the guidance of their teachers. In primary schools, which all Cuban children from five to eleven years old attend, students of both sexes participate together in sports, camping, and cultural activities. But when they play during recess, they tend to play with children of the same sex, as they did in day care.

Cuban psychologist Patricia Arés, in her studies of how masculine identities are constructed in Cuba, argues that men are not trained during childhood and adolescence to adjust to the changes in gender ideologies that they will have to confront later as a result of women's development. Boys are not allowed to cry and display pain, so grown-up men are unable to express their feelings. Boys have to fight back, creating violent behaviors. Boys do not perform household chores and are not trained to participate in the "second shift" (2002).

Girls are granted more opportunities to act less dogmatically than boys. When they make boys play with them as "school pupils," girls lead the game as "school teachers." Girls can cry their heads off, and they fight back if they wish. At school they compete with boys, getting higher marks. They are the leaders par excellence in the children's pioneer organizations.

From these reflections I infer that men in my case studies are less prepared than women to act flexibly in terms of what it means to be a man or a woman in Cuba today. Men's ideology is less flexible than women's because they have been submitted to more indoctrination both as boys and adolescents. In general, they may be as repressed as women, or even more so, in all spheres of life.

Gender Ideology in Marital Relations

Women's participation in the labor force has contributed to a change in attitude of women and men, at home and at the level of intimate relations. Yet, as a woman sociologist declared in her in-depth interview, "In the intimate sphere men are openly patriarchal, because they do not have to submit to the social rules prevailing at work and in other public spaces that are critical of such attitudes. In private men act like the superior beings they believe they are." Her opinion led me to think that Cuba perhaps repeats at the more personal level what is happening in other countries.

Cuba has gone through almost fifty years of revolutionary transformation and continuous programs to struggle against discrimination of all sorts. Measures to eliminate gender discrimination have been among the most successful, even more than those aimed at eradicating racism. Therefore, changes from the top, dedicated to women, have operated in a global framework of revolutionary transformation. There has not been a "stalled revolution," as defined by North American author Arlie Hochschild to describe what happened in the United States, where a woman's revolution occurred without a general transformation of the social structures (1989, 12). In Cuba there are macrostructures to promote women's participation in society.

Cuban women and men, mainly the former, have experienced inner changes from societal projects that intend to foster their growth as full human beings. Anguish and joy have been especially strong at the most intimate levels of many marital relations. The everyday fight between general structures pursuing equality and the patriarchal norms and values rooted in the individual is evident in this sphere of life.

Several examples illustrate how these contradictions express themselves. Women in my studies explained that their husbands were jealous of them because they dressed up to go to work. Jealousy was manifested in veiled ways or it erupted aggressively, but women always perceived it. They felt constantly observed and judged by their partners. One of them said, "People say that women are jealous, but men are more so, although some express their jealousy in subtle ways."

Women in my sample said that because they work, all men in their homes—not only their husbands—should be compelled to share domestic chores. These working women turn into examples for their daughters, because the latter want to become workers too when they grow up. The sons grow up knowing that they will have women colleagues at work and that they will probably marry a working woman. Women interviewees admit that they educated their sons with macho patterns and trained their daughters to use their liberties carefully, for they live in a highly machista society.

Women noted that working made them more independent, not only in economic terms but also in decision making. Among their decisions is a very important one: to get rid of "unwanted" husbands. Professional women said that it is difficult for them to find stable partners. They argued that they compete with their partners on professional matters. The competition increases if both have the same profession, especially when the women earn more than their husbands or, even worse, when they hold leadership positions and their husbands do not. In Cuba it is very difficult for professional women under forty to find professional men to become their partners because, for the last thirty years, professional women have outnumbered professional men. The divorce rate is high: in 2003 the divorce rate was 3.0 per 1000 inhabitants (CEPDE-ONE 2003, 161, table 5.1), while the marriage rate was 4.9 per 1000 inhabitants (130). Cuban social scientists have demonstrated that this trend has been ongoing for several years (Consulta Oficina Nacional de Estadísticas 1999; Alvarez Suárez 2008; Núñez Sarmiento 2005). Among the reasons are women's employment, housing shortages, and the fact that divorce is a relatively simple procedure. There seems to be another factor, although not one included in the divorce rates: the Cuban tradition has condoned consensual unions since colonial times.

Cuban historian María del Carmen Barcia Zequeira writes that, according to the Cuban census from 1841 to 1870, "consensual unions were the most frequent options among the members of the poorest groups in Cuban society, whether urban or rural, and this alternative had little to do with race, for it was as common among whites as among blacks" (2003, 78–79).

Both women and men in my sample thought that working women have fewer children than nonworking women. The Cuban global fertility rate has decreased in the last three decades; in 2004 it was 1.5 children per woman (Peláez 2006, 5). Cuban social scientists stress women's employment and the wide access to family planning programs since 1964 among the main causes for low fertility. Sociologist Juan Carlos Alfonso insists on the need to use a gender perspective to study Cuban fertility processes to be able to understand men's as well as women's behavior (Alfonso and Alvarez 1996; see also Núñez Sarmiento 2003). This relational approach enables scholars to understand fertility as something involving men and women, rather than concentrating only on women, as demographers often do.

Women and men in the sample considered that women's employment had affected the sexual behavior of all Cubans. Family planning policies introduced in 1964 as part of the public health system enable men and women to avoid unwanted pregnancies. Since the seventies, sex education programs in schools and for adults have given women the possibility of a more confident and free sexuality. Almost all interviewees considered that legal abortions, practiced at public health institutions at no cost, have been wrongly used by women as a contraceptive.

Men in my studies spoke little about the influence of working women on marital relations. One of the women thought that men were afraid to acknowledge their macho behavior in the private sphere, and this explained why they answer with socially accepted formulas. She said that "men should be proud of their women, for they are able to work at work and at home" and that men should "share household chores with their wives." Nevertheless, surveys conducted in Cuba since the nineties show that women spend triple the number of hours on household chores than men do. Very few men in the sample shared the "second shift" to help their wives advance professionally. Some of the men in my studies confessed that they are very attracted by professional women and at the same time fear them in intimate settings. Cuban studies on sexuality show that men feel sexually threatened by "strong" women, who they believe will challenge them to show their virility.

On the other hand, women declared that, thanks to their jobs, they have met interesting men and others who were not so interesting but that it is difficult for them to find professional men for their partners, which is frustrating. In many cases, this fact has led them to stay single or without a stable partner. When women become workers, they often mature in their sexual behaviors. They demand equal satisfaction in their sexual relations and ask men to use condoms to prevent AIDS and other sexually transmitted diseases. Some of the women declared that they feel comfortable asking men out, although they would prefer men to take the initiative.

Conclusion

Since 1959 women have lived in a society that criticizes their dependence on men. Consequently, women have reacted to these demands in their day-to-day behavior and have constructed very personal attitudes to get rid of all types of dependence. Men have not attempted to live independently of women, which is grounds for further research.

The Cuban experiences of incorporating women into jobs, keeping them in the labor force, and progressively elevating their professional qualification show that such a goal can be fulfilled in a country with scant material resources, as long as there is political will and a clear gender approach. Social scientists from Cuba and other countries could learn from these processes. Further research in this field includes identifying the spaces where machista ideology, its practices, and its means endure, as well as how and why this ideology persists culturally and politically. The implications of this phenomenon for the country at present and in the future needs to be understood to create new public policies that support women, enforce existing legal regulations, and maintain the economic and social conditions needed to promote women's equality. New mechanisms should be designed to mediate and negotiate gender conflicts that might arise in the future.

The low representation of women employed in leading managerial positions is a fundamental shortcoming concerning women's equal participation in society.

The effort to assign women to leadership positions in this area and in politics must continue, and not by imposition. In 1986 Cuba experimented with appointing women, blacks, and youth to prominent positions, without positive results. It is preferable to continue selecting candidates according to their professional competency. Studies should investigate the differences in the ways in which men and women exercise leadership and its implications for gender relations in employment, the family, and marital relations.

It is vital to continue revising Cuban programs to promote women's and men's participation in the transformation of gender relations and ideologies. Not only will women's participation be enriched but relations between men and women will be redefined, with the hope of easing many of women's difficulties.

NOTE

1. These reflections summarize case studies that I have developed from 1985 to 2007, scholarly exchanges with Cuban and foreign students and colleagues dealing with these topics, and my personal experiences as a social scientist living in Cuba who has gone through the social transformations I am studying. In particular, I used three recent studies, published in Cuban and U.S. journals, which refer to Cuban professional women and men (Núñez Sarmineto 2001a, 2003, 2005).

REFERENCES

Alfonso, Juan Carlos, and Alvarez, Mayda. 1996. Rol masculino y transición de la fecundidad: El caso cubano. Paper presented at the International Seminar on Reproductive Health in Latin America and the Caribbean (PROLAP), Brazil.

Alvarez Suárez, Mayda. 2008. La revolución de las cubanas: 50 años de conquistas y luchas. Temas, no. 56: 67–77.

Araújo, Nara. 2003. La huella y el tiempo. Havana: Letras Cubanas.

Arés, Patricia. 2002. Studies on masculinity and fatherhood in the last decade in Cuba. Paper presented at the Commission on Gender in the Fourteenth Conference of Philosophers and Social Scientists from Cuba and the United States, University of Havana, Havana, June 23.

Armand, Inessa F. 1975. Stati, rechi, pisma. Moscow, Russia.

Barcia Zequeira, María del Carmen. 2003. La otra familia: Parientes, redes y descendencia de los esclavos en Cuba. Havana: Fondo Editorial Casa de las Américas.

Campuzano, Luisa. 1996. Ser cubana y no morir en el intento. Temas, no. 5:4–10.

CEPDE-ONE. 2004. Anuario demográfico de Cuba 2003. November. Havana: Centro de Estudios de Población y Desarrollo–Oficina Nacional de Estadísticas.

Consulta Oficina Nacional de Estadísticas. 1999. Perfil estadístico de la mujer cubana en el umbral del siglo XXI. Havana: Oficina Nacional de Estadísticas.

Deere, Carmen Diana, and Magdalena León. 2000. Género, propiedad y empoderamiento: Tierra, estado y mercado en América Latina. Bogotá: Tercer Mundo.

Elwood, R. C. 1992. Inessa Armand: Revolutionary and feminist. Ottawa: Carleton University Press.

Garcia Castro, Mary, and Sherryl Lutjens. 1998. La política desde el género: La contribución feminista latinoamericana a alternativas del neoliberalismo. Paper presented at the international seminar Mundialización, Desarrollo Sostenible y Alternativas al Neoliberalismo en América Latina. Instituto de Filosofía de Cuba, Havana, June.

Gramsci, Antonio. 1971. State and civil society. In Selections from the Prison Notebooks, 206–246. New York: International Publishers.

Harris, Collette. 1995. Socialist societies and the emancipation of women: The case of Cuba. *Socialism and Democracy* 9 (1): 91–113.

Hochschild, Arlie. 1989. *The second shift*. New York: Avon Books.

Kollontai, Alexandra. 1921. The labour of women in the evolution of the economy. In *Selected writings of Alexandra Kollontai*, ed. Allison and Busby. Reprint, 1977.

Núñez Sarmiento, Marta. 1988. *La mujer cubana y el empleo en la Revolución Cubana*. Havana: Editorial de la Mujer.

———. 2000. Estrategias cubanas de empleo femenino en los 90: Un estudio de caso con mujeres profesionales. *Revista Caminos*, no. 17–18:46–63.

———. 2001a. Cuban strategies for women's employment in the nineties: A case study with professional women. *Socialism and Democracy* 15 (1): 41–64.

———. 2001b. Estrategias cubanas de empleo femenino en los 90: Un estudio de caso con mujeres profesionales. *Papers*, no. 63–64:141–170.

———. 2003. Gender studies in Cuba: Methodological approaches (1974–2002). *Gender and Society* 17 (1): 7–31.

———. 2004. Ideología de género entre profesionales cubanos. *Temas*, no. 37–38:24–36.

———. 2005. Changes in gender ideology among professional women and men in Cuba today. *Cleveland State Law Review* 52 (1–2): 173–187.

ONE. 1997. *Anuario estadístico de Cuba 1996*. Havana: National Office of Statistics.

———. 1999. *Perfil estadístico de la mujer cubana en el umbral del siglo XXI*. Havana: National Office of Statistics.

———. 2003. *Cuba en cifras 2002*. Havana: National Office of Statistics.

———. 2006. *Anuario estadístico de Cuba 2006*. Havana: National Office of Statistics.

Peláez, Orfilio. 2006. Reto inaplazable para los cubanos. *Granma*, October 30, 4–5.

Safa, Helen I. 1998. *De mantenidas a proveedoras*. San Juan: Editorial de la Universidad de Puerto Rico.

PART III

WOMEN'S AGENCY FOR PLURAL DEMOCRACY AND FULL CITIZENSHIP

5

The Mothers and Grandmothers of Plaza de Mayo Speak

INTERVIEWS BY GRACIELA DI MARCO

The Mothers' committees for the disappeared were one of the first expressions of female activism in Latin America during the 1970s and 1980s. They irrupted onto the political stage of their respective countries as a collective response to a regional policy of counterinsurgency that grotesquely violated the most basic human rights to life, to not be tortured, and to have a fair trial. The Mothers of Plaza de Mayo (May Square) of Argentina was the first and best-known group of mothers to organize in search of their disappeared children. As many other authoritarian regimes of this era, the Argentinean military dictatorship used brutal methods to eliminate a growing civil and armed opposition, tragically ending the lives of tens of thousands of people through a technique, initially employed by the Nazis in World War II, that became known as disappearance. People were illegally detained, imprisoned, tortured, and killed, without having any official paper trail that indicated to family members when they are were arrested, where they were taken, and what happened to them. The Mothers' committees were the organized expression of hundreds of mothers and other female relatives who initially searched individually for their loved ones in police stations, hospitals, and morgues. They became the first human rights organizations in Latin America and stood front and center in the national struggles for democracy.

Some years later in Argentina, the Grandmothers of Plaza de Mayo emerged from the Mothers' committees. They are dedicated to finding their grandchildren who were born in jail and given in adoption to military personal of the junta when their own parents were killed. With the help of sympathetic scientists, the Grandmothers' committee applied a sophisticated DNA procedure to identify their now-grown grandchildren, who in most cases had no idea who their real parents were. Over the years the Grandmothers have rescued the identity of almost a hundred people raised in military-dictatorship families. On February 13, 2009, the Grandmothers of Plaza de Mayo announced that they had identified their ninety-seventh grandchild. The following testimonies are firsthand stories, told by the Mothers and the Grandmothers of Plaza de Mayo.

Testimony of Nora Cortiñas: Mothers of Plaza de Mayo Founding Line

Actually, the Mothers started meeting on April 30, 1977. My son, Gustavo, was abducted on the fifteenth. I ran all over the city, from the police station, to the bishopric, to the Ministry of the Interior. Later I visited all the existing organizations, first the Liga Argentina por los Derechos del Hombre [Argentinean League for Human Rights], where relatives of the disappeared were helped. Some of them had belonged to the league and now their children were disappeared. Catalina Guagnini once said, "They took away the bad sons and daughters of the good communists." I also visited the Asamblea Permanente por los Derechos Humanos [Permanent Assembly for Human Rights], founded in December 1975, and other organizations such as the Movimiento Ecuménico por los Derechos Humanos [Ecumenical Movement for Human Rights] and the Servicio de Paz y Justicia [Peace and Justice Service], whose leader, Adolfo Pérez Esquivel, was also abducted and disappeared at the time, but who was liberated due to the international outcry demanding his freedom. He had been working for many years in defense of the unprotected in Latin America: the indigenous peoples, the peasants.[1]

After that the Mothers began to meet at Plaza de Mayo. A couple of weeks later my brother-in-law told me that a group of women gathered there wanted to know where their children had been taken to. They weren't known as the Mothers [of Plaza de Mayo] yet.

Anyway, I crazily started filling in forms and dealing with legal procedures. I talked about this at home and was told where to go. The first days I feared my husband would talk about our problems at the ministry where he worked, which was under military intervention, and I would tell myself: these people aren't going to help me find Gustavo. I tell you, they were a disaster, but I was terrified and thought that my acting might make things worse and that my son would be tortured still more. It was that kind of confusion, ambivalence, coming and going. Then I began going to Plaza de Mayo, and there I met Azucena, María Vela, María Rosario, and Juanita. Well, that's when we started. Gustavo's wife lived at home with her boy. She and Gustavo were politically active, "Peronist Montoneros."[2] At that time, 1977, Gustavo was very much engaged in politics. Although he disagreed with the leadership, he was politically active.

By then I wasn't doing any housework; my priority was to look for my son. I slipped into a spiral of growing madness. Yes. Because it's madness, but I never gave in, never. And then all that fear . . . they would phone and threaten me, they would say that they were going to arrest me, they mistreated me. As I'm an extrovert, when I went to the police station I was seen as some kind of leader, so the threats were harsher. Later, they would phone my home and repeat the threats. They wrote my name, Nora Cortiñas, on my neighborhood walls followed by the words: "terrorist mother." We went out on the streets. Azucena's idea was that we should go to Plaza de Mayo to join in our grief, anguish, and uncertainty, because grief also brings uncertainty.

The Fathers

At the end of 1977, when we began meeting, Azucena, Esther, Mary, and the French nuns were abducted. The aim was to dissolve our movement. It was like a bolt of lightning and it shook our families tremendously. Our husbands, the fathers, were afraid because, before taking our friends, they had arrested us. Entering Plaza de Mayo was symbolic, and they said, "How long will this go on? Watch out, they will disappear you." Once the fathers saw how the police stopped a bus, got all the passengers off, pushed us in, and took us away. We gestured for them not to get near, because they had to contact our lawyers. One thing was for the Mothers to be arrested, but another would be for the fathers to be arrested with us.

We could say anything to the members of military and security forces, call them names, and things like that. When we entered the army headquarters we would say, "You took our children, but your wives cheat on you." When they said, "Your son must be a stooge," we answered, "My son may be a stooge, but your wife cheats on you." The fathers couldn't. We shouted, kicked, stamped our feet, cried, and screamed. Judeo-Christian culture conditions men's behavior: they aren't supposed to cry. A man must show fortitude and endurance; he represents strength. But it wasn't like that. Men were weak. Many of the Mothers were divorced or separated, had a different attitude toward life, but many were housewives.

When we met the first time, Azucena said, "Let's go to Plaza de Mayo from Stella Maris Church." There was a small office outside, at the back of the church, for the bishop, who wore boots under his cassock.[3] So Azucena gathered the Mothers and fathers who had attended and said, "We are not coming back here; we must go to Plaza de Mayo and let everyone see us entering the government house."

She fixed a date: Saturday, April 30. Thirteen Mothers and a girl who belonged to the Communist Party and was looking for her own disappeared attended. The government house was closed. One of the Mothers said, "We'll come next Friday." Three Fridays later, one of them said, "We're coming on Fridays [in Spanish, *viernes*]; a day with an *r* is unlucky!" You see, even we Catholics are superstitious. Another Mother said, "Why don't we choose a different day?" And another one said shyly, "We still have Mondays [*lunes*] and Thursdays [*jueves*]. No, not Monday. That's laundry day; let it be Thursday." As time passes, I remember that scene very well. And the fact that we had a double role: we went out to look for our sons and daughters, but we also did the housework, even if husbands helped. In my case, not only my husband but my daughter-in-law who lived with us and my son Marcelo helped. Nevertheless, we had two roles and I thought, I've been at this meeting for hours and forgot to buy bread. Or take cooking: I would get up and cook at six in the morning because I had to be off by eight, and I wanted to leave some food at home, and my husband complained of the smell of food. And I said, "If you don't like it, you cook. I'm leaving your meal ready; you can eat it when you're hungry." Things of that sort, due to the double role we had. I would think, I'm going off, but they have this or that at home.

We never gave the fathers direct participation. At times they would express their feelings timidly—but, you know, they were fearful. Besides, we were like madwomen; we went out on the streets because we were mad. If we got phone calls, we would pick up the phone and yell, "Son of a . . ." How can you shout that on the phone? Well, let them take me. . . . You know . . . things like that could only be done by mothers. Now I understand that if the fathers had acted like that they would have been murdered or imprisoned.

After some years of gathering at Plaza de Mayo, we were about four hundred Mothers, and a few fathers accompanied us. Some have died since—some haven't. Sometimes they just sat on the benches of the square, or walked around, but they never marched with us. . . .

When we were carrying out legal procedures and any of the fathers came along, they always ended up saying something atrocious, like "I told my son or daughter not to get involved." And we said, Go away, goodbye. If you think that, you shouldn't be here." That's how it was. The fathers wanted to save their children by saying they had been naive, knew nothing about politics, and had been used. We, the Mothers, had a clear mind.

The path was marked by Azucena; she definitely had a clear mind. She had been in a union; she had courage; we learned from her. Another Mother was the daughter of an anarchist. Another belonged to a family who had escaped Nazi Europe. All this created a circle. We learned from each other, how to defend our children, vindicate their behavior without fear. At first some of us said, "I don't know what my son or daughter was up to." But that was at the beginning. You couldn't say, "My son was an activist." No! That would have buried him. Every day we learned something.

The Organization

When we began gathering at Plaza de Mayo, at first we just stood there. Azucena, an incredibly protective Mother, would bring drafts of letters to the pope, to the Episcopal conference. A draft that we read and that later would become a letter, it didn't matter what kind of paper it was written on, wrapping paper or whatever; we would sign it. Nothing was changed; we signed it as it was. Then she would produce letters to the military: the navy, the air force, and the army. She gave us copies and said, "Three Mothers will go to the Ministry of War [now the Ministry of Defense], three to the navy headquarters." In those days we were very few; three should go there, three somewhere else, and we chose who would go. It was a group experience, as in Enrique Pichon Riviere's social psychology theory. Later on, I myself started studying social psychology, because when the students of this school wrote papers, many wrote about our work. They said that we were experiencing Pichon Riviere's theory. But we didn't understand it that way. We would meet, line up to present habeas corpus, and decide who would go where; each one had a role. Later in the day we would meet again to see how things had come out. It was a very spontaneous organization in which each would choose what she was going to do: I'll go there and do that. When we met, one of us asked, "Who's going to talk?" And someone would say, "I'll speak about the babies we're looking for." For example, a Mother who wanted to know where her pregnant daughter or daughter-in-law had been taken would say, "I'll talk about pregnant women." We always went to the different institutions in threes and did our work openly: we had to arrange interviews, give our ID numbers, our home phone numbers. It was all done in the open; it wasn't clandestine work. It was like saying, "Here we are. We want to know where our sons and daughters are." And we would argue, and quarrel. . . . For many years we did not have formal roles; we worked just like that. How did things work? In 1977 Azucena was our natural leader; when she arrived at Plaza de Mayo, she inspired fortitude. She was generous; she would let everybody speak and give their opinions and considered them all. She wasn't bossy or authoritarian. She had an open mind, was spontaneous, and thought that decisions should be made by the group. She did not think of herself as the president or anything of the sort. Hers was a natural leadership. We formed smaller groups, and met at our homes or at tea rooms. At first we met for lunch at a convent in the neighborhood of Balvanera, where there was a soup kitchen and you could get a cheap meal. There we planned our work and organized different activities.

The Awakening of Consciousness

The change we went through—well, not change but transformation or learning—the awakening of our consciousness, I always say, had to do in the first place with "Why?" "What for?" and "Why did they take them?" They took them because they were politically active. That's why. As the years went by we understood this on the streets, walking together with unionists, with teachers, with doctors and medics, with those who were following in the path of the political struggle started by our sons and daughters. The reasons they took them were related to the oppressive neoliberal economic policies of hunger, unemployment, the impoverishment of a rich country. This is what we learned, but on the streets, where at first we didn't dare talk politics. That was serious; it was getting involved and we could be pointed at; they could say, "The Mothers belong to political parties." We were very careful; we still are and we don't take part in any activities that have to do with political parties. After every change of government we had to do our catharsis, because after the military dictatorship we were made all kinds of beautiful promises and we believed them, until we realized they were only promises.

The Present Situation

This government is very different from the earlier ones—up to now, and in certain respects. What is the situation? You can't be blind to all that has been achieved. After twenty years of constitutional governments, plus what we did during the dictatorship with our marches, protests, denouncing, and demands, we now have a government that listens. Surely, in the past, the president must have thought, if I become president, the first thing I will do is open the ESMA [Escuela de Mecánica de la Armada, or Navy Technical School], where there were concentration camps. That must have been one of his ideas. Still, we can also see that the dreams of our sons and daughters, like the reign of social justice, haven't been fulfilled. We understand that this country was systematically destroyed during thirty years by the military, their partners, and politicians; they destroyed it; they threw it into a ditch. You need more than one day to put it back on its feet. And you must understand that politicians who were part of former governments are responsible: they were rulers or belonged to the ruling class; they aren't innocent. When they take office they have airs at first, but later they compromise with those that hold economic power. Their commitment is with the web of politicians and businesspeople that helped them get there. So, I will not trade my son's wishes and struggle for the proposed transformation of the ESMA and the clandestine detention center Club Atlético into areas for the preservation of memory, nor for the banning of the amnesty laws. Because I'm sure that from wherever he is buried, he will follow his mother's steps and tell me to be strong. So if I had any doubts or said, "How long?" "What's the use?" I heard a voice inside me saying, "You must go on till the end; you must achieve what we did not."

Feminism and Women's Rights

We are all women. We have doubts on only one issue; we don't agree on it or haven't discussed it widely: abortion. It's a complex topic, you know; some of the Mothers are Catholic, but they are beginning to understand that the issue is that poor women die while those who are well-off can have an abortion; they can decide and their health is protected. And those poor women cannot afford contraceptive methods. Furthermore, there isn't any kind of sex education. But that took some time. At first, the topic of abortion produced uneasiness. Many said they didn't want to get mixed up in that question because woman is a life-giver. . . . But you know, we've made progress in that field. For many years I have fought for the decriminalization and legalization of abortion, although I don't support it. But I think every woman has a right to decide. I also consider that the decision to have an abortion also involves me, and unfortunately many women have to make that decision by themselves, because even if the couple gets on, well, they can't make this decision together. I wish every woman had the right to choose how many children she wants to have, how and when. This is part of the struggle for freedom we are in. The other question was accepting homosexuality, a controversial issue. Sometimes the way the media present this topic is shocking.

In a conversation with two reporters, Marta Merkin and Ana María Muchnik, one of them said, "I'm a feminist, you know," and I answered, "That's being against men." I'm married. I have two sons. I come from a patriarchal home, where masculinity was exalted. My father was very jealous, even of his daughters; we couldn't go to some places, and when we began dating, wow, well. . . . So one of them said, "Let us tell you." And they talked about the recognition of our gender's rights and gave me a lesson on feminism. Since then I've understood that what the Mothers have done was to place gender in the struggle, simply by carrying out our endeavor as women, confronting the military dictatorship, and challenging a society that had mistreated us because we were women—especially the military, the church, and the politicians. Even women who were members of political parties mistreated us, particularly those of the Unión Cívica Radical [Radical Civic Union]. A group of women belonging to this party invited us to a meeting in an apartment in Plaza San Martín [a park in the Retiro district of Buenos Aires]. They wanted us to tell them how we got organized, how we went out on the streets, but all this in great secrecy. It looked as if they were afraid to have that interview with us in case we introduced them into a world they didn't wish to know too much about. With peronist women it was different; Evita had led that movement. Although I associated Evita with machismo because she always repeated "with my general, my man," she had started walking that path. I believe this involvement scared me because my husband was such a male chauvinist, and then I had to face things I'd never done before: go out on the streets to confront the dictatorship; that made me a feminist. I had never read about feminism. I think women should be given a detailed explanation of what it means to be a feminist. This should be done on television, on the radio, when women meet. You know, I used to think it was against men, because machistas fill their wives' and daughters' heads with the idea that feminists fight for freedom, like in Europe, where women marched waving their bras, and that feminism is always a synonym of lesbianism. It's necessary to clarify this and then you understand you've got rights, equal to those of men. We belong to different genders; we walk side by side. You have the same rights, and if not, you protest. I tell you, my mother-in-law, whom I never heard use the word feminism, was a woman who did what she thought was right, and it didn't matter if her husband liked it or not. She confronted him. She would give me advice— many recommendations—she was an extraordinary woman, a beautiful, chubby lady. One day she told me that you should always have the last word, no matter if you are right or not—that's being a real mother-in-law—and that I should not allow my husband to dominate me, because otherwise I would never get him off me. Rather than a mother-in-law, she was a good mother who knew what her sons were like, and what her husband had been like. So it was good advice. That's when I understood!

I'm really an extrovert. I like to know, peek into, and read about everything, to be up to date with what's happening in the world. It was good for me to study social psychology in 1985. Social psychology is illuminating; it teaches you how to listen and analyze what you hear, to detect who says what and how it's told. My experience teaching women at my sewing workshop, although it was kind of domestic, was also important because I learned about the lives of other women and, of course, the fact that I met extraordinary women.

The Feminist Conferences

Except for a couple, I attended all the local and international feminist conferences of the past years: the Continental Conference of Women in Cuba, the New York conference, and the one held in Russia when it was still part of the Soviet Union. They have been useful in my relationship with women, taught me about the rights we are entitled to and how to use them. But sometimes women disappoint me because when they are in office they change. I also feel that we're not represented by those women in power who, after receiving our support, take no interest in gender or equality. Those who act like men are compromising, selfishly and foolishly. Nevertheless, learning is enriching for me. However, my family, my son, my daughters-in-law, and grandchildren don't belong to the feminist circle.

I would like to be remembered as a woman who wants to exalt gender, in the sense that I value myself and the struggle of women, even the most humble, in any corner of the world. The women at the pickets are an example.[4] Before these women appeared at the pickets, many other women went out on the streets of their neighborhoods to fight for drinking water or for electric power; they told me that our struggle at Plaza de Mayo was an example to them. They said "If the Mothers can go out on the streets to fight for their sons and daughters, then we can fight in our own neighborhoods for our children, for what we are entitled to, public services." Yes, I would like simply to be remembered, and maybe someone will say, "Do you remember Nora? Wow, she would go everywhere. For example, that roundtable I attended yesterday about precarious jobs. I was there saying to myself, they all talk about laws, regulations. I just have a few notes; should I talk? And I did, and they all ended up crying, even men. That was because I spoke about the essentials, what our sons and daughters wanted, and what happened.

Testimony of Estela Carlotto: President
of the Grandmothers of Plaza de Mayo

The Context

The movement of the Grandmothers of Plaza de Mayo isn't a typical movement; it's not a group of women who gathered with a particular aim, to carry out a task, or with lives, ideals, or ambitions in common. No. We founded a group summoned by grief, a struggle, and our search. The call came from a military dictatorship, not from us. We didn't know each other; we came from different cultures, religions, and economic and political backgrounds. All that was put aside; it didn't matter and our aim was the search for our sons, daughters, and grandchildren.

At the time of the coup d'état of March 24, 1976, I was the principal of a primary school. I had four children and my husband, a chemist, owned a small plant that manufactured paint. My two elder daughters, Laura and Claudia, were married and independent; both were politically active at university and in high schools; they opposed what we knew was coming. They had a clear view of the dark future that was in the making.

Our home was middle class. And I always say we raised our children with a lot of freedom, independence, and self-determination. However, we were not prepared for their political discourse and actions. We had been rebellious and had wanted change, but we had followed in the steps of our parents, and those of my generation wished their children to do the same. But this didn't happen. My husband and I did not take part in politics; we voted only when we had to, supporting the UCR; we opposed peronism. We were influenced by those who, for different reasons, had problems with Peron's politics. This issue mattered to us. When our daughters became peronists, it was a big surprise, almost unpleasant. But as I've said, with the liberty in which we raised them, we listened to them. We lived in La Plata, a university town with a strong labor movement, which was dynamic and in the opposition and, at the beginning of the troubles, suffered the actions of the Triple A, the Alianza Anticomunista Argentina [Argentinean Anticommunist

Alliance].[5] In La Plata people were abducted and murdered, and their bodies appeared anyplace or were thrown in the streets; they were not disappeared. And we could see day by day how the political milieu rarefied. It got dangerous, and we were afraid most of all for our daughters. To protect them, I tried to dissuade them from their involvement and sometimes made foolish proposals. However, if they asked for things to make their placards and posters, I helped and always listened to them in fear. I would say to Laura, the eldest of my four children, to do as I did in my daily life: if there was someone in need, give him something; if there were abandoned children, take care of them for a few hours. She laughed and said lovingly that that wasn't the way, that they wanted to do away with orphanages, that that was charity, that it lasted only for an instant, that it was only a way to cleanse our conscience, that it didn't work, and that they wanted radical changes.

And I listened, and started to understand. Both of them were married. Claudia got married when she was eighteen. They were no longer under our tutelage, but as we were a close-knit family, we were there for them and looked into their activities. Laura, the eldest, always minimized the danger she was in, as if her work weren't important. She was at the university, and belonged to the Juventud Universitaria Peronista [Peronist University Youth, the peronist youth movement in the universities], which later associated with Montoneros. She worked for this movement as a liaison with the media; she visited neighborhoods trying to awaken class consciousness; wrote political graffiti; took part in marches. My husband knew more about some of her activities. I was a little foolish, believed what I was told, and was, of course, more fearful. My husband—this I discovered later—gave refuge in his factory to many kids who were being persecuted. He took care of them and since he manufactured paint, he gave it for free for their political campaigns. Sometimes, when he saw a wall with a political slogan written by Montoneros, he would exclaim, "That's my paint." He also gave other political organizations the paint they needed—that was his contribution—and other things he did, which I won't know about because he passed away four years ago.

The problem at the time with teachers was that they were passive. We didn't confront; the union was practically inexistent. But when there were strikes, I was there. Although I was the school head, when the causes were just I even went on strike myself. I was aware of things but didn't belong formally to an organization. And I was very scared of my daughters' political engagement. When the constitutional government, a very bad one but constitutional nonetheless, was overthrown on March 24, we understood that the future was going to be hard and dangerous.

The Repression

On August 1, 1977, my husband was abducted because he was Laura's father. I was warned that if I wanted him back alive I would have to pay ransom and was given one day (Wednesday) to collect forty million pesos and save his life. They told me that on Thursday they were changing the guard and weren't turning in any prisoners; this meant they would kill him.

Obviously, I began collecting money, went to the pawnbroker, borrowed, and did everything I could and finally raised this sum and handed it to an emissary. Then I just waited, as I had no news from my husband. I read the newspapers to see if a body appeared someplace. I saw many people: lawyers who only wanted money, corrupt individuals who bargained with life. I met others who wanted to help but did not know how. Well, I did everything I could. Meanwhile I learned for the first time how to act and move in search of a disappeared person. I visited hospitals, police stations, presented a habeas corpus, spoke to politicians, and made many contacts of all kinds. Twenty-five days later he was liberated; he had lost twenty-eight pounds and, because of his diabetes, was in bad condition.

The last time I saw Laura was July 31, 1977. After my husband was freed, he went back to work, and he would meet her in Buenos Aires, where she lived. He traveled there regularly, where he had customers and suppliers for his factory. This was his cover, part of his routine. In my case it was different as I worked at a school. Laura wrote and phoned once a week. And then the letters and calls ceased. The last letter was dated November 16, 1977. So I thought, she's been abducted. We established November 26, 1977, as the day of her disappearance. She was living with her husband, so when we learned about her fate, once again I contacted politicians, the bishop, those under the bishop. The military officer Bignone, who had received me before in his office at the army headquarters, was practically out of his mind. He stated that they killed them all. I said that I did not want her killed, that if she had committed a crime, she should be tried and sentenced. That I would wait for her. He replied that I should understand what had happened in Uruguay, where the Tupamaros had been imprisoned and this had strengthened their convictions, and that this wasn't going to happen here.[6]

It was then when I thought she had been murdered, because when my husband was kidnapped he had overheard someone say that they were murdering prisoners. When he told us this, we thought he had gone mad. So I said to this man, "If you've killed her I want her body. Because I don't want to go mad like so many mothers looking for NN [No Name] initials on unidentified graves." In the past I had accompanied many mothers whose sons and daughters had disappeared or had been murdered. There were many new graves in La Plata, especially those marked NN. In April 1978, a woman who had been in prison with Laura was released. She visited my husband at the factory and told him that our daughter was alive, that her six months' pregnancy was going well—that was when I learned she was pregnant— that the baby was going to be born in June, and that I could claim it at the Casa Cuna.[7] During all these years I've gathered information from comrades who were with her and were liberated, whom I met in different countries where they were refugees, or here in Argentina. I learned that Laura had given birth to a boy on June 26, 1978, that she had been taken to the Central Military Hospital. Since then, all of us have been gathering information about what happened to her and her son. On August 25, 1978, a high-ranking police officer told us that she had resisted arrest at a road blockade and had been shot by the military. These confrontations and shootings were fabrications. The prisoners were taken from detention centers and massacred. Laura realized they were going to murder her. She said good-bye to all her comrades that day, August 25. She was twenty-three years old. Her death was the most terrible blow I've ever received in my life. It's the cross I carry, because I struggle a great deal and will continue struggling, but grief doesn't die out; it's there. And I'm also searching for her son, who is now twenty-seven years old, but I don't know where he is. The issue here is with whom he is and how. There are boys and girls who have been appropriated but don't know it. And when by various means we find them, not because they come to us but because of someone's report, then it is as if they awake to a very harsh reality. I have been introduced to boys that could have been my grandson but who weren't. Some people have told me, "There is someone who looks like you; his eyes are like your daughter's." But then, when you present the report and the blood tests are done and he isn't your grandson, it's over. Still, sometimes someone comes with reliable information and a miracle happens. That's why I have so much hope that someday I'll be lucky.

The Grandmothers

Before this happened to Laura and after some good advice I was given, I had made up my mind and thought that I should get closer to the Mothers and Grandmothers who were organized and working in La Plata, so my search wouldn't be a lonely one. I went to the Grandmothers and began attending the meetings at Plaza de Mayo and signed up for the different tasks. Since then, I have been with my *compañeras*, my sisters in grief, doing what is possible, and even the impossible. Of course, at the beginning we had no experience; we did not know what to do. We wanted to see the babies at Casa Cuna; we also watched the children going in and coming out of kindergartens in their white pinafores. If we suspected anything then we would go to their homes, pretending to be salespeople, or whatever, and tried to check our information. On certain occasions, when someone informed us that in such and such a place there lived a policeman who had taken a child of ours, we would go and see if the child was really ours. All of this was registered. But then we became well-known and couldn't go on acting this way. If you think about it, our work started as something very domestic and improved with time. Then society and bureaucracy forced us to create a nonprofit organization with a legal status, formal statutes, and a committee, inscribed in the category of human rights. Thirteen Grandmothers belong to the standing committee, and other Grandmothers who do not belong to the committee work jointly with us; we are about twenty Grandmothers in all. In the past we would meet in a tea room or in a train station and plan our strategies. Later, we had our own offices and met there. Since we have improved our organization, our meetings are more frequent, and since 1984, with a constitutional government in place and legal actions imminent, we began to work with attorneys and psychologists. We developed genetic procedures to identify our grandchildren accurately and created the National Bank of Genetic Data, a unique case in the world, at the Durán Hospital in Buenos Aires.

The Search and the National Bank of Genetic Data

We said to ourselves, "The years go by and we still can't find them." Some Grandmothers had doubts as to whether their grandchildren had been born, if they were boys or girls, if they had inherited their looks. How could we prove at a court of law that a child was one of our grandchildren? From an article in a newspaper we learned that a father had denied his paternity but it had been proven through a blood test. So we thought, if the fathers and mothers aren't here, our own blood can be used for the tests. So then we started visiting different countries: Italy, France, Sweden, and the United States. In Europe we got no answers to our questions, but in the United States we did. The person who had an important role in this, and still has, is Dr. Mary-Claire King, who, with other scientists, established in a seminar in 1983 that with the blood sample of a relative of the children, the whole genetic pattern of their parents could be rebuilt. Comparing blood samples can ascertain identity. During 1984—[we were] already in the constitutional period—Mary-Claire King came to Argentina and stated that the genetic bank was ready to operate, its experts were well prepared, and the equipment and the whole system were very modern. Clay Snow, the other doctor who came with her, created the team of forensic anthropologists. They are the pillars of this project. That way we are certain that when children are found, they are the grandchildren we were looking for. This was our contribution, and that is why many people after all these years say we were the promoters of genetic science. We promoted many initiatives, because our work, as time went by, suffered great changes. Searching for babies is very different than searching for adult men and women. The philosophy is different; the strategies have been modified. We needed teams of experts, attorneys, [and] psychologists, because children and adults were in need of care and attention. We constituted the genetic team that collaborates with the genetic bank. Later, it was the time of modern computer science, and a research team. At this point we couldn't do the work ourselves any more: receive reports, take the numerous telephone calls, visit different homes, do the follow-ups, take pictures, see the birth certificates, read the files, all that. We had different teams taking turns to do this work under our leadership. As time passed, we thought that as our grandchildren grew older, two things would happen: they might come looking for their Grandmothers, and we would continue looking for them. That is when we began carrying out different tasks that had to do with the community, because that is where our Grandchildren are.

For the past six or seven years we have been producing videos, television spots, and other programs: theater, music, tango, and dance, for identity. These programs link us to the grandchildren, to those who have doubts about their identity, and encourage them to contact us. As a matter of fact, we have a team to handle spontaneous presentations, because boys and girls come here, tell us their stories, their doubts about their identity, that they may be sons or daughters of disappeared persons, and we must help them. Most important of all are the tests; on this we work closely with the government and the Comisión Nacional por el Derecho a la Identidad (CONADI; National Committee for the Right to Identity).

The Struggle for Identity, Truth, and Justice

Eight historic organizations devoted to human rights have been doing all this work, which represents an opportunity to obtain justice, keep memory alive, unearth the history of the disappeared, and find the grandchildren. The Grandmothers work particularly with the grandchildren. We are a very specific organization but have included other topics, such as education. We have agreements with the Ministry of Education, municipalities, and universities of Buenos Aires and the provinces. These programs and tasks are like a fan that continues opening. We also intervene in matters concerning women, the elderly, and children in society.

The Grandmothers are considered a referential institution on all these issues, and these programs and the work they involve need a liaison team with the press and a team to promote our activities. These must be dynamic and have a constant presence in all the activities related with these topics, as a means of collaborating with the democratic system. Why? Because we are in need of justice and truth and, most importantly, the reconstruction of society. Our social fabric is destroyed, wounded, by hunger, unemployment, housing problems, a deficient health insurance system, and a deteriorated educational system. This concerns the Grandmothers: although we are few, we distribute the diverse tasks among ourselves and get help from our grandchildren. Many that have been found, or the brothers and sisters of those we are still looking for, work at our offices. They are our reinforcement because the Grandmothers aren't getting any younger and can't do their work as before, and, sadly, others have passed away. We are the leaders and are in good company.

The Right to Identity

During the dictatorship, between four and five hundred children were stolen. The great majority were born in concentration camps. Here, at the Grandmothers' headquarters, we have 240 reports, plus another 100 filed by CONADI, which aren't at our offices. It is a lot! Of all the missing children, eighty have been found, sadly, not all of them alive. Some were never born because their pregnant mothers were murdered, killing them as well. Others died with their families when their homes were bombed. In some cases the grandparents have found their remains.

With CONADI we have established a national network for the right to identity. We not only work in Buenos Aires and in the other five offices in our country but have developed in every province and city the means to bring our case to public notice and receive spontaneous reports from those working for nongovernmental organizations, local governments, ombudsmen, offices for Human Rights, and volunteers. These groups all belong to the network. Nowadays, with great effort, we're opening a branch office in Madrid, because we know many children were taken away, or left the country, many years ago. We have reports of boys and girls that have doubts about their identity, and some believe they might be our grand-children. They watch television, see us, listen to our concerts, and watch our films and documentaries. Our programs are worldwide.

That is why we recommended that a series of articles concerning identity be introduced in the International Convention for the Rights of the Child. Three of them are referred to as Argentinean: 7, 8, and 11. In addition, the convention has had constitutional rank in Argentina since 1994 and clearly states the proceedings that must be followed when children are stolen and the responsibilities of the state in these issues.

The Struggle against Impunity

When Alfonsín took office, the whole of society celebrated it.[8] A line was drawn after the dictatorship; the military and the security forces were in retreat, morally defeated. We supported the democratic government, although we didn't share the views of the ruling party, but the people had great hopes. We were there and expected to be contacted, but nobody called us. We asked for interviews but weren't received. And then many good things happened: the prosecution and judgment of the commanders-in-chief of the armed forces [and] CONADEP [Comisión Nacional sobre la Desaparición de Personas, or National Committee for Disappeared Persons], which published *Nunca Más* [Never Again], a national report that officially lists the disappeared. And then, the surrender and the amnesty laws, which cost us blood, sweat, and tears. Our watch at Congress was permanent, begging the representatives not to pass these laws. But well, they followed the party line and the laws were passed.[9] Our only relief was that the crimes against our grandchildren would not go unpunished. We answered, "Don't try to comfort us. Our grandchildren weren't born from a cabbage; they had mothers and fathers, and we also want truth and justice for them." Nevertheless, we continued our work and clamor for justice, and the fact is 940 military are in jail for being accomplices in the theft of babies, together with those who appropriated a child. The amnesty laws were horrendous. We felt wronged and offended because we had to live with murderers, walk on the streets not knowing if the man walking beside us had murdered our son or daughter. And something that worried us was the continuity of barbaric acts, because crimes committed by the police, gangs of extortionists, and paramilitary groups weren't investigated. That is why we have always demanded the repeal of these laws. But now this new government is doing things that give us hope once again.[10] I think that these are good times that we must take advantage of. We have a government that has made a political decision in this sense, and has done what we have asked for before without success. We now are received, they ask for our advice, we are in permanent contact with them, and, furthermore, our requests are answered.

Gender Consciousness

Two things have changed: women and the knowledge of their rights. In the past they accepted given roles in life: kept home and raised children, and the husbands had their jobs, held office, etc. This has changed. But men have changed too, recognizing women as their peers, their right to be at the same level, neither higher nor lower, neither behind nor in front, but side by side. I believe that the compulsory percentage of 30 percent women as political candidates on electoral slates should be raised to at least 50 percent. Also, in many companies you can see women's leadership.

We are for everything that represents women's rights: the right to hold public office, have economic and social responsibilities, intervene in society beside men, and not be subjugated, mistreated, discriminated against. That is part of our work. Nowadays we're struggling for the ratification of the protocol of the CEDAW [Convention on the Elimination of All Forms of Discrimination against Women], which hasn't been approved by our Congress. Last year I visited the United Nations, commissioned by our Ministry of Foreign Relations, so you can imagine how important our institutional work is.

I believe that the society that condemned us was saying, consciously or not, "Well, that did not happen to me; they must have been up to something or their family didn't look after them." There was no distinction between sons and daughters. At first we felt discriminated against by a society that ostracized us, but especially by the military, who called us "madwomen" and said, "Don't worry. They will get tired of all this and just cry; they're women." They were wrong and, well, here we are. They could have disappeared many more people if they had been clever enough to acknowledge that women are strong. I can't say if it was courage, or mere love, but it was defying a situation in which it was impossible to keep still. I think no mother in our place could keep still. Those that kept quiet were afraid, or sick, or were restricted by their families: "Don't go," "I don't want you to go." But a great majority went out on the streets. It was a challenge to verbalize that they had taken away part of our souls and that this leaves an empty space. But you just can't stay at home crying. Every one of us did what she could and what we knew best. The miracle is that we're still together, because it's not easy. And time passed, fatigue and ailments came, but we did not reduce our efforts. Of course we have our problems like any family or organization. But we will continue working, I hope, while we have the strength and energy.

I would like to be remembered as a woman who did what had to be done; who was not a heroine, nor different, nor special, but a woman with a lot of love and grief, with memory; who did her part; who needed to do her part, and still does; a woman committed to that struggle.

ACKNOWLEDGMENTS

Edited by Alejandra Brener and translated by Esteban Moore.

NOTES

1. Adolfo Pérez Esquivel founded the Servicio de Paz y Justicia, which in those years promoted an international campaign denouncing the atrocities committed by the military regime. In 1977 he was arrested by the federal police in Buenos Aires, held a prisoner for fourteen months in the police headquarters without due process, and was tortured. While he was imprisoned he received the Pope John XXIII Peace Memorial and in 1980 he was awarded the Nobel Peace Prize.

2. The Movimiento Peronista Montonero (Montonero Peronist Movement) was a political military organization that emerged as an armed movement in defense of the third administration of General Domingo Perón, who was elected in 1973 but died in 1974. He was replaced by his widow, Isabel Perón, who had previously been elected vice president. Montoneros went underground in 1976 to fight against the military coup that had overthrown Isabel Perón's government. The group was finally crushed through state and paramilitary repression.

3. The boots imply that he was linked to the military.

4. Editor's note: see Graciela Di Marco (this volume, ch. 9) on women's participation in the picket movement in the 1990s.

5. The Triple A was a paramilitary organization that was instrumental in carrying out the repression of the "dirty war." Created in 1974 by José López Reja, secretary of social security during the administration of Isabel Perón, it controlled political forces that were considered to be threats to this government and continued to be part of the repressive apparatus during the military coup.

6. The Tupamaros, or the Movimiento de Liberación Nacional (National Liberation Movement), was a left-wing political organization in Uruguay that emerged in the sixties and evolved into a guerrilla movement at the end of that decade. It was severely repressed during the military regime of the seventies and early eighties, with most of its members assassinated, in exile, or in jail. It became a political movement again with the return to democracy, actually forming part of the ruling Frente Amplio (Broad Coalition).

7. Casa Cuna, formerly Casa de Niños Expósitos (Home for Abandoned Children), was founded in Buenos Aires in 1779. Since 1961 it has become a children's hospital, Hospital General de Niños Dr. Pedro de Elizalde.

8. Raúl Alfonsín was president of Argentina from 1983 to 1989.

9. The Law of Final Point and the Law of Due Obedience were sanctioned in 1986 and 1987, which liberated hundreds of oppressors from charges and guilt. In 2003 those laws were repealed. In June 2005 the nation's Supreme Court of Justice resolved the nullity of these laws. As a consequence, new rulings could be started against military officers accused of human rights violations during the last military dictatorship.

10. She is referring to President Nestor Kirchner's administration.

6

Gender Politics in Nicaragua

FEMINISM, ANTIFEMINISM, AND
THE RETURN OF DANIEL ORTEGA

KAREN KAMPWIRTH

> The Sandinista Front made an opening to establish a
> new basis for relations. . . . They treated [women] as
> important.   —María Lourdes Bolaños

> There was a [Sandinista] discourse about women but
> I think there was a strong fear of the word "feminist."
> I think that more than anything it is a fear of losing
> power, of having to share power with a woman.
>   —Hazel Fonseca

> The autonomy of the family was heavily attacked in my
> country under the Marxist government of the 1980s. . . .
> In that decade the Constitution established the recogni-
> tion of common law marriage as equal to legal marriage
> and also unilateral divorce. . . . Today the class struggle
> has converted itself into a struggle for the elimination of
> sexual classes and the triumph of the "neutral sex."
>   —Max Padilla

Nicaragua has the most significant feminist movement in Central America today, thanks in part to the Sandinista Revolution (1979–1990). But, according to María Lourdes Bolaños, Hazel Fonseca, and many other activists in the women's move-ment, many leaders of the revolution were also responsible for impeding the emer-gence of feminism. So it is somewhat ironic that the opponents of today's feminist activists, people I call antifeminists, often frame their opposition to feminism in terms of the Sandinista Revolution.[1] Antifeminist activists such as Max Padilla see the revolution and feminism as part of the same process, a process they oppose.

But ironically, in 2006, the antifeminists accomplished one of their long-term goals—the abolition of the right to abortion to save the life of the woman—with the help of the same revolutionary party that they had blamed for the emergence of feminism in Nicaragua.

The Emergence, or Reemergence, of Feminism in the 1980s

One of the few things that feminists and antifeminists agree about is that Nicaraguan feminism was a product of the Sandinista Revolution. However, as Victoria González-Rivera (2001) has shown, Nicaraguan feminism was not born with the revolution. Instead, it can be traced back to the nineteenth century. Moreover, many of the most independent and politically active women of the twentieth century were supporters of the Somoza dictatorship, and so the Sandinista Revolution was not the first time that women were mobilized behind a partisan or feminist project. Nonetheless, historical memory is typically constructed by history's winners and so the history that González-Rivera uncovered is truly a lost history. In the dominant story, told by feminists and by their opponents, feminists first began organizing in the 1980s.

This feminist organizing was possible in large part because of the mass mobilization of men and women, especially young women, in the early 1980s. They were mobilized by the Sandinista government for a variety of purposes: to teach others to read, to immunize children, to harvest coffee, to guard their neighborhoods at night. Those campaigns played a critical role in the challenge to traditional authority that was the revolution (Kampwirth 2004, 26–28).

In the early years of the revolution, the Sandinista-affiliated national women's organization, Asociación de Mujeres Nicaragüenses Luisa Amanda Espinoza (AMNLAE; Luisa Amanda Espinoza Association of Nicaraguan Women) played an important role in challenging traditional authority. Founded in 1977 as the Asociación de Mujeres ante la Problemática Nacional (AMPRONAC; Association of Women Confronting National Problems) it was one member of the Sandinista coalition that helped bring down Somoza. With the revolution it changed its name but its mission did not change significantly. Still a support group of the Frente Sandinista de Liberación Nacional (Sandinista Front for National Liberation), the most significant changes were due to the development in the FSLN itself, from a guerrilla movement to a political party.

AMNLAE's work included advocating for legal changes to help women and providing services through Casas de la Mujer (Women's Houses), which numbered more than fifty nationwide by the end of the revolutionary decade. These Casas provided services in the areas of health and psychological and legal counseling, at the same time as they offered workshops in areas such as sexuality, contraception, and job training. Yet despite all the important work it did, AMNLAE's role as support for the male-dominated FSLN impeded its ability to challenge sexual inequality. With time, even women who stayed with AMNLAE began to question the relationship between the association and the party (on AMNLAE and the FSLN, see Criquillón 1995; Kampwirth 2004, 28–36, 54–57; Murguialday 1990, 101–148).

AMNLAE's work promoting reforms in gender-related laws, and internal pressures within the women's organization in the 1980s, provides reasons to believe that AMNLAE would have evolved into a more independent and more feminist organization had the revolution continued on its original course. But there is no way to know for sure. The relatively easy years of the revolution came to an end with Ronald Reagan's inauguration as president of the United States in 1981 and his funding of the contras shortly thereafter.

With the onset of the war, gender politics in Nicaragua entered a new phase. Within the evolving women's movement, there were at least two different responses to the war, that of what Nicaraguans call "the sectors" (labor unions or other economically organized groups) and that of AMNLAE. And their responses to the very same war could not have been more different.

The Secretarías de la Mujer (Women's Secretariats) were founded in all the major labor unions in the early to mid-1980s. The first Secretaría was created within the rural wageworkers union, the Asociación de Trabajadores del Campo (ATC; Association of Rural Workers) in 1983. The women of the ATC Secretaría successfully made the case that the key to increasing rural women's productivity—and therefore raising funds necessary for the war effort—was to address gender inequality. Perhaps because of the power that came out of their important role in the national economy, the women of the ATC succeeded in pressuring the FSLN to open hundreds of day care centers, collective corn mills, and wash basins and to address issues like sexual harassment and access to contraception. At the same time as the women of the Secretarías insisted that the war could never be won without more gender equality, the women of AMNLAE accepted an ever more subservient relationship with the FSLN, on the grounds that the war could never be won without softening demands for gender equality, at least temporarily (on the emergence of feminism within the sectors, see Criquillón 1995, 215–225; Murguialday 1990, 155–188).

The final years of the 1980s were a time when elements of the revolution were institutionalized; they were also the years when another sort of women's organizing began to emerge. Joining the Sandinista-affiliated women's movement, AMNLAE, whose roots could be traced to the guerrilla period, and the Secretarías, which grew in response to the contra war, was a third branch: independent or autonomous feminism. This third way—that explicitly rejected links to parties and unions—responded to two occurrences: the debates that led up to the 1987 Constitution and the 1987 Encuentro Feminista de América Latina y el Caribe (Latin American and Caribbean Feminist Encuentro) that was held near enough— in Taxco, Mexico—to allow forty to fifty Nicaraguan women to attend.

By 1987 one of the earliest autonomous feminist groups, the Colectivo de Mujeres de Matagalpa (Matagalpa Women's Collective), was formed. Initially it broadcast over the radio and performed feminist theater on topics such as abortion, and soon added classes in literacy, midwifery, and the law. The Centro de Mujeres de Masaya (Masaya Women's Center), founded in 1988, and the Centro de Mujeres IXCHEN (IXCHEN Women's Center), founded in 1989, were women's centers that provided a range of legal, health, and psychological services, at the same time as they advocated for gender equality.

Groups like the Centro de Mujeres de Masaya and IXCHEN (which soon had centers in many Nicaraguan cities) were in many ways like AMNLAE's Casas, except that they operated independently from the FSLN. But a very different model of women's organizing—an autonomous feminist organization that sought to change state policy rather than provide services—was founded by many of the women who participated in the Encuentro. Upon their return from Mexico in 1987, they founded the Partido de la Izquierda Erótica (PIE; Party of the Erotic Left).

The PIE was a lobbying group that succeeded in promoting gender equality as a constitutional value. In the 1987 Constitution, at least ten articles make specific mention of women's rights (compared with none in the 1974 Constitution). Couples in common law marriages (which are more common than legal marriages among Nicaragua's poor majority) were protected from discrimination, and no-fault divorce was permitted. The PIE did not last into the 1990s, but it left its mark on the Constitution and on the women's movement. After the FSLN lost the 1990 election, all twenty-some members of the PIE became founding members of the autonomous feminist organizations that emerged in the early 1990s (on gender issues and Sandinista law making, see Kampwirth 1998; Stephens 1988, 1990).

After the Revolution: Autonomous Feminists
Respond to State Antifeminism

The war was the central topic of the 1990 presidential campaign and the language with which both leading candidates spoke of war and peace was highly gendered. Daniel Ortega, "the fighting cock," was portrayed simultaneously as a loving father, hugging his baby daughter Camila, and as a horse-riding cowboy leading a charge of other men on horses. These masculine images were tied together with the slogan "everything will be better," a very poor choice for a party that had already governed for ten years.

Ortega's major challenger, Violeta Barrios de Chamorro, or doña Violeta, as she was consistently called, always dressed in white, invoking the image of the Virgin Mary. Through her words and image, she made the claim that she, a woman with almost no formal political experience, would be able to end the war and reconcile the Nicaraguan family, just as she had reunited her own politically divided children. Instead of formal political experiences, doña Violeta promised to draw on her experiences as wife, widow, and mother. Appealing to an imagined past in which men protected women in exchange for their loyalty and subservience, a past in which families were not divided by politics, she promised to end the war, reunite families, and end the suffering of mothers (Kampwirth 2004, 48–54). Running on that platform, she won with almost 55 percent of the vote.

When doña Violeta took office in April 1990, she fulfilled many of those promises. Ending the war, the central promise of the campaign, largely did occur that same year as the contras demobilized, mainly because their main source of funds—the U.S. government—withdrew its support. Sporadic political violence continued for several years after doña Violeta took office, but the draft was abolished and, for the most part, the war ended. To a significant extent doña Violeta also came through on her promise of reconciliation, even making an alliance with some FSLN legislators against more radical right-wing members of her own political coalition. And doña Violeta also carried through the implicit antifeminist promise of her political campaign by seeking to overturn many Sandinista-era gender reforms, especially in the areas of health, education, and social welfare (on those policies, see Kampwirth 2004, 48–54).

The early 1990s brought major changes for Nicaraguan feminists. The electoral loss of the party of the revolution, the FSLN, meant that they lost an ideological ally in government, and many of the laws and social programs that had promoted gender equality were overturned or underfunded. But they were also freed from the constraints that the vanguardist FSLN had tried to place on feminist activists. The most unanticipated result of the 1990 election was not the peaceful end of the Sandinista Revolution or the demobilization of the contra forces but the explosive emergence of autonomous feminism, including lesbian feminism.

The official coming-out party of the new branch of women's organizing was held, appropriately enough, on International Women's Day. The Festival of the 52 Percent, held at the Piñata fairgrounds in Managua during the weekend March 8, 1991, was a critical turning point.[2] It represented a definitive and public break between AMNLAE and other currents within the women's movement. While the break did not mean the end of AMNLAE, it did signal a mass exodus of AMNLAE dissidents to the new independent feminist movement. Among those dissidents were members of a new lesbian-feminist rights movement that made its first public appearance at the Festival of the 52 Percent. While a few gay and lesbian rights organizations existed as early as the mid-1980s, they occupied a precarious space during the revolution, ordered by FSLN leaders to lie low and refrain from making waves.

Many lesbians were loyal revolutionaries who accepted those limits. For example, Mary Bolt, who helped found the sexual rights organization Fundación Xochiquetzál in 1991, had a long history as a Sandinista, having become an urban guerrilla in 1974. I asked if she was an open lesbian when she joined the FSLN:

> They never asked me, what sort of thing are you? Never [laughing]. You simply joined and, period, it isn't as though they asked me what I thought, what I believed. I simply joined. . . . So before the triumph [of the revolution] I didn't have problems. . . . And after the triumph, I still wasn't very interested in lesbian organizations. For me the fundamental objective was the defense of the revolution. (interview, July 1994, Jamaica Plain, MA)

But after the Sandinistas lost the 1990 election, she reconsidered her political goals. "After, with the new election, an emptiness opened up and I think this happened to a lot of Nicaraguan men and women. It was a political emptiness. . . . for us it was very strong; it was a cause for grieving. . . . So for me this emptiness was filled by the feminist movement" (interview, July 1994, Jamaica Plain, MA).

A single thread tied together Mary Bolt's life as guerrilla, party activist, and autonomous feminist. She never rejected the earlier activism; instead, she moved on from one form to another when circumstances changed: from guerrilla to party activist after Somoza was overthrown, and from party activist to autonomous feminist after the Sandinistas lost the 1990 election. Many gays and lesbians did the same in the early 1990s. Freed from the constraints of the FSLN, which tried to limit their activism, and faced with a hostile new government, many gays and lesbians organized themselves. The year 1990 saw the founding of the gay rights organization SHOMOS, the anti-AIDS organization Fundación Nimehuatzín, and the lesbian feminist collective Nosotras (We Women).[3] In 1991 the sexual minority rights organization Fundación Xochiquetzál opened its doors. It was soon followed by the lesbian organizations Entre Amigas (Among Friends) and Grupo por la Visibilidad Lésbica (Group for Lesbian Visibility). And, in 1992, more than twenty-five groups united in the Campaña por una Sexualidad Libre de Prejuicios (Campaign for Sexuality Free of Prejudice) (on the gay and lesbian rights movement, see Arauz 1994; Babb 2003; Thayer 1997).

If the March 1991 Festival of the 52 Percent was a declaration of independence for the autonomous feminist movement and the lesbian rights movement, that independence was ratified less than a year later. In January 1992 more than eight hundred women attended the first national feminist conference, which was titled Diversas pero Unidas (Diverse but United). By early 1992 the autonomous feminist movement was large, diverse, capable, and increasingly daring.

The major disagreement that divided the newly autonomous activists was autonomy itself. Some activists—the majority—were so afraid of being controlled once again by an organization like the FSLN or AMNLAE that they rejected proposals to form any sort of coordinating organization. Yet efficiency required them to be able to unite their individual groups in some way, and so they agreed to form a series of networks. Eight were formed at the conference, to work on issues such as sexuality, economics, and environmentalism. By the early twenty-first century, two of the networks formed in early 1992—the Red de Mujeres contra la Violencia (Women's Network against Violence) and the Red de Mujeres por la Salud María Cavallieri (María Cavallieri Women's Health Network)—still were active and large. There were 120–150 member organizations in the network against violence and 96 alternative clinics, collectives, and Casas in the network for women's health (Kampwirth 2004, 64).

Those who preferred the network model were the majority at the 1992 conference. But there was a large minority that feared that failing to create something more centralized than the networks was risky. Without a coordinating body and without an explicit commitment to feminist goals, the new autonomous movement might stagnate. So they formed the Comité Nacional Feminista (National Feminist Committee) in May 1992. To join the committee, groups had to agree to support a set of feminist demands: that they were against violence, domestic and otherwise; that they were in favor of gay rights; and that they were prochoice. Although the committee disbanded in 1994, it recreated itself with twenty-five organizations and five individual members in November 1998. By the mid-1990s, the autonomous feminist movement in Nicaragua was influential, not just in Nicaragua but in the whole region (see Kampwirth 2004, 96–108; Blandón 1997). So when the five-country Corriente Feminista Centroamericana (Central American Feminist Current) was created in 1995, it was no surprise that its office and staff were based in Managua, Nicaragua.

But the internationalization of Nicaraguan feminism was not the only innovation of the 1990s. Another major change in women's organizing was the beginning of coalition building across partisan and class lines, forging alliances that would have been unimaginable in earlier decades. Two of the most visible examples of the new cross-partisan, cross-class alliances for gender justice were the Comisarías de la Mujer y la Niñez (Women's and Children's Police Stations) and the Coalición Nacional de Mujeres (National Women's Coalition).

In 1993 a number of groups whose relations were often hostile came together behind a project that helped to make legal protections against domestic violence a reality. The plan was to create a series of Comisarías that would be staffed by women and would offer a holistic range of services including legal, psychological, and medical support, very much like the Casas that had been originated by AMNLAE in the 1980s and like similar women's police stations in Brazil. Nineteen organizations sponsored the pilot project. That these nongovernmental organizations and government agencies united behind the Comisarías was surprising, given their often opposing roles in the revolution, contra war, and gender battles of the 1980s and early 1990s (see Kampwirth 2004, 68–69).

Yet despite the apparent instability of the coalition, the Comisarías continued to grow: four years after the beginning of the pilot project, there were twelve centers in operation nationwide, three of them in the capital. By 2000 thousands of women had been served at one of the fourteen centers nationwide (Kampwirth 2004, 66–69). Nicaragua stood out among Central American nations with regard to women and law enforcement: "Nicaragua currently boasts a higher percentage of women police officers, more women officers in the highest ranks, the most institutionalized system of women's police stations, and the most extensive police training on gendered crimes in Central America" (Fitzsimmons 2000, 225).

Another cross-class and cross-partisan women's coalition was formed in 1995. The Coalición Nacional de Mujeres sought to extract promises from all the parties in the months leading up to the 1996 national election, which was the first election for any national office since 1990. The coalition included women who belonged to the two biggest parties—Arnoldo Alemán's Alianza Liberal (Liberal Alliance) and Daniel Ortega's Sandinista Front—along with women from many of the smaller parties, including the Movimiento de Renovación Sandinista (MRS; Sandinista Renewal Movement), the Partido Conservador (Conservative Party), the Partido Resistencia Nicaragüense (the contras; Nicaraguan Resistance Party), and Proyecto Nacional (PRONAL; National Project), an alliance of centrist parties. All three currents within the women's movement—AMNLAE, the Secretarías, and the autonomous feminist organizations—were also well represented.

Three parties and coalitions—the FSLN, the MRS, and PRONAL—eventually signed the Minimum Agenda of the Coalición Nacional de Mujeres, committing themselves to a series of gender reforms. Of course, the most controversial demands—abortion, contraception, gay rights—did not appear on the agenda. But even so, had the demands on the agenda been met, politics would have been transformed in some important ways at the level of the nation and the family. As it happened, the big winner of the 1996 election, Arnoldo Alemán of the Alianza Liberal, refused to sign the agenda or to even meet with members of the coalition, even though it included many women from his own party (Blandón 2001).

The Antifeminist Response from the State

Why did Alemán refuse to even consider signing the Minimum Agenda? Although he never really explained, his response to the Coalición Nacional de Mujeres was consistent with the general patterns of his political career. Both as a young man in the Juventud Somocista (Somoza Youth) and as the mayor of Managua from 1990 to 1996, his political style was one of right-wing populism: appealing to excluded groups, especially the very poor, and seeking to mobilize those groups from above.[4] Arguably, Alemán refused to sign the Minimum Agenda of the Coalición Nacional de Mujeres because the Coalición could not be squeezed into his political framework. It was nonpartisan while he was fiercely partisan; it was an autonomous organization while his organizations were all controlled from above; it demanded rights with no strings attached while he preferred to dole out privileges in exchange for loyalty. Finally, the coalition's demands for gender equality might have been problematic; Alemán was very closely allied with the most conservative sectors of the Catholic Church.

During the first year of the new administration, that church-state alliance was strengthened. In one of his first acts as president, Alemán named a new cabinet, replacing all the ministers from the Chamorro administration with the exception of the minister of education, Humberto Belli. Belli, a member of the right-wing Catholic organization Opus Dei—and one of the most nationally and internationally prominent opponents of the feminist movement—had been at the forefront of efforts to combat various revolutionary legacies. Although the Constitution of 1987, ratified under the Sandinistas' watch, had guaranteed free public education, Belli led the drive to privatize public education. While the women's movement promoted sex education, AIDs awareness, and egalitarian gender roles, Belli promoted legal matrimony, abstinence, and traditional gender roles.

Of course, the retention of Belli did not signal a break with Violeta Chamorro's administration, quite the opposite. Yet despite her efforts to turn back the clock on gender politics, doña Violeta also was committed to reconciliation. Thus the Instituto Nicaragüense de la Mujer (INIM; National Women's Institute), an agency that was formed under the Sandinistas, continued to exist. In fact by the end of the Chamorro administration, the INIM was one of the central actors in the coalition that created the Comisarías. However, under Alemán, there was far less ambivalence toward the feminist movement and feminist NGOs.

During his 1996 campaign for president, Arnoldo Alemán accused the NGO sector of being a primary cause of Nicaragua's underdevelopment and poverty. But a public campaign against prominent NGO leaders did not begin until after the worst natural disaster to hit Nicaragua during the Alemán administration: massive flooding as a result of Hurricane Mitch in late 1998 and early 1999.

Following Hurricane Mitch, President Alemán greatly accelerated his attacks on the NGOs. Accelerating the campaign against the NGOs was logical in the context of the administration's goals: capitalizing on opportunities, while minimizing the political risks associated with Hurricane Mitch. There was even more of a need, from Aleman's perspective, to increase his attacks against the NGO sector once it transformed in response to Mitch, forming a Coordinadora Civil (Civil Coordinating Committee) in November 1998, composed of more than three hundred organizations. Once the NGO sector had united, it had the ability to carry out studies of the unmet needs of people in regions hit by Hurricane Mitch, studies that clearly were irritating to Arnoldo Alemán.

In addition to the irritation of the Coordinadora studies, Alemán could not have been pleased to realize that many foreign funders seemed to deem the groups that belonged to the Coordinadora more trustworthy than his administration. Alemán might have relied on the tried-and-true populist strategy of blaming powerful foreigners, especially the members of the European Union, for his problems in responding to the devastation of Hurricane Mitch. In fact, he was critical of some powerful foreigners, but the main focus of his attacks was on local foreigners, that is, prominent members of the NGO sector, and especially on women (on the individual women he targeted, see Kampwirth 2003, 141–146).

In fact, Arnoldo Alemán's campaign against prominent NGO activists mainly targeted women who were identified in one way or another with the feminist movement. In addition to attacking feminist NGO leaders, "the more than 200 private medical clinics that offer services to low income women" were harassed and investigated "under the pretext that abortions were carried out there," according to Ana Quirós (quoted in Cuadra 2000, 5). Although the administration never found evidence that any of those centers performed abortions, many Nicaraguan feminists did support the right to safe, legal abortion. Ultimately, the campaign against women's health providers was not primarily a campaign against their actions (since claims that they performed abortions were unfounded) but rather a campaign against their ideas (that is, their belief in reproductive rights).

In the campaign against the NGOs, Arnoldo Alemán united the church and state on one side, while he and his allies conflated foreigners and feminists on the other side. Marching in a September 2000 demonstration with Cardinal Obando y Bravo of Managua, Alemán asserted his support for a proposal to abolish article 165 of the Constitution, a nineteenth-century provision of the civil code that permitted abortion to save a woman's life. Supporters of banning abortion under all circumstances asserted that the church and Alemán administration, not those NGO activists who defended women's right to life, were the real Nicaraguans. According to "Dr. Rafael Cabrera of the Catholic University [Universidad Americana], the

NGOs 'are foreigners who do not represent Nicaraguans, feminist movements that promote lesbianism and organizations that promote sexual licentiousness and homosexuality'" (Infopress Central America 2000, 2).

Journalist Sofia Montenegro has suggested that, of all the sectors of civil society, the feminist movement is the most threatening to the interests of the Catholic Church. According to Montenegro, "the Church has demanded the head of the feminist movement" as part of its pursuit of the "reevangelization of the continent [which is necessitated] by secularization and, on the other hand, [by] competition with the Protestants." She suggested that the very close ties between the Alemán administration and the hierarchy of the Catholic Church could be seen as an unofficial pact, with the ultimate goal of forming a hegemonic alliance between the Partido Liberal Constitucionalista (PLC; Liberal Constitutionalist Party), the FSLN, and the church. Given that the 1999 pact between the PLC and the FSLN undercut all other parties' ability to compete and given the weakness of private enterprise and unions in neoliberal Nicaragua, the main impediments to the PLC/FSLN/church alliance were the feminist movement and the press. Arnoldo Alemán largely succeeded in co-opting and controlling the FSLN through the 1999 pact, but the feminists were not so easily persuaded (interview, August 7, 2001, Managua, Nicaragua).

Antifeminist Organizations

The antifeminist organizations do not constitute a movement in the same sense as the feminist movement. While hundreds of organizations identify with the feminist movement, there are a relatively small number of antifeminist groups. The most extensive list of organizations I have seen in writing was composed of nine organizations that identified themselves as prolife and profamily. They signed an open letter to George W. Bush, calling on him to put a stop to many of the United States Agency for International Development (USAID)'s programs, which, they said, "gravely attack our cultural identity and mock our moral and spiritual principles, at the same time as they promote, especially in children and adolescents, the addiction to sex, homosexuality, prostitution, promiscuity, [and] the deceptive and irresponsible use of immoral methods, like the condom and contraception" (Vida Humana Internacional 2002).

I do not claim that the signers of the letter comprise a complete list of antifeminist groups in Nicaragua, just as my previous discussion of feminist groups is incomplete. But I think it is accurate to claim that there are hundreds of feminist groups and a much smaller number of antifeminist groups, because I used the same research methods when I interviewed antifeminists as when I had interviewed feminists.

Of these organizations only one of them, the Asociación Nicaragüense de la Mujer (ANIMU; Nicaraguan Women's Association), founded in 1996, is composed exclusively of women and, unlike most Nicaraguan women's organizations, never makes even momentary alliances with other women's groups. When I asked ANIMU Vice President Evangelina de Guirola if ANIMU ever collaborated with other women's groups, she quickly answered no, suggesting with her tone that the very question was objectionable. According to the then president Elida de Solórzano, ANIMU "seeks ways to benefit women . . . so that they have access to an education, to protect them in all that pertains to women . . . not just our organs but our psychology, which is based on motherhood" (interview, December 18, 2002, Managua, Nicaragua; quote from phone interview, December 19, 2002). In the course of talking about her work, ANIMU vice president Evangelina de Guirola brought up the topic of feminism without my asking her about it (in fact, all the antifeminists I interviewed brought up the topic of feminism on their own). She told me that feminists sought unnatural solutions to imaginary social problems: "I have heard some who say that they want equality but they want the sort of equality that goes against nature, like Marxism. . . . The first thing the radical feminists do is to make you feel like a victim. It is Paolo Freire's system. . . . Never in my life have I felt discriminated against for being a woman (interview, December 13, 2002, Managua, Nicaragua).

But even though it is easy to identify hundreds of feminist groups and only a few antifeminist groups, it does not follow that feminists are hundreds of times more powerful. Counting the number of organizations is not the only way to measure the strength of a movement. When measured by another criterion—the extent to which activists have access to powerful institutions—Nicaraguan antifeminism is quite significant. In the years following the 1990 electoral defeat of the Sandinistas, until Sandinista Daniel Ortega was reelected president in 2006, opponents of feminism enjoyed direct access to the state. In fact, many prominent antifeminists directed or held powerful positions within state agencies under presidents Chamorro, Alemán, and Bolaños, especially those agencies that were directly involved with the issues that most concern opponents of the feminist movement: sexuality, inculcation of values, and access to contraception and abortion.

In fact, one could argue that opponents of feminism in the 1990s did not need to organize as feminists have because they enjoyed often direct access to two very powerful institutions: the state and the Catholic Church. In fact, this access was so good that individual activists tended to move back and forth between the state and civil society. A good example is Elida de Solórzano: A participant in the charismatic Catholic movement since 1974 and a member of the charismatic organization Ciudad de Dios (City of God) since its founding in 1978, she lived in Nicaragua throughout the revolution, even though she and her family were harassed for being charismatic Catholics rather than liberation theology Catholics.

After the Sandinistas were voted out of office, Solórzano worked closely with Humberto Belli as his adviser (1990–1996) when he served as vice-minister and then as minister of education. She sought to directly confront the legacy of the revolution: "Education [under the Sandinistas] was devoid of a lot of traditional family values that Nicaragua had known under the Somozas. . . . Christian values were lost" (interview, January 31, 1991, Managua, Nicaragua). Solórzano participated in the governmental delegations to the United Nations International Conference on Population and Development (both the preparatory conference in Mexico City in

1994 and the later conference in Cairo), and she served as head of the Nicaraguan delegation to the Beijing +5 conference. From 1999 to 2002 she worked within the Ministry of the Family as an adviser to ministers Humberto Belli and Max Padilla. Finally, at the time of the 2002 interview, she was president of the women's organization ANIMU.

During the years 1990–2006, when the right largely controlled the state, one major goal of the antifeminists was to abolish article 165 of the penal code, the article that gave doctors the right to perform therapeutic abortion. Dr. Rafael Cabrera, president of Asociación Nicaragüense Pro Vida (ANPROVIDA; Nicaraguan Prolife Association) told me that the abolition of article 165 in 2006 was a good thing, because it was a nineteenth-century anachronism. In that time, before the invention of antibiotics, before tuberculosis had been brought under control, before cardiac problems could be treated, Nicaragua was characterized by what he called "a hostile environment" (interview, November 28, 2006, Managua, Nicaragua). In the nineteenth century, pregnancy could threaten a woman's life, and so therapeutic abortion was permitted to allow doctors to try to save patients faced with life-threatening pregnancies. But over the course of the twentieth century, that medical environment became less hostile, until the point when, according to Cabrera, all pregnancies could be safely carried to term.

I told Cabrera of a case of a Nicaraguan woman I knew personally who died at the age of twenty-seven after her first pregnancy caused irreparable heart damage. He dismissed that example, telling me that since she died months after the baby was delivered by cesarean, her death could not be attributed to the pregnancy. Cabrera's position—that therapeutic abortion was never medically necessary and article 165 was just a loophole to permit abortion for social reasons—was the most common position among the antitherapeutic abortion activists that I interviewed, although it was not the only position.

Abortion and the Return of Daniel Ortega

The most public battle between feminist and antifeminist forces in Nicaragua, prior to the overturning of therapeutic abortion in 2006, revolved around a nine-year-old rape victim, who was known as Rosa. Feminists ultimately won that struggle, in a couple of ways: first, because after months of public conflict, Rosa had a therapeutic abortion in the dead of the night and, second, because most Nicaraguans (64 percent according to one poll) thought that a nine-year-old should not be forced to carry a pregnancy to term (Villegas 2003; also Kampwirth 2006, 73–74). But the next time the issue of therapeutic abortion became a matter of public debate, feminists lost. And in 2006 the battle was not about the life of one little girl but about the lives of the hundreds of girls and women who faced life-threatening pregnancies every year.

Arguably, the abolition of therapeutic abortion is the logical outcome of three separate occurrences in Nicaraguan politics in the years since the end of the revolution in 1990, two of which I have analyzed in this chapter. First, the autonomous feminist movement—which as I have shown emerged both because of the revolution and despite the efforts of revolutionary leaders to control the movement—was divided over tactics in 2006, and those disagreements undermined their effectiveness to some extent (Kampwirth 2008). But therapeutic abortion, as much as it is a life-and-death issue, should not cloud our vision of the real accomplishments and real strength of the autonomous feminist movement. At the beginning of the twenty-first century, feminism in Nicaragua is a powerful social movement, including hundreds of organizations and thousands of activists. It is a movement that may touch the lives of millions through its networks of Casas de la Mujer, through its legal lobbying efforts, through advocacy work for people like Rosa, and through its role in the mass media.[5]

The second major factor that explains how Nicaragua came to be one of a tiny handful of countries that does not permit abortion to save the woman's life is the antifeminist movement, which emerged in the 1990s as a backlash against the legacy of the revolution and against the autonomous feminists. The considerably smaller antifeminist movement turned out to be a formidable foe in 2006, as it had never been so united and sophisticated. Over the course of the years following the Sandinista Revolution, it had taken full advantage of its strong ties to the state, especially to the state ministries that dealt most directly with personal politics: the ministries of health, education, and family. These activists had opposed therapeutic abortion for many years prior to 2006. That they succeeded in abolishing that nineteenth-century medical reform in 2006 cannot be understood outside the electoral context, which abortion opponents had not taken advantage of previously. But, just as importantly, Catholic and Evangelical abortion opponents had rarely worked together.[6] That started changing in the late 1990s.

Elizabeth de Rojas, a minister with Alianza Evangélica (Evangelical Alliance), explained that her work first came to the attention of traditional Catholic leaders in December 1998, when she helped organize a "crusade" called Festinavidad. That festival involved distributing to Nicaraguan children more than three hundred thousand gifts that had been provided by supporters of U.S.-based evangelical minister Franklin Graham and culminated in a two-day cultural event in the Dennis Martínez National Stadium, in which an estimated 160,000 children participated. Rojas told me that through Festinavidad they hoped "to introduce them to the word of God [and] to strengthen family values" (interview, December 4, 2006, Managua, Nicaragua; Tórrez 1998).

That massive event attracted press coverage and "Max Padilla, the minister of the Family at that time, saw the great gathering of children on TV" (Rojas, interview, December 4, 2006, Managua, Nicaragua). Believing that the evangelical organizers of this event shared values with traditional Catholic opponents of feminism, Padilla invited Elizabeth de Rojas to a meeting at his office in the Ministry of the Family. It was there that she met Elida de Solórzano, adviser to Padilla and founder of ANIMU), Evangelina de Guirola of ANIMU and founder of Sí a la Vida (Yes to Life), and Dr. Rafael Cabrera of ANPROVIDA. That was the beginning of the alliance between Catholic and evangelical abortion opponents that culminated in a mass march against therapeutic abortion on October 6, 2006, and the vote in the National Assembly a few days later, to abolish the life-of-the-mother exception to the civil code.

The third and final factor that explains the abolition of therapeutic abortion in 2006 is the transformation of the FSLN. In 2006 the FSLN seemed to reimagine the legacy of the revolution. That new vision of what it meant to be a revolutionary was traditional Catholic rather than liberation theology Catholic, antifeminist rather than feminist. One could question in what sense this legacy of the revolution was revolutionary. On the billboards that sprung up everywhere in Nicaraguan cities in the months leading to the November election, there was little of the FSLN's traditional red and black, replaced instead with an array of brilliant colors, especially hot pink. Daniel Ortega, the Marxist-Leninist in military uniform, was replaced with Daniel the practicing Catholic in white shirt and jeans. The rhetoric of anti-imperialism and class struggle was replaced with the rhetoric of peace and reconciliation. In fact, many historical enemies of the FSLN were incorporated into the Sandinistas' electoral coalition, most prominently, vice presidential candidate— and former contra commander—Jaime Morales Carazo.

But despite the unlikely breadth of the Sandinista electoral coalition, many traditional revolutionaries—most notably the feminists—were left out as Ortega chose to ally himself and his very disciplined party with the right in voting to abolish therapeutic abortion. Despite long-standing tensions between the leadership of the FSLN and autonomous feminists, I think it is highly unlikely that the FSLN would have voted to abolish the life-of-the-mother exception if not for the fact that the election was days away. In other words, the FSLN's new-found opposition to therapeutic abortion does not necessarily indicate a shift to the right. What it does show is that, after a decade and a half out of power and close to a decade of political pacts with the right—with Arnoldo Alemán's Partido Liberal Constitucionalista (Liberal Constitutionalist Party) and with Obando y Bravo's faction within the Catholic Church (Hoyt 2004; Torres-Rivas 2007, 6–7)—the FSLN was quite willing to oppose its former base in the women's movement, to say nothing of the vast majority of Nicaragua's medical establishment, if that is what it took to return to power. Rather than a shift to the right, it was a shift to cynicism. It was part and parcel of the FSLN's long-term evolution from a revolutionary party to one that was often a personal vehicle for Daniel Ortega and his family. But whether right-wing or cynical, the return of Nicaragua's revolutionary party does not look very left-wing, at least not from a feminist perspective.

NOTES

1. The activists I identify as "antifeminist" rarely use that term to describe their own work, instead calling it profamily or prolife. But I contend that the term "antifeminist" is appropriate for at least three reasons. First, feminist activists are also in favor of families (albeit egalitarian families) and their work against maternal mortality and domestic violence is also prolife work. Second, activists in this movement are not simply social conservatives any more than feminist activists are simply social liberals. In both cases, the movements are centrally concerned with the politics of intimacy and daily life. Finally, the term "antifeminist" identifies it as a backlash movement.

2. The "52 Percent" in the name of the festival refers to the fact that women are a majority of Nicaraguans.

3. SHOMOS is a play on words: *somos* means "we are"; by adding the "h"—which is silent in Spanish—the pronunciation remains the same but the meaning changes to "we are homosexuals."

4. The Juventud Somocista was an organization of young people that supported the Somoza dictatorship (1936–1979).

5. The feminist magazine *La Boletina* (available at http://boletina.puntos.org.ni/), which has been published approximately every other month since 1991 by the Fundación Puntos de Encuentro (Common Ground Foundation), has a circulation of twenty-six thousand. That is larger than the circulation of any other magazine in Nicaragua. The feminist soap opera *Sexto Sentido* (Sixth Sense)—which addresses issues such as domestic violence, rape, abortion, and homophobia—is produced by the staff of Fundación Puntos de Encuentro. It drew 70 percent of the audience in its time slot in 2001, which was its first year on the air.

6. Evangelicals are a significant and growing minority. "At the end of the 1970s, only five percent of Nicaraguans were evangelicals. Now they account for more than twenty percent— some say more than thirty percent—of the population" (Miller Llana 2006). But evangelicals, which in Nicaragua is a synonym for "Protestants," were divided. Many evangelicals, especially those belonging to the Consejo de Iglesias Pro-Alianza Denominacional (CEPAD; Council of the Ecumenical Alliance of Churches), an alliance of thirty-three denominations, favored protecting the right to therapeutic abortion (Ramona López, CEPAD, interview, November 30, 2006, Managua, Nicaragua; Sirias 2006).

REFERENCES

Arauz, Rita. 1994. Coming out as a lesbian is what brought me to social consciousness. In *Sandino's daughters revisited: Feminism in Nicaragua*, ed. Margaret Randall, 265–285. New Brunswick, NJ: Rutgers University Press.

Babb, Florence. 2003. Out in Nicaragua: Local and transnational desires after the revolution. *Cultural Anthropology* 18 (3): 304–328.

Blandón, María Teresa. 1997. *Movimiento de mujeres en Centroamérica*. Managua: Programa Regional la Corriente.

———, ed. 2001. The Coalición Nacional de Mujeres: An alliance of left-wing women, right-wing women and radical feminists in Nicaragua. In *Radical women in Latin America: Left and right*, ed. Victoria González and Karen Kampwirth, 111–131. University Park: Penn State University Press.

Criquillón, Ana. 1995. The Nicaraguan women's movement: Feminist reflections from within. In *The new politics of survival: Grassroots movements in Central America*, ed. Minor Sinclair, 209–237. New York: Monthly Review.

Cuadra, Scarlet. 2000. Tintes políticos en la polémica sobre el aborto en Nicaragua: Unidos, la iglesia y el presidente Alemán. *Proceso*, no. 1246:1–6.

Fitzsimmons, Tracey. 2000. A monstrous regiment of women? State, regime, and women's political organizing in Latin America. *Latin American Research Review* 35 (3): 216–229.

González-Rivera, Victoria. 2001. Somocista women, right-wing politics and feminism in Nicaragua, 1936–1979. In *Radical women in Latin America: Left and right*, ed. Victoria González and Karen Kampwirth 41–78. University Park: Penn State University Press.

Hoyt, Katherine. 2004. Parties and pacts in contemporary Nicaragua. In *Undoing democracy: The politics of electoral caudillismo*, ed. David Close and Kalowatie Deonandan, 17–42. Lanham, MD: Lexington Books.

Infopress Central America. 2000. NGOs under attack. *Central American Report (CAR)*, March 10. www.infopressca.com/CAR/magizi/2710-2.htm (accessed March 10, 2000).

Kampwirth, Karen. 1998. Legislating personal politics in Sandinista Nicaragua, 1979–1992. *Women's Studies International Forum* 21 (1): 53–64.

———. 2003. Arnoldo Alemán takes on the NGOs: Antifeminism and the new populism in Nicaragua. *Latin American Politics and Society* 45 (2): 133–158.

———. 2004. *Feminism and the legacy of revolution: Nicaragua, El Salvador, Chiapas.* Athens: Ohio University Press.

———. 2006. Resisting the feminist threat: Antifeminist politics in post-Sandinista Nicaragua. *NWSA Journal* 18 (2): 73–100.

———. 2008. Neither left nor right: Sandinismo in the anti-feminist era. *NACLA Report on the Americas*, January–February.

Miller Llana, Sara. 2006. Evangelicals flex growing clout in Nicaragua's election. *Christian Science Monitor*, November 2. www.csmonitor.com (accessed November 4, 2006).

Murguialday, Clara. 1990. *Nicaragua, revolución y feminismo (1977–1989).* Madrid: Revolución.

Sirias, Tania. 2006. Presidente de Universidad Evangélica y el aborto terapéutico: Fuera electorerismo y escuchar a mujeres. *El Nuevo Diario*, October 13. www.elnuevodiario.com.ni (accessed October 13, 2006).

Stephens, Beth. 1988. Changes in the laws governing the parent-child relationship in postrevolutionary Nicaragua. *Hastings International and Comparative Law Review* 12:137–171.

———. 1990. A developing legal system grapples with an ancient problem: Rape in Nicaragua. *Women's Rights Law Reporter: A Rutgers Law School Publication*, no. 12:69–88.

Thayer, Millie. 1997. Identity, revolution, and democracy: Lesbian movements in Central America. *Social Problems* 44 (3): 386–407.

Torres-Rivas, Edelberto. 2007. Nicaragua: El retorno del sandinismo transfigurado. *Nueva Sociedad*, no. 207:4–10.

Tórrez, Joaquín. 1998. Un puente infantil de amistad EU-Nicaragua. *El Nuevo Diario*, December 9. www.elnuevodiario.com.ni (accessed December 20, 2006).

Vida Humana Internacional. 2002. Grupos provida de Centroamérica felicitan a Bush. *Boletín Electrónico de Vida Humana Internacional (VHI)* 5, no. 15. www.vidahumana.org/news/26MARZ002.html (accessed March 26, 2002).

Villegas S., Jairo. 2003. Reaparece Rosa. *La Prensa*, March 16. www.laprensa.com.ni (accessed March 16, 2003).

7 Haiti

WOMEN IN CONQUEST OF FULL AND TOTAL CITIZENSHIP IN AN ENDLESS TRANSITION

MYRIAM MERLET

For some years now, almost all analytic texts on Haiti take as a point of departure the difficult junction of transition that the country has been experiencing. In fact, since the fall of the Duvalier dictatorship in February 1986, Haiti has been seeking and continues to seek paths leading to democracy. In late May 2005, nineteen years later, Haiti is still bogged down and in an endless crisis. So any attempt to present and to analyze is perforce marked by the parameters of this transition, punctuated by a series of crises. The most recent, precipitated among other things by the contested elections of 2000, is not without economic and social consequences. For several years the Haitian economy has posted disturbing macroeconomic indicators and negative growth in real terms. The longevity of such a crisis increases the difficulties of Haitians living together in a national community where they historically have not enjoyed full citizenship. Poverty, inequality, the permanence of anti-democratic structures, totalitarian temptations, and state violence are among the many motifs that push feminist thought to question the exercise of citizenship in this country, which, for the moment, receives a great deal of media coverage but remains nevertheless poorly understood. A presentation of Haiti, however brief, is indispensable as an introduction. To understand the geopolitical stakes and the terms of the current issue, it is important to also understand the context of the situation.

Haiti is a former French colony, which gained independence in 1804 after a long slave revolt and a bloody war of independence. Many believe that it is from this bellicose past that the practices of violence stem, practices that taint social relations both between individuals and between individuals and state institutions. I strongly doubt this. Aside from the fact that similar situations do not necessarily produce this effect, I believe that violence is a cultural phenomenon that results from certain conditions prevalent in a given society, and that is what accounts for its hegemony. In the case of Haiti violence is more likely observed in interpersonal relationships and in relationships that power structures hold with men and women citizens.

Since its independence Haiti has had a very stormy political history. From 1957 to 1986, the country lived under the hold of the dictatorship of the Duvaliers.

This most bloody dictatorship brought about the massive exodus of thousands of Haitian men and women to Africa and to the large metropolitan areas of North America and Europe.

The Postdictatorial Resurgence

The year 1986 was the year of all hopes. After about thirty years of dictatorship, the confluent effect of popular pressures and international negotiations forced Duvalier the younger to step down from power. This departure opened a whole era of struggle for the reconquest of fundamental rights. The Haitian women's movement would itself see a renewal. The ability to mobilize, demonstrated by women during this period, was a signal element on the Haitian sociopolitical landscape. On the occasion of the historical April 3, 1986, demonstration—where thousands of women took to the streets of the capital and of the provincial towns—women reaffirmed under various forms their refusal to be excluded and their wish not to accept that the construction of democracy come about without them, or worse, at their expense. Since then, the women's movement has not stopped moving, with an expansion of groups and associations of various tendencies.

A new constitution was worked out in 1987, which sheds light on the trends of the time. It finally seemed that Haitian men and women were going to afford themselves the means to live together in, what the preamble describes as, a "socially just Haitian nation," where discrimination is prohibited and the respect for fundamental liberties is postulated as guaranteed from the "right to progress, to education, to health, to work," and so on. Gender relations are also taken into consideration, inequalities between the sexes are banned, and the principle of the equality of the different forms of union is proclaimed.

The ability of women's groups to organize so promptly comes, as in the case of other social movements, from being rooted in certain ideals. The people as a whole, since the construction of the Haitian state in 1804, have aspired to better their conditions. These aspirations explain an entire set of social movements that from 1987 to 1990 (date of the first democratic elections in the country, allowing Jean-Bertrand Aristide to be elected president), attempted to choke off the various successive crises by refusing certain forms of arbitrariness.

The holding of democratic elections nonetheless does not betoken a break with these successive crises. The post-1990 period was specifically marked by a bloody military coup d'état (1991–1994), during which women in particular were in the crosshairs, for the insurgents often used collective rape as a fearsome political weapon.

A Transition without End

Under the banner of the military contingents of so-called multinational forces (but in fact principally made up of U.S. GIs), the constitutional government of Aristide came back to power. Although establishing a Truth and Justice Commission, this era, known as the return to constitutional order, did not at any rate bring the awaited redress. Notably, no reparation came about concerning specific violations of which women were victims, despite the fact that women's organizations had spared no effort to assemble dossiers and to submit them to the authorities. On the other hand, the Haitian army was dissolved. Moreover, women disappeared from spheres of power. The lone cabinet position occupied by a woman was that in the new Department of the Condition and Rights of Women. During this period of international military occupation, women's organizations denounced the sexual abuse of women, and especially of girls, by military personnel. The government pursued none of the complaints filed. This government would nevertheless adhere to the Beijing Platform of Action.

The two administrations that followed this return to constitutional order once again did not keep their promises. In 1995 René Préval won against Aristide in a close race, consolidating the power of the Lavalas party. The second Aristide administration—whose election was contested by all political groups for its lack of popular participation—accentuated the crisis that was brought on by the closing of Parliament in 1999. The contesting of the elections of 2000 that brought Aristide to the presidency plunged the country into another crisis. Political repression became widespread and a climate of state terrorism was established, especially after *chimères* (criminal gangs close to the Lavalas regime) led attacks on several campuses of the state university in December 2003. Women's organizations, in this context of war waged by the Lavalas government on the civilian population, drew up an index of the rapes, often collective, of women by Aristide's paramilitary. The use of sexual violence as a weapon of terrorism became consolidated and generalized. The government was declared outlawed by the Coordination Nationale de Plaidoyer pour les Droits des Femmes (National Coordinating Committee of Advocacy for Women's Rights)—a position that would produce unanimity and accompany the mobilization against the Aristide government. During this period, the women's movement succeeded in getting Parliament to vote and ratify the Inter-American Convention on the Prevention, Punishment, and Eradication of Violence against Women, or the Convention of Belém do Pará, and proclaimed April 3 the National Day of the Movement of Haitian Women.

Beginning in March 2004, Haiti entered once again into another phase of its recent, tumultuous history. The apprentice dictator Aristide was constrained under the pressure of various forces to resign and went into exile. Another United Nations mission, composed of men and women civilians and military personnel, was enacted. Thus began a new so-called transition phase, with the installation of a government charged with establishing a climate conducive to running elections at every level of the state apparatus. The elections were to be held before the end of the year 2005.

Following a scenario well-known to the Haitian populations since the fall of the dictatorships of both Duvaliers (father and son), Haiti continues on its seemingly endless cycle, consisting of alternating periods of political crisis followed by periods of so-called transition.

The War against Citizenship

Since the question of democracy became the center of the aspirations of the Haitian people, they have been implicated in a struggle without respite for access to full citizenship. From the very start of the nineteenth century, the Haitian state and the Haitian nation have been built and rebuilt, but not without considerable difficulty. After each gain made by the citizens, there followed long periods of repression, when the body of social, political, and economic rights was again called into question. There has long been a permanent war against citizenship. Even though it has not taken the usual form where factions square off, arms in hand, this war against the Haitian people has been very real. More often than not, it has donned the clothing of state terrorism, as illustrated by the last moments of the Lavalas regime.

In the grips of galloping inflation and a drastic devaluation of the local currency, Haitians watched their living conditions deteriorate more each day, thereby threatening all social and economic rights. One characteristic of this impoverishment has been the phenomenon of the feminization of poverty, in a country where, according to the 2003 Institut Haïtien de Statistique et d'Informatique census, women head 42 percent of households. The poverty of women in an economy in regression for more than a decade is tantamount to social injustice. Women are the poorest among the poor and the existence of a dual labor market is manifested by intra- and interprofessional segregation. Women find themselves in jobs in the sectors on the periphery and/or at the bottom of the salary hierarchy (Bureau du TAG 2000b). Despite the weaknesses of the data on revenues, those available reveal significant gaps between men and women (UNICEF 2000). Women find themselves overwhelmingly at the lower echelons of the wage hierarchy.

The situation seems to go from bad to worse. Between the two Enquêtes Budget-Consommation des Ménages (Household Budget-Consumption Studies) (EBCM 1986–1987, 1999–2000), a noticeable rise in food expenditures has been observed (from 49.4 percent to 72.6 percent) (Ministère de L'Economie et des Finances 2000, 113). The worsening of household poverty has added considerably to the weight of the efforts made by people to obtain access to basic services. An analysis of the dynamics of basic social services revealed that, given the minimal contributions of the state and its partners in the public sector (NGOs and foreign assistance), "the relation between household budget items is deteriorating: preference is being given more and more to food to the detriment of other household budget items" (Rouzier 2001).

The situation is even more serious for women. They are the first victims of these shortfalls. Not only does the discrimination practiced against them put them in a difficult position, but very often they are obliged to compensate by engaging in additional nonremunerated activities (Merlet 2003a).

Citizenship defines who we are, our way of living together. This concept refers to "a sociological object, like a process of collective life characterized by two states, that of the political citizen man [and woman] and that of the social citizen man [and woman]" (Thériault 1999). Worldwide, women's first demands attacked matters of political rights, a struggle that gained the ability to vote in many countries during the first half of the twentieth century. Nonetheless, this membership among the enfranchised will not, for all that, guarantee the full freedom of women citizens and, even less, equality with their male counterparts. Indeed, citizenship possesses a gendered dimension (Del Re and Heinen 1996, 12). Considering the citizenship of women, one is forced to take into account two essential dimensions: citizenship as a mode of belonging to national space and citizenship as a set of rights and duties. A few facts suffice to illustrate the urgent need for social rights:

- Illiteracy is certainly a signal phenomenon of the Haitian landscape, yet recent data show that the gap between men and women has widened, growing from the order of three to ten points between 1982 and 2000. There are still 9 percent more girls (than boys) not attending school and the male/female ratio stands at seven to three at the collegiate level.
- The morbidity rate remains disturbing for the population on the whole, from 21 percent to 36 percent, according to socioeconomic level: the lower the level, the higher the rate. However, with respect to the specific material needs of women, the decrease of services offered by the state, both in quality and in quantity, dangerously increases their vulnerability. Thus, Haiti continues to post the highest maternal mortality rate in the Americas (523 deaths per 100,000 births). The deficiencies of the health care system have social as well as individual costs. Principally women, as the ones responsible for the health of the family unit, must compensate for the structural deficiencies with supplementary domestic work, which aggravates the situation of poverty, defined in terms of one's access to choice and possibilities of action in one's own life and environment.
- Access to certain basic services, such as electricity and water, remains the appanage of some privileged city dwellers. And, as a function of the sexual division of labor, the seeking of water is a task principally reserved to the female sex, notably to girls. This fact has grave consequences: many reported cases of violence against women count attacks perpetrated during these times.

Normatively speaking, legislation has long neglected women in Haiti: "Since the formation of the Haitian state, women have been treated like second-class citizens. . . . Even though different adopted constitutions declare that the law is the same for all, one must admit that prior to 1950 [when women's suffrage was won], women were not regarded as actual persons and, as such, did not enjoy the same rights as men" (Magloire 2004, 101).

It was at the beginning of the 1930s that the exclusion of women was brought into public view. The struggles of the Ligue Féminine d'Action Sociale (LFAS; Feminine League of Social Action) to gain political rights attacked the very foundations of the status of women in Haiti. These arduous struggles resulted in political rights as much for voting as for eligibility in 1950, and Haitian women were able to exercise their citizenship for the first time in 1957.[1] Nevertheless, full citizenship for Haitian women still remains to be introduced into legal texts. Women did not obtain the equality of rights in marriage until 1982, discrimination regarding women in terms of adultery has only very recently been lifted, and, even today, paternal authority and marital supremacy remain.

Women's access to the same civic and civil rights as men is possible only with the recognition by the law of their right to control their own reproduction. Legal recognition of reproductive rights makes women fully autonomous individuals not subject to forced pregnancy and able to decide for themselves (Tahon 1998).[2] In such a way, citizenship can be in harmony with freedom and can finally be a fact of equality. In Haiti no text of law, no policy or other document, treats the right of women to control their reproduction. The only reference to women's reproduction has to do with abortion, and this text of the penal code is far from guaranteeing women control of the act of reproduction. So, on the strictly normative level, it is possible to state that for as long as Haitian women do not have reproductive rights, full and whole citizenship will remain a pious wish (Merlet 2003b).

The question of abortion is worth a pause for consideration on more than one account. On the one hand, it holds weight in the very construction of women's citizenship, and, on the other, the problem of public health is engendered by the consequences of recourse to clandestine services. According to Haitian legislation in effect, abortion is considered a crime. Stipulated penalties are heavy (imprisonment); they pertain as much to the woman in question as to the person performing the abortion and his or her auxiliaries. Hence, abortions are all carried out in secret, as much in commercial hospitals as in the offices of qualified practitioners. It goes without saying that, given the weak socioeconomic conditions of the great majority of Haitian women, most abortions are carried out under risky conditions with grave consequences, the responsibility of which is not assumed by the hospital system.[3]

In this war waged against the citizenship of the Haitian people, the question of rights takes its full measure and, as in any patriarchal society, the state of subordination of Haitian women is marked by discrimination and violence. The laws in force in Haiti derive from the Napoleonic code and hence do not consider women as full citizens. Even though the 1987 Constitution recognizes the equality of both men and women, its provisions are not reflected in the law, and that is what counts in court.

The war against citizenship aims at women in particular. In a situation of generalized repression, such as the coup d'état and the last days of the Lavalas reign (a situation comparable to a war), sexual violence against women is used as a punitive and dissuasive weapon. This weapon is certainly aimed at women, but men also abuse the women of other men to make the latter feel worthless and powerless, since they generally consider women to be "property." A positive correlation has been observed between the use of force as a political weapon and in domestic violence. During periods of high political repression, domestic violence increased quantitatively, as well as on the level of forms and degree of cruelty recorded (Merlet 2001a).

Violence against women is an everyday phenomenon. The women of Haiti, like those of all patriarchal societies, must daily confront situations of violence in the privacy of their dwellings as well as in public places. Yet the absence of viable official statistics on violence against women greatly limits any attempt at evaluating the situation in Haiti. Moreover, the silence in which society cloisters women aggravates the situation, to the extent that still too few women dare to denounce the violence victimizing them. Haitian society is one that considers violence against women as a normal, unexceptional act, a behavior that does not shock in and of itself. Haitians react according to a certain threshold of tolerance that seems to accept this violence as a manifestation of Haitian culture.

Nevertheless, the efforts of sensitizing and consciousness raising carried on by women's groups have fostered a wider circulation of information. Thus, more and more women are breaking the silence and daring to report the violent acts they suffer. Encouraged by the effort of individual women, women's organizations are systematizing the recording and the analysis of data.

Actions of the Women's Movement

Since the fall of the Duvaliers' dictatorship, like many men and women social activists, Haitian women have understood that they must make their voices heard to avoid changes being made at their expense. During the period of the coup d'état of September 1991, the question of violence committed specifically against women by the forces of repression was one of the principal spearheads in the denunciation of the military dictatorship.

On this occasion, women's organizations were able to call attention to the specificity of violence against women. In the very midst of the coup d'état period, a coalition formed of more than one hundred women's organizations, called the Première Rencontre Nationale contre la Violence (First National Meeting against Violence), where more than three hundred women denounced and analyzed the violence of which they were victims and sought to organize networks to fight against this reality.

With this action and those that followed, women's organizations brought the struggle against violence directed at women to the forefront of the nation's political agenda. Witness, for example, the interest generated by the Tribunal International contre la Violence Faite aux Femmes Haïtiennes (International Tribunal against Violence Done to Haitian Women), held in November 1998. The principal media of the capital and of provincial towns broadcasted conclusions and excerpts from these sessions during the three days it lasted and continued to speak about the event for more than two months afterward.

Women's appeals for justice are numerous and urgent. Since 1998 a platform of women's organizations has established a Comité de Négociation (Negotiation Committee), charged to work with members of Parliament, with an eye toward changing the laws most unfavorable to women. Work was carried out within the frame of an agreement duly signed between the parties (a first in Haiti from which other groups of civil organized society would subsequently draw inspiration). Negotiations culminated in the rendering of drafts of laws on adultery, sexual aggression, domestic work, and the partial liberalization of abortion.

Box 7.1

Report of the Negotiation Committee of Women's Organizations

(Excerpt)

September 1998

The negotiations with members of Parliament—specifically with the Health, Population, Family Social Affairs, and Women's Condition Commission—arrived at the formulation of three (3) new proposed laws to submit to the Parliament:

1. Modification of certain articles of the civil code relating to divorce (Articles 215 and 216 of Law no. 7)
2. Modification of certain provisions of the penal code (articles relating to rape and other sexual aggressions, to abortion, and to adultery)
3. Modification of Article 257 of the work code, relating to men and women domestic workers (referred to as "servants" by the current Article 257)

PROPOSALS SUBMITTED TO PARLIAMENT

1. On abortion
   The proposal submitted to the parliamentary assembly permits the practice of Voluntary Termination of Pregnancy (IVG) during the first twelve weeks of pregnancy, in the event
   • of danger to the life and health of the mother and the infant to be born;
   • of rape or incest.
   The new law also provides that only authorized persons (physicians, nurses, aides) with a certification of competent authority may perform the abortion in a hospital, a health center, or a clinic.
2. On rape and other sexual aggressions
   The new proposed legislation constitutes an innovation to the chapter dealing with murders and other assaults on persons. More precisely,
   • The notions of sexual aggressions, rapes, and sexual harassments are defined.
   • Rape is no longer defined from the point of view of the male aggressor. As a result, rape is no longer limited to a matter of penetration.
   • Penalties are established for different types of sexual aggressions.
   • The position of authority of the aggressor (male or female) is equally taken into account.
   • The notion of community service is introduced as a new penalty in cases of sexual harassment.
3. On domestic work
   The new legislation proposes a somewhat broader social coverage:
   • Days off every week.
   • Annual paid vacations.

- An annual bonus. This last point respects the constitutional stipulations on the matter.
4. On adultery

The proceedings of the commission's goals are strictly limited to seeking to lift "discrimination against women." According to this principle, the commission refrains from removing penalties for adultery. It limits itself to subjecting the male spouse to the same sanctions as those currently reserved for the female spouse and allows that divorce may be requested by either party.

Two (2) significant changes must be noted:

- Proof of adultery is uniform, regardless of the sex of the person concerned.
- Homicide of the adulterous spouse is not excusable, except in the case of self-defense.

THE POSITION OF THE COMMITTEE

1. On abortion

Considering that women should remain the sole mistresses of their bodies, the committee salutes the lifting, even partially, of the penalty for abortion. The committee remains convinced that this new legislation heads in the direction of protecting the health of women. Nonetheless, the requirements for the practice of IVG (authorized places and persons) are not in keeping with the situation of the country. There still exists today a high number of zones and regions of the country that do not have authorized personnel and / or sites. In light of this fact, a high number of women will be unable to benefit from these new provisions. It would be fitting, therefore, to provide for transitional arrangements to permit greater application of the new rule (inclusion of midwives, after training, and extension of sites at all levels of the health system).

2. On rape and other sexual aggressions

The new proposal of law constitutes a praiseworthy attempt to face the different cases head-on and to lift the ambiguity of crime against honor, placing sexual aggressions in the chapter of crimes against a person. This proposal offers the merit of forearming women against forms of aggression of which they are first and almost exclusively the victims. It also offers the benefit of covering individuals of both sexes, outside of any consideration of age or situation.

3. On household work

Working conditions to which domestic personnel are generally subjected disparage them to the rank of nonperson. This category of personnel is not paid or considered as full-time workers, and as such does not benefit from

(continued)

Box 7.1 (*continued*)

the set of rights legally afforded the other categories. In taking up the cause to raise this thorny social question, the committee seeks to highlight the importance and the social value of household work. Such work is ordinarily done for free by women for the benefit of the whole society. The fundamental problems that household work raises, and more particularly the situation of domestic personnel in Haiti, cannot be posed in the framework of these negotiations. The latter essentially deals with a limited expansion of social coverage. Despite the evident limits of the proposed law, the concern that has been injected into the work of the legislature constitutes a first step toward the state taking into consideration the situation of one of the categories of the most disadvantaged men and women workers.

4. On adultery

The simple fact of providing, in the case of adultery, the same penalties for both sexes can in no way be satisfactory. Binding men to the same legal provision as women cannot at all be considered a step forward. Male adultery is not stigmatized by our society. On the contrary, it is given value as an expression of virility. Adultery is cast as a problem only when it is the act of women. Consequently, even if legal recourse is offered to women, it will be difficult for them to avail themselves of it. One can safely bet that the cases that the courts will have to hear will remain principally cases of adulterous women. This being so, to penalize male adultery does not change the feminine condition.

Unfortunately, the vicissitudes of Haitian political life did not permit the enactment of these laws by the Chamber of Deputies and the National Assembly because of the dissolution of Parliament at the beginning of 1999 and the monopolizing of the legislature by the Lavalas power structure.[4] Moreover, the situation of impunity that currently prevails in the judicial system exposes women even more to the risks of conjugal and sexual violence.

In various forms, such as the initiative committees, the ad hoc committees, or even brainstorming groups and action groups, women's collectives are consolidating and functioning in a somewhat systematic manner; the last example to date is that of the Coordination Nationale de Plaidoyer pour les Droits des Femmes (CONAP; National Coordinating Committee for the Advocacy of Women's Rights. The Executive Committee of CONAP—which brings together five principal feminist organizations: Information Femmes (Women News), Présence des Femmes / FanmYo La (Women's Presence), Les Femmes Décidées de Jacmel Fanm Deside de Jacmel (Determined Jacmel Women), La Maison des Femmes Kay Fanm (Women's House), and Solidarité Femmes Haïtiennes (Haitian Women Solidarity)—was able to impact the last mobilization of women citizens by inscribing women's strategic demands in the global political context. CONAP's constitutive organization, the Comité de Négociation des Organisations de Femmes (Negotiation Committee of Women's Organizations), developed a five-year Plan for the Defense of Women's Rights to pursue the process of negotiation with the Haitian parliament and the executive powers. CONAP intends to bring about modifications at the level of certain texts of law particularly unfavorable to women and to appeal to the state for the enactment of programs and regulations answering to the specific needs of women.

This sort of action is the fruit of a long process of maturation, during the course of which women's organizations learned to act strategically. The process contributed to demystifying certain spaces of struggle. Thus, contrary to the years 1986–1990 when women's organizations did not invest in official political spaces, they no longer reject direct involvement. Their strategy now involves all spaces and is based on preoccupations statutory in nature. The status of women returns—as in the first Haitian feminist organization, LFAS, during the fifties—to the center of discourse and action in women's organizations.

The Mobilization for Citizens' Rights

The last transition phase initiated in March 2004 was rich with anticipation. The people, who had just experimented with their mobilizing capacity, were hoping that this new transition would be seized on for the installation of a new order, specifically in terms of governance. They wanted to see the coordination of the diverse forces constituting this nation eventually segue to the construction of the foundation of a viable citizenship for all men and women. Alas, constraints of all kinds, notably linked to practices of bad governance, came to sap these hopes once again. The movement of Haitian women, which had acquired a certain enfranchisement at the height of women citizens' mobilizations in 2003 and 2004, is presently confronting strategies of marginalization on the part of traditional sociopolitical figures. Another swing of the pendulum seems to be in the offing.

The present situation, characterized by an aggravation of the climate of insecurity, the generalization of rape as a weapon of terrorism, widespread impunity, and a drastic deterioration in living conditions, brings back into question the very principles of citizenship. Economic and social rights are not respected and political rights are denied. The situation calls into question "the exercise of citizenship as the possibility of existing and living in a positive relationship with a community" (Trouillot 2002, 10). Wishes to curtail citizenship are given pride of place, and the people's aspirations for a better life are being postponed for the foreseeable future.

The government's evident scorn for citizens' rights remains a constant. It is vital for men and women citizens to mold society to guarantee fundamental rights. Thus, feminist action, conscious of the danger, owes it to itself to link up with a vast citizen movement for the defense of fundamental rights. Women's organizations in synergy with those of students, unions, and activists fighting for human and economic rights must mobilize for the right to education, health care, food, and life in a healthy environment. Once more, the people, in organized fashion, owe it to themselves to formulate petitions for good governance to provide better living conditions and guarantee the rights of citizens. These petitions must be channeled through demands against the high cost of living and in favor of social policies, the creation of jobs, and respect for political rights, including free speech and freedom of expression. Thus, the petitions must demand a redefinition of the legal and regulatory framework guaranteeing economic and social rights.

ACKNOWLEDGMENTS

Translated by Lawrence Gregorio, Gettysburg College.

NOTES

1. For an analysis of the participation of women, see Merlet (2002b).

2. For a consideration of women's rights to control their sexuality, see Merlet (2002a).

3. Despite the existence of family planning programs—programs that address themselves primarily to women—the so-called modern availability of contraceptives still shows meager success. Only 13.2 percent of women use modern methods of contraception (EMMUS III, 76). The great majority of them therefore do not, for diverse reasons (notably, the accessibility of contraceptives and gender relations), use means to control their reproduction. As a result, unwanted pregnancies are legion. Given the unfavorable socioeconomic situation faced by most women many decide to abort (see Bureau du TAG 2000b).

4. Women in both chambers of the Haitian Parliament number fewer than 4 percent. The fall 1998 elections, which were supposed to renew the Parliament, never took place. In January 1999 President Lavalas dissolved the parliament under false pretenses, and it did not return until 2000.

REFERENCES

Bureau du TAG. 2000a. *Effets de l'intégration des femmes dans les caisses populaires, Etude.* Port-au-Prince: Fonds Kore Fanm de l'ACDI (Agence Canadienne de Développement International).

———. 2000b. *La problématique de genre en Haïti.* Mimeograph document.

———. 2004. Abortion in Haiti and its consequences. *Chemins Critiques* 5, no. 2.

Del Re, Alisa, and Jacqueline Heinen, eds. 1996. *Quelle citoyenneté pour les femmes? La crise des Etats-providence et de la représentation politique des femmes en Europe.* Paris: L'Harmattan.

EBCM 1986–1987, 1999–2000. Institut Haïtien de Statistique et d'Informatique. Port-au-Prince.

EMMUS III. 2000. *Mortalité et Utilisation des Services.* Port-au-Prince: Ministère de la Santé Publique et de la Population (MSPP).

Magloire, Danièle. 2004. La violence faite aux femmes: Une violation constante des droits de la personne. *Chemins Critiques* 5 (2): 101–130.

Merlet, Myriam. 1998. La subcontratación internacional en Haití: Un estrangulamiento para las mujeres. In *Posibilidades de incidencia en la elaboración y ejecución de política sobre "Maquila y Equidad Genérica".* Paper presented at the Maquila y Equidad Genérica conference, Seminar of Christian Aid, UNICEF, Antigua, Guatemala, January 20–23.

———. 2001a. Between love, anger and madness: Building peace in Haiti. In *The aftermath: Women in post-conflict transformation*, ed. Sheila Meintjes, Anu Pillay, and Meredeth Turshen, 159–171. London: Zed Book.

———. 2001b. Le portrait des femmes dans l'audiovisuel Haïtien. *Le Nouvelliste.* November 9–11.

————. 2002a. Lorsque le tabou social se cache derrière la foi! Paper presented at the workshop on sexual and reproductive rights of the Ninth Latin American and Caribbean Feminist Encuentro, Punteras, Costa Rica, December 1–5. www.campanha28set.org.

————. 2002b. *La participation politique des femmes en Haïti: Quelques éléments d'analyse.* Port-au-Prince: Fanm Yo La.

————. 2002c. Pauvreté, inégalité et exclusion. In *Bilan économique et social de l'année 2001.* Port-au-Prince: UNDP.

————. 2003a. Le fardeau de la croissance négative, L'accès des femmes à l'économie à l'heure de l'intégration des Amèriques: Quelle économie? Conference, Montreal. April 23–26.

————. 2003b. Société, es-tu capable d'être juste? (envers les femmes, les enfants, les pauvres, les handicapés-es. . .). In *Les actes du colloque La Participation Citoyenne, la Démocratie Participative et la Gouvernance Décentralisée*, ed. Imprinerie Déchamps, 14–17. Port-au-Prince: ActionAid.

————. 2004. Impact de l'impunité et de la violence sur les femmes. Presentation at the International Droits Humains, Justice, Réconciliation et Paix, l'ActionAid. NCHR. November 24–26.

————. 2005. Vyolans politik pote vyolans sou fanm. *Ayiti Fanm* 15 (61): 6.

Merlet, Myriam, and Danièle Magloire. 1997. Agir sur la condition féminine pour améliorer les situations des femmes. In *Homme et femme, Dieu les créa: Du féminisme au partenariat no. 2; Conférence Haïtienne des Religieux-ses*, 33–40. Port-au-Prince.

————. 1999. *L'avortement en Haïti et ses conséquences: Analyse de la situation.* Technique d'Administration, d'Animation et de Gestion. Mimeograph document.

————. 2000. *Cahier national des revendications des femmes.* Port-au-Prince: National Haitian Coordination of the 2000 World March of Women.

Ministère de L'Economie et des Finances. 2000. *Enquête Budget-Consommation des Ménages (EBCM 1999–2000).* Preliminary results. Port-au-Prince: IHSI. www.mefhaiti.gouv.ht.

Rouzier, Philippe. 2001. *La dynamique des SSB.* Mimeograph document. Port-au-Prince: UNDP.

Tahon, Marie Blanche. 1998. *Citoyenneté et parité politique.* Paper presented to the Congrès des Sociétés Savantes, Ottawa, Canada, May.

Thériault, Joseph-Yvon. 1999. La citoyenneté: Entre normativité et factualité. *Sociologie et Sociétés* 31 (2): 193.

Trouillot, Lionel. 2002. *(Re)penser la citoyenneté.* Port-au-Prince: Haïti Solidarité Internationale.

UNICEF. 2000. *Analyse de la situation des femmes et des enfants en Haïti, 1980–1993.* Port-au-Prince: UNICEF-Haïti.

8

From Urban Elite to
Peasant Organizing

AGENDAS, ACCOMPLISHMENTS, AND
CHALLENGES OF THIRTY-PLUS YEARS OF
GUATEMALAN FEMINISM, 1975–2007

ANA LORENA CARRILLO

NORMA STOLTZ CHINCHILLA

First Phase, 1975–1985

The First United Nations World Conference on Women, held in Mexico City in 1975, served as a catalyst for and accelerated the second wave of feminism in a number of Latin American countries. In Guatemala, however, it took more than a decade before women's groups—particularly those with an explicitly feminist perspective—began to play an important and visible role in civic and political life.

The fact that feminism and a gender perspective are relatively new in Guatemala does not mean that women only recently became actors in Guatemalan history. Throughout the decade following the United Nations conference, for example, women of all ages and social classes, ethnic groups and religious perspectives, mobilized in unprecedented numbers around issues of democracy, human rights, social justice, greater economic equality, and peace. The majority did not join union, peasant, or student movements; Christian-based communities; or Communities of Population in Resistance and exile organizations as a result of an explicit gender consciousness or elaborated critique of women's subordination in general. However, the very act of violating traditional rules proscribing public sphere participation for "good women" stimulated many women activists to reflect on their identities and abilities as women. The sense of personal power that many women felt on becoming active protagonists, capable of influencing history instead of being merely recipients of it, caused profound personal transformations.

Cristina Calel, an indigenous Quiche woman and activist with the Comité de Unidad Campesina (CUC; Committee of Peasant Unity) tells how CUC organized the whole family, including the women:

> At first there were problems because, [people would say] how is it possible for a woman to talk about politics with men? Little by little they saw that women also had the ability and the men wanted their wives to do the same type of

[activist] work that we did. Many women felt happy when they saw us. The ladies brought their *petites* [woven mats] to the classes and they sat and asked us about this and that. Catholic Action helped them a lot to come out of their homes and to start getting organized. (Stoltz Chinchilla 1998, 322)

Elena Tecún, a young indigenous woman from the *altiplano* (highlands) who joined the guerrilla movement, showed her pride at being able to do what the male combatants did in the mountains:

My life in the guerrilla movement was totally different from when I was at home. At home I couldn't run, or walk long distances, but in the guerilla you get used to it as a result of the training. When we had to carry things on our backs, the women were able to carry as much as the men. We all carried our part of the load. Some of our leaders were women. . . . When people [plantation workers] saw that some of us were women, they were very happy and they approached us. The women workers especially were happy to see other women in the guerrilla forces, because this proved that women are capable, and that it wasn't true that women were good for nothing. (Stoltz Chinchilla 1998, 395–396)

The participation of hundreds of women—rural as well as urban—in revolutionary and in mixed-gender civil organizations from 1975 to 1985 lead to a transcendent break in Guatemalan women's history. Women partaking in public life, exercising their citizenship, is widely recognized as having fertilized the ground for the present period. But the fierce response from the government's counterinsurgency army and its economically and politically powerful allies was a heavy price to pay. An estimated two hundred thousand Guatemalans were killed or disappeared as a result of the conflict and approximately one hundred thousand Guatemalan peasants (84 percent of them indigenous) were forced to flee to Mexico between the early and mid-1980s.

Taking into consideration the context of governmental repression and revolutionary insurgency that characterized Guatemala during this period, it is not difficult to unravel the reasons for the delay in the development of explicitly feminist and gender-conscious organizations. The first, and probably most important, reason was the repressive atmosphere that restricted the free circulation of ideas, silenced debate, and kept cultural revolutions within certain limits. In the mid- and late 1960s, for example, when there were cultural and political revolutions in different parts of the world, the framework of political repression was already in place in Guatemala, as a result of the reaction of the elites to the Jornadas of March and April 1962.[1] These early protests proved to be a defining moment in Guatemalan history, one in which many women participated. Violeta Alfaro has observed,

For the urban youth—and *ladinas*—March and April of 1962 were like 1968 in France or Mexico.[2] The difference was that in Guatemala the young people took up arms. Among them were the first women who took up arms, going up to the Sierra de las Minas in the eastern part of the country; many of them were barely twenty years old at the time. (Stoltz Chinchilla 1998, 11)

There had been other moments in Guatemalan history—moments of national political crises in 1920 and 1944—when women played an important public sphere role and defined new forms of female political activism. But the Jornadas were important because they opened up a limited space for debate in an otherwise repressive culture. At the same time, it is important to recognize that the restricted cultural and social patterns in Guatemala from the midsixties until the mideighties were the result of not solely political repression but also the notoriously conservative dominant culture of Guatemalan elites and the hierarchy of the Catholic Church, as well as the hegemony of orthodox leftists who resisted theoretical and practical challenges to the primacy of social class (Monzón 2003, 16; Carrillo 2004, 131–136).

Despite the restrictions on public sphere debate and organizing, feminist ideas circulated in Guatemala as early as the 1960s. During this time, small groups of activists and intellectuals, mainly women, read, debated, and spoke about the ideas of Simone de Beauvoir and Betty Friedan in study groups, trying to contextualize the readings within the Guatemalan and Latin American environment. The meetings, however, appear to have been isolated experiences that were neither followed nor encouraged by the majority. According to one of the participants,

> What was happening was that there was no clarity on the issue of women [in the left], and the men made you feel guilty for taking on a problem that was only a "secondary conflict." They said that the women's situation would be resolved when the revolution was achieved, and moreover, in a society like the Guatemalan society, with so much conflict and such fundamental problems, dedicating time to this was detracting from the real conflict. There were warnings [about those ideas], not so much from our partners, but from other *compañeros* and even from women. They also told us that we were assimilating everything that came from abroad and they asked us when we were going to go to the park to burn our bras. (Mariel Aguilar, interview in Stoltz Chinchilla 1998, 7–8)

An example of these first efforts was the publication in Guatemala of the book *Mujer y Lucha Social* (Women and Social Struggle) (Aguilera 1979), a compilation of different texts on feminist theory and history, as well as statements from members of Latin American and global feminist movements. The editors conceived of it as a manual for the use of "study groups" and "feminist movements." Their visions and plans for change were never realized, having been eclipsed by other political events and the generalized repression.

Later in the seventies, some of these same women, together with academics, journalists, and activists, used the opening that preparations for the United Nations conference in Mexico provided them to obtain national and international support for the struggle of women workers and to write articles on domestic work, double shifts, women in politics, prostitution, health, education, and women's wage work for daily newspapers such as *Prensa Libre*. Violeta Carpio and Amalia Rivera, for example, wrote about the struggles of women workers in the U.S.-owned Outer

Limit jeans factory; their articles were published in Guatemalan newspapers and a U.S. journal, *Latin American Perspectives*. They spoke about their findings at the tribunal of the 1975 United Nations conference and participated actively in the conference, together with other Guatemalan activists and writers such as Raquel Blandón, Luz Méndez de la Vega, and Eunice Lima.

Another attempt at spreading the feminist perspective during this period was the column Femina Sapiens, published in the independent weekly magazine *¿Qué Pasa Calabaza?*, which began to circulate in Guatemala in 1977, two years after the United Nations conference. The column, often signed by "Amaranta," the pseudonym of the young feminist writer Viviana Fanjul, openly and frankly discussed topics such as sexuality, abortion, reproductive health, and love that even today are still often considered taboo in the Guatemalan media. The column Femina Sapiens, whose name emphasizes the importance of the written word and knowledge in service of the emancipation of women, appealed to popular common sense and spoke about such subjects in a tone that was not only frank or natural but openly defiant. In 1978 alone, despite its limited allocation of space, the column covered subjects such as maternity, the commercial use of the female body in advertising, the questioning of the canons of female beauty and its commercial use, women's health, maternity, sexuality, orgasm, domestic work, pain-free birth, and the different types of abortion, underground and legal, accompanied by graphics and photographs. Despite its courageous and pioneering character, escalating levels of violence from conflicts between the army and armed revolutionary groups in the late 1970s limited the magazine's ability to generate a wider discussion of women's issues and it ceased publication.

During the sixties and seventies, women played increasingly more visible and important roles in mixed-gender organizations, including in the revolutionary organizations that pushed for fundamental social change in rural and urban areas in a context of growing repression. In these organizations, women of all ages earned political experience and organizing skills that proved useful in pushing for a women's and gender-conscious agenda once the war ended. Some women revolutionaries recall having been exposed to feminist ideas through reading books such as *The Second Sex* by Simone de Beauvoir, articles written by Italian and Latin American feminists, and works by socialist authors like Alexandra Kollantai (1977), Clara Zetkin (1984) and Margaret Randall (1974) during this time. More often than not, however, women revolutionaries who pushed for a deeper analysis of the causes and consequences of women's subordination or who demanded a more important role in the decision making within their organizations during the 1970s and 1980s were discouraged from pursuing their concerns and labeled egocentric or divisive.

Beyond the ideological resistance that revolutionary organizations had to second-wave feminist ideas, the climate of violence itself at the end of the 1970s and beginning of the 1980s made it difficult to discuss and mount challenges to the dominant patriarchal culture. The growing challenge of armed revolutionary groups to ruling elites and the military's brutal but sophisticated counterinsurgency campaigns, particularly in the rural areas of the altiplano (where indigenous populations are concentrated), were not favorable to public debates about new paradigms or deep questioning about traditional gender relations (Monzón 2004b, 16). When the Primer Encuentro Feminista de América Latina y el Caribe (First Latin American and Caribbean Feminist Encuentro) took place in 1981 in Bogotá, many Guatemalan women were literally struggling for their lives and those of their families and communities. It was not until six years later, at the fourth Encuentro in Taxco, Mexico, that a Guatemalan delegation was able to participate in a hemispheric feminist gathering in a significant way.

Second Phase, 1985–1994

The first second-wave feminist organizations in Guatemala began to appear as the war began to draw to a close and Vinicio Cerezo, the first civilian president in more than thirty years, was elected. Many of the founders of the first postwar women's organizations, explicitly feminist or not, had been in exile, where they had developed relationships with feminists from throughout Latin America—including Sandinista Nicaragua—Europe, and North America. Furthermore, they brought with them a wealth of organizing experience and lessons gained from working in unions, political parties, and revolutionary groups. One of the first explicitly feminist women's groups, Tierra Viva, founded in 1988, insisted from the beginning on the principle of autonomy and independence and the importance of developing feminist theory in a Guatemalan context. The idea for the formation of the group emerged among the Guatemalan women attending the fourth Encuentro in Taxco in 1987, a decisive moment for the consciousness of many of Central American women who attended. In the same year, the Grupo Guatemalteco de Mujeres (GGM; Guatemalan Women's Group) was organized to raise consciousness about women's lives and needs and to serve women in need, especially those affected by domestic violence. Two years earlier, in 1986, the Grupo Femenino por Mejoramiento de la Familia (Women's Group for Family Improvement), aligned with the Unidad de Acción Sindical y Popular (Unity Group for Popular and Labor Union Action), had emerged to promote women's organizing, to develop the leadership skills of working women, and to support the needs of workers and their families.

Together, these three pioneering groups established the Coordinación de Agrupaciones de Mujeres de Guatemala (Coordinating Body of Women's Groups of Guatemala), which collaborated, in turn, in the creation of the Asamblea Permanente de Mujeres Centroamericanas por la Paz (Permanent Assembly of Central American Women for Peace), an organization that existed for four years. After the assassination of Dinorah Pérez, political activist and director of the Instituto de la Mujer María Chinchilla (María Chinchilla Women's Institute), these and other groups formed the Red de la No Violencia contra la Mujer (Network for Nonviolence against Women), which helped to direct public attention to the need for laws, public policies, and social services to help reduce violence. It also served to link Guatemalan activists to other regional and international networks that worked to develop public consciousness about and organize resistance to violence against women. The leading role that the founders of these three groups played in the creation of coordinating bodies and networks can be directly linked to their experiences in exile or in the refugee camps during the war, particularly in Mexico.

During the same period, other women participated in women's groups that focused on human rights, the resolution of armed conflict through negotiation, and the demilitarization of society in favor of respect for civil law. In some groups, indigenous and ladina women organized around specific problems stemming from the conflict. These included the Coordinadora Nacional de Viudas de Guatemala (CONAVIGUA; National Coordinating Committee of Guatemalan Widows) and the Grupo de Apoyo Mutuo (Mutual Support Group), a mixed-gender group made up of relatives of the disappeared, with significant female leadership and membership.

For some women, experiences in mixed ladino-indigenous organizations engaged in discussions about gender laid the basis later in the 1980s and early 1990s for the formation of indigenous women's organizations with a women's agenda and gender consciousness (Carrillo 1991, 118). For other indigenous women, it was their experience in indigenous refugee organizations in Mexico, such as Mamá Maquín, Madre Tierra, and Ixmucané, that informed their demands for women's empowerment and greater equality, including for the first time in the history of Guatemala, the demand that peasant women's right to land ownership be recognized (Hernández 2005, 76). This process was accelerated by indigenous women's participation in the first regional and continental indigenous conferences in the early 1990s, including the Conferencia del Quinto Centenario (Fifth Centenary Conference) in 1992 and the Enlace Continental de Mujeres Indígenas (Continental Network of Indigenous Women) in 1993.

During this same period, another new initiative, *Otra Guatemala*, a magazine published between 1988 and 1990 by exiles in Mexico, helped to spread feminist ideas by articulating them with leftist projects and concepts as a means of resolving the old debate about the relevance of the women's demands. The magazine sought to bring together different positions on the left but also served as a forum for the dissemination of Guatemalan feminist ideas and the activities of women's organizations in Guatemala, as well as for the recovery of women's history. Women who published articles in the magazine and/or were on its editorial board, such as Carmen and Victoria Álvarez, Lucia Pellecer, Lorena Carrillo, Ana Cofiño, and Yolanda Urizar, later went on to found or were linked to feminist groups, indigenous organizations, and women's groups in Guatemala.

Despite the tensions and contradictions inherent in the relationship between more autonomous women's organizations and those that were related to leftist organizations at the time, and between the leftist-affiliated women's organizations and their parent organizations, the most important achievement of this period was "to take feminism out from the 'underground' in which it had been entombed during all the preceding years" (Aguilar 2001, 73).

Third Phase, 1994–1999

The third phase of women's organizing in Guatemala was characterized by several milestones. One of the most important occurred during the first debates of the Asamblea de la Sociedad Civil (ASC; Assembly of Civil Society), an organization created so that civil society could support the Peace Accords, which were finally signed by the government and the insurgent forces in 1996.[3] The assembly, composed of more than thirty organizations and some individuals, was originally based on the assumption that women's needs and demands would automatically be included as part of the other social groups of which they formed a part: workers, peasants, professionals, students, businesspeople, the indigenous, the religious, political parties, and so on. A coalition of women's organizations, mainly the Convergencia Cívica Política de Mujeres (Women's Civic Political Convergence), GGM, Coordinadora por el Desarrollo Integral de la Mujer (Coordinating Body for Women's Comprehensive Development), Familiares de Detenidos y Desaparecidos de Guatemala (Relatives of the Detained and Disappeared of Guatemala), Tierra Viva, and Coincidencia de Mujeres came to an agreement, not without struggle, that women should be included as one of the founding sectors of the assembly (Jimeno 1996; Berger 2006).

The creation of a Women's Sector in the ASC produced a forum in which twenty-two women's organizations (some working exclusively with women and others interested in promoting women's issues within mixed-gender organizations) and five independent women could debate different versions of gender-specific demands to be included in the negotiations and, if successful, in the agreements that resulted from them. The task was not an easy one. Arriving at agreement among the members of the Women's Sector meant having to negotiate among a diverse group of women who did not have a common agenda or experience with women's issues and who lacked the trust that comes from having worked together previously. In the end, however, the members of the Women's Sector were able to get the rest of the assembly to take their demands seriously and to add a number of them into the final agreement. Among the demands were the incorporation of a gender focus in development programs and programs for the resettlement of uprooted populations; the creation of legislation recognizing sexual harassment and domestic violence as punishable crimes; measures favoring the expansion of women's citizenship and political participation; special protections of indigenous rights; and increasing women's access to land, credit, housing, and education.

Political activist and active participant in the Women's Sector, Georgina Navarro, describes the negotiation process that characterized this challenging but important effort:

> In the Women's Sector, the contributions of the feminists gave theoretical support and valid arguments to the proposals that later sustained them at the negotiating table, with the political parties and the other sectors. [In the beginning] indigenous women did not identify with them; they were surprised that we would come up with things that had not been spoken of publicly here, at least

they had not heard about them … but little by little the indigenous women began to identify. Rosalina Tuyuc, for example, who handled the issue of human rights very well, began identifying with some proposals in which she saw herself reflected. CONAVIGUA began to join the Sector when they heard the proposals and identified with some of the issues. They didn't endorse everything, just what they believed in. And since we had to present consensus proposals, things they didn't endorse, didn't pass, like abortion [an issue that didn't have agreement from some other women either because they continue to consider it a taboo topic (ASM)]. The issues [with which] they identified were, for example, the problems faced by widows due to the armed conflict, the situation of the women victims of the armed conflict [an experience already shared in Mexico with other ladina refugees]; it was not feminism as such, but certain issues that united us. (Monzón 2004a, 62)

The agreement to include women as a sector with specific interests and direct representation was a milestone in the history of women and democracy in Guatemala and of peace accords in the world. It deserves to be recognized as such despite subsequent disappointments resulting from the government's inability or lack of will to implement fundamental provisions of the accords. Similarly, the establishment of the Foro Nacional de la Mujer (National Women's Forum), an attempt to ensure that women's issues were not overlooked in the implementation of the accords, deserves recognition for being a pioneering effort in spite of the fact that rural women's groups were insufficiently represented in it (Berger 2006). According to one observer, "It can be said, then, that it was during this period that feminism and feminists decisively influenced the discussions of the main leaders of the broader women's movement and the content of the demands expressed in the Peace Accords through the constant and dynamic participation of organized women in the spaces and mechanisms defined for this process" (Aguilar 2001, 73).

Other milestones during this period included the coordination of an increasingly more varied collection of women's groups and the organization of public debates related to preparations for regional, hemispheric, and international conferences, such as the Primer Encuentro Centroamericano de Mujeres (First Central American Women's Encuentro), held in Montelimar, Nicaragua (1992); the Sexto Encuentro Feminista de América Latina y el Caribe (Sixth Latin American and Caribbean Feminist Encuentro), in Costa del Sol, El Salvador (1993); and, sponsored by the United Nations, the World Conference on Human Rights, in Vienna (1993); the International Conference on Population and Development, in Cairo (1994); and the World Conference on Women, in Beijing (1995).

The public debates conducted by women's groups and their desire to have political influence and negotiate with the government, as well as with different sectors of civil society, generated a strong reaction at times. Such was the case of the proposed Law on Population and Development (Decree 3-93), which focused on the reproductive health of men and women, including family planning, gynecological and obstetric treatment, and the treatment of sexually transmitted diseases.

Opposition to the law—passed by Congress but eventually vetoed by the president—came not only from the Catholic Church hierarchy and conservative groups who saw family planning as a cover for abortion but also from some Catholic women activists and indigenous women.

Another significant event during this period was the establishment of the first monthly feminist newspaper in Guatemala, *La Cuerda*, in 1998. It started out some years before as a monthly page in a nationally circulating daily paper. The most important contribution of the newspaper to praxis and theory of progressive social movements in Guatemala is its emphasis on articulating the ethics of the body and feelings to politics. Picking up the trail of Femina Sapiens but taking it further and updating it in Guatemalan time and space, *La Cuerda* pays homage to its predecessor with a column of the same name. *La Cuerda*, however, reinterprets the intention of the original column by emphasizing an integration of the theoretical and political. The newspaper defines itself as "a feminist look at reality" and seeks to balance analysis with reporting information, as well as to stimulate opinion and debate on national matters from a feminist perspective. The newspaper's vision derives from an integrated concept of feminist thought and social reality and originates in the debate with the left, summarized in the principle of "the personal is political." Together with the radio program *Voces de Mujeres* (Women's Voices), established in 1993, *La Cuerda* is the result of the postwar democratic opening that has brought about more favorable conditions for the creation of alternative means of communication and knowledge creation and transmission. In 2007 *La Cuerda* expanded its vision to form Agenda Feminista (Feminist Agenda), a space where women can share the history of their experiences in the women's movement, hammer out a common language, and support feminist political action throughout the country. Although the project is still in its early stages, the goal is to convene a Congreso de Feministas (Feminist Congress) in 2009.

A contradictory trend that accelerated during this period was the progressive NGOization of Guatemalan women's organizations and the women's movement overall. On one hand, beginning in the nineties, there was growing international pressure from the United Nations conferences and public and private donors to include women's issues in the programmatic initiatives of governmental agencies and nongovernmental organizations, both of which depended heavily on external financing. This created a certain demand for people trained in gender issues and for workshops on subjects related to women. Many women activists believe, however, that it also increased fragmentation, duplication, and competition for scarce resources, resulting in a lack of long-term, coherent goals. Many of the critics also believe that increasing NGOization weakened the most political aspects of the feminist movement in favor of the "institutionalization of the movement, the establishment of administrative and accounting systems . . . the creation of impact indicators and the drawing up of logical frameworks for the execution of projects," while "negotiating and influencing became the same . . . as not confronting and abandoning political mobilization and denunciation" (Aguilar 2001, 82–83).

Other women activists, although they recognize the contradictory effects of NGOization, have pointed out a positive development during this period, not entirely unrelated to NGOization. That is, for the first time, by the end of the period the Guatemalan women's movement, particularly its feminist current, no longer had a majority of members from the ladina-mestiza or urban population or the upper and middle classes. It was no longer only rural and indigenous women who were creating spaces for themselves and their concerns but also women with other ethnic identities (Garifuna and Xinca, for example), young women, religious women, and women with different sexual orientations.

Fourth Phase, 2000 to the Present

By the year 2000 there was once again an increase in violence (due mostly to crime), government corruption, a climate of impunity, insecurity in the public sphere, and the fragility of the legal system, which, together with economic deterioration, helped to undermine the implementation of the Peace Accords and state policies related to the accords. The creation of the Secretaría Presidencial de la Mujer (Presidential Secretariat for Women) opened up some avenues for the institutionalization of policies favoring women and paved the way for the Guatemalan Congress to ratify the Protocolo Facultativo (Optional Protocol) of the Convention on the Elimination of All Forms of Discrimination against Women (CEDAW). But the relevant state agencies have still not publicized the content of CEDAW and have not acted on other reforms stipulated in the Peace Accords, including the law of electoral and political parties reform, the law against sexual harassment, and the integration of women into the Consejos de Desarrollo Urbano y Rural (Urban and Rural Development Councils). The incorporation of a gender perspective into the packet of educational reforms and into the expansion of rural women's rights to land and credit has also not progressed.

On the positive side, a diverse group of women have been able to come to agreements on certain political agendas and specific projects. During the election campaigns of 2003, women's groups joined the protests against the constitutional court's approval of the candidacy of the ex-president General Efraín Ríos Montt (who was responsible for the "scorched earth" counterinsurgent campaign). They joined the Nosotras las Mujeres (We, the Women) campaign to convince other women to exercise a well-informed vote, reminding them of the impact that the war of the 1980s had on women and their communities (Monzón 2004b, 26).

For the first time there was discussion between indigenous and ladina-mestiza women of approximately twenty proposals for inclusion in the election platforms of the political parties. The symposia organized around these proposals focused attention on the problems women faced and demands for action by the state that would benefit the common good, including "the creation and strengthening of institutional mechanisms for the advancement of women, the allocation of state funds to specific women's programs, as well as the approval of laws and/or legal reforms that contribute to eliminating the barriers that limit the effective participation of women in political and management spaces and the execution of public policies" (Monzón 2004c, 27).

Although the proposed reform in the law governing elections and political parties that would have provided for quotas for women in party electoral slates seems to have stagnated and women still seem to be required to have higher educational levels and more experience to be selected as political party candidates than men do (Garcia 2007), the pressure to get more women involved in electoral politics appears to have born fruit in the 2007 elections. More indigenous women participated than before, including as candidates, and a number of them have been elected to Congress and several more as mayors. Indigenous women also presented local agendas to the political parties and, for the first time, organizations of women affiliated with the left emerged to push women's issues and candidacies in their parties' elections. Formed in 2006, the Colectiva Feminista de Mujeres de Izquierda (Feminist Collective of Leftist Women), allied with the Unidad Revolucionaria Nacional Guatemalteca–Movimiento Amplio de Izquierda (URNG-MAIZ; Guatemalan National Revolutionary Unity–Broad Leftist Movement) party, and the Núcleo de Lucha contra el Patriarcado (Nucleus of Struggle against Patriarchy) gave leftist women visibility, a defined identity, and a mechanism through which to sustain a debate about feminism and women in the context of electoral politics. The selection of feminist Walda Barrios as vice president on the URNG-MAIZ ticket in 2007 represented a landmark in the history of women and left parties in Guatemala and was the result of left women having organized as women.

This new effort to think concretely and strategically about legislative and policy reform agendas, increase women's participation in electoral politics, and form the necessary alliances is not without its critics. There are feminists who believe that pressuring the government to implement and supervise reforms, given the problematic political atmosphere and the weakness of the Guatemalan state, distracts from a more militant feminist effort to transform the social order.

The most important new development during this period has been the unexpected and historically unprecedented diffusion of women's organizations and feminist perspectives outside of Guatemala City. The coordinated public marches that began in the capital with the signing of the Peace Accords on March 8, 1996, are celebrated more and more frequently in the departmental administrative centers, under the leadership of coordinating bodies that bring together diverse groups. Mayan, Garifuna, and Xinca women, the main ethnic groups in Guatemala, are increasingly active in several regional and hemispheric networks as well as in many local and national organizations. Garifuna women began to develop their hemispheric ties as a result of the Primer Encuentro de Mujeres Negras Latinoamericanas y del Caribe (First Latin American and Caribbean Black Women's Encuentro) in 1992 and indigenous women did the same after the Enlace Continental de Mujeres Indígenas in 1993.

Indigenous women who had been in exile or refugee camps during the war have faced a number of organizational challenges upon their return. During the 1980s and early 1990s, indigenous women who were in refugee camps had strong support from the Mexican NGOs (Blue 2005) and were successful in organizing their nine thousand or so women members into three main groups: Mamá Maquín in 1990, Madre Tierra in 1993, and Mujeres en Resistencia Ixmucane in 1993. When they returned to Guatemala in 1993, and in the years that followed, the women encountered a more conservative and hostile environment. Branded as members or sympathizers of revolutionary organizations (brought together in URNG) and often rejected by local male leaders with a much less progressive mind-set compared to that to which they were accustomed, the women found it difficult to continue with the same agenda of empowerment that they followed when they were refugees. Nevertheless, in 2000 the three groups mentioned earlier formed the Alianza de Mujeres Rurales por la Vida, la Tierra, y la Dignidad (Rural Women's Alliance for Life, Land, and Dignity), which operated out of Quiché, Huehuetenango, Alta Verapaz, Suchitepéquez, and Petén. After a period of focusing primarily on "productive projects," their current agenda tries to combine preparing for employment or income generation with a political agenda that has "a transformative character" and foments "broader relationships" (Hernández 2005, 82).

Some indigenous women work actively for land rights in mixed-gender groups such as the Coordinadora Nacional de Organizaciones Campesinas (National Coordinating Body of Peasant Organizations) and the Coordinadora Nacional Indígena y Campesina (National Indigenous and Peasant Coordinating Body), which since 1996 has had a Secretariat for Women that pressures for greater representation of women in positions of power. Other indigenous women organize around a particular focus: cultural (Consejo de Mayas, or Mayan Council, formed in 1993); political (Comité de Mujeres Coordinadora de Organizaciones del Pueblo Maya de Guatemala, or Women's Coordinating Committee of the Mayan Organizations of Guatemala, formed in 1996; and the Asociación de Mujeres Tejedoras del Desarrollo, or Association of Women Weavers of Development, formed in 1997); self-knowledge (Grupo de Mujeres Mayas Kaqla, or Kaqla Mayan Women's Group, formed in 1998); and women's leadership and citizenship development (Asociación Política de Mujeres Mayas Moloj, or Moloj Political Association of Mayan Women, formed in 2001). Others struggle for a more visible role and against discrimination (Asociación de Mujeres Garífunas de Guatemala, or Association of Garífuna Women of Guatemala, formed in 1995) or to bring together women of diverse ideological positions to push for a broad political movement of Mayan women and their increased representation in the state apparatus (Asociación Moloj, or Moloj Association, formed in 1999). These organizations, whether consisting of mixed groups or organizing women around a particular focus, are playing an increasingly important role in the education and mobilization of rural indigenous women (Monzón 2004a, 34–35). This mobilization, in turn, has motivated other governmental and nongovernmental organizations, such as the Foro Nacional de la Mujer (National Women's Forum), created in 1989, to restructure themselves along regional, linguistic, and sociocultural lines, so as to facilitate more diverse participation.

Perhaps the most innovative of the new groups is Grupo de Mujeres Mayas Kaqla, made up of Mayan women with experience in the revolutionary movements of the 1980s, along with some younger women. What is interesting about Kaqla's project is the creative appropriation and updating of a wide range of cultural, intellectual, and political traditions, in a dialogic approach that keeps the channels open for a wide range of debates, with the goal of combining both the private and the public. These include Western European and U.S. traditions such as psychoanalysis and socioanalysis, feminism, deconstructionism, and theoretical paradigms of development, integrated with cultural points of reference from indigenous peoples and languages and Guatemalan popular culture. Although the Mujeres Maya de Kaqla want, in this initial phase of their process, "to talk to themselves" (Grupo de Mujeres Mayas Kaqla 2004, 28), particularly around issues of internalized oppression, their ultimate goal is dialogue in the search for new ways of configuring—at least on the discursive level—a multiple and heterogeneous subject.

Another important initiative is the effort that some historic organizations, such as CONAVIGUA, are making to guarantee a new generation of leaders. CONAVIGUA has created the Movimiento de Jóvenes Maya (MOJOMAYA; Maya Youth Movement), an autonomous organization of young activists who are linked with a growing youth movement in Guatemala.

While some activists look with consternation at what they view as the depolitization of Guatemalan women's movements over these past eight years and a decrease in influence at the national policy level, others focus on the historically unprecedented spread of women's organizations and feminist perspectives in rural areas. It is indisputable that in Guatemala today there is a growing diversity of projects that give voice and space to women who historically have not had it. In a country that is just beginning to accept its identity as a multiethnic nation and explore all the ramifications of that identity, and in which, until very recently, effective citizenship was denied to the majority of its population, this diffusion of women's organizations, activities, and consciousness can be seen as a preexisting condition for a new moment of protagonism.

Weakness and Challenges

The most remarkable part of the past thirty years of activism by Guatemalan women has been its continuity in spite of threats, deaths, a genocidal war, and a postwar period characterized by high levels of impunity and official corruption, as well as by increasing hunger and poverty, elites that resist democratic reforms, and a valiant but fragile civil society. Women's activism during and after the wars of the 1970s and 1980s has helped to bring about a concept of citizenship that is more active and inclusive and a concept of the nation that is more pluralistic and multiethnic. It has created a more holistic concept of progressive social change that combines reproduction with production, and feelings and desires with economic and political transformation. It has encouraged more democratic and less sectarian practices in progressive coalitions and, most importantly, it has brought into public life a core group of women—some who have been activists since their teens and others who have been organizing for decades—with extensive knowledge of the art of mobilizing and organizing, even under the most adverse conditions. These experienced women work alongside new generations of activists who did not directly experience the war and the more orthodox traditions of leftist organizations; together they combine the transmission of experience with the creation of new spaces and experiments in new organizing styles.

At the same time, the fragility of the changes that have been achieved, the emergence of new forms of terror and intimidation such as the wave of femicides—1,049 women killed between 2002 and 2004—and problems generated by civilian governments that conciliate the right-wing Catholics of Opus Dei or attempt to co-opt feminist discourse without genuinely believing in it make it difficult to carve out time to collectively reflect on the achievements of Guatemalan women's organizations and the lessons they have learned.[4]

The goal of fully integrating women and feminist ideas into democratic political culture in Guatemala has been constantly challenged by conditions of violence, limited access to education and public debate, and intolerance and discrimination on the basis of gender, class, and ethnicity. But responding to these challenges has also been the strength of the Guatemalan women's movement. The failure of the left to develop women's organizations and a framework for feminist analysis during the war gave a certain freedom to postwar feminist groups to experiment with ideas and organizational forms. On the other hand, the continuing presence of large numbers of women in mixed organizations, or the women's organizations linked to them, has made it possible for these women to develop critiques, based on their experiences, of gender approaches that lack feminist theory or politics and of feminist approaches that minimize the importance of class.

Women refugees and peasants have challenged their organizations to develop strategies that promote improvement not only in women's economic conditions but also in political empowerment. Recent research in communities of returnees confirms that "access to land for isolated groups, through credits and timely support, is insufficient to turn back poverty and does not generate development" (Hernández 2005, 82). This concurs with the evaluations of peasant women's organizations who now propose goals with a more political character. The airing of debates about theory and practice with regard to women, within and among leftist organizations and between leftist organizations and feminists, has resulted in feminist agendas that are closely tied to political issues and the social problems of Guatemala, far removed from those elsewhere that might be viewed by Guatemalan feminists as self-absorbed and elitist. While the ability of women with a feminist perspective to influence national politics and the programs of leftist political parties is still relatively weak, recent developments have occurred, such as the selection of Walda Barrios as the vice presidential candidate of the URNG-MAIZ in the 2007 elections and the unprecedented collaboration of women congressional representatives with rural and urban women's groups in the passage of the new Law against Femicide in April 2008.

Guatemalan women's movements currently face a number of challenges, some of which are more related to their particular context and others similar to those of other Latin American women's groups. Like movements elsewhere, Guatemalan women's organizations face an ongoing challenge to determine how much effort to invest in organizing public actions versus the internal development of the movement, what types of relationships women's organizations should maintain with the state, and how to maintain autonomy and independence while depending on international financial support.

On the other hand, of particular importance in a multiethnic country like Guatemala is the articulation of differences, particularly within and among ethnic groups. The recent geographic dispersion and political decentering of Guatemalan women's organizing activities makes this articulation more important than ever before. In parts of Latin America where academic feminism is well institutionalized, the challenge is to bridge the gap between academic and rank-and-file feminists. In Guatemala, however, the challenge is to generate more theory that sustains and encourages women's activism and to create and permanently sustain academic institutions, research centers, and civil organizations that can help teach gender issues, shape feminist thought, and generate ongoing financial support for these projects.

And finally, in Guatemala, as elsewhere in Latin America, there is the need to effectively confront the resurgence of a religious right adamantly opposed to women's right to reproductive choice. How to respond to the right-wing offensive while still constructing a women's movement that respects and allows for differences among women—especially between some indigenous and nonindigenous women when it comes to state reproductive policies—has created tension among women around public policy issues. This potential division highlights once again the overarching challenge of how to construct a movement that teaches women how to negotiate among their differences, as well as with the state and their nonstate allies. Throughout these challenges, the fundamental task of finding ever more creative ways of "subverting, transgressing and subverting again" still remains (Aguilar 2001).

NOTES

1. The Jornadas, a series of political campaigns and public protests against the military government of Ydigoras Fuentes, developed into an insurrectionary moment in Guatemalan political history.

2. The term *ladinos*, as used in Guatemala, refers to mestizos or, in many cases, any non-Indians.

3. The peace negotiations between the government, the army, and the Unidad Revolucionaria Nacional Guatemalteca (URNG; Guatemalan National Revolutionary Unity), an umbrella group that brought together an array of armed and civilian revolutionary organizations, began in Mexico on April 26, 1991, with the signing of the agreement that included the participation of civil society.

4. The figure of 1,049 exceeds the total cases attributed to femicide in Ciudad Juárez as of 2004 (see Grais-Targow 2004). The brutal killings of women with only minimal efforts to investigate the perpetrators and virtually no prosecutions in Ciudad Juarez, Mexico, is a phenomenon that has received extensive media attention and international campaigns on behalf of

the murdered women, while the situation in Guatemala has received much less attention. In a number of the Guatemalan women's cases there are indications of involvement by government security forces.

REFERENCES

Aguilar, Ana Leticia. 2001. El movimiento feminista y el enfoque de género en las instituciones nacionales e internacionales: Balances y desafíos. In *Feminismos en América Latina*, ed. Edda Gaviola Artigas and Lissette González Martines, 69–91. Guatemala City: FLACSO.

Aguilar, Urízar, and Yolanda de la Luz. 2003. Identidades políticas feministas en Guatemala: Etnología de la trasgresión. Undergraduate thesis, Área de Antropología, Escuela de Historia, Universidad de San Carlos, Guatemala City.

Aguilera, P. Gabriel, ed. 1979. *Mujer y lucha social*. Guatemala City: Instituto Centroamericano de Estudios Políticos, INCEP.

Berger, Susan. 2006. *Guatemaltecas: The women's movement, 1986–2003*. Austin: University of Texas Press.

Blue, Sarah A. 2005. Including women in development: Guatemalan refugees and local NGOs. *Latin American Perspectivas*, no. 32:101–117.

Carrillo, Lorena. 1991. Indias y ladinas: Los ásperos caminos de las mujeres en Guatemala. *Revista Nueva Sociedad*, no. 111:109–118.

———. 1994. El voto de las mujeres. *Revista Otra Guatemala*, no. 13:17–19.

———. 1995. Las formas de participación fémina el trabajo y la política en Guatemala (1920–1980). Master's thesis, UNAM, Mexico City.

———. 2004. *Luchas de las guatemaltecas del siglo XX: Mirada al trabajo y la participación política de las mujeres*. Guatemala City: Pensativo.

García, Diana. 2007. Agendas políticas desde la pluralidad de las mujeres: Elementos para un futuro debate. Guatemala City: PNUD / Letra Negra Editores / Cuaderno de Desarrollo Humano.

Grais-Targow, Risa. 2004. *Femicide in Guatemala*. Report for the Center for Gender and Refugee Studies. Berkeley: University of California, Hastings Law School.

Grupo de Mujeres Mayas Kaqla. 2004. *La palabra y el sentir de las mujeres mayas de Kaqla*. Guatemala City: Novib / Hivos / Oxfam / PCS.

Hernández Alarcón, Rosalinda. 2005. *Las campesinas y su derecho a la tierra (realidad y emancipación)*. Guatemala City: Cuerda.

Jimeno, Clara. 1996. The role of Guatemalan women's organizations in the peace process. Paper presented at the Twenty-seventh Congress of the Canadian Association for Latin American and Caribbean Studies (CERLAC), Cork University, Toronto, November 1–3.

Kollantai, Alexandra. 1977. *Selected writings of A. Kollantai*. Westport, CT: Lawrence Hill.

Monzón, Ana Silvia. 2003. *Memoria del porvenir: 10 años de voces de mujeres*. Guatemala City: Friedrich Ebert Stiftung–Christina Aid.

———. 2004a. Entre mujeres: La identidad étnica, factor de tensión en el movimiento de mujeres en Guatemala, 1990–2000. Master thesis in social sciences, Programa Centroamericano de Postgrado, FLACSO-Guatemala, Guatemala City.

———. 2004b. Los estudios de la mujer y de género en Guatemala: Balance y perspectivas. Paper presented at the Encuentro Nacional de Investigación en Género y Feminismo, Guatemala City, November 11–12.

———. 2004c. Y sin embargo se mueven . . . del movimiento de mujeres a la construccion de agendas en Guatemala (1985–2003). *Dialogos*, special issue. Universidad de Costa Rica, Escuela de Historia.

Peláez Aldana, Ligia. 2007a. Descubriendo la fuerza que tenemos para luchar. In *Aproximación a los imaginarios sobre organización campesina en Guatemala: Ensayos sobre su construcción histórica*. Paper presented at the Twenty-seventh Congress of the Latin American Studies Association, Montreal, Canada, September 5–8.

———. 2007b. Mujeres y organización campesina: La experiencia de las retornadas. In *Aproximación a los imaginarios sobre organización campesina en Guatemala: Ensayos sobre su construcción histórica*, 199–224. Textos para Debate 19. Guatemala: AVANCSO.

Randall, Margaret. 1974. *Cuban women now: Interviews with Cuban women*. Toronto: Women's Press.

———. 1983. *Sandino's daughters: Testimonies of Nicaraguan women in struggle*. Vancouver: New Star Books.

Rivera, María Amalia Irías de, and Irma Violeta Alfaro de Carpio. 1979. Guatemalan working women in the Labor Movement. *Latin American Perspectives*, 156–164.

Stoltz Chinchilla, Norma. 1998. *Nuestras utopías: Mujeres guatemaltecas del siglo XX*. Guatemala City: Terra Magna / Agrupación de Mujeres Tierra Viva.

Zetkin, Clara. 1984. *Selected writings by Klara Zetkin*, ed. Phillip S. Foner. New York: International.

PART IV

BROADENING THE CIRCLE OF WOMEN'S ACTIVISM

New Meanings from
Intersecting Oppressions

9 Women's Movements in Argentina

TENSIONS AND ARTICULATIONS

GRACIELA DI MARCO

There are, therefore, by necessity, many feminisms and any attempt to find the "true" form of feminist politics should be abandoned.　　　　—Chantal Mouffe

This chapter focuses on the relations between Argentinean women's movements and the state between the nineties and the early twenty-first century. In this period, processes of structural adjustment and globalization dramatically changed the social structure of Argentina. A significant corpus of law was passed to support women's rights; however, a gap remains between the laws on the books and an effective defense and protection of such rights.

My approach to trace the developments that took place from the mid-nineties to the present takes the vast literature about women's movements in Latin America into account, starting from considerations of both public and private organizations as spaces where gender discourses are constructed and negotiated in their linguistic and practical implications.[1] Gender is constructed; that is to say, legitimized and nonlegitimized gender relations are sanctioned and gender is performed. The state is an organization where different discourses and practices coexist, because it is the result of social processes rather than a unified apparatus pursuing well-defined, homogeneous strategies. Rather than a monolithic, uniform whole, it is a battlefield where different interests fight one another. Pervaded by asymmetric gender relations, the state nevertheless plays a role in the construction of these same unequal power relations between genders. In Argentina, social movements interrelate with the state in countless ways, and these relations also give rise to negotiations of new meanings (Di Marco 1997a). The messages generated by collective action are related to the actors' demands for subjectivity and visibility at the intersection with other social forces and interlocutors (political parties, religious organizations, and the state). Any attempt at examining the connections among various social movements, women's movements, and the Argentinean state will necessarily be only partly successful, because it requires fragmenting a relation in progress within a field of democratic conflicts and potentialities.

My approach is also based on the tenet that "feminist politics should be understood not as a separate form of politics designed to pursue the interests of women *as* women, but rather as the pursuit of feminist goals, and aims[,] within the context of a wider articulation of demands" (Mouffe 1992, 382). I therefore start from the existence of numerous forms of feminism, bearing in mind the articulation between feminist politics and that of other social movements rather than establishing an a priori definition of a "suitable" form of feminist politics. Strategies and the identity of actors in social movements implicate one another; we may therefore conclude that different modes of women's participation in social movements articulated with other issues—whether or not exclusively feminist—may lead to struggles to lessen gender subordination (Cohen 1985; Alvarez 1990, 23; Molyneux 2000, 225). Women's movements have always featured a relative autonomy compared to other organizational forms, such as political parties and trade unions. The movements that emerged in Argentina during the neoliberal era are similar to the many ways in which women have mobilized around gender interests, whether through women's organizations, groups composed of both men and women, or associations to demand justice for crimes committed against their children (the Mothers of Plaza de Mayo is a case in point).

Women's collective action during the nineties should be viewed within the context of economic adjustment, the ensuing impoverishment of the population, and its response to this economic situation.[2] Both urban and rural movements emerged, which resulted in the growing visibility of working-class women in the public sphere.

Collective Action in the Nineties

The nineties were marked by numerous social responses to the socioeconomic, political, and cultural model that was setting in. These responses were characterized by the increasing complexity of social and political identities, the steady dislocation of trade unions, and the emergence of a matrix of citizenship and rights (Scribano and Schuster 2001).

Mobilizations were composed of workers affected by the industrial rationalization processes and of various middle-class sectors injured by market reforms. Likewise, cities of the interior, immersed in a crisis related to the implementation of provincial fiscal adjustment together with market reforms, organized demonstrations in which entire towns came out into the streets in defense of their interests (*puebladas*).[3]

The first roadblocks were carried out by inhabitants of Cutral-Co and Plaza Huincul in the province of Neuquén in June 1996, followed by similar actions in several provinces. Roadblocks in General Mosconi and Tartagal, Province of Salta, in May 1997 were the most important ones. There were a total of 104 roadblocks in various Argentinean provinces during 1997. Around the same time several movements appeared: the Movimiento de Mujeres Agropecuarias en Lucha (Agricultural Women in Struggle Movement); the Movimiento Campesino Santiagueño

(Peasants' Movement in Santiago del Estero); Coordinadora contra la Represión Policial e Institucional (Coordinating Committee against Police and Institutional Repression) and Mothers of Grief (Madres del Dolor).

Mothers and Grandmothers of Plaza de Mayo

Whether explicitly or not, many of these organizations follow the legacy of human rights movements such as the Madres y Abuelas de Plaza de Mayo (Mothers and Grandmothers of May Plaza), whose political practices grew out of individual grief and evolved into open confrontation with the military government.[4] Eventually, their mode of action influenced Argentinean politics, including the practices of the parties that ruled the country over the last few decades. The movements redefined motherhood and grandmotherhood through the discourse and practice of *social motherhood*, which, rather than focusing on personal blood ties, involves a public demand for the government to publicly answer for the torture and disappearance of their sons and daughters (Schmukler and Di Marco 1997).

The movement rooted its political practice in motherhood rather than using motherhood as a paradigm of women's participation in politics. Mothers' discourses and practices claiming for justice, as well as their struggles against authoritarianism, endow motherhood with a new meaning. Such a practice politicizes motherhood, no longer a private exercise in the privacy of the home subjected to male authority. Although twenty-five years have elapsed since constitutional restoration, the Mothers keep up their defense of human rights as a criticism of all forms of oppression, including the adjustment programs implemented in the nineties, unemployment, and social fragmentation resulting in ever more differentiated sectors. In so doing, the Mothers contribute to the deepening of democratic citizenship which, in Mary Dietz's words, is collective, inclusive, and generalized (1985).

The fact that the Mothers accepted their children's militancy and decided to keep on fighting for the very same ideas their children upheld enables us to grasp a new aspect of the movement: an inverted generational transmission in which the Mothers learned from the example set by their offspring. According to one of the leaders, Hebe Bonafini, "We are the first mothers to have been born to their children" (Di Marco 1997b, 134). Their politicization, the struggles that ensued, and articulations with other human rights organizations impelled the Trials for Truth and Justice and the 2005 decision of the Supreme Court of Justice to declare the amnesty laws (Law of Final Point and Law of Due Obedience) unconstitutional and void, thus putting an end to twenty years of impunity.

Although the military rulers repressed the Mothers and attempted to abort the movement as it emerged, the Mothers pressed on with their demands. Their tenacity made them one of the most important twentieth-century movements both in Argentina and in the rest of the world.[5] They retained their prophetic, countercultural potential in later actions and coalitions with other movements, thus ensuring their own continued relevance. They continued to struggle for the recognition of the right to truth and justice, for trials of the main parties responsible for their children's appropriation, and for compensation from those who had cashed in on property stolen from their victims. Finally, in 1995 the government committed itself to guarantee the right to truth and to uphold norms regarding all investigations concerning the disappeared.

Movements and NGOs

Like in most Latin American countries, in Argentina the women's movement has been classified into three offshoots: participation in human rights movements, the collective actions undertaken by women from the popular sectors (i.e., women organized to confront economic hardship, especially during the adjustment era), and women in feminist movements, with a strong component of middle-class women in their initial and mature phases (Jaquette 1994; Molyneux 2000).

In the eighties the debate began about women's citizenship and the need to demand legal reforms and public policies. Several networks of nongovernmental organizations (NGOs) wove a weft in which women became aware of issues such as subordination, violence against women, sexual harassment, reproductive rights, health care, and the need for various laws to be passed.[6] The United Nations conferences, notably the World Conference on Women, held in Beijing in 1995; regional conferences (e.g., CEPAL 1994); and the mandates from multilateral agencies, which in the nineties began to establish requirements regarding gender equity for poverty reduction policies, drove most countries in the region to adopt diverse but favorable positions incorporating women into development policies (Molyneux 2000).

The gradual increase in the number of women in executive and legislative state institutions, as well as the elaboration of gender-equity agendas, resulted from the intertwining of the activism of women's movements and the new agenda adopted by the states in the region to comply with international pressure and show some sort of leadership in issues of citizens' rights (Molyneux 2000, 305).

More than half of the women's organizations were founded in the nineties. Of these, half were in the province of Buenos Aires. Besides addressing women's issues, most of them are engaged in issues such as childhood, youth, and old age. Very few declare to be working for gender equity. These figures point to a gradual, belated, NGOization of feminist organizations, compared to Brazil and Mexico, for example, where this process began in the eighties (Alvarez 1999; Lebon 1997, 7). Still, we cannot overlook the emergence of NGOs and the role played therein by international cooperation agencies. In fostering projects aimed at citizenship, participation, and empowerment, these international connections promoted the creation of numerous groups in search of funding, even if these groups lacked a feminist orientation and reproduced state efforts to deal with social problems.

Women's Participation in Social Movements

To explore women's participation in the various social movements emerging in the mid-nineties, I focus specifically on three of them: the Movimientos de Trabajadores Desocupados (Movements of Unemployed Workers); Asambleas Populares (Popular Assemblies); and Empresas Recuperadas y Autogestionadas

(ERAs; Recovered and Self-Managed Enterprises), although this does not lessen the importance of the others mentioned earlier.[7]

Unemployed workers' movements started in the interior of the country, in areas affected by job cutbacks resulting from privatizations. Members of these movements chose to act by establishing roadblocks, or "pickets," which led to their label of *piqueteros* (picketers). They garnered more visibility than other social movements (assemblies and ERAs) because of their scope and their strategy. The main purpose of these mobilizations was to obtain subsidies and food. In 2002 most picket organizations obtained subsidies for their members through the Plan Jefes y Jefas de Hogar Desocupados (Unemployed Heads-of-Household Program) and several other organizations, especially those implemented by the province of Buenos Aires.[8]

The various picket movements presented a mosaic of groups with distinctive characteristics, a consequence of their alliances and origins in political parties, trade unions, or independent organizations. About 70 percent of the people involved in the picket movement were women, especially dedicated to the management of community projects, participation in demonstrations, and the occupation of open spaces. In this type of collective action, the political, the economic, and the communal are solidly intertwined in a complex web.

Popular assemblies stemmed from a variety of protests that started on December 19 and 20, 2001. The triggering events behind their emergence were multiple: a few days before December 19 and 20, the population staged protests in front of banks after an announcement of restrictions on the amount of money the public was allowed to withdraw, a measure meant to stop the run on banks. That same week, supermarkets in the greater Buenos Aires area and other cities were looted. The government declared a state of siege, reviving the painful collective memory of the repression suffered under the military state of siege. The protests turned to widespread riots, leaving more than twenty people dead because of police repression, and resulting in President de la Rua's resignation.

One of the assemblies' most striking characteristics was that they appropriated public space.[9] Besides gathering at Plaza de Mayo, the traditional space for popular protest, the population gathered in parks and at centrally located corners in the various neighborhoods of Buenos Aires. On the one hand, assemblies focused on a profound criticism of the political regime and elaborated proposals for a deepening of democracy. On the other hand—and this is not so well known—they strove to articulate their proposals with new socioeconomic models (Di Marco and Palomino 2003). The distinctive feature of the assemblies was that their actions were not coordinated by a central body; they were instead articulated in a network. Their actions expressed each assembly's autonomy and their criticism of representative democracy. The assemblies deepened the politicization of civil society, reopening the issues of power and authority relations in society and in the political sphere.

The recovery of enterprises was one of the responses chosen by male and female workers facing the threat of closedowns resulting from owners not complying with their social and legal obligations. The beginning of workers' self-managed cooperative modes of production stemmed from the events of December 2001.[10]

Confronted with the likely loss of their jobs, workers could have chosen to try to obtain an employment subsidy and, when it expired, enroll in programs such as the Plan Jefes y Jefas de Hogar Desocupados. Instead, they had another option: to recover and manage their former workplace. This was a positive bet on the future because their jobs would be preserved and they would earn some income. Certainly, at the beginning, they would be earning much less than before the crisis, but even so it would be more than what unemployment subsidies and other plans had to offer. The challenge lay in cooperative organization and in production, bearing in mind their wishes for increased income.[11] Male and female workers became partners, because they managed the enterprises themselves. In many cases everyone agreed to receive the same income regardless of their type of work. ERAs base their actions on the defense of the right to employment, emphasizing the notion of the public value of work (Di Marco and Moro 2004).

Women's Discourses about Participation

It is important to inquire into the various discourses developed by women to understand their collective practices, but care must be taken to avoid lumping them together under one common denominator. Movements of unemployed workers, assemblies, and ERAs each produce different discourses, due to both their heterogeneous strategies and their distinctive goals.

In the assemblies, mainly composed of those from the middle class, both men and women participated equally, both in terms of their number and the frequency and quality of their interventions. More than a third had a history of prior militancy. At this stage, male and female assembly members deepened their political and social education and were extremely critical of social injustice but, on the whole, tended to maintain the gender discourses that, in this particular social sector, were marked by the denial of women's subordination and by discrimination against them. However, it should be noted that female assembly members did not perceive their work on social projects as a form of assistentialism, nor as an extension of motherly altruism, but rather as part of their struggle for social justice. This thinking sets them apart from maternalistic and patriarchal ideology. Many of the methodologies adopted by the popular assemblies—horizontality, politicization, and the democratization of the public sphere—are related to methodologies favored by feminist movements. The assemblies attempted to exercise egalitarianism between genders and generations during discussions, when making decisions, and when tasks were carried out. However, practices furthering equality between men and women were unevenly followed and were difficult to differentiate from those in the prevailing patriarchal culture, because it is not easy to renounce the traditional approaches to norms and values at play in gender relations.

In some of the assemblies, feminists spoke loud and clear about abortion and organized a workshop on this subject at the Porto Alegre Foro Social Mundial (World Social Forum), held in Buenos Aires in 2002. The Red de Salud (Health Network) created by the assemblies included such issues as contraception, sex education, and the legalization of abortion. On March 8, 2002, feminists and neighborhood assemblies marched to Plaza de Mayo to claim their rights.[12] At the end of that same year, the Asamblea por el Derecho al Aborto (Assembly for the Right to Abortion) was created.[13]

In unemployed workers' movements, women account for over 70 percent of members. Most of the participants, unlike their leaders, lack activist experience, whether in political parties or trade unions. Practices successful over time—especially marching for their demands in open spaces and the community work they undertake in their own areas—have provided them with tools to connect individual and collective needs. Women tend to perceive community work as a job, and so do young people, above all because this is their first opportunity to experience what a job feels like.

Economic support is also deemed a right. While at the beginning this need kindled women's commitment to the various movements, so their participation might be regarded as part of a strategy for family survival, there is no denying that women entering the public sphere have experienced countless interactions with other social actors that help to rethink gender relations, particularly violence against women. The appearance of women in the public arena (borrowing Hannah Arendt's [1993] concept) makes them visible as subjects fighting for their rights. This kind of visibility, in the public spaces at the heart of urban centers, was the vehicle with which they expressed their identity as *piqueteras*. For some groups of women engaged in collective learning, the crux lies in the struggle for the right to work and dignity. The end of domestic isolation, through their community activities and their participation in roadblocks and on the streets, has gradually helped them to appropriate the idea that rights can be obtained through struggle.

Most (male) movement leaders claim that now is not the time to set off a debate about the inequality between men and women with regard to power, authority, and resources, because it could generate divisions within the collective. On the other hand, some women think that it is important to posit the right to abortion and to a life free of violence. Such disagreements bring about conflicts in these organizations, especially between men and the women whose ideas about gender have started to change and who are seeking more influential positions within the movement. In this complex reality—despite the fact that female protagonism in picket struggles has become common in the discourse of the organizations themselves, of those that support them, and of the media that disseminate their activities—leadership is still in the hands of men.

For female workers of ERAs, the closedown of their workplace was particularly grim, as they risked losing unionized jobs. This meant resorting to domestic work—either poorly paid or not paid at all—or informal sector jobs, which spell poverty and social helplessness. They would have exchanged stable jobs for housekeeping and no economic resources of their own, a situation still worse in the case of female heads of households. Pay equality and rotation across factory jobs have benefited women, even though the functions they perform may be defined as gender-typed. On the other hand, equal pay and participation in decision making lead to higher levels of commitment with production.

Some women hold leadership positions in ERAs, and not only in companies where the majority of the workers are women, as is the case with the textile industry. The glass ceiling was broken by women with no previous political or trade union leadership or militancy at two levels (and here no differences are found in the case of men). First, they participated in collective decision making; second, they led some of these decisions in the capacity of chairpersons, deputy chairpersons, or consultants to the cooperatives. They have developed leadership and negotiation skills in the face of eviction threats, and this has extended to their dealings with judges, lawyers, legislators, and government officials. At present, a factory is a place to work, to struggle, and to seek social recognition. As happened in other movements before, participation in collective action gradually modified women's perception of their own abilities outside the private household.

Female workers' participation in the new cooperatives, together with their relations with those in social movements, political parties, academic institutions, and the legislative branch, has given rise to greater awareness and contributed to widen the scope of rights and citizenship for women workers. They have also started to take part in the Encuentros Nacionales de Mujeres (Women's National Encuentros), joining workshops about labor problems, as well as others dealing with gender-specific claims: the legalization of abortion, distribution of contraceptives, policies to fight violence against women, and so on.

The historical experiences of the Madres and Abuelas de Plaza de Mayo or of women in community organizations who got together in their respective neighborhoods to fight for their family's and their own needs show that experience in the public sphere causes subjective changes. Of course, individual timing and personal differences do matter. Some women experience changes in the way they view themselves and in how they think and act with their partners and children, developing a discourse of rights in family relationships as well as in organizations. These transformations have evolved from practices of denouncing injustice, defending rights, and acknowledging their own abilities, so often ignored or belittled, to earning power and commanding authority when confronted by men in the movement and by their families at home. In spite of the differences, to many women the process resulting from their involvement in collective action may indicate a point of no return regarding the transformation of their identities, facilitated by the interaction between participation and the development of social awareness.

Women in Movements and Women's Movements

The confluence between the women's movement and feminism had its ups and downs throughout the nineties, and so did the articulation between different women's organizations. The difficulties arose from the fact that it was necessary to build new ways of relating that ensure mutual respect and acknowledgement, not traditionally present in the existing party or association systems.

During the second half of the nineties, women's participation in the movements of the time generated a seed of change still at work today. It became apparent that these movements, characterized by the presence of women and men alike, struggled in favor of more comprehensive rights. Depending on the sort of movement they belong to, women define themselves differently regarding their interests and rights, as well as deploy different strategies. In some cases, we can observe the advent of a popular feminism made up of picket women, female workers in ERAs, mothers fighting against police repression, and women in aboriginal and peasant movements. Popular feminism finds its expression in Encuentros Nacionales de Mujeres, demonstrations, the struggle for the legalization of abortion, and endeavors to release women imprisoned because of their participation in protests.[14] Over the last ten years, feminist Encuentros have provided a privileged space for debate within the movement.

The rise of the movements just described is heralding a new historical phase in women's movements. It may contribute to the consolidation of popular feminism in Argentina, together with an alliance among women coming from different social, urban, and rural sectors. Moreover, unprecedented tension has been arising between women fighting for their rights in the public arena and more conservative sectors within the Catholic Church. As long as feminism was viewed as a bearer of the demands of a small group of urban, middle-class women, the latter sectors did not feel threatened, but the ongoing process accounts for a rise of new conflicts and responses by women in the movement. Maxine Molyneux considers the difficulty in defining women's movements (2000, 226). Women in movements—those who join forces to reach common objectives, whether or not these are feminist issues—make for a significant part of feminine solidarity in the world, even when their actions are not strictly regarded as women's movements (Vargas Valente 2002; Alvarez 1999; Molyneux 2000, 269).

Popular feminism in the eighties in parts of Latin America is expressed by activists from low-income neighborhoods using feminist strategies and discourses. This practice seems to have become consolidated in present times in Argentina, with the participation of a large number of women coming from the social movements presented here. The members of these movements articulate their stands with feminists and, from their own needs and interests, posit their priorities, which may or may not coincide with feminist claims.

One way of grasping the multiplicity of meanings present in Argentinean women's movements is to follow the milestones of the Encuentros, held once a year in a province chosen and run by an ad hoc committee. These yearly meetings started in 1986 at the initiative of a group of Argentinean feminists who had taken part in Nairobi's Third International Conference on Women, called by the United Nations in 1985. Argentina's national Encuentros are attended by women, whether feminists or not, from both popular and middle-class sectors. The Encuentros are autonomous, self-promoted, pluralistic, massive, uninstitutionalized, and critical of the establishment (opposing structural adjustment programs, corruption, and the foreign debt, among other issues). This is a space for women to ponder, debate, discuss, and establish networks related to a wide range of demands regarding contraception, abortion, health, education, life standards, unemployment, and the consequences of structural adjustment. While two thousand women were present at the first Encuentro, attendance has steadily increased to reach more than twenty thousand participants each in the latest Encuentro held at Mendoza (2004), Mar del Plata (2005), Jujuy (2006), Córdoba (2007), and Neuquén (2008).

Women from the newly founded unemployed workers' organizations started participating in the Encuentros in 1997, along with women from various provinces who told about the hardships they were going through. Women from other organizations created during the second round of protests also started attending. At the same time, they started to draw attention from the more conservative sectors.

It is no surprise if the 1997 meeting held in San Juan, a province with powerful traditional forces, grabbed the Catholic Church's attention to the extent that it called a parallel meeting to spell out its standpoint concerning such matters as sexuality, contraception, abortion, the family, education, and the preservation and redefinition of women's traditional roles. The Catholic Church enlisted the participation of female parishioners who were especially trained for the event. In the 2001 Encuentro, held in the La Plata, the capital of the Buenos Aires province, outside sectors exercised their pressure before the Encuentro even took place. Political parties on the extreme left tried to interfere with the collective by promoting the idea that feminism had no connection with the current social crisis. Moreover, they argued that a debate over gender-strategic interests would only postpone or minimize the more urgent discussion of the country's extensive social problems.[15]

At subsequent Encuentros, the consolidation of new expressions of women's activism was shown through the presence of picket women, female workers in ERAs, and aboriginal and peasant women. They all brought new struggles and protagonism into the picture; "new facts and points of view were voiced, and even slogans were rewritten, like the one that went: 'Let's make a socialist country, but also a picket and feminist country'" (Dauness 2002, 1). Rights related to reproductive health held center stage. Just like on other occasions, the Madres de Plaza de Mayo were there. The use of green headscarves to indicate a prochoice position was inspired by the Mothers' white scarves.

According to one of the organizers of the Rosario Encuentro in 2003, the event stood out for the increase in popular women's participation, as compared to Encuentros prior to 1997. While these had been attended by women from popular sectors, a majority came from the middle classes: " the organizations that emerged in the last few years offered new experiences to women who, until then, had been only mothers and wives" (RIMA 2003, 1).

The Mendoza Encuentro in 2004 was attended by more than fifteen thousand women, whereas the demonstration gathered twenty thousand. There was a strong presence of women coming from rural and urban areas and from poor neighborhoods, unemployed women, feminists, lesbians, and women fighting impunity. Workshops dealing with employment, small businesses, emergency contraception, strategies to legalize abortion, and ways to fight violence against women were the best attended. Regarding labor rights, demands were made for equal conditions for men and women, an earlier retirement age for women, and adoption of the corresponding legislation all over the country. There were also claims for active policies aimed at the protection of women against violence at home and at work. The workshops on strategies for the decriminalization of abortion gave rise to the National Campaign for the Right to Abortion, the first one with federal scope in Argentina. The idea was to create awareness of and spread information about the issue, respecting the strategies implemented by women's organizations in every city and province. Women attending the latest Encuentros in Mar del Plata (2005), Jujuy (2006), Córdoba (2007), and Neuquén (2008) have intensified the demands. Legal abortion and suitable measures to duly act on violence against women are still a priority.

Final Remarks

This short overview focuses on tracing the multiple relations between social movements, women's movements, and the state, with the purpose of shedding light on the new trends that point to changes in the way they relate to each other, without overlooking the coexistence of old practices that correspond to more traditional notions about neighborhood work, patronage systems, and the naturalization of gender domination. The social movements I have described—both those that I discussed in more detail and others that have been emerging since the mid-nineties— brought to the public agenda new issues and practices, stemming from a revisiting of the actors' needs and demands. The movements contributed to changes in the hegemonic social and political discourse because these social actors found a way to express their needs in the public sphere and to claim satisfaction from the state. Their discourse, understood within the framework of a politics of needs interpretation (Fraser 1991), criticizes recourse to the market as the only possible regulator. Although their practices are not free of contradictions, the movements developed a language of needs, translated into the demands for rights, and politicized the market just as they politicized private family life and turned women's needs into actual policies toward gender equity (Di Marco and Palomino 2003).

The new discourses of rights and citizenship explore and include—though in a necessarily conflictive fashion—fundamental rights, a handful of women's rights, the recognition of difference, and the construction of interdependence between actors and organizations, all of which contribute to positing politics from a different perspective. Pluralist democracy is grounded on that very same conflictive process. Participation in the public sphere does not presuppose that social inequality has been solved beforehand. Still, it is in the public sphere where new meanings are agreed on and where subordination may be confronted, encouraging interpretations that oppose the hegemonic view of the identities, interests, and needs of every subaltern group (Fraser 1997, 116).

The process gathered unprecedented momentum on December 19 and 20, 2001, when Argentina burst in search of new social and political relations, new collective subjects, and new citizenships by rejecting the state of siege and chanting "They all must go" (Que se vayan todos). Analysis of the representational crisis and the motto reveal that the latter may have been signaling both a request for politicians to resign their leadership and the need to prevent these leaders from invading a real and symbolic space in which society was trying to resolve its problems (De Ípola 2004). Another interpretation considers that the roots of new citizenship practices are to be found in the crisis of representative democracy, as well as in democratic expectations of a different type of representation and in the legacy of the human rights movement, "which created the conditions for symbolically elaborating a critique of all discretionary forms of the exercise of political authority" (Torre 2004, 76).

In neighborhood assemblies, men and women took into their own hands the redefinition of the very concepts of citizenship, democracy, and collective interests. In the unemployed workers' movements, men and women basically demanded the right to work and women added the claim for a life free of violence. The workers in ERAs defied capitalist labor relations, organizing themselves without bosses. Women workers have an important leadership role in these businesses. Therefore, these movements multiplied the spaces in which "relations of power are open to democratic contestation" (Mouffe 1999, 17).

The politicization of society and culture is about the transformation of unequal relations and about a new culture of rights in both the private and the public spheres, redefining and broadening relations with the state (Escobar and Alvarez 1992). When the movements imposed new interests on the public agenda, they opened the possibility of exploring ways to strengthen citizenship beyond the rhetoric exploited by government and political parties alike. One of the confluences among movements' demands resulted in the emergence of a popular feminism that articulates various struggles aimed at extending women's rights and at the consolidation of a pluralist democracy.

ACKNOWLEDGMENTS

Translated by Marta Merajver Castillo.

NOTES

1. For an array of literature about women's movements in Latin America, see for example Feijóo (1998, 2000); Feijóo and Gogna (1985); Jelin (1985, 1987b, 1990); and, more recently, Feijóo's revision (2000) of contemporary feminism in Argentina.

2. In 2002, 57.5 percent of the population had become poor and 27.5 percent were paupers. In the seventies Argentina had displayed social indicators resembling those of European countries (IDESA 2007). For more on the socioeconomic conditions in Argentina during this period, see Di Marco (2006a).

3. In 1993 the inhabitants of the capital city in the province of Santiago del Estero held Santiagazo. As a protest against fiscal adjustment, demonstrators set fire to the seat of the provincial government and attacked other state offices and private homes of legislators and politicians.

4. By "Madres de Plaza de Mayo" I mean both the association known by that name and Línea Fundadora, a group of mothers who constituted an independent movement in 1986.

5. The military government sought to discredit the Mothers by calling them "locas de la plaza" (crazy women in the square), as well as to destroy the movement. In fact, members Azucena Villaflor de Deventi, Esther Ballestrino de Careaga, and María Ponce del Bianco were abducted in December 1977, tortured, and thrown alive into the sea. Later on, their bodies appeared on the Atlantic coast.

6. In the eighties and the early nineties a set of laws was passed aimed at the democratization of families (Law of Joint Custody and Law of Civil Marriage) and of women's political representation (Law of the Minimal Quota of Women's Participation). In the second half of the nineties, the Egalitarian Treatment of Public Officials and the Plan for Equal Job Opportunities were decreed. The Programa Nacional de Salud Sexual y Procreación Responsable (National Program for Sexual Health and Responsible Procreation) was created in 2002, and the National Congress endowed the Convención Interamericana para Prevenir, Sancionar, y Erradicar la Violencia contra la Mujer (Inter-American Convention for the Prevention, Sanctioning, and Eradication of Violence against Women) in 2004.

7. Information about these three movements is based on Di Marco and Palomino (2004a, 2004b), Di Marco and Moro (2004), and Di Marco and Palomino (2003). Parts of this text have been published in Di Marco (2006b).

8. In April 2002 the national government implemented a national subsidy program called Plan Jefes y Jefas de Hogar Desocupados. This plan is granted to unemployed men and women from poor households that have disabled family members, children under eighteen, or pregnant women. In exchange, beneficiaries were expected to devote four hours a day to work at community and training activities, finish high school, learn a trade, or find formal employment. In 2002 two million people were subsidized. The unemployed workers' movement received about 10 percent of this money.

9. Assemblies were held in Buenos Aires, Greater Buenos Aires, La Plata, Mar del Plata, Rosario, Santa Fe, Córdoba, and some smaller cities. We counted about 150 in early 2002. By the end of the year, their momentum had dwindled, as they started intense internal work about their political differences and participation decreased. At present very few assemblies are still active: one example is the environmental assemblies organized by neighbors from different cities, specifically the city of Gualeguaychu, regarding the serious environmental conflicts Argentina has with Uruguay, because of Uruguay's unilateral decision to permit the construction of a Finnish mill on the shore of the shared Río Uruguay. From the opposite side of the political spectrum, roadblocks and *cacelorazos* (protests by banging pots, pans, and other utensils) similar to those used against President Salvador Allende in Chile in 1974, were used in March 2008 by protesters reacting to restrictions in the reimbursement of income from the external trading of their products, especially soy.

10. Brukman's textile factory was taken over by female workers on December 18, 2001, when the owners left without paying them. The following day, when the state of siege was established some of the workers were afraid: "We were the first to burst; then the country burst . . . and I felt much more frightened, sort of defeated. . . . We burst all right, but now that the country burst . . . Who's going to pay attention to us? Who's going to care about a little factory?" (Di Marco and Moro 2004a, 113).

11. Studies from the last two years claim that, at present, there are more than 130 ERAs, with about eight thousand to ten thousand workers. A total of 75 percent are cooperatives and most of them deal with manufacturing (Fajn 2003; *Sin patrón* 2004; Programa Facultad Abierta 2005).

12. In Plaza de Mayo, feminists handed out flyers stating, "We are struggling to achieve such economic, social, political, cultural, and sexual changes as will enable justice, solidarity, equality, liberty, respect for differences, a respectful use of natural resources, and a fair, equitable distribution of wealth, for a world free of violence, exploitation, and oppression" (D'Atri 2004, 2).

13. The Asamblea por el Derecho al Aborto (Assembly for the Right to Abortion) was composed by the Comisión por el Derecho al Aborto (Commission for the Right to Abortion), the Foro por los Derechos Reproductivos (Forum for Reproductive Rights), the Asociación Pan y Rosas (Bread and Roses Association), the Asociación para la Lucha en Favor de la Identidad Travesti (Association for the Struggle in Favor of Transvestite Identity), Asociación de Trabajo y Estudio de la Mujer (Women's Association for Work and Study), Coordinadora de Unidad Barrial (Coordinating Body for Neighborhood Unity), Secretariado de Género del Congreso de Trabajadores Argentinos (Gender Secretariat of the Congress of Argentinean Workers), female members of the Partido Obrero (Workers' Party), along with a group of young anarchists,

young members of student centers, the groups of left-wing women, independent women, and assembly members.

14. President Nestor Kirchner adopted, as a state policy, the condemnation of human rights violations perpetrated during the last military dictatorship (1976–1983) and fostered a policy of memory, meant to ensure the atrocities of the past are not forgotten. The policies addressed at social protests consist of the systematic isolation of protesters and the prevention of violent deaths of militants.

15. These pressures were contested by the ad hoc group Feministas en el Encuentro (Feminists at the Encuentro).

REFERENCES

Alvarez, Sonia. 1990. *Engendering democracy in Brazil: Women's movements in transition politics.* Princeton, NJ: Princeton University Press.

———. 1998. El estado del movimiento y el movimiento en el estado. Paper presented at the international seminar Experiencias de Investigación desde una Perspectiva de Género. Programa de Estudios de Género, Mujer y Desarrollo, Universidad Nacional de Colombia, Santa Fé de Bogotá, Colombia, May 6–9.

———. 1999. Advocating feminism: The Latin American feminist NGO "boom." *International Feminist Journal of Politics* 1 (2): 181–209.

Alvarez, Sonia, Evelina Dagnino, and Arturo Escobar, eds. 1998. *Cultures of politics/politics of cultures: Revisioning Latin American social movements.* Boulder, CO: Westview.

Arendt, Hannah. 1993. *La condición humana.* Buenos Aires: Paidos.

Cohen, Jean L. 1985. Strategy or identity: New theoretical paradigms and contemporary social movements. *Social Research* 52 (4): 663–716.

D'Atri, Andrea. 2004. Obreras, movimiento de mujeres y movimiento feministas: Dos años de lucha y solidaridad con Brukman. www.rimaweb.com.ar/feminismos/andrea_datri _obreras2.html (accessed July 2, 2005).

Dauness, Liliana. 2002. Encuentro de Mujeres en Salta. Red Informativa de Mujeres de Argentina (RIMA). August 25. www.rimaweb.com.ar/encuentros/nac_salta_daunes.html.

De Ípola, Emilio. 2004. Política y sociedad: ¿Escisión o convergencia? In *Reflexiones sobre los movimientos sociales en Argentina,* comp. Graciela Di Marco and Héctor Palomino, 55–72. Buenos Aires: Baudino / UNSAM.

Dietz, Mary. 1985. Citizenship with a feminist face: The problem with maternal thinking. *Political Theory* 13 (1): 19–37.

Di Marco, Graciela. 1996. Ciudadanía femenina. In *Relaciones de género y exclusión en la Argentina de los '90s: ¿El orden del desorden o el desorden del orden?* 204–213. Buenos Aires: ADEUEM / Espacio.

———. 1997a. Feministas en los gobiernos: ¿Un espacio para ampliar la ciudadanía femenina? Paper presented at the preliminary conference on Female Citizenship, Twentieth International Congress of the Latin American Studies Association, Guadalajara, Mexico, April 17–19.

———. 1997b. Las mujeres y la política en los '90s. In *Madres y democratización de las familias en la Argentina contemporánea,* ed. Beatriz Schmukler and Graciela Di Marco, 127–150. Buenos Aires: Biblos.

———. 2001. La constitución de nuevas identidades en los procesos de formación de las políticas públicas. Paper presented at the Twenty-third International Congress of the Latin American Studies Association, Washington, DC. September 6–8.

———. 2006a. Relaciones de género en los movimientos sociales. *La Aljaba* 3:15–36. Edición de las Universidades de Luján, La Pampa y Comahue, Argentina.

————. 2006b. Social justice and gender rights. Presented at the workshop proceedings at the UNESCO International Forum on Social Science. Global Issues and Dynamics, Women's Human Rights, Research/Policy Nexus, Social and Human Sciences, Human Rights, and Gender and Equality Development. Buenos Aires, February.

Di Marco, Graciela, and Javier Moro. 2004a. Experiencias de economía solidaria frente a la crisis argentina: Estudio desde una dimensión de género. In *Políticas de empleo para superar la pobreza*, ed. María Elena Valenzuela, 111–160. Santiago: Andros.

Di Marco, Graciela, and Héctor Palomino. 2003. *Movimientos sociales en la Argentina: Asambleas; La politización de la sociedad civil.* Buenos Aires: Baudino / UNSAM.

————. 2004a. *Construyendo sociedad y política: Los proyectos del movimiento social en acción.* Buenos Aires: Baudino / UNSAM.

————, eds. 2004b. *Reflexiones sobre los movimientos sociales en la Argentina.* Buenos Aires: Baudino / UNSAM.

Escobar, Arturo, and Sonia Alvarez, eds. 1992. *The making of social movements in Latin America: Identity, strategy and democracy.* Boulder, CO: Westview.

Fajn, Gabriel, coord. 2003. *Fábricas y empresas recuperadas: Protesta social, autogestión y rupturas en la subjetividad.* Buenos Aires: Centro Cultural de la Cooperación, Ediciones del IMFC.

Feijoó, María del Carmen. 1998. Democratic participation and women in Argentina. In *Women and democracy: Latin America and central and eastern Europe*, ed. Jane Jaquette and Sharon Wolchick. Baltimore: Johns Hopkins University Press.

————. 2000. El feminismo contemporáneo en la Argentina: Encuentros y desencuentros en un escenario turbulento. In *Cuadernos de investigación social.* Research report. Lima: Departamento de Ciencias Sociales, Pontificia Universidad Católica del Perú.

Feijoó, María del Carmen, and Mónica Gogna. 1985. *Las mujeres en la transición a la democracia.* Vol. 1 of *Los nuevos movimientos sociales*, ed. Elizabeth Jelin. Buenos Aires: CEAL.

Fraser, Nancy. 1991. La lucha por las necesidades: Esbozo de una teoría crítica socialista-feminista de la cultura política del capitalismo tardío. *Debate Feminista* 3:3–41.

————. 1997. *Iustitia interrupta: Reflexiones críticas desde la posición "postsocialista."* Caracas: Siglo del Hombre.

Giarracca, Norma. 2001. *La protesta social en la Argentina: Transformaciones económicas y crisis social en el interior del país.* Buenos Aires: Alianza.

Grüner, Eduardo. 2004. Subjetividad y política. In *Reflexiones sobre los movimientos sociales en Argentina*, ed. Graciela Di Marco and Héctor Palomino, 129–140. Buenos Aires: Baudino UNSAM.

Gutiérrez, M. Alicia. 1998. Mujeres autoconvocadas para decidir en libertad (MADEL): La experiencia reciente del movimiento de mujeres. *Instituto de Pensamiento Socialista Karl Marx.* www.ifcs.ufrj.br/jornadas/papers/09st0404.rtf.

IDESA. 2007. La distribución del ingreso en el 2006. www.idesa.org/v2/noticias.asp?idnoticia =142.

Jaquette, Jane, ed. 1994. *The women's movement in Latin America*, 2nd ed. Boulder, CO: Westview.

Jelin, Elizabeth. 1985. *Los nuevos movimientos sociales.* 2 vols. Buenos Aires: CEAL.

————, ed. 1987a. *Ciudadanía e identidad: Las mujeres en los movimientos sociales en América Latina.* Ginebra: UNRISD.

————. 1987b. *Movimientos sociales y democracia emergente.* 2 vols. Buenos Aires: CEAL.

————, ed. 1990. *Women and social change in Latin America.* London: Zed Books.

Lebon, Nathalie 1997. Volunteer and professionalized activism in the São Paulo women's movement. Paper presented at the Twentieth International Congress of the Latin American Studies Association, Guadalajara, Mexico, April 17–19. www.pitt.edu/~lasa.

Molyneux, Maxine. 2000. *Women's movements in international perspective: Latin American and beyond*. Basingstoke, England: Palgrave.

Mouffe, Chantal. 1992. Feminism, citizenship and radical democratic politics. In *Feminists theorize the political*, ed. Judith Butler and Joan W. Scott, 369–384. New York: Routledge.

————. 1999. *El retorno de lo político: Comunidad, ciudadanía, pluralismo, democracia radical*. Buenos Aires: Paidós.

Los panuelos verdes. 2005. www.rimaweb.com.ar/aborto/index.html.

Programa Facultad Abierta. 2005. *Las empresas recuperadas en la Argentina*. Informe del segundo relevamiento del Programa Facultad Abierta. Buenos Aires: SEUBE / Facultad de Filosofía y Letras, UBA.

RIMA. 2003. *El Ciudadano* (Rosario, Argentina). August 18. http://www.rimaweb.com.ar.

Schmukler, Beatriz, and Graciela Di Marco. 1997. *Madres y democratización de las familias en la Argentina contemporánea*. Buenos Aires: Biblos.

Schuster, Federico, and Sebastián Pereyra. 2001. La protesta social en la Argentina democrática. Balance y perspectiva de una forma de acción política. In *La protesta social en la Argentina: Transformaciones económicas y crisis social en el interior del país*, ed. Norma Giarracca, 85–97. Buenos Aires: Alianza.

Scribano, Adrián, and Federico Schuster. 2001. Protesta social en la Argentina de 2001: Entre la normalidad y la ruptura. *Observatorio Social de América Latina, Consejo Latinoamericano de Ciencias Sociales* 2 (5): 14–22.

Sin patrón: Fábricas y empresas recuperadas por sus trabajadores; Una historia, una guía. 2004. Buenos Aires: Lavaca.

Torre, Juan Carlos. 2004. La movilización de las expectativas democráticas. In *Reflexiones sobre los movimientos sociales en Argentina*, comp. Graciela Di Marco and Héctor Palomino, 73–78. Buenos Aires: Baudino / UNSAM.

Vargas Valente, Virginia. 2002. Los feminismos latinoamericanos en su tránsito al nuevo milenio (una lectura político personal). In *Estudios y otras prácticas intelectuales latinoamericanas en cultura y poder*, comp. Daniel Mato. Caracas: CLACSO / CEAP / FACES / Universidad Central de Venezuela.

Vasallo, Marta. 2001. Mis impresiones del Encuentro de Mujeres. Especial para RIMA. www.rimaweb.com.ar/encuentros/mvasallo_encuentro01.html.

————. 2002. Existir contra el aniquilamiento. *Le Monde Diplomatique* 38 (August): 15–18.

10

Advocating for Citizenship and Social Justice

BLACK WOMEN ACTIVISTS IN BRAZIL

KIA LILLY CALDWELL

This essay examines the emergence of the black women's movement in Brazil since the early 1980s and focuses on the ways in which activists in the movement have sought to redefine and expand norms of democracy and citizenship in the country. Black women's political activism during Brazil's most recent transition to democracy has played a key role in calling for new conceptualizations of equality and justice that seek to redress long-standing processes of social, economic, and political exclusion. By calling attention to the intersectional nature of racial, gender, and class dynamics, black women activists have challenged both progressive social movements and the state to address the specificities of black women's life experiences and social identities. Black women activists have been instrumental in developing a gendered critique of Brazilian racism that highlights the ways in which racist discourses and practices are implicated in the perpetuation of contemporary social inequalities, as well as their role in preventing the full achievement of democracy and citizenship for all sectors of Brazilian society.

Formation of the Black Women's Movement

In recent decades black women have played a crucial role in the development of Brazil's black movement, women's movement, and leftist political parties, most notably the Partido dos Trabalhadores (Workers' Party). The women's movement and black movement both emerged during the 1970s as the country gradually returned to democratic rule. The military regime that ruled Brazil from 1964 to 1985 initiated a process of political liberalization (*abertura*) that allowed for greater political involvement by various sectors of civil society. Moreover, the process of political opening that began in 1974 also generated increased demands and contestation from marginalized social groups and led to the establishment of a number of significant social movements, including the women's movement and black movement.

Although black women were involved with the contemporary Brazilian women's movement from its inception in the 1970s, racial divisions within the movement caused a number of black women to feel alienated from it. The Manifesto of Black Women, which was presented during the Congresso de Mulheres Brasileiras (Congress of Brazilian Women) in July 1975, marked the first formal recognition of racial divisions within the women's movement. The manifesto critiqued the notion of universal female identity by highlighting the ways in which black women's experiences of racial, gender, and economic subordination were rooted in the colonial slave era. It also underscored the ways in which race and gender have interacted to produce black women's long-standing sexual exploitation (Nascimento 1978).

Early black feminist Lélia Gonzalez followed this line of critique in an essay about the 1979 Encontro Nacional de Mulheres (National Encontro of Women). In her written reflections, Gonzalez notes the ways in which activists in the women's movement denied the significance of race and its impact in black women's lives (1982). Gonzalez's essay highlights the existence of racial divisions in the Brazilian women's movement and charges that white women's complicity in racial domination made them reluctant to acknowledge racism as a problem. Her criticisms are particularly unique and path-breaking because they point to the racial privilege of white women by suggesting that they benefited from hegemonic discourses on race relations in the country, most notably the claims that Brazil was a racial democracy.

Gonzalez further criticizes activists in the women's movement for being oblivious to the sexual exploitation experienced by black women, particularly those who work in domestic service, and called for analysis of the interrelationship between race, gender, and class. As Gonzalez notes, "The exploitation of the black woman as a sexual object is something that is still very far from what the Brazilian feminist movements, generally led by middle-class white women, think or speak about. For example, 'senhoras' still exist who seek to employ pretty young black women to work in their homes as domestics, but the principal objective is to have their sons be 'initiated' sexually with them" (1982, 99–100). Gonzalez's statements provide a powerful critique of social practices that made black women vulnerable to ongoing sexual and economic exploitation. This critique also highlights white women's complicity in the subordination of black women.

While the racial question created divisions in the Brazilian women's movement during the 1970s, the relationship between race and gender was also inadequately addressed in many black movement organizations that began to be formed during the mid-1970s.[1] The founding of the Movimento Negro Unificado (MNU; United Black Movement) and a host of other organizations in major cities throughout Brazil during the mid- and late 1970s signaled the emergence of new political responses to the country's racial predicament. However, black women who participated in the black movement during this time often found that their concerns about gender and sexism were not adequately addressed. Although black women played an active role in establishing many of the black movement organizations that were formed during this period and were vital to their long-term survival, they encountered sexism within many groups and were often relegated to support rather than leadership roles. The observations of Luiza Bairros, a former MNU leader in the state of Bahia and national MNU coordinator, are useful in understanding some of the possible reasons why black women were not viewed as equals in black movement organizations. According to Bairros, black women's subordination in the MNU, in particular, can be attributed to the fact that their male colleagues saw them as competitors and regarded it as a space in which their authority should go unchallenged (Ribeiro 1995). Bairros's commentary on gender politics in the black movement highlights the prevalence of sexism and patriarchal attitudes among male activists.[2]

Due to their marginal status vis-à-vis both white women and black men, black women began to organize separate groups within women's organizations and black movement organizations during the 1980s. However, their attempts to focus on their specific needs and interests were often met with resistance and led to increasing tensions within both movements. When I interviewed her in 1997, Fátima Oliveira, a longtime activist in the women's movement, black movement, and black women's movement, commented on the initial difficulty that activists in the women's movement and black movement had in understanding the *"questão da mulher negra"* (the question of the black woman) (interview, August 6, 1997, Belo Horizonte). Oliveira noted that black women who were active in the women's movement during the 1980s often began to have problems when they raised the issue of race. A similar outcome was common when black women raised gender issues within the black movement.

Oliveira's reflections highlight how black women's attempts to address racial issues within the women's movement and gender issues in the black movement were viewed as problematic by activists in both movements. Most black women who have participated in the black women's movement have also been involved with militancy in at least two of the following areas: the black movement, the women's movement, political parties, and labor unions. Furthermore, in their attempts to call attention to the relationship between race and gender, black women have argued that their experiences could not be adequately addressed by focusing on only one form of oppression.

Activists in the black women's movement have long asserted the importance of recognizing the specificities of black women's experiences and the ways in which they differ from those of black men and white women. As Sueli Carneiro, a longtime activist in the black women's movement and director of Geledés, has noted,

> The marriage of racism and sexism against black women and the lack of solidarity among some feminists and black activists has meant that the victories of the women's movement end up benefiting white women and the victories of the black movement tend to benefit black men. This has imposed a double militancy on black women: from their own perspective, they must take up the causes of both the black movement and the women's movement. But for double militancy to be meaningful, they need their own independent organization of black women in order to constitute themselves as a political force capable of dialogue on an equal basis with other social movements and social institutions. The construction of the black woman as a new social actor has called for creativity in demarcating a political identity in dialogue with women's issues and black issues. (1999, 224)[3]

The increasing difficulty of having their specific needs and interests be acknowledged by activists in the women's movement and black movement caused black women to form autonomous groups in the early 1980s. One of the first black women's organizations, Nzinga / Coletivo de Mulheres Negras (Nzinga / Collective of Black Women), was founded in Rio de Janeiro in 1983. The Coletivo de Mulheres Negras de São Paulo (Black Women's Collective of São Paulo) was formed in early 1984 in response to black women's exclusion from the newly formed Conselho Estadual da Condição Feminina (State Council on the Feminine Condition). It is important to note that in their attempts to achieve representation on the State Council on the Feminine Condition, members of the collective opened a dialogue with the Brazilian state before either black male activists or the larger black movement did (Roland 2000). The collective also played a key role in forging ties among black women activists by organizing the Primeiro Encontro Estadual de Mulheres Negras (First State Encontro of Black Women) in 1984.

During the mid- and late 1980s, black women's collectives and groups were formed throughout Brazil. Organizations such as the Coletivo de Mulheres Negras da Baixada Santista / Casa de Cultura da Mulher Negra (Black Women's Collective of Baixada Santista / House of Black Women's Culture), Grupo de Mulheres Negras Mãe Andresa (Mãe Andresa Black Women's Group), Centro de Mulheres de Favela e Periferia (Center for Women from the Shantytown and Periphery), Grupo de Mulheres Negras de Espirito Santo (Black Women's Group of Espirito Santo), Maria Mulher (Maria Woman), Coletivo de Mulheres Negras de Belo Horizonte / N'zinga (Black Women's Collective of Belo Horizonte / N'zinga), Geledés, and Comissão de Mulheres Negras de Campinas (Commission of Black Women of Campinas) were formed between 1986 and 1989 in the states of Minas Gerais, São Paulo, Maranhão, Espirito Santo, Rio de Janeiro, and Rio Grande do Sul (Roland 2000).

The Primeiro Encontro Nacional de Mulheres Negras was held in 1988, the centennial anniversary of Brazilian abolition, with subsequent meetings occurring in 1991, 1994, 1997, and 2000. In the bulletin for the first Encontro, activists in the black women's movement expressed a collective desire to shape Brazil's future:

> All of us, black women, must understand that we are fundamental in this process of transformation, revindicating (*reivindicando*) a just and equal society where all forms of discrimination are eradicated. . . . We would like to clarify that it is not our intention to cause a division in the social movements, as some sectors accuse. Our objective is that we, black women, begin to create our own references, that we stop seeing the world through the lens of men, black or white, or that of white women. The significance of the expression "create our own references" is that we want to be side-by-side with our female and male companions in the struggle for social transformation. We want to become spokespersons for our own ideas and needs. In sum, we want a position of equality in this struggle. (quoted in Ribeiro 1995, 450)

Black women's organizations continued to be formed throughout Brazil during the 1990s.[4] Black women's organizations such as the Coletivo de Mulheres Negras do Distrito Federal (Black Women's Collective of the Federal District), Coletivo de Mulheres Negras de Salvador (Black Women's Collective of Salvador), Criola

(Creole/Black Woman), Associação Cultural de Mulheres Negras (Black Women's Cultural Association), Quilombolas (Female Quilombo Residents/Maroons), Eleeko-Instituto da Mulher Negra (Eleeko Black Women's Institute), Associação de Mulheres Negras Obirin Dudu (Obirin Dudu Black Women's Association), and Fala Preta! (Speak Black Woman!) were established in Brasília, as well as in the states of Bahia, Rio de Janeiro, São Paulo, and Rio Grande do Sul between 1990 and 1997 (Roland 2000).

Black women's organizations have ranged in size and type from small informal groups to larger nongovernmental organizations that have paid staff and receive funding from international donors. Black women's organizations have developed innovative programs that seek to address and ameliorate the effects of gender, racial, and class domination at the microlevel (i.e., self-esteem and personal empowerment) as well as at the macrolevel (i.e., the state, unions, political parties, and other social movements). Areas of focus in many black women's organizations range from self-esteem, personal identity, and intimate relationships, to employment, violence, and sexual and reproductive health.

Through collective organizing, activists in the black women's movement have sought to challenge black women's political invisibility and lack of adequate representation in the political sphere. In recent decades black Brazilian women have worked to develop a collective voice at the national level, as well as at the regional level, throughout the Caribbean and Latin America. Since the late 1980s black women's collective organizing at the national level has been instrumental in the development of policy proposals that lie at the intersection of race, gender, and class.

In addition to the Encontros, activists have also participated in regional meetings of the Rede de Mulheres Afrolatinoamericanas e Afrocaribenhas/Red de Mujeres Afrolatinoamericanas e Afrocaribeñas (Network of Afro-Latin American and Afro-Caribbean Women) in 1992 and 1995. These meetings provided activists in the black women's movement with an opportunity to identify common areas of concern and struggle. Such shared moments of dialogue and reflection also enabled activists in the black women's movement to define and consolidate a collective political voice.

The Paradoxes of Black Feminism in a "Racial Democracy"

In many ways, Afro-Brazilian women's experiences vis-à-vis the women's movement and black movement have paralleled the experiences of women of African descent in other countries, most notably the United States and England, whose concerns have often been marginalized by white feminists and black male antiracist activists (Carby 1983; Collins 2000; Crenshaw 1995; hooks 1984). Like Afro-descendant women in other national contexts, Afro-Brazilian women have struggled to bring an intersectional perspective to both feminist and antiracist politics. In doing so, they have had to point out the importance of addressing questions of race, gender, class, and sexuality simultaneously to achieve social justice and reorder social relations in Brazil.

While it is important to highlight the similarities in black women's activism in diverse national contexts, it is also essential to underscore the specificities of the

Brazilian situation, particularly with respect to dominant discourses on race and nation and to black women's continuing struggle to achieve full citizenship and democracy in the country. In many ways, activists in Brazil's black women's movement have had the difficult task of calling attention to racial inequalities and racialized forms of discrimination in a society that has largely denied the role of racism in shaping social, economic, and political structures. The Brazilian ideology of racial democracy has also played a fundamental role in shaping interaction between white and black women and has provided white women with an excuse for not addressing their racial privilege or their complicity in racial domination.[5]

Critical examination of Brazilian discourses on race and nation are essential to understanding the cultural and social particularities of racism in the country. The writings of Brazilian sociologist Gilberto Freyre played a central role in the consolidation of racial democracy as the dominant view of race and national identity in the country. Since the 1933 publication of his *Casa Grande e Senzala*, Brazil has been represented as a "racial democracy" in official and popular discourses, both domestically and internationally. Brazilian notions of racial democracy have been based primarily on the lack of legalized forms of racial segregation and racial discrimination in the country. Furthermore, the country's high incidence of racial miscegenation (*mestiçagem*), in the past as well as the present, has also been cited as proof of racial harmony.

In recent decades an increasing number of scholars and black activists have critiqued the Brazilian variant of racial democracy as being a dominant ideology, as well as a myth, that denies the existence of racism and racial discrimination in the country. In an important critique of the ideology of racial democracy, black Brazilian feminist scholar and activist Lélia Gonzalez argues,

> The notion of racial democracy, developed by Gilberto Freyre in the 1930s, has constituted the public and official view of this [black] identity. Accordingly, blacks are citizens like any other citizen and, as such, are not subject either to prejudice or discrimination. The Brazilian images of carnival and soccer are widely used (especially abroad) as "concrete proof" of Brazilian "racial harmony." What does predominate in Brazil's "racial democracy" is *the prejudice of not being prejudiced*." (1995, 313)

Gonzalez's comments link dominant discourses on Brazilian national identity to questions of citizenship and highlight the ways in which the ideology of racial democracy has served to obscure racialized processes of social and political exclusion. Her critique of racial democracy also centers on the ways in which individual and collective self-denial of racist beliefs and practices perpetuates racial inequalities in the country.

Gender, Race, and Public Policy

In recent decades black Brazilian women have been involved in policy advocacy at both national and international levels. During the early 1990s activists in the black women's movement began to call for social movement organizations, policy makers, unions, and political parties to acknowledge the relationship among gender, race, and class in the development of policies and initiatives to address social inequality and discrimination. These efforts exemplify activists' attempts to promote macrolevel social transformation that centers on the needs and experiences of black women.

Activists in the black women's movement participated in the 1994 United Nations International Conference on Population and Development, using the conference as a springboard to develop a self-defined agenda for reproductive rights. In preparation for the conference, a Seminário Nacional de Políticas e Direitos Reprodutivos das Mulheres Negras (National Seminar on Black Women's Reproductive Rights and Policies) was organized by Geledés, a black women's nongovernmental organization based in São Paulo. This historic event was held in August 1993 and included participants from the black women's movement, the black movement, the women's movement, research centers, and the health sector. Discussions during the seminar resulted in the subsequent publication of the *Declaracão da Itapecerica de Serra das Mulheres Negras* (Itapecerica da Serra Declaration of Brazilian Black Women), a policy document that outlines key issues and proposals related to black women's health and reproductive rights (Geledés 1993). This unprecedented document gave voice to black women's long-silenced aspirations for reproductive autonomy and culturally competent health care.

While a number of important social issues affect black Brazilian women's lives on a daily basis, health care and reproductive rights have an especially profound impact on their well-being and survival. Black women's contemporary struggles for reproductive autonomy can be traced to colonial patterns of racial, gender, and class subordination that denied enslaved women control over their bodies and sexuality (see Giacomini 1988). In recent decades a growing number of black women health activists have called attention to the ways in which Brazil's alarmingly high rate of female sterilization reflects ongoing racial, gender, and class inequalities. Since the 1980s activists in the black women's movement have asserted that the promotion of nonreversible birth control methods, such as female sterilization, has a greater impact on impoverished women, many of whom are Afro-Brazilian. These activists have also pointed to the higher incidence of sterilization in the Brazilian northeast, a region in which Afro-Brazilians constitute the majority of the population (Roland 1999).[6]

Activists in the black women's movement have developed policy initiatives focused on health issues that disproportionately affect black women, including female sterilization, maternal mortality, sickle-cell anemia, and HIV/AIDS.[7] These policy initiatives reflect activists' commitment to ensure that black women are able to exercise full bodily integrity and reproductive autonomy. Moreover, activists have used the struggle for health, sexual, and reproductive rights as part of a broader effort to reconceptualize the relationship among gender, race, class, and citizenship.

Following their participation in the 1994 United Nations International Conference on Population and Development, activists in the black women's movement grew increasingly familiar with the policy advocacy process through their participation in the Fourth United Nations World Conference on Women, which was held in Beijing, China, in 1995.[8] As a result of black women's involvement in the preparatory process for this conference, the issue of race was included in the declaration of Brazilian women that was prepared by the Brazilian women's movement, as well as in the official document prepared by the Brazilian government. The declaration of Brazilian women stands as one of the first official acknowledgments of the impact of racism on women's experiences by members of the Brazilian women's movement. Moreover, the inclusion of race in this document demonstrates the impact that black women's collective organizing began to have on the larger women's movement in Brazil during the 1990s (Roland 2000).[9]

In recent decades the marked growth in the number of black women's organizations and black women's increasing involvement in policy advocacy have both reflected and contributed to the black women's movement's increasing clout as an autonomous political force. Although black women activists struggled to gain legitimacy in relation to the women's movement and black movement during the 1980s, by the mid-1990s the black women's movement was increasingly recognized as an important political actor. Moreover, black women's activism during the 1980s and 1990s laid the groundwork for activists in the black women's movement to play a leading role in the preparatory process for the Third United Nations World Conference against Racism, Racial Discrimination, Xenophobia, and Related Intolerance, which was held in Durban, South Africa, in 2001.

By 2000 dozens of black women's organizations existed in various states throughout Brazil. Members of these organizations highlighted the intersection of race and gender and the specificities of black women's experiences during events that were organized by black movement entities during the preparatory process for the Durban conference. By this time a number of activists in the black women's movement had become familiar with the policy advocacy process as a result of their participation in previous United Nations conferences.[10] These activists were thus poised to play a leading role in shaping the agenda for black movement organizations from Brazil during the preparatory process for the Durban conference. Black women's concerns were also given greater visibility by leading Brazilian women's organizations during the preparatory process. During 2000 and 2001 two leading national women's associations, the Articulação de Mulheres Brasileiras (AMB; Network of Brazilian Women) and the Rede Nacional Feminista de Saúde, Direitos Sexuais e Direitos Reprodutivos (RedeSaúde; Feminist Network on Health, Sexual Rights, and Reproductive Rights) produced lengthy publications focusing on black women (AMB 2001; *Jornal da RedeSaúde* 2000). These publications provide evidence of the increasing recognition of black women's issues within the larger women's movement in Brazil (Oliveira and Sant'anna 2002).

The preparatory process for the 2001 Durban conference was a signal moment in the consolidation of the black women's movement. One of the most important outcomes of the conference preparatory process was the formation of a national network of black women's organizations, the Articulação de Organizações de Mulheres Negras Brasileiras (AMNB; Network of Black Brazilian Women's

Organizations) in 2000. A national meeting of black women was held in September 2000, at which time the Executive Secretariat of the AMNB was charged with producing "a document that would gather in one place all current and relevant information and proposals for the struggle of black women as they lobby on public policy" (AMNB 2001, 7). The document *We, Brazilian Black Women: Analysis and Proposals (Nós, Mulheres Negras: Análise e Propostas)* was subsequently published and endorsed by thirty entities representing the black movement and black women's movement in the country. Versions of this document were published in Portuguese, English, and Spanish, and copies were presented to governmental and nongovernmental representatives for all of the countries participating in the Durban conference.

We, Brazilian Black Women is an important source for understanding the aspirations and objectives of activists in the black women's movement, particularly as they relate to policy development. By providing statistical evidence of black women's unfavorable status within Brazilian society, this document seeks to challenge the Brazilian government's historical silence about the discrimination experienced by black women. As Nilza Iraci, a representative from Geledés, noted in a July 2001 newspaper interview, "Whenever we go abroad, we hear that racial democracy exists and that in our country there is no racism. When we bring up the reality of black women, there is always a suspicion that we are exaggerating the facts. With this document we are showing that we are not working with a 'victimization' [mentality], but with data that reflects reality" (Almeida 2001).

We, Brazilian Black Women reflects activists' understandings of the significance of the United Nations process for the development of policy and the promotion of progressive cultural change at the national level.[11] Activists in the black women's movement hoped that their documentation of black women's status would be used to prompt the Brazilian government to align its discourse and practice, particularly with regard to racism, and to recognize the plight of black women within international arenas. *We, Brazilian Black Women* was also viewed by activists as a tool that could be used by the official delegation to the 2001 United Nations conference in Durban and by members of Brazilian civil society in their negotiations for specific public policies at the state and national level (Almeida 2001).

Following the World Conference against Racism, unprecedented changes began to take place in the development of public policies for the black population in Brazil. This policy shift began during the second term of President Fernando Henrique Cardoso (2000–2003). In a 2001 report to the Committee on the Elimination of Racial Discrimination—a body of experts that monitors implementation of the United Nations International Convention on the Elimination of All Forms of Racial Discrimination—the Cardoso administration admitted to the existence of racism in Brazil, making it the first presidential administration in the country to officially acknowledge racism in a government document (Telles 2004, 62). In December 2001 President Cardoso announced an affirmative action program in the Instituto Rio Branco, Brazil's foreign diplomacy school, which provided twenty scholarships annually for black students. On May 13, 2002, the 114th anniversary of Brazilian abolition, he signed a presidential decree that instituted a national affirmative action program in Brazilian public administration.

During his first term in office (2003–2006), President Luis Inácio Lula da Silva enacted significant measures to combat racism. One of his most notable accomplishments in this regard was the creation of the cabinet-level Secretaria Especial de Políticas de Promoção da Igualdade Racial (SEPPIR; Special Secretariat for the Promotion of Racial Equality Policies) in March 2003. The creation of SEPPIR made Brazil the first country in Latin America to have an organ within the federal government focused on challenging racism. President da Silva appointed long-time feminist and antiracist activist Matilde Ribeiro to head SEPPIR, signaling increasing recognition of black women's contributions to Brazilian politics. Nonetheless, while leading political figures such as President Cardoso and his successor President da Silva have played an important role in facilitating greater public acknowledgement of racism in Brazil, the shifts that have taken place should be viewed as the fruit of long-standing efforts by black activists, particularly black women, to call attention to racial injustice in the country.

Conclusion

Afro-Brazilian women's social location at the nexus of intersecting processes of gender, racial, and class domination provides them with a unique vantage point from which to experience, view, and critique everyday practices of discrimination and exclusion. In recent decades activists in the black women's movement have taken on the challenge of contesting dominant discourses on racial democracy and mestiçagem (racial intermixture)—which promote Brazil's image as a racially mixed and nonracist society—by drawing on their individual and collective experiences of racial, gender, and class oppression. Both the political praxis and writings of activists in the black women's movement have been instrumental in developing analyses and critiques of black women's status in Brazil and proposing alternative models of social relations that seek to achieve racial, gender, and economic justice. Nonetheless, continuing challenges to the full inclusion of black women as political actors in Brazil include institutionalized sexism and racism and long-standing practices of political exclusion and patronage.

ACKNOWLEDGMENTS

I would like to thank Karla Slocum, Bayo Holsey, Nathalie Lebon, and Elizabeth Maier for useful feedback and suggestions for this essay.

NOTES

1. The Sociedade Intercambio Brasil Africa (Society for Brazil-Africa Exchange) and the Instituto de Pesquisa das Culturas Negras (Institute for the Study of Black Cultures) were both founded in Rio de Janeiro during the mid-1970s.

2. It is useful to consider the similarities in the gender politics of the black movement in Brazil and the U.S. civil rights and black power movements. Black feminist critiques of the U.S. civil rights and black power movements include hooks (1981), Springer (2005), and Wallace (1979).

3. Like Carneiro, a number of other activists in the black women's movement have emphasized the inseparability of race, gender, and class concerns in ways that resonate with conceptualizations of intersectionality that have been developed by and about women of color in the United States (see, for example, Collins 1998 and Crenshaw 1995). U.S. legal scholar Kimberlé Crenshaw developed the concepts of political and structural intersectionality to describe women of color's subaltern positioning vis-à-vis white women and men of color. The concept of intersectionality is a useful tool for understanding the ways in which interlocking processes of race, class, and gender domination co-construct the experiences and identities of racially marginalized women.

4. See Safa (2005) for a recent discussion of autonomous organizing by indigenous and Afro-descendant women in Latin America. Caldwell (2007) also provides an in-depth discussion of the development of the black women's movement in Brazil.

5. White liberal beliefs in racial democracy in Brazil share a number of important similarities with U.S. discourses on colorblindness. See Frankenberg (1993) for a discussion of white feminists and colorblindness in the U.S. context.

6. Until recent years, activists' claims that black women are targeted for population control have been difficult to prove, given the Brazilian government's failure to include the category of race or color in most health data.

7. See Lebon (2007) and Caldwell (forthcoming) for detailed analyses of black women's health advocacy in Brazil.

8. See Alvarez (2000) for a discussion of the role of policy advocacy in Latin American women's movements.

9. Lebon (2007) examines the role of Afro-Brazilian women scholars and activists in challenging racism and sexism in Brazil.

10. Werneck (2003), of Criola, has criticized black women's relative lack of representation during United Nations conference processes prior to the World Conference against Racism, Racial Discrimination, Xenophobia, and Related Intolerance.

11. Alvarez (2000) discusses the significance of transnational advocacy networks and the United Nations conference process for Latin American feminists in terms of both gender-conscious policy development and broader cultural change.

REFERENCES

Almeida, Eliana Fonseca. 2001. Mulheres documentam o racismo no Brasil. *O Tempo*, July 4.

Alvarez, Sonia. 2000. Translating the global: Effects of transnational organizing on local feminist discourses and practices in Latin America. *Meridians* 1 (1): 29–67.

AMB. 2001. *Mulheres negras: Um retrato de discriminação racial no Brasil*. Brasilia: AMB.

AMNB. 2001. *We, Brazilian black women: Analysis and Proposals*. Report prepared for the Third UN World Conference against Racism, Racial Discrimination, Xenophobia, and Related Intolerance (English Version), Durban, South Africa, August 31–September 7.

Caldwell, Kia Lilly. 2007. *Negras in Brazil: Re-envisioning black women, citizenship, and the politics of identity*. New Brunswick, NJ: Rutgers University Press.

———. Forthcoming. Black women and the development of intersectional health policy in Brazil. In *The Intersectional Approach: Transforming women's and gender studies through race, class, and gender*, ed. Kathleen Guidroz and Michele Tracy Berger, 118–135. Chapel Hill: University of North Carolina Press.

Carby, Hazel V. 1983. White women listen! Black feminism and the boundaries of sisterhood. In *The empire strikes back*, ed. Centre for Contemporary Cultural Studies, 212–234. London: Hutchinson.

Carneiro, Sueli. 1999. Black women's identity in Brazil. In *Race in contemporary Brazil: From indifference to inequality*, ed. Rebecca Reichmann, 217–228. University Park: Pennsylvania State University Press.

Collins, Patricia Hill. 1998. *Fighting words: Black women and the search for justice*. Minneapolis: University of Minnesota Press.

———. 2000. *Black feminist thought: Knowledge, consciousness, and the politics of empowerment*. New York: Routledge.

Crenshaw, Kimberlé. 1995. Demarginalizing the intersection of race and sex: A black feminist critique of antidiscrimination doctrine, feminist theory, and antiracist politics. In *Critical race theory: The key writings that formed the movement*, ed. Kimberlé Crenshaw, Neil Gotanda, Gary Peller, and Kendall Thomas, 357–383. New York: New Press.

Frankenberg, Ruth. 1993. *White women, race matters: The social construction of whiteness*. Minneapolis: University of Minnesota Press.

Freyre, Gilberto. 1933. *Casa grande e senzala: Formação da família brasileira sob o regimen de economia patriarcal*. Rio de Janeiro: Maia and Schmidt.

Geledés. 1993. *Itapecerica da Serra Declaration of Brazilian Black Women*. English version of document resulting from the Seminário Nacional Políticas e Direitos Reprodutivos das Mulheres Negras, São Paulo, Brazil, August.

Giacomini, Sonia Maria. 1988. *Mulher e escrava*. Petrópolis, Brazil: Vozes.

Gonzalez, Lélia. 1982. A mulher negra na sociedade brasileira. In *O Lugar da Mulher*, ed. Madel T. Luz, 87–104. Rio de Janeiro: Edições Graal.

———. 1995. The black woman in Brazil. In *African presence in the Americas*, ed. Carlos Moore, Tanya R. Saunders, and Shawna Moore, 313–328. Trenton: Africa World.

hooks, bell. 1981. *Ain't I a woman: Black women and feminism*. Boston: South End.

———. 1984. *Feminist theory from margin to center*. Boston: South End.

Lebon, Nathalie. 2007. Beyond confronting the myth of racial democracy: The role of Afro-Brazilian women scholars and activists. *Latin American Perspectives* 34 (6): 52–76.

Nascimento, Abdias do. 1978. *O genocídio do negro brasileiro: Processo de um racismo mascarado*. Rio de Janeiro: Paz e Terra.

Oliveira, Guacira Cesar de, and Wânia Sant'anna. 2002. Chega de saudade, a realidade é que. . . . *Estudos Feministas* 10 (1): 199–207.

Ribeiro, Matilde. 1995. Mulheres negras brasileiras: De Bertioga a Beijing. *Revista Estudos Feministas* 3 (2): 446–457.

Roland, Edna. 1999. The soda cracker dilemma: Reproductive rights and racism in Brazil. In *Race in contemporary Brazil*, ed. Rebecca Reichmann, 195–205. University Park: Pennsylvania State University Press.

———. 2000. O movimento de mulheres negras brasileiras: Desafios e perspectivas. In *Tirando a máscara: Ensaios sobre o racismo no Brasil*, ed. Antônio Sérgio Alfredo Guimarães and Lynn Huntley, 237–256. São Paulo: Paz e Terra.

Safa, Helen. 2005. Challenging *mestizaje*: A gender perspective on indigenous and afrodescendant movements in Latin America. *Critique of Anthropology* 25:307–330.

Springer, Kimberly. 2005. *Living for the revolution: Black feminist organizations, 1968–1980*. Durham, NC: Duke University Press.

Telles, Edward. 2004. *Race in Another America: The Significance of Skin Color in Brazil*. Princeton, NJ: Princeton University Press.

Wallace, Michele. 1979. *Black macho and the myth of the superwoman*. New York: Dial.

Werneck, Jurema. 2003. O dia seguinte: A conferência mundial contra o racismo e suas consequências. *Revista Articulação de ONGs de Mulheres Negras Brasileiras*, no. 1:10–13.

11

Itineraries of Latin American Lesbian Insubordination

NORMA MOGROVEJO

When you live on the border, people walk through you;
the wind steals your voice; you're a she-burro, an ox, a
scapegoat, the harbinger of a new race, half and half—
both woman and man, and neither—a new gender.

—Gloria Anzaldúa

The lesbian movement came to Latin America in two ways: first, in the case of Mexico, Brazil, Argentina, and Puerto Rico, through the gay struggle influenced by the 1969 Stonewall Rebellion in the United States. In Chile, Peru, the Dominican Republic, and Costa Rica the lesbian struggle emerged in the second half of the 1970s, thanks to the influence of the Latin American feminist movement and its conferences. Because of similarities in their circumstances, Latin American lesbians have maintained strategic alliances—sometimes close and other times contentious—with the gay, transgendered, and bisexual movement, which I call "sexual dissidence."[1] Along the itinerary of this struggle, two kinds of demands emerge, the symbolic and the material, embodied in three currents: (1) equal rights, or the moment of universality; (2) difference and the rejection of the masculine symbolic order; and (3) shifting identities.[2]

The Early Days

Throughout Latin America, the 1960s and 1970s were particularly violent, with the outbreak of many social and political conflicts. An embryonic civil society sometimes responded by forming guerrilla groups seeking the violent overthrow of authoritarian regimes to set up better, more egalitarian, and just living conditions. Other sectors of society such as workers, women, homosexuals, young people, and shantytown dwellers responded by building social movements to achieve change. Although the idea of the revolution as a single act, a transformation of epic proportions, was very seductive, year after year its actual result, the supposed socialist utopia, was increasingly questioned. Most social movements actually set their sights on more short-term goals—sometimes material and sometimes symbolic of their relationship to those in power—and worked from inside the institutions. That is why they demanded democratic rights and respect for human rights simultaneously.

187

The Equal Rights Current

Politically motivated repression, persecution, and forced disappearances also touched gay milieus. Police raids and arbitrary arrests not only violated the right to mobility and individuality but also discouraged mobilization.[3] Together with police blackmail, the threat of a scandal-mongering press could be fatal for people's families and jobs. Thus, the gay movement included its own demands around sexuality as part of a general protest against political repression. For many activists the demand had to be equal rights with heterosexuals. Thus, the quest for recognition as subjects was accompanied by public appearances, statements to the media, leafleting, denunciations, organizing, or marches to raise their demands and analyses of antigay discrimination.[4]

For many sectors of civil society, including gays, the transition to democracy in countries just coming out from under military dictatorships and the political reforms created to strengthen burgeoning democracies were rays of hope for a change from the persecution and social exclusion they had experienced. Democracy brought with it the concept of legal equality, which lesbians and gay men considered an ethical ideal. Inspired by feminist thinking about equality—that of suffragists and existentialist feminists—they sought to win a place in history by becoming part of the logic and the values of the dominant nation-state rationality. The state had previously denied them citizenship status and now they demanded it recognize them as persons with equal rights. Celia Amorós analyzes the private/public duality and uses the demand for equality and the concept of universality as an ethical reference point to define the subject: all human beings are equal because they share rational structures and intersubjectivity. She thinks that the morality of the law lies in its validity for all rational subjects. But the issue at the time was how it was possible to make men and women equal if thousands of years of socialization had marked substantial differences between them (1994, 14, 26, 55). Equally, given open exclusion and discrimination, the question for implementing public policies would be how to make lesbians, gays, transgendered people, bisexuals, and other dissident identities be treated as equal to heterosexuals when the essentialist supposition of dissidence as abnormal still prevails.

In the first stage of the organization and consolidation of the movement's discourse through its initial public activities, it formulated its first symbolic demands for inclusion and equality. In the next stage, these demands transformed into legislative changes to protect human rights and establish social rights.

Dialogue and Visibility through Candidacies

While society pinned its hopes on democracy, activists put their money on ways of relating to the state for changing the situation. Thus, it was important to achieve recognition as political subjects. The first forms of political dialogue with the state created by the burgeoning gay movement were established through certain political parties. While these parties did express a certain sensitivity about the demands of marginalized sectors such as women and gays, they were not immune from the desire to get more votes and stay in the electoral game. The movement did manage to register some openly gay candidates, who, though then perhaps thought of as almost stridently audacious, paved the way for building a new kind of gay image, committed to solving the social problems of their time and place.

The legal struggle began in Mexico with the movement's participation in the 1982 elections. The Partido Revolucionario de los Trabajadores (PRT; Revolutionary Workers Party) offered its presidential slot to Rosario Ibarra de Piedra, a representative of the Frente Nacional contra la Represión (FNCR; National Front against Repression), one of the country's leading opposition groups, and, for the first time, seven candidacies for federal deputy were given to gay activists. The proposal was a challenge because it offered a surefire strategy for coming out of the closet politically. To support Rosario Ibarra, activists created the Comité de Lesbianas y Homosexuales en Apoyo a Rosario Ibarra (CLHARI; Lesbian and Gay Support Committee for Rosario Ibarra). Until then, the political parties had not needed to take a position about sexuality, but with the work of CLHARI, the Nineteenth Congress of the Moscow-affiliated Partido Comunista Mexicano (Mexican Communist Party) gave its support to the gay struggle, defending respect for sexual freedom (PRT 1989, 5). Although none of the gay candidates won, the results were positive because the campaign allowed the movement to send its message to a broader audience. The movement began to win a place in the public eye; marches increased in size, and cultural activities began to be widely disseminated (Mogrovejo 2000, 109).

In 1986 in Brazil, Herbert Daniel, a former 1970s guerrilla fighter who had come out while exiled in France, ran for State Congress on the Partido dos Trabalhadores (PT; Workers' Party) ticket. Even though he didn't win, the campaign was a model for future candidacies and opened up room for lesbians and gays in the PT (Green 2004, 79). It was not until 2002 that an openly lesbian deputyship was won in Mexico. Enoé Uranga ran on the feminist group Diversa's (Diverse) ticket on the slate of proportional representation candidates and was elected, thanks to the alliance between Diversa and the Partido de Convergencia Democrática (Democratic Convergence Party).

Legal Protection against Discrimination

Many forms of violence are brought to bear against sexual dissidents, from everyday practices making them invisible, mockery, jokes at their expense, all the way to fascist-style attacks aimed at exterminating the gay population. Given this, the gay community has demanded the state provide protection and set policies to discourage different kinds of discrimination.

In the 1980s and 1990s important strides were made in the Latin American struggle to achieve legal guarantees both on a constitutional level and in legislation against discrimination for reasons of sexual orientation. Between 1987 and 1988 the Brazilian gay movement organized a campaign to amend the Constitution to prevent this type of discrimination. On January 28, 1997, about 25 percent of the Constituent Congress voted in favor of the change. Nine years later, in 1997, Ecuador became the first country in Latin America and the second in the world after South Africa to include in its Constitution specific protection against discrimination based on sexual orientation.

In Mexico, as a result of the 1999 Foro de la Diversidad Sexual y los Derechos Humanos (Forum on Sexual Diversity and Human Rights), the Mexico City Federal District's criminal code was changed to prohibit discrimination against individuals because of their sexual orientation. Two years later the state of Aguascalientes followed suit. Another important achievement was the passage in 2003 of the Federal Law to Prevent and Eliminate Discrimination and the establishment of the Consejo Nacional para Prevenir la Discriminación (National Council to Prevent Discrimination). In July 2003 Uruguay outlawed homophobia nationwide.

In December 2004 Peru saw a new law come into effect (Law 28237, the Code of Constitutional Procedures) that allows individuals to get injunctions against discrimination based on sexual orientation. This makes Peru the fourth country in Latin America with this kind of protection on a national basis, after Ecuador (in its Constitution), Uruguay (in its criminal code) and Mexico (in federal legislation). As a result, on June 9, 2004, the Peruvian constitutional tribunal handed down a decision declaring Article 296 of the Military Code of Justice unconstitutional for explicitly prohibiting homosexual acts. In November of that same year, the court ruled in favor of a soldier who had been ousted from the armed forces for marrying a transsexual, ordering that he be reinstated and that the time he was out of the service be computed as part of his time served.

Decriminalization of Homosexuality

The struggle against the criminalization of homosexuality is a special chapter in the Latin American movement. Historically, in Ecuador, Chile, Nicaragua, Puerto Rico, and Jamaica, just being homosexual brought with it the threat of imprisonment. This made the decriminalization of homosexuality a priority. The movement organized letter campaigns to heads of state, congresses, courts, and international bodies; organized marches and rallies; and, above all, followed through on bills repealing repressive legislation. After more than ten years of struggle by the Ecuadorian and international gay communities, on November 25, 1997, Ecuador's constitutional tribunal unanimously found that Article 516, paragraph 1, of the criminal code, which penalized homosexual relations among adults, was unconstitutional. In Chile, the gay movement fought for seven years to throw out constitutional Article 365, which penalized homosexual relations; they won in December 1998.

The new century brought new victories. Puerto Rico's LGTB movement fought a long, hard battle to repeal Article 103, which criminalized homosexuality.[5] It celebrated the U.S. Supreme Court decision in the case of *Lawrence v. the State of Texas* that any law criminalizing sodomy between two consenting adults was unconstitutional.[6] At the same time, this questioned the state's ability to classify as a crime anything that happens between the sheets between two consenting adults and forced at least thirteen states to take crimes involving sodomy and oral sex between two adults of the same sex off the books. As a commonwealth of the United States, Puerto Rico benefited from this decision in June 2003.

Nicaragua's National Assembly passed a new criminal code on November 13, 2007, replacing the one that had been in effect for the previous 104 years. In 1992 Violeta Chamorro's government had approved Article 204, criminalizing "being," "practicing" or "propagating" sodomy, with sentences of three to five years in jail. The new criminal code, which went into effect in May 2008, does eliminate the "crime" of sodomy. However, it has not been completely to the liking of most sexual dissidents or of civil society in general because it continues to criminalize therapeutic abortion (establishing sentences of one to three years in jail for doctors and women who interrupt a pregnancy for medical reasons) and reduces sentences for money laundering.

Jamaica remains the only country in the region that continues to legally persecute dissidents to the heterosexual norm.

Social Rights

The struggle for social rights became important in this century, not only because activists sought equal rights with heterosexuals but also because the new international order brought with it a tendency to cut back social spending. However, some important policy achievements included in the human rights agenda can be cited, even if they have been slow in coming.

In Costa Rica, the Instituto Nacional de Seguridad Social (National Social Security Institute) system began to accept registering same-sex couples as beneficiaries for life and health insurance and as joint applicants for public housing mortgages. Important advances were made in Brazil, such as the Instituto Nacional do Seguro Social's (National Social Security Institute) decision to make lesbian widows and homosexual widowers eligible for pension benefits. Brazil's National Immigration Council also recognizes the legal status of the permanent same-sex life partner of a male or female Brazilian citizen as the basis for granting permanent residence to foreigners, as well as in civil partnerships formalized abroad. Seven Brazilian cities have passed ordinances guaranteeing equal rights for government employees who live as a couple with same-sex partners. The Instituto Nacional do Seguro Social in the state of Bahia considers anyone listed in the Registry of a Stable Homosexual Union, begun by the Grupo Gay da Bahia (Bahia Gay Group), as eligible for benefits. In Porto Alegre, in the state of Rio Grande do Sul, the mayor has given male and female municipal employees the right to guarantee their same-sex partners pensions.

In 2004 Colombia's constitutional court handed down a decision giving foreigners the right to permanent residency status on the basis of their being part of a homosexual couple. And on October 2, 2007, the court recognized health rights for same-sex couples, meaning that employees can now register their same-sex partners as beneficiaries for health care. Courts in Argentina and Uruguay have also handed down decisions recognizing pension rights for members of same-sex couples.

Civil Partnership Laws

In many countries, legislators have presented bills recognizing basic civil rights such as inheritance, guardianship, maintenance allowance, and permission to continue renting the home in the case of the partner's absence. However, the Catholic Church has become a political actor regulating the state's role and, using strictly moral-religious arguments, has blocked the recognition of civil rights for couples who live together.

In the case of Brazil, a woman PT deputy presented the Same-Sex Civil Partnership Bill in 1995, but thirteen years later, it continues to be used as a political football for exchanging favors among congresspersons. Members of the community had hoped that the Lula administration would push for its passage. Now, however, they say they're seeing the administration drift toward the right because of Lula's campaign alliances with the conservative sectors of the Catholic Church who are currently blocking the bill's discussion.

Despite church opposition, in May 2003, for the first time in Latin America, the local Buenos Aires legislature passed regulations stipulating how the Civil Partnership Law would work, which allows for the legal recognition of couples regardless of sex. The law gives same-sex couples the right to legalize their partnership if they can show they have lived together at least two years, that neither is married, and that at least one partner has resided in the capital for at least two years. The rights and obligations of partners under this law are the same as those of married couples, except that they are unable to inherit or adopt children. It took two years for this bill to pass, two years of intense polemics. In its wake, several Argentinean provinces passed their own civil partnership laws.

In Mexico pressure from the Catholic Church blocked a discussion of the Partido de Convergencia Democrática's (Democratic Convergence Party) Joint Living Arrangement Law, presented before Mexico City's Legislative Assembly in 2001. It was the Mexico City mayor who, in late 2003, concerned about his approval ratings, caved into church pressure and opposed the bill's being discussed, arguing the need to submit it to a public consultation. This contradicted the position the Mexican left had held since the 1980s in support of gay rights and caused a serious backlash in several sectors of the mayor's own party and the gay community itself, who argued that principles are not matters for consultation or negotiation. Finally, on November 9, 2006, after almost seven years of debate, the Joint Living Arrangement Law was passed in Mexico City after a new bill was introduced by the Partido Alternativa Social Demócrata (Social Democratic Alternative Party), supported by the Partido de la Revolución Democrática (Democratic Revolution Party), Partido de Convergencia Democrática (Democratic Convergence Party), and Partido del Trabajo (Labor Party. The bill stipulates that people living together, whether of the same or different sexes, have rights to maintenance, inheritance, and guardianship. Months later, the Coahuila state Congress passed a law called the Civil Solidarity Pact, which recognizes same-sex domestic partnerships.

In Colombia, Law 152, offering social guarantees to same-sex couples, traveled a bumpy road. It garnered support in the Senate, from the public defender, and from three former presidents, plus a letter from the United Nations to the sitting president. However, the Catholic Church brought pressure to bear, writing letters to each and every senator, calling on them to vote against the bill. This led the minister of justice to speak against the bill; the day of the vote, legislators stayed away in droves, resulting in the lack of quorum, and the administration reversed its opinion. Finally, after thirty months of debate, everything pointed to a victory when the Chamber of Representatives gave a green light to the bill on June 14, 2007. But on June 19 the Senate used a political maneuver to turn things around and sink it. Thanks to activist efforts, however, on September 19, Colombia's constitutional court legally recognized same-sex partnerships between couples who have been living together for at least two years. Colombian law mandates the Higher Judicial Council to instruct family court judges and the directors of conciliation centers to implement the decision. The ruling does not cover issues such as social security, health care, retirement pensions, and adoption rights. However, couples will have the right to divide community property fifty-fifty (counting nonpaid labor as an investment in accumulated joint property) and also to inherit or divide assets in the case of death or separation. Similar bills have been introduced in other Latin American countries (Chile, Peru, and Panama), sparking sharp reactions by right-wing political parties and their religious allies, who call the bills "attacks on marriage and the family."

Although there is not a complete consensus among the different currents of the lesbian, feminist, or sexual dissident movement about demands for the recognition of joint living arrangements, a large part of the gay community defends legalizing it. However, the press and society have interpreted this demand as promoting "gay marriage." This is mainly due to the Catholic Church and right-wing offensive that clearly aims to cause confusion and sabotage the proposals; they talk about marriage and adoption, despite the fact that none of the proposals actually include these legal concepts. Joint living arrangements, civil solidarity agreements, or civil unions are typical cases of legal discrimination because they give same-sex couples an inferior, unconstitutional status compared with married couples. However, at this moment in Latin America, they seem to be a goal that can actually be achieved. Activists for equality think the most important battle is against inequality: the legalization of marriage, they say, would bring mutual protection and citizenship. They emphasize that, for this region, it would imply a profound change in the culture, because a large part of the public sees homosexuality as a crime; so, equality activists are betting that cultural changes will come about more easily with legal changes as the basis.

The Politics of Difference Current

Although demanding that the state recognize rights in the face of rampant exclusion and homophobia would help guarantee many people their very existence and thousands more the decent life that the state is obligated to provide, it is not a homogenous proposal in the sexual dissidence movement. A large part of the movement, albeit perhaps not a majority, was inspired in the 1970s by the feminism of difference and based itself fundamentally on the idea of recovering so-called women's values. Members of this group proposed the idea of searching for an identity of their own that would mark their difference vis-à-vis men or the male construct. Difference is an existential principle involving the ways of being human and the specificities of each person's experiences, aims, and possibilities (Lonzi 1981, 23). The theory of sexual difference stipulates that, as a hierarchical relationship, the gender system ties women to men, making it impossible for women to become corporeal subjects and to express their difference with dominant male thought. Historically, the pejorative use of everything female and feminized is structurally necessary for the patriarchal system to function. Therefore, this current also considers that defending the fundamental value of female difference is the most profound way of achieving the deconstruction of the order presenting itself as the only existing model (Gargallo 2005b, 2). This theory's proponents are critical of demands for equal rights because they think they propose no new values.

Lesbians participating together with gay men or heterofeminists in the 1980s were the first to put forward expressions of difference politics in Latin America. They did not feel the movement was including their demands because the men were phallocentric and the feminists were heterocentric, so they began to organize autonomously. Another expression of difference politics was the emergence of a group of bar-frequenting, transvestite, queen, and homosexuals who called themselves the gay lumpen proletariat, rejecting the construction of an ideal type of revolutionary subject that conformed to the social canons that sought equality with heterosexuals. They demanded the construction of a countercultural or denigration-based subject, representing the most marginal of the marginalized (Mogrovejo 2000, 117).

In 1993 a group of Mexican and Chilean feminists created a group they called the Accomplices, to differentiate themselves from what they thought was becoming a hemisphere-wide movement of nongovernmental organizations demanding legislation to achieve equality without questioning the origins of their funding or world economic policy after the 1989 fall of the Berlin Wall. They said that rejecting patriarchal canons should not be used to dialogue with the world of men or to demand something from them, but to reflect about feminist action and recognize the differences among women as the right to be different and not something that makes them unequal. The Accomplices Manifesto was launched during the preparations for the Fourth United Nations World Conference on Women, held in Beijing in 1995. It was a statement that distanced its signers from the politics of the possible and expressed the first positioning against what five years later would be called globalization. This statement by the group, also known as the "autonomous feminists," attracted autonomous lesbians because they agreed on the politics of sexual difference and on rejecting the category of gender, because it always remits women to their relationship with men. It also attracted anarchist feminist currents (Gargallo 2006, 203).

For Chilean manifesto signer Margarita Pisano, one of the main challenges continues to be the reconstruction of the symbolic sphere of masculinity, which encompasses femininity (1999, 20). Sometimes, women enter a sphere of male power, such as politics, but always at the service of the interests of masculinity. These "great steps forward" are ways of rearranging masculine structures; negotiating in unequal conditions is a transaction in which members submit to the rules of the game of whoever is in power, because the only people who negotiate are those who recognize each other as having equal power and needs (Fischer 2005, 55).

In this same sense, in her critique of identity and performance politics, Yuderkys Espinosa Miñoso writes that feminism's theoretical debates changed under the influence of different donor agencies. They moved toward a sexual and reproductive rights agenda—part of the state's interests in response to the new economic situation—in a perverse relationship among the population, economy, and development. This gave rise to the emergence of new identities recognized as "sexual minorities." To fit into the government and international agencies' financial categories, activists regrouped under the heading "sexual diversity," which even included heterosexuality. Thus, the feminist critique of those in political power imposing obligatory heterosexuality was lost, and the agencies instead turned to a political agenda, reclassifying the struggle to fight for the issues of health (HIV/AIDS), antidiscrimination legislation, the right to maternity and paternity, the right to marriage, and even Miss Gay Universe pageants. Far from contributing new epistemic realms, all of this traps us in binary relationship, reproducing gender norms based on the supposed break with stereotypes (2007, 125).

Amalia Fischer analyzes the limits of the feminist movement's institutionalization, which is also useful for analyzing the LGTB movement. She argues that this process has been neither good nor bad but rather that it allows for making relations of domination visible, denouncing them, and then doing research and producing knowledge about them. The negotiation of public policies to improve living conditions does not guarantee a real transformation because changing people's mentalities is a slow process. Funding and institutionalization allows feminist ideas to spread and women to be better informed about their health, bodies, and rights, as well as better treated by the courts when they suffer from violence. Funding makes alternative media, feminist local and regional networking, and meetings and conferences possible. In general, it has benefited some currents more than others. But the lack of clear, objective mechanisms for representation and leadership; influence peddling with funding agencies; or negotiating with the government in the name of the movement have also contributed to turmoil, produced competition, information hoarding, clashes, and distrust. Not all funding agencies are the same, nor do they have the same objectives. There is a big difference between the World Bank, the International Development Bank (IDB), the Agency for International Development (AID), and a feminist women's fund anchored in trust among women. Some agencies impose their rules and are increasingly pegged to their governments' policies. Activism has become a commodity that must be efficiently produced and turned in on schedule just like in management-labor relations. Funding has also strengthened power groups and produced loyalties based on economic rather than ethical or political rewards (2005, 63).

In the ideological, epistemic sphere, this current also seriously questions marriage and other forms of conjugality put forward as the only acceptable form of social organization. Or, what is the same thing, it considers them an institution whose aim is control and social stratification to subordinate women and the socially vulnerable by reproducing the heterosexual relationship model, now in crisis even for heterosexuals. Therefore, demanding them for oneself makes no sense. Francesca Gargallo states that while the main objective of marriage has been social and biological reproduction, secular marriage can utilize a gay couple or a "married" lesbian in the same way it uses heterosexual marriage to order society, forging obedience to institutions stemming from the male subject in his relationship with capitalist production (2005a, 3).

Jules Falquet argues that despite the diversity of families, neoliberal globalization tends to impose the ideal of the neonuclear family, in some cases reorganized around persons of the same sex. The stable couple seems to be the main guarantee of minimal stability. In the ideological sphere, we are witnessing a real victory of the heterosexual couple and its distillation into its essence. The symbolic significance of a monogamous, heterosexual couple has transcended the models of so-called diversity. Conjugality as a model for the couple is conservative and not very compatible with taking part in collective struggles for social change. Therefore, it is clear that love must be redefined, and we must ask ourselves whether we need the authorization of the state to organize our emotions and our daily learning processes. For Yan María Castro, love should be taken out of the individual, personalized sphere and linked to a collective feeling of social justice; we should examine the patriarchal system, the role of the state and its laws, the capitalist system, and the international division of labor (2006, 53).

While communal experiences have not been massive, stable, or permanent, they have expressed forms of resistance to the monopolistic conjugal form of organization and have avoided seeking government authorization. Communities based on love, economic production, solidarity, or any other organizing principle can function outside the capitalist logic, the fundamental value of which is private property. Thus, questioning conjugal partnerships and marriage implies rethinking the entire organization of society. Our socialization inside monogamy, ruled by the principles of privately owning our partner, has prevented us from visualizing the dimensions of the situation. Therefore, we can say that monogamy is held up by the pillars of jealousy and violence, just as heterosexuality is held up by homophobia, that is, by compulsion and compulsoriness.[7]

While the most important expression of the politics of difference is its theoretical production, experiences do exist of quite different kinds of group action. Some are absolutely critical of any form of dialogue with the state from "the outside," because they think there is nothing to negotiate, while others are formally organized in NGOs and work to create visibility through the media or in study circles. Still others are organized in collectives and are critical of the institutionalization of feminism and sexual dissidence. They also critique the movement's neoliberal bent, most obviously expressed in the LGTB pride marches, which have become increasingly commercial and carnivalesque and less and less political, linking freedom more to consumption than to self-determination. To counter this, in some countries, parts of the movement have convened lesbian marches, marches of the dissidents, or "the other march," in an attempt to recover the political, rebellious significance they originally had.

While the autonomous current has created spaces for reflection, activism, cultural creation, and Encuentros, it has also caused contradictions, ghettos, and fundamentalist positions. Differences among the small groups have made it more and more difficult for the movement to advance and have often created exclusionary, intolerant dynamics and practices, making vigorous, plural, coordinated work impossible. Arrogance may well be one of the most serious—and least understood—problems. Like with most small political opposition groups, the struggle to survive leads to isolating, self-destructive dynamics. However, what should be underlined is the movement's critical sense and profound desire to change society.

The Shifting Identities Current

The shifting identities current, inspired in poststructuralist feminism, gender technology, and queer theory, puts forward a critique of the theory of sexual difference because it includes certain aspects of biological determinism, by stating, "We women are different as women." Defenders of shifting identities question whether biology is a determining factor in forging identity. Teresa de Lauretis argues that identity means self-situation, a choice determined by experience that can be assumed either involuntarily or in the form of political consciousness (1991, 165). In this sense, gender is in and of itself a cultural fiction, a performance effect of repeated acts, without an origin or an essence. Gender should not be interpreted as a stable identity or a place where the ability to act is located. Rather, it should be understood as an identity feebly constructed over time, instituted in an exterior space through a stylized repetition of acts (Butler 2001, 23).

Poststructuralist feminism rejects the possibility of defining women as such and tries to deconstruct all the possible conceptions of women. It maintains that the very concept is a fiction, and that feminism should turn its efforts to dismantling it. This is why its proponents prefer to talk about the category of gender and not women. Nevertheless, this current, also known as nominalism, poses serious difficulties for its own feminism. What would be the basis for a feminist politics that deconstructs the female subject? Nominalism threatens to annihilate feminism itself (Alcoff 1988, 16). More than a search for a collective sexual identity, it is a matter of breaking with fixed identities, deconstructing the established genders and assigned sexes. From the standpoint of queer theory, identities are mutable; they depend on strategic, political, even playful moments, and this nomadism throws into stark relief the futility of searching for definitive stability with regard to the body, gender, or sexuality, which can dissolve the deployment of normalization (Butler 2001, 169; Sáens 2004, 52).

The Sexto Encuentro Lésbico Latinoamericano y del Caribe (Sixth Latin American and Caribbean Lesbian Encuentro) (Mexico, 2004) and the Décimo

Encontro Feminista Latino-Americano e do Caribe (Tenth Latin American and Caribbean Feminist Encontro) (Brazil, 2005) put front and center the discussion of allowing lesbian feminist man-to-woman transgendered people to participate.[8] Although some of the advocates of allowing them to participate had an electoral agenda, three clearly different positions could be distinguished: (1) those who criticized naturalizing gender constructions, (2) those who defended that naturalization, and (3) those who, though not denying the criticism, defended the need for differentiated political spaces and the right of self-determination as the exercise of autonomy, allowing people to organize themselves as they wished. The transgendered persons' demand to be able to participate once again posed the question of what it means to be a woman. How is the concept defined? If it is a cultural construct, it is possible to leave aside the rules and construct an identity in dissidence.

Monique Wittig stated that "lesbians are not women" (2006, 43), just as no female who is not personally dependent on a man is a woman, since the concept of "woman" has been constructed by men and as a function of men. This statement reaffirms the notion that gender identities are cultural constructs with political directionality. If gender and sexual identity is determined by the body, this also merits dissidence. We lesbians, deprived of bodies of our own, trapped in the bodies of stereotypical women, have not yet been able to reconstruct or reinvent a lesbian corpus that would include a history as different as ours is from that of the colonized woman.

Wittig may be one of the few theoreticians who try to reconstruct that identity and that disarticulated corpus (1977). Following in her footsteps, I would add that women's bodies have been constructed in the service of heterosexuality, for social and biological reproduction. They are imprisoned bodies, with sizes, measurements, and forms harmful to our health, which in many cases have led women to their deaths from anorexia. Then, what is a lesbian body? This meaning continues to be undefined, a need under construction based on a negation: "I don't want a body for others; I need a body for myself." Lesbians and transgendered people share the rejection of an imposed body. In this process of deconstructing "being" a woman and what a woman "should be," lesbians have also felt they were transgendered (Tron n.d., 2).

The search for a lesbian body primarily rejects the one imposed by hegemonic male power. However, it seems paradoxical that it is precisely that stereotypical body that is the object that male-to-female transgendered people identify with. A great many of them resort to self-medication, hormones, silicone, or kitchen or motor oil injections to get that colonized body, running the risk of serious health problems or even death. But, if a transgendered person identifies herself as a feminist lesbian, there is no "lesbian-ometer" or "feminist-ometer" that can deny her identity. In that sense, the dispute over political spaces also implies the challenge of constructing and inventing other spaces, differentiated ones, for coming together and providing autonomy. It's a wide world, and it's ours, ready for us to make new breaks.

The struggle for the change in legal identity, far from questioning the binary order, seems to reinforce it. According to Espinosa Miñoso (2007), going from one gender to the other or from one body to another refunctionalizes the binary. However, male and female transgendered people are not the only ones who participate in that recycling. All of us, male or female, who are aware of it and do not renounce our gender framework, collaborate with it. Certain unavoidable questions arise: What does the concept "woman" mean for lesbians, then? Is it impossible for us to escape gender or the binary system? Does not escaping from the binary system but questioning it necessarily mean that we refunctionalize it? Why, then, does persecution have an effect, and why is it expressed so violently?

If we agree with the premise that gender is a nonessential social construct, the concept of "woman" cannot be defined biologically or socially. It must be defined by the position women occupy in a web of relationships where the biological, the social, the economic, the cultural, and the historical take place, by affirming the fact that their position in that web lacks power and mobility and requires a radical change. Thus, de Lauretis says that a woman's identity is the product of her own interpretation and her reconstruction of her own history, permeated by the discursive cultural context she has access to (1992, 167).

In this regard, I think it is very necessary that we recover Adrienne Rich's concepts of "lesbian continuum" and "lesbian existence," which suggest both the historical presence of lesbians and our continual creation of the meaning of that existence. The lesbian continuum includes a range of women-identified experiences and solidarity, in the face of male tyranny, that has been out of our reach because of the limited definitions—most of them clinical—of "lesbianism." Practically all the historic forms of women's resistance to the model of social relations between the sexes propping up the patriarchal order could be included in this continuum: from Sappho to inseparable little girls, China's communities of women resisting marriage, nineteenth-century English spinsters, or the survival solidarity networks of women in Africa (2003, 30). Only in this way, by recognizing a history of resistance, can we once again find a place in that web of power relations. Although many feminists think that in the sphere of politics, sexual difference should not be a relevant distinction, it is important to avoid the thesis of the universal, neutral, generic human being that shuts our eyes to racism, androcentrism, and obligatory heterosexuality. What we need is a theoretical and corporal rearticulation in the reconstruction of a political identity as women and feminist lesbians in the face of a new global context and face-to-face with ourselves.

While what we have gained might make us visualize a more democratic, libertarian horizon limiting yesterday's authoritarianism, we must not get carried away, because with the new international order and the reordering of the economy, that authoritarianism has not been eradicated. Although state functions have been reduced, its discretionary power has been maintained in the form of a state of emergency. Giorgio Agamben traces a relationship between the new international order and the continuity of the 1970s authoritarian political system. Today's democracies make possible the unlimited opening of markets and the accommodation to multi-national capital, the impunity of murdering, genocidal governments carrying out repression, and the disarticulation and disorganization of civil society. Left political alternatives have been eliminated by co-optation, which forced their demands to the right, assimilating them in the new ruling global order in place since the 1970s.

It is not possible to conceive of transforming Latin American states independently of state reorganization taking place worldwide; that would situate us in a conditioned, subordinate position vis-à-vis supranational state bodies or the most powerful nations (Agamben 1998, 25). For this reason, our struggles cannot escape that reorganization and those economic interests.

Latin American feminism is faced with the challenge of incorporating a more complex, postcolonial, analytical vision and political posturing that, for example, fully supports the resistance of the original peoples of this continent as they defend their natural resources and cultural knowledge from neoliberal policies that have facilitated transnational encroachment. It is by identifying with this multicultural perspective (nuestramerica; our-america) that feminism can reconfigure a more integral—and therefore truly universal—cultural proposal. The challenge for lesbians is to use our experience to critically advise alternatives to oppressive hierarchical relations that exist because of habit or imposition.

ACKNOWLEDGMENTS
Translated by Heather Dashner.

NOTES

1. There are many different ways of naming the group of subjects involved in the movement: lesbians, homosexuals, gays, transgendered people, transvestites, bisexuals, intersexuals, and others that may arise who question the system of obligatory heterosexuality. Acronyms such as LGTB (lesbian, gay, transgendered, and bisexual) and LGTTB (lesbian, gay, transgendered, transvestite, and bisexual) vary according to the importance assigned to the different components (GLTB, TLGB, etc.) I think "sexual dissidence" is a more political concept than "sexual diversity" because it underlines the objection to a system of obligatory heterosexuality, an idea I have examined in other essays.

2. The phrase "moment of universality" refers to the search for equal rights for all, which since the French Revolution has been an ethical component of the definition of all subjects; all human beings are considered equal because of the commonality of rational structures and intersubjectivity.

3. Even though police raids were a long-established persecutory strategy in Latin America, the 1970s distinguish themselves for linking them to political activism.

4. Argentina's Nuestro Mundo (Our World) group, led by a former Communist Party member who was expelled for his homosexuality, spent two years bombarding the Buenos Aires media with mimeographed bulletins calling for gay liberation. In 1974 Puerto Rico's Comunidad de Orgullo Gay (Gay Pride Community) began publishing the newspaper *Pa' Fuera* (Out). In 1978 a group of Brazilian gays launched *Lampião da Esquina* (Corner Lamppost), whose name refers to gay street life; the publication gave rise to the group Somos: Grupo de Afirmación Homosexual (We Are: Group of Homosexual Affirmation). The Mexican group Frente Homosexual de Acción Revolucionaria (Homosexual Front for Revolutionary Action) published *Nuestro Cuerpo* (Our Body) in 1979.

5. Margarita Sánchez de León, pastor of the Comunidad Metropolitana Cristo Sanador (Christ the Healer Metropolitan Community Church) and member of the Coalición contra el

Artículo 103 y Pro-Derechos a la Intimidad (Anti–Article 103 and Pro–Intimacy Rights Coalition) in the city of Santurce, turned herself in to the public prosecutor's office, admitting that she had violated Article 103 of the criminal code, known as the Sodomy Law, which carried a sentence of ten to twelve years in prison. Prosecutor Ramón Muñiz Santiago told her she could not be prosecuted because the article did not apply to lesbians since, to be guilty of the crime, the perpetrator had to have a "male member." He added that even if two male homosexuals came in to confess their crime, they could not be prosecuted either because there was no victim of their acts. With this, he was saying that the law was not enforceable if there was no victim, and since there was no victim or injured party, there was no crime. However, the fact that the law established punishment meant that prosecution could be discretionary and could, therefore, discriminate against and endanger the rights of an important sector of the population. For that reason, the movement demanded that the state amend the law to clearly stipulate that it did not intend to prosecute consenting individuals who decided to have sexual relations with persons of the same sex.

6. The 1998 Texas case was about a homosexual couple surprised during anal sex when a neighbor called the police complaining that a man was "going crazy" in the house. The defendants argued that the neighbor had called the police to get them in trouble. The state of Texas argued that keeping the antisodomy statute on the books helped foster marriage and family values. The accused, John Geddes Lawrence and Tyron Garner, were fined two hundred U.S. dollars each and spent the night in jail after being convicted of a sexual offence.

7. Jealousy as an expression of distrust implies a sentiment of appropriation, and that is a form of violence, even though it manifests in distinct degrees.

8. The Décimo Encuentro Feminista de América Latina y el Caribe (Tenth Latin American and Caribbean Feminist Encuentro) accepted the participation of male-to-female transgender people in successive conferences.

REFERENCES

Agamben, Giorgio. 1998. *Homo sacer.* Valencia, Spain: Pre-textos.

Alcoff, Linda. 1988. Cultural feminism versus post-structuralism: The crisis in feminist theory. *Signs: Journal of Women in Culture and Society* 13 (3): 16–32.

Amorós, Celia. 1994. *Feminismo: Igualdad y diferencia.* Mexico City: UNAM.

Butler, Judith. 2001. *El género en disputa: El feminismo y la subversión de la identidad.* Mexico City: Paidós.

De Lauretis, Teresa. 1991. Estudios feministas, estudios críticos: Problemas, conceptos y contextos. In *El género en perspectiva,* comp. Carmen Ramos, 165–193. Mexico City: Universidad Autónoma Metropolitana, Iztapalapa.

———. 1992. *Alicia, ya no: Feminismo, semiótica y cine.* Madrid: Cátedra.

Espinosa Miñoso, Yuderkys. 2007. *Escritos de una lesbiana oscura: Reflexiones críticas sobre feminismo y política de identidad en América Latina.* Buenos Aires: Editorial en la Frontera.

Falquet, Jules. 2006. *De la cama a la calle: Perspectivas teóricas lésbico-feministas.* Bogotá: Brecha lésbica.

Fischer, Amalia. 2005. Los complejos caminos de la autonomía. *Nouvelles Questions Feministes* 4 (2): 54–78.

Gargallo, Francesca. 2005a. Para ahondar en la práctica política de la diferencia sexual. Paper presented at the Seminar Nuevos y Grandes Retos del Feminismo en el Siglo XXI, Colegio de México, Mexico City, June 29.

———. 2005b. *Unos apuntes sobre la teoría lésbica de Norma Mogrovejo.* Mexico City: Book Launch.

———. 2006. *Ideas feministas latinoamericanas.* Mexico City: UACM.

Green, James. 2004. Deseo y militancia: Lesbianas, gays y el Partido de los Trabajadores de Brasil. In *Arco iris diferentes,* ed. Peter Drucker, 70–85. Mexico City: Siglo Veintiuno.

Lonzi, Carla. 1981. *Escupamos sobre Hegel: La mujer clitórica y la mujer vaginal*. Barcelona: Anagrama.

Mogrovejo, Norma. 2000. *Un amor que se atrevió a decir su nombre: La lucha de las lesbianas y su relación con los movimientos feminista y homosexual en América Latina*. Mexico City: CDAHL Plaza y Valdés.

Pisano, Margarita. 1999. Una larga lucha de fracasos. *ALAI* 7 (November): 20–22.

PRT. 1989. Sexualidad y política. Paper presented at the Foro de Derechos Humanos, UNAM, Mexico City, October 1989.

Rich, Adrienne. 2003. La heterosexualidad obligatoria y la existencia lesbiana. *Existencias lesbianas*, no. 1:28–32.

Sáens, Javier. 2004. *Teoría queer y psicoanálisis*. Madrid: Síntesis.

Tron, Fabiana. n.d. Che ¿vos te diste cuenta que sos una mujer? Una no nace mujer. Gully. www.thegully.com/espanol/articulos/gay_mundo/031113_una_no_nace_mujer_1.html (accessed July 4, 2008).

Wittig, Monique. 1977. *El cuerpo lesbiano*. Valencia, Spain: Pre-textos.

———. 2006. No se nace mujer. In *El pensamiento heterosexual y otros ensayos*, trans. Javier Sáez and Paco Vidarte, 31–59. Madrid: Egales.

12

Respect, Discrimination, and Violence

INDIGENOUS WOMEN IN ECUADOR,
1990–2007

MERCEDES PRIETO

ANDREA PEQUEÑO

CLORINDA COMINAO

ALEJANDRA FLORES

GINA MALDONADO

In the 1970s illiterate indigenous women in Ecuador received the right to vote, a right that years later would open the way for their active participation in indigenous movements. Indeed, by the 1990s indigenous movements, with significant participation by women, besieged centers of state power as the country experienced a growing economic and political crisis.[1] This public presence initially took the shape of an uprising that paralyzed much of the country and led to lengthy negotiations, with "native peoples" and nations demanding respect for their rights. As a result, the rights of indigenous peoples were recognized, both in the Constitution and in the creation of intercultural public policies in the fields of health, education, and the administration of justice. An extensive bibliography examines the nature, strategies, and achievements of the various stages of indigenous movements. However, this literature has been by and large blind to the relevance of gender as well as to the participation of women in the process of indigenous revitalization. While the country has been shaken by the voices of indigenous peoples, white and mestizo women—especially educated urban women—have lobbied for the inclusion of their agendas and interests in public debate. It is within this context that we pose the following question: how has the subject of indigenous women been treated inside these concurrent movements? The evidence points to divisions between the women's and indigenous movements, and this problematic is the focus of our essay.

Women's groups have found it difficult to build solid bridges with indigenous women.[2] In many cases, indigenous leaders, both men and women, openly reject an agenda centered exclusively on women or on gender relations, arguing external or imperialist meddling (Morocho 1998, 223–224) or the potential for division in the politics of indigenous peoples. However, within the indigenous movement itself, there are efforts—albeit strained—to create a women's agenda in the midst of the struggles for recognition as peoples and as nations. Analysts have interpreted this complex game in various ways. Some have read it as a counterresponse to the homogenizing state discourse on femininity and masculinity (Radcliffe 1993) or as an effort to combat gender discrimination by assigning new meanings to the traditional roles and values ascribed to women (Cervone 2002). Others have seen it as a strategy to postpone dealing with women's issues to strengthen the struggle for the recognition of indigenous peoples' rights or as an expression of the masculine power that controls the indigenous renaissance (Minaar 1998). And—from a perspective that deserves our attention—it is plausible to view it as part of a process leading to an "indigenous feminism" aligned with the multiracial and postcolonial models critical of white Western middle-class feminism (Baca Zinn and Thornton Dill 1996; Mohanty 1986, 2003).

This essay emphasizes practices and statements by Kichwa women from the Ecuadorian highlands, confirming that feminism is not a single, universal language to express gender inequalities and the interests of women. The search for new codes in the struggle against ethnic and racial inequalities is palpable. Indigenous women have begun declaring themselves feminists in recent years (Reuque 2002; Sánchez 2005) and in Ecuador are constructing autonomous spaces for themselves, articulated around the Consejo Nacional de Mujeres Indígenas (CONMIE; National Indigenous Women's Council), whose members work for gender equity within the framework of the rights of native peoples. These various trends clearly attest to the existence of factors that have prevented the alliance between the women's movement and indigenous women. The divisive factors include different constructions of gender relations and of relations between individual and community, racism and discrimination, and class status. We argue, therefore, that these disagreements are the result of the specific articulation of gender, class, and ethnicity, expressed in the notions of respect, discrimination, and violence.

These divisions merit further analysis, given the pronounced economic and social marginalization of indigenous women in Ecuador (Larrea and Montenegro 2005). Like other indigenous women in the region, they endure profound disadvantages in their access to public and societal resources, particularly in terms of educational opportunities and health services.

The Gender Division of Labor and Gender Ideologies

Various studies have argued the existence of gender relations particular to indigenous Andean societies, both in terms of the gender division of labor and gender ideologies. This literature emphasizes the flexibility of the gender division of labor and the strategic roles that women fulfill in reproduction—in the home, the family, and the community (Hamilton 1998; Prieto 1998). Moreover, it suggests that women can draw on diverse sources of power and negotiation (i.e., productive factors and knowledge). The hypothesis is that indigenous women's work has never been exclusively domestic; they have always been involved in production and commerce. In this context, the notion of complementarity is offered as connective between this flexible gender division of labor and gender ideologies derived from a worldview in which men and women are equivalent and equal. However, this idea of complementarity as an idealized expression of equality and interchangeability between genders has been questioned by scholars who attest to the complex interplay of hierarchies, exclusions, and equality in gender relations (Harvey 1989; Crain 2001; De la Cadena 2000) that open and close options available to indigenous women.

Complementarity and Hierarchies: The Communal Web

Complementarity denotes a harmonious, balanced construction of the indigenous community, as well as its egalitarian nature. Women and men are said to be interdependent; political and economic participation of each is based on their different sources of power. This duality constitutes the backbone of community relations; moreover, the collectivity is seen as prevailing over other social and cultural factors. At the same time, the idea of an underlying equality implies the potential for hierarchy, which in turn requires a constant negotiation between the two (Canessa 1997, 237). As a result, the practices and ideologies of complementarity are not free of tensions and violence.

It is worth asking whether such relations of complementarity and hierarchy are still operating. Our observation among transnational textile saleswomen in Otavalo, for example, reveals a play of hierarchical roles, with both symbolic and generational elements, that weigh heavily in decision making and in the assignment of responsibilities and privileges. This complex web of interrelations comes together to form the family and community fabric; it implies an exchange of positions that assures the survival of the collectivity, economic and social continuity, and the cultural identity of the group. Given these dynamics, the boundaries between the roles and abilities of men and women and the hierarchy among them become blurred.

Moreover, in recent times, socioeconomic status has increasingly become one of the most important determinants of hierarchical relations in families and communities. Faced with changing social relations, women strive to balance divisions of various types—gender, status, wealth—but, as Lynn Sikkink (1997, 122) observes, a true integration may remain forever "incomplete." In our opinion, it is in this space, marked by an absence of completeness and by growing fissures, that women raise questions about their lives in indigenous communities and society. Indeed, one of the current discussions among indigenous women themselves focuses on the character of such complementarity. Questions have been raised about its very existence within a highly individualistic context and about the extent to which it forms part of an indigenous ideational construct harmful to the interests of women.

In the Andean worldview, all elements, human and earthly have, at the same time opposite and complementary features. Thus, for example, among the Aymará, the duality *chacha-warmi* (male-female) is essential for societal reproduction. Duality, though weakened, remains part of the collective imagination (Painemal 2005, 78) and thus can be used to criticize masculine power (Hernández and Sierra 2005, 108). If this is so, duality can act as a powerful magnet to develop unity and a sense of belonging; in other words, it can become a tactical element in struggles for the recognition of indigenous rights.

Women as Guardians of Their Peoples' Identity

In documents and public statements, indigenous rhetoric assigns to women the mission of preserving their peoples' culture. But political discourse is not alone in emphasizing their role as guardians of collective identity. Much of the academic literature on the subject also represents indigenous women as reproducers and transmitters of their group's culture. This conception links women to a universe of traditions, characterized by the conservation of habits (language, dress, adornments, and customs) and its association with rural life and settings. Women therefore can be "more Indian" (De la Cadena 1992) given their social and economic positions, their ability to preserve culture, and their reticence toward foreign contacts; in sum, they are the vehicles of ethnic identity. In this context the bodies of indigenous women become "practical sites for social control," an identity matrix for the entire people: "through their routine customs, these women create identities of vital importance for the group's cultural reproduction" (Crain 2001, 353). However, control of the body and behavior of women is not a univocal process; it results from a field of negotiation among dominant sectors, the state, indigenous peoples, and women—all of whom create new meanings for women's assigned roles.

The conception of indigenous women as guardians can be traced in statements by women leaders and intellectuals, as well as in the production of indigenous peoples. A forerunner, for example, is the Andean creation myth that Luz María de la Torre (1999) calls *The Story of Man and Woman*. According to this tale, woman's tasks are directly related to nature in a communion that emphasizes her role as caretaker and in which she is charged with "protecting that which exists"—a task implying the survival of living things and the transmission of knowledge.

Maruja Barrig suggests that the role of guardian and reproducer is useful to leaders and, in general, to the indigenous political discourse, as it offers a "symbolic territory . . . that provides leverage in the political arena" (2001, 100). We believe, however, that this role also opens new opportunities for women. The role of cultural guardian is vital to the group's survival and well-being. It is not a minor function; in fact, the Ecuadorian indigenous movement assigns to the community, and the networks woven within it, a predominant place for it in its struggle for recognition. Female indigenous leaders make use of a variety of images, in which they figure in this role as guardians and reproducers of culture and community, as the basis for sociopolitical action and legitimacy (Chuma and Lema 2000). Such expressions are not the simple acceptance of representations and functions assigned by others but rather a discursive strategy that corroborates their place within the collectivity and the movement. Thus, in a strategic essentialism, women use the guardian image as a political tool to have a voice, to be recognized as a people, and to emphasize the importance of their role.

These expressions also function as a rhetorical strategy aimed at a nonindigenous audience. One such appeal is found, for example, in the use of traditional dress by women leaders, a political action that reinforces the sense of belonging while it marks boundaries with mestizo society. For instance, former congresswoman and minister of foreign relations Nina Pacari has stated that, on entering the university, she recognized that when dressed as a mestiza she was denying "her being" (Bulnes 1994, 56). From then on, she has emphasized her indigenous ancestry (name, dress, and language); that is, she crafted an image and, through that act, exercised the power of the social and political representation of herself and her identity as a member of an indigenous people. This "constructing her self" outside the dominant society and through a struggle to reestablish autonomous spaces (Richards 2002) would grant the indigenous world, and especially its leaders, a capacity to act and to resist that which has tended to be ignored.

These rhetorical and expressive strategies, in addition to giving new meaning to assigned images and roles, are also the vantage point of many indigenous demands. Rooted in an image of women as guardians of the people's culture and identity, demands generally prioritize the indigenous collectivity. The discourse of women active in indigenous organizations is therefore about the struggle for justice for the entire people, an effort that involves men and women. Nevertheless, this group effort has opened avenues for improving women's lives and contesting male power, which make it possible to talk about a path toward gender equity.

Itineraries toward Gender Equity

In this section we explore the paths of indigenous women who are leaders and intellectuals, with special reference to the roles played by education and by women's demands. Gender discrimination and access to education have been important driving forces in the creation of narratives and discourses about the rights of peoples and of women, as well as in their active participation in indigenous politics. These routes speak of practices seeking gender equity and the creation of agendas benefiting women.

Careers of Women Leaders and Intellectuals

An outstanding feature of indigenous movements in Ecuador is the presence of female leaders and intellectuals. What are their histories and how did they earn their credentials? According to a pioneering study by Muriel Crespi (1976), mid-twentieth-century Ecuadorian women leaders possessed strategic leadership. Living in a highly repressive atmosphere, like that of the haciendas, women had greater mobility than their masculine peers, as they did not have access to the owner's land and resources. Subsequent research has demonstrated that roles and knowledge linked to health and sickness and membership in prestigious families seem to have been complementary factors in the constitution of these leaderships. Emma Cervone (1998, 171) points out that the gift of eloquence was also a key element in the traditional leadership of women. By contrast, contemporary leadership by indigenous women is mostly linked to education, community projects, and political representation. At the same time, today the experience of violence and discrimination within the educational and labor systems challenges them to politicize their identities as indigenous people and as women. Education, as a strategic element in cultural struggles, goes hand in hand with community practices. These practices facilitate the legitimation of new cultural capital gained through schooling.

The extension of public schooling to indigenous areas has been a long and conflict-ridden process that began in the 1940s, with indigenous organizations playing a relevant role, both in expanding coverage and in curricular development. However, for indigenous women, the road to schooling has been especially difficult. For cultural and economic reasons, families have prioritized the education of male children. The disadvantages for women are evident in high rates of illiteracy and low rates of schooling, as well as in the predominance of male indigenous leaders. But, in addition to gender discrimination, those who have managed to get schooling have had to face the strong ethnic-racial discrimination that exists in those settings. "When I went to school, I felt the force of discrimination directed toward me and my culture. The teachers were mestizos and did not want us to speak in Quichua (the language of savages, it was said); if we did, they beat us with a pine branch. . . . [They] encouraged only men to study; we women held no interest for them, as we existed solely to do housework. I also felt discriminated by male and female mestizo classmates, who made fun of us . . . and mistreated us" (Tene 2000, 211).

There are many testimonies like this one from women indigenous leaders. They show us that everyday life tensions due to ethnic-racial identity and gender relations have turned education into a fundamental pillar in the formation of female indigenous leaders. Another important factor is the will of some leading indigenous families to educate both sons and daughters. Several biographies illustrate the ties of female leadership to education, paternal guidance, and community organizing.

Together with educational barriers, women leaders and intellectuals have encountered obstacles in their access to communal, social, or political leadership. In these spaces, they have had to face sociocultural norms that restrict their ability to act in public spheres. Nina Pacari remembers that, in her first incursions into political work, her parents did not give their permission, because "as a woman, I had to be at home; it was madness to leave the house and to attend meetings" (Bulnes 1994, 56). Such experiences have led to a variety of efforts to strengthen female leadership, based on the recovery of cultural identity and community improvement.

The educational processes have made it possible, at the same time, to reflect on indigenous peoples' identity and thus on women's rights. For Lourdes Tibán, "education has to be seen as a process of reconstruction of identity and the strengthening of who we are" (interviewed by Alejandra Flores, November 12, 2004, Quito). In turn, this reconstruction of identity makes possible a reconsideration of women's roles (Masaquiza 2004, 14). In sum, the educational experience appears to be a strategic tool that facilitates advances and transformations in modes of action by and for indigenous women.

Women's Agendas

Women have not remained silent in the politics of indigenous movements. Women leaders and intellectuals have made themselves heard as they structured a narrative that has empowered them on the political and community stage. In addition, they are attempting to create an agenda that reflects and publicly recognizes their practices. Such an agenda has changed over the years with the dynamic of the indigenous movement itself, the specificities of different native peoples, international women's meetings, and ties to the state.[3]

THE RIGHTS OF PEOPLES AND WOMEN

In 1979 the Ecuadorian Constitution extended political rights to the illiterate population—in large part, indigenous and female. This opening mobilized and politicized the indigenous peoples whose members came together in the Confederación de Nacionalidades Indígenas del Ecuador (CONAIE; Confederation of Indigenous Nationalities of Ecuador). The creation of this coalition coincided with the beginning of an organizational process, leading women's secretariats within the various levels of the confederation—local, regional, and national. Within this framework, at the first meeting of the women of CONAIE, a decision was made to create a Women's Leadership Committee as a mechanism to involve women in the process. Bringing women together and integrating them into the organization was justified on the basis of their central role in the cultural reproduction of the group: defense of lands and territories, maintenance of native languages, and revival of medical and other traditional practices.

The women of CONAIE also saw themselves as having a vital role in the family's economic reproduction, especially in rural settings. Because of male migration, women work the land, care for children, and find the resources necessary for the family's survival; they have effectively become providers. Land is thus the conceptual block on which the argument is constructed, as it articulates both economic and cultural reproduction: "without mothers and without land, neither humans nor food would exist. Without land we run the risk that even the language will disappear" (CONAIE 1994, 40).

These women decided that the best way to position their interests is by participating in the struggles for the recognition of their rights as a people and a nation. Thus, the fundamental pillars in their declarations have been the demands related to land, territory, natural resources, and language, synthesized in turn in the struggle for the recognition of Ecuador as a plurinational and multicultural country, the eradication of racial and ethnic discrimination, the provision of state services that recognize their customs, and the local administration of justice and municipal life.

The basic strategy has been, and continues to be, to prepare women for leadership positions. In this way, they hope to persuade men to change some gender injustices but mostly to have greater access to the web of relations of indigenous power and of society as a whole, in a language and style that emulates that of men. At the same time, this effort to be a part of the networks of power has allowed women leaders to recognize the limitations they experience—as women—in achieving greater participation in community and political decision making. Occasionally, from this position, women explore their devaluation not only by society but also by their male peers. Thus, for example, they acknowledge disagreements with masculine family members regarding their participation in community life and in organizations, as well as a lack of time due to their excessive workload. They also criticize men for not valuing women's work in the home, and leaders for abandoning their families. But some indigenous women leaders have intentionally put their interests on the backburner. A former leader, for instance, made it clear that, while women have too much work, now is not the time to clash with men on the issue (Tamia Porate, interview, September 28, 1996, Otavalo, Imbabura). Most women believe that the main problems they face are ethnic discrimination, ethnic violence, and inadequate recognition of their rights as a people and a nation.

In this context, interpretations of gender hierarchies reveal two contradictory patterns: while some documents emphasize the existence of community relations based on an imagined male-female complementarity, others maintain the existence of a patriarchal order in present-day communities. Nevertheless, both views put forth the violent and discriminatory interrelations with nonindigenous institutions and actors as determinants of gender hierarchies. From this vantage point, a tension arises between the discourse of women indigenous leaders and the discourse of wider women's movements, considered as foreign.

INDIGENOUS WOMEN'S RIGHTS

The debate about creating women's secretariats in various indigenous associations surfaced in the midst of local preparations for the Beijing conference and the organization of a continental meeting of indigenous women in Quito. Although indigenous women took on a central role, they nonetheless saw themselves as marginalized from decision making in their organizations. A group of militant female members of the indigenous movement, interested in greater autonomy and power, proposed that the women's secretariats of five mixed organizations come together to create CONMIE, while remaining part of their original organizations. The motivation behind this new entity was to reinforce the self-esteem of the movement's women (Blanca Chancoso, interview, July 25, 2003, Quito) and to openly question certain male privileges (Teresa Simbaña, interview, June 23, 2003, Quito).

This proposal generated, and continues to generate, disagreements and resistance. As a result, officers of the secretariats remained in their leadership positions within the secretariats while militants from a number of organizations created CONMIE. According to its creators, CONMIE does not intend to compete with CONAIE but to recognize and analyze practices harmful to women's rights. According to one of the women involved, this is a struggle to bring indigenous men to recognize the values women hold; however, as she is quick to emphasize, it is not about feminism but about the search for gender equity (Ana María Guacho, interview, June 1, 2003, Columbe, Chimborazo). This network, though still weak, reflects a new stage in the creation of discourses on indigenous women. While there is an attempt to maintain ties with the structures of the indigenous movement, bridges have also been built with women's organizations, especially with the state office charged with promoting the well-being of women, CONAMU.

Noteworthy in this context are the demands presented to CONAMU (2004) in a joint effort to create a plan for equal opportunities for indigenous women. This effort reveals a new emphasis on women's interests, while remaining linked to the recognition of indigenous rights. The document does not contain a new narrative to explain gender hierarchies, nor does it present new images of indigenous women; nevertheless, its central concern is ethnic-racial and gender discrimination. In the gaze of indigenous women, discrimination unfolds in family and community life as well as in relations with the state and other nonindigenous actors. Thus, for example, in addition to proposing the eradication of illiteracy, the strengthening of intercultural bilingual education, and the ancestral worldview, women discuss their discrimination and mistreatment in educational institutions. They refer to sexual violence and teenage pregnancy as problems particularly relevant to indigenous students. They also consider institutional racism and gender violence in the health system. The proposal to address violence and discrimination is linked to discourses about the recognition of native peoples' and women's rights. Thus, they call for strengthening public intercultural services, the implementation of indigenous justice, and greater participation in different decision-making arenas.

LOCAL POWER RELATIONS: NEW VOICES

In recent years a variety of indigenous women's agendas have appeared in the process of rebuilding a strongly divided indigenous movement and as a response to the participation of indigenous women in local governments. The discourses permeating these recent sets of demands show a renewed concern with the redistribution of state resources and seem to openly question gender violence and discrimination in indigenous communities, families, and culture. The 2006 agenda of Kichwa women of Chimborazo, for example, includes a strong, explicit reference to processes of exclusion within indigenous communities: "they experience this marginalization in the flesh when their own parents, spouses, and leaders . . . see them as inferior beings, incapable of assuming responsibilities other than exhausting domestic chores; or when culture is used to allow domestic violence to go unpunished" (CEDIS 2006, 5).

As indigenous women question gender subordination in different spheres of daily life, they directly bring up issues of access to education, housework and the use of time, violence within the family, participation, leadership and decision making, sexuality, and indigenous justice. In doing so, they unmask the existence of a harmonious "good life." In fact, the discourse of complementarity is criticized precisely for being "a political discourse" that covers up practices that subordinate and exclude women; complementarity is seen instead as an ideal that has yet to become a reality in women's daily lives, a condition that may have existed in a mythical past and should be recovered. Demands and proposals refer to everyday relationships characterized by respect and understood in relation to ethnic and gender identities within families, indigenous communities, public services, and so on. In this sense, women ask for interventions by the state and local governments, as well as by indigenous men and women, to change a way of being that, for them, is tremendously exclusionary and violent.

On the other hand, CONMIE (2007) guidelines emphasize both recognition and redistribution (Fraser 1997) but seem to stress these realities within indigenous communities and the movement itself more than the issue of discrimination and violence by mestizo society and the Ecuadorian state. Thus, for example, they discuss the exclusion of women within indigenous organizations—which they accuse of having a "lack of support for the advancement of women"—and call for gender equity within peoples and nations. Such initiatives point to a basic pillar of their struggle: gaining political presence and significant political leadership in decision making. In addition, we find demands for projects to strengthen ethnic identity, indigenous medicine, and the provision of health services, as well as resources for women, their families, and their communities. It is precisely in the issue of access to economic and technical resources that we find a break with nonindigenous women's organizations. Indigenous women generally see them as a threat and reject their intermediacy; they seek an autonomous path. Indeed, within the context of gender identity, leaders of the women's indigenous movement link the demands for recognition and redistribution by reiterating the more universal demand against poverty and violence, which indigenous women are exposed to in contemporary society (CONMIE 2007b).

Gender Violence: A Field Where Women Can Come Together?

During the 1990s women achieved significant gains in the legislative sphere, including the 1995 Law Prohibiting Violence against Women and the Family. This process entailed the creation, organization, and implementation of women and family courts in cities throughout the country—though this has not benefited indigenous women, especially those living in rural areas.[4] Members of women's movements have argued that gender violence affects all women as a structural phenomenon that is directly related to hegemonic models of masculinity and femininity and to patriarchal structures. For that reason, the law was based on a universalistic logic, with no differentiation in its definitions or procedures in reference to specific ethnic and racial groups.

It is this same universalistic language that has led many indigenous women to feel excluded. Leaders and intellectuals complain that the law does not protect them (Tene 2000, 220). In the year 2000 researchers began to study the so-called critical path followed by victims of violence and the quality of the response they receive from the various services available. One of these studies, undertaken among indigenous women in Guamote (Chimborazo), concludes that victims do not have access to adequate orientation for themselves or for their husbands and family members. Many women know that a "law for women" exists and seek out the special courts but, in spite of extensive efforts, in the end their problems go unresolved. Although many indigenous women declare that they are subject to physical and psychological violence in the home, both as wives and as daughters (CEPAR 2005), services for battered women reveal that only 8 percent of all their complaints come from indigenous women (Ardaya and Ernst 2000, 59).

It is interesting to note that the national imagery paints indigenous women as natural and systematic victims of violence, which they resist in a passive fashion.

There is a classic phrase repeated among urban women about the attitude of indigenous women who face violence: "Even if he hits me, even if he kills me, he is still my husband." But, contrary to this image, a number of studies have shown forms of resistance and protest by women subject to aggression that strive to create a sense of respect. Thus, for example, in Zumbahua women manipulate food to give their husbands indigestion after an episode of violence (Weismantel 1994). In other areas women who have been abused go back to their own families to negotiate their return with the support of their family (Muratorio 2002). At the same time, through the administration of justice at the community level, local authorities and family members intervene in the resolution of problems by counseling those involved and punishing aggressors with, for example, corporal punishment and the payment of compensation (García 2002). The complexity of these practices of resistance and conflict resolution has not been taken into account by public and private institutions in their attempts to come up with strategies to combat violence.

While the law makes no explicit mention of the diversity of women and of community responses to violence among indigenous peoples, and in spite of its urban logic, its application has created opportunities to consider and confront gender violence in indigenous and rural collectivities. Local authorities have recognized, for example, that women and family courts do not have the capacity to respond to complaints from residents far from urban centers. As a result, the police and justices of the peace have been empowered to receive complaints of mistreatment. In other cases, mobile courts have been created to receive complaints. Likewise, women are working with local authorities to test new models of response. These processes have made possible a critique of current legislation.

Critics have pointed out that although the law is generally recognized as a significant tool for the protection of women, its application often involves the mistreatment of indigenous women by intimidating and biased authorities. In addition, indigenous women face significant language barriers. The common perception is that public servants are unable to communicate with women in their native languages, demanding that they speak Spanish. This suggests that, rather than disinterest, what is involved is a series of problems concerning the meaning of and the access to justice. In this regard, many indigenous women are proposing that the law require an intercultural approach, along with improvements in the quality and access to services.

Additional evidence that contradicts the resignation and passivity attributed to indigenous women who experience violence comes from a variety of initiatives to provide attention to battered women, while making an effort to respect cultural differences and use distinct mechanisms for the resolution of problems. Examples include the Centro de Atención Integral a la Mujer y Familia (Comprehensive Care Center for Women and Families), created by Cotacachi's local government, as well as initiatives by organized indigenous women in the provinces of Sucumbíos and Chimborazo.

But strategies for dealing with violence are not the only elements distinguishing indigenous from other cultural contexts. Another crucial point involves the fact that gender violence in the indigenous world touches on a complex web of community and collective relations, including, as we have seen, the discourse of complementarity. Gender relations construct the fabric of collective relations and, in this respect, intervening in gender violence has an impact on the relations among, and the identity of, indigenous groups. This is why women insist that they do not want to struggle against men but to invite them to work together for a new relation that will strengthen collective life.

Respect, Discrimination, and Violence

> *Our struggle is not only to achieve equality between men and women, it is to achieve respect; and to end the problem of discrimination and violence that exists from woman to woman.*   —CONAIE

Respect, discrimination, and violence synthesize the meaning of indigenous women's political agendas and in turn provide the connections between gender, ethnic, and class relations involved. We have argued that the gender division of labor and gender relations and ideologies speak to the cultural particularities of the indigenous worlds. On the one hand, we have emphasized the flexibility of the division of labor that goes beyond the univocal process of the domestication of women. On the other, we have demonstrated that gender relations underlie the community web, with special reference to the collective rather than the individual identity of women. Finally, we have proposed that, according to gender ideologies, women are central to the conservation of traditions and communal construction for indigenous peoples. We have also argued that a number of these roles and responsibilities limit and confine women while simultaneously opening opportunities for education and participation in indigenous politics. It is precisely these opportunities that have moved indigenous women to develop practices that will lead to gender equity and to reflect on gender discrimination. The transformation of women's agendas reflects this complex process.

In effect, these agendas are the result of two superimposed moments. The first one refers to the discrimination and violence experienced by sectors who identify themselves as native peoples and who want to be recognized as such, in a language that minimizes gender hierarchies but opens the way for practices leading to equity for women. The other interweaves issues of racial, ethnic, and gender violence and discrimination. Ideas of respect, discrimination, and violence connect these two moments.

Initially, as is evident in the epigraph to this section, such notions were constructed with particular reference to conflictive interrelations between indigenous and mestizo societies. Such a primordial sense of respect becomes a powerful tool to act against all ethnically motivated violence and discrimination affecting persons and groups, while it also underlines the particular tensions that exist among women of different origins. Experiences of mistreatment at the hands of employers—for example, under the hacienda system or as household maids—or derogatory treatment in social institutions or public places highlight differences with regard to middle-class and well-off white and mestizo women, while they blur gender hierarchies in the indigenous world. Within this framework, a female indigenous leader remembers that initially they did not see inequality between men and women but rather between Indians and mestizos; but it was in the process of that very struggle that they were able to see "that as women we were also marginalized" (Ana María Guacho, interview, June 1, 2003, Columbe, Chimborazo).

During the second moment, ideas related to respect, violence, and discrimination became more complex as indigenous women tackled both conflictive interrelations with the nonindigenous world as well as gender relations within indigenous society, also marked by aggression and prejudice. While seeking respect for cultural diversity, they call for respect for women within the framework of their relations with members of indigenous and mestizo societies. But the construction of respect also questions complex family and community relations, because gender relations are at the base of these collective webs. In this sense, women's agendas represent a precarious balance between their interests and those of their peoples, a dynamic that helps to explain their differences with women's movements.

For indigenous peoples of the highlands, respect means achieving a general state of moral order and harmony (Lyons 2001, 9). Within this interpretative framework, we suggest that, in their emphasis on respect, indigenous women are looking to create a social order that includes complementarity and male-female harmony, the preeminence of the community, and decent treatment of women by other groups as well as from their male peers. It is a search that points to differences with movements lead by white, urban, middle-class women. With their emphasis on violence and discrimination, indigenous women express their interests and acknowledge the gender hierarchies woven into racism and class hierarchies. Echoing proposals for a multiracial, postcolonial feminism, we suggest that this set of concepts reiterates the fact that there are a number of languages in which to express the interests and dreams of women and to question gender relations.

ACKNOWLEDGMENTS

This text is the result of a collaboration among indigenous and mestiza academics at the Ecuadorian campus of the Facultad Latinoamericana de Ciencias Sociales (Latin American Faculty of Social Sciences). We are thankful for comments by Gioconda Herrera, Nathalie Lebon, and Elizabeth Maier.

NOTES

   1. The history of contemporary indigenous movements in Ecuador has several moments. The initial stage, 1979–1990, structured the movement, a process implying the creation of both a discourse and mechanisms for action. The years 1990–1998 were characterized by intervention in the wider political arena, where the demands presented during the 1990 uprising were discussed and negotiated, including the demand that the Constitution define Ecuador as a plurinational, multicultural country. The most recent stage, 1998–2007, represents a juncture marked by the transformation from a social to a political movement, leading to a splintering of and distancing among movements.

   2. While a number of efforts have been made to carry out joint actions, these have not been sustained. At the same time, the agendas of two significant women's collectives—the Coordinadora Política de Mujeres Ecuatorianas (Ecuadorian Women's Political Coordinating

Committee) and the Foro Permanente de la Mujer (Permanent Forum on Women)—do not recognize indigenous women or women of African descent, although they have women of different racial and ethnic backgrounds within their ranks.

3. For this analysis we use documents created in diverse contexts. The first was produced during preparations for alternative celebrations of the five-hundredth anniversary of the Spanish arrival in the Americas, an event marked by the effects of the 1990 indigenous uprising and by discussion of a complex negotiating platform with the Ecuadorian government and state regarding indigenous rights (Minutes 1990). The second is part of a series of meetings sponsored by CONAIE in preparation for the Beijing conference, accompanied by a heated discussion of the Agrarian Reform Law and a call to the March for Life (CONAIE 1994). The third is an effort to work on an equal opportunity plan between a national indigenous women's organization (CONMIE) and the state entity dealing with gender-equity policies (CONAMU-CONMIE 2004). Finally, we use texts produced within the context of the recomposition of indigenous movements (CONMIE 2007a, 2007b) and by a local women organization of Chimborazo (CEDIS 2006).

4. In spite of these efforts, only 47 percent of women say that they ask for help after experiencing physical or sexual violence and, of these, only 8 percent appeal to institutions created within the context of this law (CEPAR 2005).

REFERENCES

Ardaya, Gloria, and Miriam Ernst. 2000. *Imaginarios urbanos y violencia intrafamiliar.* Quito: CEPAM.

Baca Zinn, Maxine, and Bonnie Thornton Dill. 1996. Theorizing difference from multiracial feminism. *Feminist Studies* 22 (2): 321–331.

Barrig, Maruja. 2001. *El mundo al revés.* Buenos Aires: CLACSO.

Bulnes, Marta. 1994. *Me levanto y digo: Testimonio de tres mujeres quichuas.* Quito: El Conejo.

Canessa, Andrew. 1997. Género, lenguaje y variación en Pocobaya, Bolivia. In *Más allá del silencio: Las fronteras de género en los Andes,* ed. Denise Arnold, 233–249. La Paz: CIASE-ILCA.

CEDIS. 2006. *Agenda de las mujeres Kichwas de Chimborazo.* Riobamba, Ecuador: CEDIS.

CEPAR. 2005. *Encuesta demográfica y de salud materna e infantil: Informe preliminar.* Quito: CEPAR.

Cervone, Emma. 1998. Prof. Abelina Morocho Pinguil: Entre cantares y cargos. In *Mujeres contracorriente: Voces de líderes indígenas,* ed. Emma Cervone, 163–207. Quito: CEPLAES.

———. 2002. Engendering leadership: Indigenous women leaders in the Ecuadorian Andes. In *Gender's place: Feminist anthropologies of Latin America,* ed. Rosario Montoya, Lessie Jo Frazier, and Janise Hurtig, 177–196. New York: Palgrave Macmillan.

Chuma, Vicenta. 2004. Las mujeres en la construcción del estado plurinacional. Speech to the Indigenous Parliament of America, Ecuador. Instituto Científico de Culturas Indígenas. www.icci.nativeweb.org/boletin/cumbre2004/chuma.html (accessed May 25, 2005).

Chuma, Vicenta, and Josefina Lema. 2000. Construimos la vida, llamando a la paz. *Instituto Científico de Culturas Indígenas* 2, no. 14. www.icci.nativeweb.org/boletin/mayo2000/chuma .html (accessed May 25, 2005).

CONAIE. 1994. *Memorias de las jornadas del Foro de la Mujer Indígena del Ecuador.* Quito: CONAIE.

CONAMU-CONMIE. 2004. Document prepared for the Taller Mujeres Indígenas en el Plan de Igualdad de Oportunidades, La Merced, Ecuador, March 20.

CONMIE. 2007a. Informe de actividades 2005–2007, Quito, Ecuador, November.

———. 2007b. Vicepresidencia, planificación estratégica, 2005–2009. Quito, Ecuador.

Crain, Mary. 2001. La interpretación de género y etnicidad: Nuevas autorepresentaciones de la mujer indígena en el contexto urbano de Quito. In *Antología: Estudios de género,* ed. Gioconda Herrera, 351–381. Quito: FLACSO.

Crespi, Muriel. 1976. Mujeres campesinas como líderes sindicales: La falta de propiedad como calificación para puestos públicos. *Estudios Andinos* 5 (1): 151–170.

De la Cadena, Marisol. 1992. Las mujeres son más indias: Etnicidad y género en una comunidad del Cuzco. *Revista Isis Internacional: Ediciones de las Mujeres*, no. 16:25–45.

———. 2000. *Indigenous mestizos: The politics of race and culture in Cuzco, Peru, 1919–1991.* Durham, NC: Duke University Press.

De la Torre, Luz María. 1999. *Un universo femenino en el mundo andino.* Quito: INDESIC-Fundación Hanns Seidel.

Fraser, Nancy. 1997. *Justitia interrupta: Reflexiones críticas desde una posición "postsocialista."* Bogotá: Universidad de Los Andes.

García, Fernando. 2002. *Formas indígenas de administrar justicia.* Quito: FLACSO.

Hamilton, Sarah. 1998. *The two-headed household: Gender and rural development in the Ecuadorian Andes.* Pittsburgh: University of Pittsburgh Press.

Harvey, Penélope. 1989. *Género, autoridad y competencia lingüística: Participación política de la mujer en pueblos andinos.* Documentos de Trabajo, no. 33. Lima: IEP.

Hernández, Rosalva A., and María Teresa Sierra. 2005. Repensar los derechos colectivos desde el género: Aportes de las mujeres indígenas al debate de la autonomía. In *La doble mirada: Voces e historias de mujeres indígenas latinoamericanas,* coord. Martha Sánchez, 105–120. Mexico City: Instituto de Liderazgo Simone de Beauvoir / UNIFEM.

Larrea, Carlos, and Fernando Montenegro. 2005. Ecuador. In *Indigenous people, poverty, and human development in Latin America: 1994–2004,* ed. Gillette Hall and Harry Patrinos, 67–105. New York: Palgrave Macmillan.

Lyons, Barry J. 2001. Religion, authority, and identity: Intergenerational politics, ethnic resurgence, and respect in Chimborazo, Ecuador. *Latin American Research Review* 36 (1): 7–48.

Masaquiza, Miriam. 2004. Mujeres indígenas fuertemente unidas a pesar de los riesgos. *Yamaipacha Actualidad* 23 (40): 14–15, 40. Internal bulletin of FHS-INDESIC.

Minaar, Renée. 1998. Género dentro de un discurso étnico: El ejemplo del movimiento indígena en el Ecuador. In *Ciudadanía y participación política,* ed. Guadalupe León, 69–79. Quito: Abya-Yala.

Minutes. 1990. Encuentro Nacional de la Mujer Indígena, Riobamba, Ecuador, February 9–11.

Mohanty, Chandra T. 1986. Under Western eyes: Feminist scholarship and colonial discourses. In *Third world women and the politics of feminism,* ed. Chandra Mohanty, Ann Russo, and Lourdes Torres, 51–81. Bloomington: Indiana University Press.

———. 2003. Under Western eyes revisited: Feminist solidarity through anticapitalist struggles. In *Feminism without borders: Decolonizing theory practicing solidarity,* ed. Chandra Mohanty, 221–251. Durham, NC: Duke University Press.

Morocho, Abelina. 1998. Historia de la vida de la profesora Abelina Morocho Pinguil, primera alcaldesa indígena de América Latina. In *Mujeres contracorriente: Voces de líderes indígenas,* ed. Emma Cervone, 209–226. Quito: CEPLAES.

Muratorio, Blanca. 2002. Violencia contra mujeres en comunidades indígenas del Napo: Historia y cultura en un contexto de globalización. Paper presented at LASA's Ecuatorianists' meeting, LASA, Quito, July 18–22.

Pacari, Nina. 1998. La mujer indígena: Reflexiones sobre su identidad de género. In *Ciudadanía y participación política,* ed. Guadalupe León, 59–79. Quito: Abya-Yala.

Painemal, Millaray. 2005. La experiencia de las organizaciones de mujeres mapuche: Resistencia y desafíos ante una doble discriminación. In *La doble mirada: Voces e historias de mujeres indígenas latinoamericanas,* coord. Martha Sánchez, 77–88. Mexico City: Instituto de Liderazgo Simone de Beauvoir / UNIFEM.

Prieto, Mercedes. 1998. El liderazgo en las mujeres indígenas: Tendiendo puentes entre género y etnia. In *Mujeres contracorriente: Voces de líderes indígenas*, ed. Emma Cervone, 15–37. Quito: CEPLAES.

Radcliffe, Sara H. 1993. People have to rise up—like the greatest women fighters: The state and peasant women in Peru. In *Viva: Women and popular protest in Latin America*, ed. Sarah A. Radcliffe and Sallie Westwood, 197–235. London: Routledge.

Reuque, Isolde. 2002. *Una flor que renace: Autobiografía de una dirigente mapuche*. Santiago: DIBAM.

Richards, Patricia. 2002. Expandir el concepto de la ciudadanía de las mujeres: La visión del pueblo y la representación de las mujeres mapuches en SERNAM. In *Impactos y desafíos de las crisis internacionales: Chile 2001–2002*, 267–297. Santiago: FLACSO.

Sánchez, Martha, and Alma Gilda López Mejía. 2005. Ser mujer indígena en México: Una experiencia personal y colectiva en el movimiento indígena en la última década. In *La doble mirada: Voces e historias de mujeres indígenas latinoamericanas*, coord. Martha Sánchez, 89–104. Mexico City: Instituto de Liderazgo Simone de Beauvoir / UNIFEM.

Sikkink, Lynn. 1997. El poder mediador del cambio de aguas: Género y el cuerpo político condeño. In *Más allá del silencio: Las fronteras de género en los Andes*, ed. Arnold Denise, 94–122. La Paz: CIASE / ILCA.

Tene, Carmen. 2000. Ruptura de la exclusión de mujeres indígenas. In *Mujer, participación y desarrollo*, 201–223. Quito: CORDES.

Weismantel, Mary J. 1994. *Alimentación, género y pobreza en los Andes ecuatorianos*. Quito: Abya-Yala.

PART V

SHAPING PUBLIC POLICY WITH A GENDER PERSPECTIVE

13 Peace Begins at Home

WOMEN'S STRUGGLES AGAINST VIOLENCE AND STATE ACTIONS IN COSTA RICA

MONTSERRAT SAGOT

Several studies have shown that violence against women is a major social problem—stemming from a social organization based on gender inequality—that systematically affects millions of women all over the world.[1] An endemic form of such violence is the abuse of women by their partners. According to research carried out in Latin America, 25 percent to more than 50 percent of women report having suffered this type of abuse.[2] In Costa Rica results of the National Survey on Violence against Women show that 58 percent of women have experienced at least one incident of physical or sexual violence after age fifteen and, in most cases, that violence was exercised by men close to them (Sagot 2004).

Violence against women is a structural component of the system of gender oppression. Recourse to violence is not only one of the most effective means to keep women under control but also one of the most brutal, explicit ways in which domination is expressed. The relative positions of females and males involve a hierarchical organization in which males control both the main resources of society and women. There are many ideological, political, economic, and legal supports to the exercise of authority of men over women. Although these vary historically and culturally, the use of violence is one of the main and generalized forms that helps the exercise of such authority.

As Rebecca and Russell Dobash state, while the legal right of men to exercise violence against women is no longer explicitly recognized in most Western societies, the heritage of ancient laws and openly sanctioned social practices continue to generate the conditions that allow the pervasive existence of this type of violence (1979). While these practices currently lack explicit legal endorsement, the inaction, indifference, and contradictory policies of social institutions still reflect the ideal of women's subordinate position and of men's right to dominate and control, even by using the means of violence. Likewise, the state's inaction regarding this issue is related to the notion that certain aspects of social life, particularly those pertaining to the home or the so-called private sphere, should not fall within the control of the state.

This phenomenon is the outcome of notions dating back to Aristotle, whose theory of justice relegated women to the household, a place populated by persons who are not equal to free men, those who actively participate in political justice. In fact, Western political theory as a whole, and consequently the shaping of its social institutions, has been influenced by these notions, which regard women as the keepers of areas of life defined as lying outside the scope of justice (Okin 1989).

On the other hand, Western societies have established a strong association between peace and safety and the institution of the family, to the extent that some conservative thinkers such as Talcott Parsons have called it "a haven in a soulless world" (1976, 89). Consequently, it has not been easy to admit that most violations of women's human rights occur in the home or in the context of next-of-kin relationships. But for women, the family is the most violent social group, and the home the most dangerous place. The Costa Rican National Survey on Violence against Women proved that men with whom women have a close relationship are to blame for more than 65 percent of the acts of violence against them. The danger of the private sphere is also confirmed by the fact that more than 80 percent of the incidents of violence, including most murders of women or femicides, are perpetrated in the home, mainly by intimate partners (Sagot 2004; Carcedo and Sagot 2002; Pola 2002).

Starting in the 1970s the women's movement began to make such violence visible as a social and political problem stemming from a hierarchical gender system. A large theoretical and empirical production shows that the inclusion of this problem into the public agenda, together with the subsequent passing of legislation and the development of public policies to confront it, is a direct result of the actions undertaken by the feminist movement.[3] Thus began a process that intends to erase the myth that this type of violence is a private, even normal pattern within human family dynamics, which translates into the belief that such violence should remain outside the scope of justice and the state. Through testimonials, research findings, demonstrations, and other interventions, the feminist movement succeeded in bringing the problem to light, which contributed to show the artificiality of the dichotomies public/private and personal/political. As a result, the road was cleared for concrete claims for state intervention.

This chapter explores the Costa Rican feminist movement's experiences and contributions to the field, as well as the latest breakthroughs and achievements. It also deals with the permanent tensions between the movement's proposals and claims and their social impact. In other words, I will discuss the efficacy and relevance of the new laws, policies, and institutions in the pursuit of the ultimate goal of building a society free of violence against women.

Giving Visibility to the Ignored: The Contributions of the Feminist Movement

It was in the 1980s that the Latin American feminist movement began to publicly denounce violence against women as a major problem with serious consequences. In 1981, during the Primer Encuentro Feminista de América Latina y el Caribe (First Latin American and Caribbean Feminist Encuentro), held in Bogotá, the problem was identified as a priority, and November 25 was declared the International Day for the Elimination of Violence against Women.[4] In 1990, during the fifth Encuentro held in Argentina, the Red Latinoamericana contra la Violencia Doméstica y Sexual (Latin American Feminist Network against Domestic and Sexual Violence) was established. At a varying pace throughout the decade, feminist organizations in the various countries developed awareness campaigns, drafted legislation and public policies proposals, and opened the first support programs.[5] In practically every country, the 1990s also witnessed the creation of national networks to confront violence against women, mostly composed of feminist organizations and NGOs.

One fundamental factor in this process was the positioning of violence against women as an issue related to power, that is, as the outcome of a structural system of gender oppression. Along these lines, various institutions and social practices were analyzed as the par excellence manifestation of male domination. In Ana Carcedo's words,

> We have spoken of laws made by men with the purpose of retaining their gender domination; of the police as safe-keepers of the patriarchal order; of State institutions insensitive to the suffering and needs of abused women; of an upbringing that produces aggressive men and disempowered women; of Churches and their forgiveness-oriented discourses; of Judeo Christian morality fostering guilt and renunciation to happiness on Earth. . . . We have also spoken of the structure of property and credit that leaves economic resources in the hands of men; of the formal political structure that excludes women, and of customs and traditions which amount to stereotyped practices, maintenance rituals for the established order between genders. (Carcedo and Molina 2003, 7)

The Latin American feminist movement has also stated that the problem must be understood as a denial of citizenship rights and as a social exclusion issue. In this sense, violence against women has been regarded as a matter of justice, that is to say, not as an individual, private, or family problem but as a public issue closely related to the social distribution of duties and rights, of burdens and benefits. Women, especially those who are abused, are denied their rights and benefits.

Feminists have demanded that their respective country's political institutions implement a broad notion of social justice to enable the construction of a society that contains the necessary conditions for all its members to develop and exercise their capacities, express their experiences, and participate in determining their living conditions. There is no reference to a universalizing concept of justice, but to one that considers the distinctive features and differences that social and sexual hierarchies produce in each individual and that rule their differential access to society's material and symbolic resources. Along these lines, the claim entails a "genderization" of the state—a state that will explicitly acknowledge that some citizens are men while others are women (Lazarus-Black 2003)—and a change in the relations of power to ensure women's control over society's material and social resources as well as over their own bodies, which means control over their lives.

The 1990s witnessed some of the most outstanding conquests achieved by the feminist movement. It was then when violence against women was brought into the global agenda and the problem was introduced into several international declarations. After several resolutions were issued by the United Nations and the Organization of American States, the United Nations World Conference on Human Rights, held in Vienna in 1993, created an opportunity to crystallize a political consensus on the fact that the various forms of violence against women, whether in the context of armed conflict, other public scenarios, or in private life, should be understood as blatant violations of human rights (Sullivan 1994). Also, as a result of feminist actions in the Americas, in 1993 the Pan-American Health Organization declared violence against women to be a public health issue, and in 1994 the Organization of American States approved the Inter-American Convention on the Prevention, Punishment, and Eradication of Violence against Women (Convention of Belém do Pará), which is binding to the OAS member states. Moreover, as a result of proposals by Latin American participants, violence against women was included in the twelve-point Platform for Action agreed on at the Fourth United Nations World Conference on Women, held in 1995 in Beijing.

Such international instruments and declarations have proved most useful for the feminist movement to demand that particular actions be taken in every country, arguing that the state is ultimately responsible for its actions and its inactions (Isis Internacional 2002). Consequently, in the 1990s all the countries of the continent, with the sole exception of the United States, ratified the Convention of Belém do Pará and passed legislation and public policies on some forms of violence, particularly intrafamily violence. National plans and training programs for public and private institutions have multiplied, along with shelters for battered women.

Thus, the feminist movement of the region became a vehicle for broadening democracy and, at the same time, it succeeded in bringing about a rupture in the patriarchal system, by allowing the voices of the most excluded women in society—that is, the abused ones—to inspire proposals for state policies and legal reforms. In other words, the problem of violence against women gave birth to a counterhegemonic discourse that disseminated new concepts and ideas and propitiated changes in the state agenda (Young 2000; Weldon 2004). In this sense, the discourse about violence against women, more than any other feminist discourse, has played a fundamental role in efforts to politicize the private sphere.

This was possible because the state, far from being a monolithic, instrumental entity, is a differentiated set of institutions, a territory in dispute enjoying relative autonomy to represent and reconstruct gender relations (MacDowell Santos 2004; Schild 1998). The relationship between the feminist movement and the state is dynamic, contradictory, and conditioned by the political and historical conjuncture (MacDowell Santos 2004; Molyneux 2000). Like any other social movement attempting to influence the state, the feminist movement has a better chance of being influential in progressive places and times and when there are democratic openings. So, opportunities for feminist influence fluctuate between moments of liberating change and receptivity and times of harsher conservatism and repression (Lengermann and Brantley 2000). There is, besides, a permanent tension between the feminist movement's proposals and visions and its capacity to influence the powers that be. In other words, in the field of social transformations related to violence against women, "there are no definitive achievements, nor progress devoid of contradictions" (Carcedo 2003).

Furthermore, according to Sonia Alvarez's definition (1998, 265), the feminist movement should be understood as a "discursive field of intervention/action" rather than as a social movement in the classic sense of the term, that is, one that involves mass demonstrations, mobilizations, and so on. The feminist movement should be seen as a political field that goes beyond the borders of groups or organizations. Alvarez also posits that feminists scattered over the field are always engaged not only in "classically political" struggles but also in discursive struggles about the meaning of citizenship, human rights, violence, and so on. At the same time, women who operate within the feminist field relate to each other in a number of public, private, and alternative spaces through various ways and means of communication.

Peace in Central America and at Home: Feminism and State Action in Costa Rica

In the 1980s, at the close of the United Nations' Women's Decade (1975–1985), Costa Rica initiated the first activities to confront violence against women. As was the case in other countries, these initiatives stemmed directly from women's organizations. In 1988 the Mujer No Estás Sola (Woman: You Are Not Alone) program was created in the framework of the Centro Feminista de Información y Acción (CEFEMINA; Feminist Center for Information and Action). This was the first Central American program that provided support to women abused by their intimate partners. In 1990 the Fundación para la Promoción, Capacitación y Acción Alternativa (Foundation for Promotion, Training, and Alternative Action) opened its first shelter for sexually abused and pregnant adolescents and, in that same year, the Fundación Ser y Crecer (Being and Growing Up Foundation) was established as the first Latin American organization dedicated entirely to dealing with the problem of incest and sexual abuse (Carcedo 2003).

In the 1990s other women's organizations such as the Colectiva Feminista Pancha Carrasco (Feminist Collective Pancha Carrasco) and the Alianza de Mujeres Costarricenses (Alliance of Costa Rican Women), as well as some collective initiatives, such as the Colectiva 25 de Noviembre (November 25 Collective) in 1991 and the Agenda Política de Mujeres (Women's Political Agenda) in 1997, also included the issue of violence against women in their working agendas. Since then, there has been an enormous increase in the number of organizations that work on the various manifestations of violence in particular populations, such as sex workers, the GLBT population, and domestic workers.[6]

Given the state of war and systematic violation of human rights experienced in Central America in the seventies and eighties, it is no coincidence that Costa Rica was the place where social and economic conditions allowed a wider initial development of actions intended to publicly address this form of violence. This country boasts relative economic stability and a long-standing formal democratic tradition.

Moreover, it is the seat of several supragovernmental institutions, such as the Instituto Interamericano de Derechos Humanos (Inter-American Institute for Human Rights) and the Instituto Latinoamericano de Naciones Unidas para la Prevención del Delito (United Nations' Latin American Institute for Crime Prevention), all of which provide a receptive environment for the visions and claims of the feminist movement.

Because of Costa Rica's particular conditions, feminists did not have to face the obstacles that hindered other Central American activists at a time when it was commonly believed that these manifestations of violence were not a priority if compared to the violence generated by war and repression that prevailed in the region (Carcedo and Verbaken 1992). Taking full advantage of the proposal for the Central American peace process in which the president of Costa Rica Oscar Arias (1986–1990) was actively involved, some feminist organizations posited that the peace and democratization processes must guarantee a life free of violence and abuse for the entire population, regardless of where and by whom that violence is perpetrated.[7] As was expressed by a Costa Rican feminist, it was vital to promote this idea because "in daily life, all forms of violence are firmly intertwined, and sometimes the aggressors themselves engage in different forms of violence as they exercise the different powers with which they have been endowed" (Carcedo and Verbaken 1992, 12).

So in light of the peace proposals for Central America, feminists proclaimed that no peace was possible unless it began at home. The juncture was also favorable to advance some legal changes, because First Lady Margarita Penón was interested in furthering reforms leading to gender equality. A joint effort by the government and some women's organizations resulted in the Real Equality for Women Bill (1988). The bill was passed by Congress in 1990 and signed into law the same year. For the first time ever, a piece of legislation responded to a series of feminist demands related to domestic and sexual violence against women. This law established that when charges are pressed against an aggressor, he must leave the shared home and pay mandatory provisional alimony. The law also created the Ombudswomen Office and other measures to improve the assistance and protection of women during judicial procedures (García et al. 2000). While the enactment of the Real Equality Law has been viewed as a great step forward, particularly because of the public debate that it aroused around discrimination and gender equity, the law actually contains only a few restricted measures dealing with violence against women. In addition, many of these measures, such as the removal of the aggressor from the home, were not implemented due to the lack of regulatory instruments (Carcedo 2003).

It was not until 1991 that, at the initiative of a feminist organization, state institutions and civil society organizations gathered to develop proposals for a new public policy (CEFEMINA 1992). This was the first effort aimed at responding to the needs for new legislation, victim protection measures, and overall care, education, and sensitivity training. In the same year the Primer Encuentro Centroamericano y del Caribe sobre Violencia contra las Mujeres (First Central American and

Caribbean Encuentro on Violence against Women) was held in Costa Rica, with the objective of developing a framework proposal to design public policies related to violence against women and within the family. The conference was attended by representatives from all over Latin America and the Caribbean, who agreed that all proposals involving public policies should be guided by the principle that "violence against women is neither natural nor spontaneous, but learnt, chosen, and encouraged" (CEFEMINA 1991, 1).

Expansion of State Actions on Gender Equity: 1994–1999

In Costa Rica the development of norms for the protection of women's rights, particularly those concerning their defense against violence, reached its climax between 1994 and 1999, when most of the laws and legal reforms on the matter were approved and enacted. A large number of the norms approved at that time were fostered within the framework of public policies and their respective nationwide plans, such as the Plan de Igualdad de Oportunidades entre Mujeres y Hombres (Equal Opportunity Plan for Women and Men) and the Plan Nacional contra la Violencia Intrafamiliar (National Plan against Intrafamily Violence) (García et al. 2000; Ramellini and Mesa 2000). In 1995 Congress ratified the Convention of Belém do Pará and passed a large corpus of new legislation on sexual harassment, domestic violence, alimony and child support, civil union, sexual exploitation, and sexual and reproductive rights, among other issues concerning the expansion of rights for women and other specific groups.[8]

During the same period, the national machinery for the advancement of women—first the Centro Nacional para el Desarrollo de la Mujer y la Familia (National Center for the Development of Women and Families) and then its successor, the Instituto Nacional de las Mujeres (Women's National Institute)—developed an integrated strategy to face the problem through the establishment of the Sistema Nacional para la Atención de la Violencia Intrafamiliar (National System to Address Intrafamily Violence) (1997).[9] The creation of this system enabled the development of intervention models for the health, education, and municipal sectors, and for workers helping women in shelters. Another beneficial offshoot of the system was the strengthening of training programs for service providers in the health and judicial sectors.

The Costa Rican state extended its action to address this form of violence thanks to a combination of various factors. First, the impact of the United Nations' international conferences on human rights (Vienna, 1993), population and development (Cairo, 1994) and women (Beijing, 1995), whose platforms for action reconfigured the discourse and practice of human rights. This influenced many progressive states, including the Costa Rican state, which went on to implement some normative and institutional changes to adapt its practices to the new international claims.

Second, in the early 1990s, feminist activism experienced an increase in the region, reflected in the appearance of new groups and in the development of various initiatives, such as the creation of magazines and videos, the organization of collectives, the opening of programs for abused women, and the institutionalization of women's studies within universities (Sagot 2002). This process was strengthened by the Primer Encuentro Feminista Regional Centroamericano (First Central American Regional Feminist Encuentro), held in 1992 in Nicaragua under the name Historia de Género en Centroamérica (History of Gender in Central America), and by the Sexto Encuentro Feminista de América Latina y el Caribe (Sixth Latin American and Caribbean Feminist Encuentro), held in El Salvador in 1993, which paved the way for the discussion and definition of joint strategies. While the feminist movement in Central America has never been homogeneous, its quantitative and qualitative expansion in the early 1990s provided those feminists interested in advocacy with greater legitimacy and political power. This was critical in giving them the ability to influence the proposal and approval of new legislation and public policies regarding violence against women.

Finally, all of these processes occurred during a politically favorable period, since President José María Figueres (1994–1998), a member of the Partido de Liberación Nacional (National Liberation Party), made social equity—including gender equity—a priority in his administration. Likewise, First Lady Josette Altmann was personally committed to the advancement of women, particularly when it came to adopting measures against violence. In collaboration with the Instituto Nacional de las Mujeres, her office engineered the first national sensitization campaigns in the media. The campaigns, launched through the radio, television, and the printed press, represented an effective means to support the claims for new legislation and public policies, to encourage the demand for services, and to increase the population's awareness of the problem (García et al. 2000).

A Conservative Wave Sweeps through the World

By the year 2000 there was a notable decrease in new laws and public policies regarding gender equity and violence against women. This was due to a change of direction on the part of the local government and to the reemergence of international conservative and fundamentalist movements that promoted new forms of women's subordination and the reproduction of traditional gender roles. Nevertheless, in 2001 Congress ratified the Optional Protocol to the Convention on the Elimination of All Forms of Discrimination against Women (CEDAW) and passed a law on responsible paternity. This law, which is the only one of its kind in the world, reverses the burden of proof regarding paternal filiation. In other words, when a man does not want to take on parental responsibilities, he is the one who must prove he is not the father of the child.

Before the enactment of that law, when a man denied paternity, the woman had to undergo long, cumbersome judicial proceedings involving various manifestations of violence: male, family, and institutional. The Law on Responsible Paternity is considered a significant breakthrough because it not only frees the woman from having to prove who the father is but also establishes that, once paternity has been determined, the father is legally bound to reimburse pregnancy and delivery expenses, as well as all other child-care expenses over a twelve-month period following delivery (Carcedo 2003).

A bill to criminalize violence against women was submitted to Congress in 1999, resulting from a joint effort by a group of feminists who worked within civil society and the state. The bill was inspired by the commitments assumed by the Costa Rican state when it ratified the Convention of Belém do Pará and by the need to guarantee special protection and justice for women. It was also intended to fill a legal void, as there were no penal provisions regarding violence against women. It would apply to adult women related to the aggressor through relationships of power or trust, regardless of where the violence occurred—the home, the workplace, public spaces, and so on. In other words, the bill addressed more than domestic or family violence.

After eight years of heated debates, the Law to Criminalize Violence against Women (Law 13874) was finally passed in April 2007, but in a substantially modified form. First, it only applies to women who are married or in civil unions. Thus, a law that intended to cover all forms of violence against women was reduced to intimate partner violence. Second, the proposed penalties were drastically reduced, because legislators did not accept the argument that the unequal relations of power between the sexes should be regarded as an aggravating circumstance. While the approval of this law implied significant progress, such as the differentiation between femicide and homicide as separate criminal categories, legislators still tended to downplay the consequences of violence against women and to regard aggressors' behavior as minor offenses. There was also a tendency to consider as violence only those acts that occur within the domestic or intimate spaces and to exclude from criminalization any other forms of violence against women.

This bill was more strongly and passionately opposed than any other reforms or laws addressing violence or gender equity. Not even the Responsible Paternity Law, which affects a long-standing male practice, confronted such resistance. Apart from the fact that the law was passed during a much more politically conservative period, as illustrated by the election of legislators from new ultra right-wing parties, this law seems to have touched the core of male hegemony and some essential elements of the gender oppression structure.[10]

During the previous debates, detractors of the bill argued—among other matters—the unconstitutionality of a norm exclusively benefiting women, thus ignoring Costa Rica's ratification of CEDAW and of the Convention of Belém do Pará, both of them being sets of norms specifically addressed at women. Contrary to all empirical evidence, detractors also argued that the law failed to recognize that men and women were equally violent and that it would leave men with no legal tools to defend themselves from supposed female aggressors. They even claimed that, although statistics might not show the existence of a significant number of women who murder their partners, women were the masterminds behind such murders. (This argument has validity—except that the murder has little to do with power differentials between men and women when it is the result of women defending themselves against past abuse.) Further arguments stated that family men who abuse their wives should not be incarcerated, as they would be mixed up with common criminals, as though abusive men are not themselves criminals.

Legislators also said that not all manifestations of violence can be penalized, as many of them result from "normal, natural conflicts" in the relations between the sexes. One speaker went as far as to publicly declare that the bill should not be passed because men holding positions of authority would be at risk of being punished for calling their secretaries "stupid," something they were naturally entitled to do if the secretaries made mistakes.

The feminist movement's experience regarding this law leads to the conclusion that while Costa Rica has approved a large number of legal norms and public policies addressing violence—many more than in other Central American countries—most of the laws do not directly address the unequal relations of power between men and women. In other words, there has been significant progress regarding services and legal resources, which shows the commitment of some state agencies with abused women. There has also been some degree of cultural change, thanks to which violence is no longer invisible or considered a private issue.

However, the approval of these laws and policies did not provoke much opposition because of their limited nature (they are quite reformist), not having specifically addressed violence against women. In other words, they were gender neutral, and as such they only partially disturbed the system of gender oppression. On the other hand, the Bill to Criminalize Violence against Women was submitted in a much more conservative social climate, characterized by the appearance of both religious and political organized groups that tried to put the breaks on feminist progress and even to undo previous feminist efforts to expand women's rights as citizens. From this perspective, debates that revolved around this law are emblematic of the new conditions in which feminists try to advance their transformative agenda: confronted by a far less receptive society, ever more influenced by the actions and discourse of traditionalist groups that fight to protect the traditional gender order.

Violence against Women and State Action: The Limits of Reform

The feminist movement's new conceptualization of violence against women as a justice and human rights issue implies major social breakthroughs. However, there is a permanent tension between the proposals of any progressive movement and its influence on the public agenda. In other words, as the feminist movement's proposals earn social recognition, they risk losing their profoundly subversive, transformative nature. The institutions begin to appropriate feminist tenets and discourse but to adapt them to their logic and interests. This has been the case of the Costa Rica's laws and public policies on violence against women.

While laws have been approved and public policies have been put in place, the Costa Rican state is still unable to guarantee women's personal integrity or their right to full justice. Evidence of this is found in the dozens of women murdered each year in Costa Rica, victims of violence against women. Additionally, according to the National Survey on Violence against Women (Sagot 2004), only 4 percent of the women who reported an act of violence at the hands of their intimate partner succeeded in having the perpetrator convicted.

Moreover, the approval of legislation has not followed the guidelines established in the Convention of Belém do Pará. With the exception of the criminalization law, all the norms and policies enacted are related to domestic or family violence, in which protection is granted to the family in the abstract rather than to family members as concrete people with specific bodies. Furthermore, their main focus is on prevention and assistance; in other words, they ignore the unequal power relations that lie at the root of the problem. Insofar as these laws and policies are gender neutral, they do not only blur the special features characterizing violence against women but also act in detriment of the victims, for their aggressors can use the same norms as an extra instrument of abuse and the institutions can turn them into a mechanism of revictimization (CEFEMINA 2003).[11]

Many opposed criminalizing this form of violence, claiming that these laws would be discriminatory and even unconstitutional because they protect women only. This discourse remains unchanged, even though the Convention of Belém do Pará clearly establishes that the state parties must adopt the necessary "criminal, civil, and administrative norms" that will prevent, punish, and eradicate violence against women (1994, Article 7). As a result, many women have lacked access to justice and, in many cases, aggressors have enjoyed impunity, as illustrated by the results of the National Survey on Violence against Women.

The Costa Rican state's reluctance to address violence that specifically targets women can be seen both in the nature of formal laws and policies and in the way various institutions carry them out. Most of the state institutions operate according to the logic of charity, without a perspective of rights or a clear vision in which the end goal is the elimination of violence. Women are regarded as "beneficiaries," "individuals in need of help," or "victims" that have to be assisted or tolerated out of kindness, not because they are citizens with the right to protection, due process, physical integrity, justice, and a life free of violence. These institutional practices and ideas place women at great disadvantage in relation to service providers, which foster impunity and the revictimization of women through indifference, trivialization, and even mockery (Sagot and Carcedo 2000).

Programs that are controlled by bureaucrats within state agencies are often ineffective and limited. The way in which abused women are treated when they request help from the various state services indicates that training programs have not led to substantial changes in institutional practices, and certainly not to true cultural transformation, especially regarding the judiciary and the police (Sagot and Carcedo 2000; CEFEMINA 2003). Many service providers still embrace the patriarchal idea that this form of violence is not an actual risk for women, which translates into prejudiced, insensitive, and inappropriate responses to the problem (Sagot and Carcedo 2000).

In addition, the laws and policies do not account for the diversity of women and the multiple ways in which violence manifests itself. In this sense, the specific forms of violence that affect women from different social classes, ages, ethnicities, religions, skills, and sexual orientation are not reflected in the laws. For example, the laws addressed to children and adolescents are not gender specific, and there is little legislation to prevent and respond to sexual violence and sex trafficking (Claramunt 2003). At the same time, Costa Rica has not repealed laws, such as the one that criminalizes the voluntary interruption of pregnancy, which openly represent a form of violence against women and against their right to autonomy and self-determination.

In general, the Costa Rican state has not provided the necessary material or logistic resources to enforce laws and policies. For example, the budget of the Instituto Nacional de las Mujeres, the leading institution in violence issues, has been cut down by more than 40 percent over the last few years (García et al. 2000). Neoliberal policies that call for cutbacks in public expenditure and downsizing of the social sector have a very negative impact on the state's ability to address violence against women.

Public policies regarding violence occupy a marginal role in national politics. They have not even been incorporated into national development plans, nor are they seen as a matter of long-term state policies; instead, they are considered temporary issues that do not require long-term national commitments. Moreover, existing plans lack sufficient resources and do not have monitoring and evaluation mechanisms that could determine whether the country is actually moving toward the construction of a society that will guarantee women a life free of violence.

From this perspective, it is possible to conclude that the relations between the state and the feminist movement are problematic and riddled with contradictions. On the one hand, the state incorporates some of the movement's claims into its agenda. But, on the other hand, feminist proposals are drained of their most important contribution and analytical tool: the understanding that violence against women is a matter of power, the product of a society characterized by inequality and gender oppression. The feminist movement's radical, transforming approaches are then recycled by the state and returned to society as socially acceptable laws, policies, and programs that do not represent a threat to the establishment. In that sense, rather than bring about social and cultural change, the institutionalization of feminist demands leads to the co-optation of those demands and even of the movement itself.

Nonetheless, most Costa Rican feminists believe in the importance of keeping up the struggle for the enactment of laws and policies, because these resources have opened options for abused women, expanded their rights as citizens, and saved many lives (Carcedo and Molina 2003; CEFEMINA 2003). In the words of a local activist: "Our efforts are not pointless. Far from it, even if we fail to achieve the eradication of violence and do not reach our final goal, we win all the same. Many women live better; we live better, much better lives" (Carcedo and Molina 2003, 82).

Finally, it is necessary to acknowledge that despite the problems and the contradictions, the advances and setbacks, processes of social transformation usually evolve slowly, registering modifications on a day-by-day basis. The changes promoted by the feminist movement have already led to new societal ideas and practices regarding violence against women, something that would have been unthinkable twenty-five years ago. Nevertheless, the goal of the feminist movement is not—and should not be—merely to struggle for better policies, laws, and programs. These should be viewed as part of the tools used in a struggle that began over two hundred years ago, aimed at building a society that can guarantee women's autonomy, well-being, integrity, and the right to live free from all forms of violence.

ACKNOWLEDGMENTS
Translated by Marta Castillo.

NOTES

1. On this particular point, see the following studies: Heise et al. (1994), Ellsberg et al. (1996), Carcedo and Zamora (1999), Kennedy (1999), Sagot and Carcedo (2000), and Johnson et al. (2008).

2. See, for example, Johns Hopkins University, Center for Health and Gender Equity (1999), United Nations (2000), Güezmes et al. (2002), and Sagot (2004).

3. See, for example, Pleck (1987), Gordon (1988), Dobash and Dobash (1992), Sullivan (1994), Rivera (1995), Sagot and Carcedo (2000), Lazarus-Black (2003), Weldon (2004), and MacDowell Santos (2004).

4. The date was chosen in commemoration of the vicious murder of the three Mirabal sisters, political Dominican activists who were killed in 1960 by order of dictator Rafael Trujillo (1930–1961). Following the commemoration established by the feminist movement, in December 1999 the fifty-fourth session of the United Nations General Assembly adopted Resolution 54/134, declaring November 25 the International Day for the Elimination of Violence against Women.

5. The first program of this kind was the Julia Burgos Protected Home, opened in Puerto Rico in 1979.

6. Among the new groups stand out La Sala, which organized and supported sex workers; Instituto Latinoamericano para la Prevención en Salud (Latin American Institute for Health Prevention); Triángulo Rosa; Centro de Investigación y Promoción para América Central en Derechos Humanos (CIPAC; Center for Research and Advocacy for Human Rights in Central America), which took on the defense of the rights of the GLBT (gay, lesbian, bisexual, and transgender) populations, just as Las Entendidas had done before with lesbians; and Asociación de Trabajadoras Domésticas (ASTRADOMES; Domestic Workers Association), which takes care of domestic workers.

7. Oscar Arias's participation in the peace process earned him the Nobel Peace Price in 1987.

8. The following legislation was passed in the period: Law against Sexual Harassment in the Workplace and Educational Institutions (1995), Regulatory Law for Civil Union (1995), Law against Domestic Violence (1996), Alimony Law (1996), Childhood and Adolescence Code (1997), General Law for the Protection of Adolescent Mothers (1997), Law for the Creation of the Women's National Institute (1998), Law against the Sexual Exploitation of Minors (1999), and a decree establishing the mandatory recording of intrafamily violence at the Costa Rican Social Security System (1999).

9. The executive decree that created the system established the following programs: Gender Violence Area within the National Institute for Women, which opened a women's police station and began a hotline; Violence Commission at the Costa Rican Social Security System; Ministry of Public Education's Commission for the Prevention of Violence; Judicial System's Commission for the Follow-up of Domestic Violence; and Ministry of Planning and Economic Policy's Commission for Domestic Violence. In addition, women's municipal offices were opened and support networks were organized.

10. In the last few years, organizations of conservative males have appeared, which oppose all legislation geared at promoting changes in gender relations. They argue that such changes contribute to discrimination against men and alter traditional gender roles. In their opinion,

such roles must be kept at any cost, since they are "natural" and "complementary" and protect social and political order.

11. Some aggressors, foreseeing that a woman will request protection from them under the provisions of the Law of Domestic Violence, make the first move and, resorting to the very same law, file a report against the woman. There are also child abusers who file a domestic violence complaint against their female partner and request protection. As a consequence, she is the one who has to leave the shared home.

REFERENCES

Alvarez, Sonia E. 1998. Feminismos latinoamericanos. *Estudios Feministas* 6 (2): 265–284.

Carcedo, Ana. 2003. *Violencia contra las mujeres: Aportes para la discusión sobre un sistema de vigilancia y protección del derecho de las mujeres a vivir libres de violencia.* San José: Proyecto Estado de la Nación.

Carcedo, Ana, and Giselle Molina. 2003. *Mujeres contra la violencia: Una rebelión radical.* San José: Royal Netherlands Embassy / CEFEMINA.

Carcedo, Ana, and Montserrat Sagot. 2002. *Femicidio en Costa Rica, 1990–1999.* San José: Instituto Nacional de la Mujer / Pan American Health Organization.

Carcedo, Ana, and Karin Verbaken. 1992. *La violencia contra las mujeres en Centroamérica y la Cooperación Holandesa.* San José: CEFEMINA.

Carcedo, Ana, and Alicia Zamora. 1999. *Ruta crítica de las mujeres afectadas por la violencia intrafamiliar en Costa Rica.* San José: Pan American Health Organization.

CEFEMINA. 1991. *Memorias del Encuentro Centroamericano y del Caribe sobre Violencia Contra la Mujer.* San José: CEFEMINA.

———. 1992. *La política contra la violencia ha sido no tener políticas: I Consulta Nacional para Elaborar Propuestas de Políticas Públicas en Relación a la Violencia contra la Mujer.* San José: Feminist's Center of Information and Action.

———. 2003. *Políticas públicas sobre violencia contra las mujeres: Un balance desde las organizaciones de mujeres.* San José: Feminist's Center of Information and Action.

Claramunt, María Cecilia. 2003. *Situación de los servicios médico-legales y de salud para víctimas de violencia sexual en Centroamérica.* San José: Unidad Género y Salud / Pan American Health Organization.

Dobash, Rebecca E., and Russell P. Dobash. 1979. *Violence against wives: A case against patriarchy.* New York: Free Press.

———. 1992. *Women, violence and social change.* London: Routledge.

Ellsberg, Mary, Rodolfo Peña, Andrés Herrera, Jerker Liljestrand, and Anna Winkvist. 1996. *Confites en el infierno: Prevalencia y características de la violencia conyugal hacia las mujeres en Nicaragua.* Managua: Department of Preventive Medicine / UNAM-León.

García, Ana Isabel, Enrique Gomáriz, Ana Lorena Hidalgo, Teresita Ramellini, and Manuel Barahona. 2000. *Sistemas públicos contra la violencia doméstica en América Latina: Un estudio regional comparado.* San José: GESO.

Gordon, Linda. 1988. *Heroes of their own lives: The politics and history of family violence.* New York: Penguin Books.

Güezmes, Ana, Nancy Palomino, and Miguel Ramos. 2002. *Violencia sexual y física contra las mujeres en el Perú.* Lima: Flora Tristán / World Health Organization / Cayetano Heredia Peruvian University.

Heise, Lori, Jacqueline Pitanguy, and Adrienne Germain. 1994. *Violencia contra la mujer: La carga oculta sobre la salud.* Washington, DC: World Bank.

Isis Internacional. 2002. *Violencia contra las mujeres en América Latina y el Caribe español 1990–2000: Balance de una década.* Santiago: Isis Internacional / UNIFEM.

Johns Hopkins University, Center for Health and Gender Equity. 1999. *Para acabar la violencia contra la mujer.* Population Reports, vol. 1, no. 11. Baltimore: Johns Hopkins University.

Johnson, Holly, Natalia Ollus, and Sami Nevala. 2008. *Violence against women: An international perspective.* New York: Springer.

Kennedy, Mirta. 1999. *Violencia intrafamiliar: Ruta crítica de las mujeres afectadas en Honduras.* Tegucigalpa, Honduras: PAHO / World Health Organization.

Lazarus-Black, Mindie. 2003. *The (heterosexual) regendering of a modern state: Criminalizing and implementing domestic violence law in Trinidad.* Chicago: American Bar Foundation.

Lengermann, Patricia M., and Jill N. Brantley. 2000. Teoría feminista contemporánea. In *Teoría sociológica contemporánea,* ed. George Ritzer, 353–451. Mexico City: McGraw-Hill.

MacDowell Santos, Cecilia. 2004. En-gendering the police: Women's police stations and feminism in São Paulo. *Latin American Research Review* 39 (3): 29–55.

Molyneux, Maxine. 2000. Twentieth-century state formations in Latin America. In *Hidden histories of gender and the state in Latin America,* ed. Elizabeth Dore and Maxine Molyneux, 33–82. Durham, NC: Duke University Press.

Okin, Susan Moller. 1989. *Justice, gender and the family.* New York: Basic Books.

Organization of American States. 1994. *Inter-American Convention on the Prevention, Punishment, and Eradication of Violence against Women (Convention of Belém do Pará).* Washington, DC: Organization of American States.

Parsons, Talcott. 1976. *Ensayos sobre teoría sociológica.* Mexico City: Amorrortu.

Pleck, Elizabeth. 1987. *Domestic tyranny: The making of social policy against family violence from colonial times to the present.* New York: Oxford University Press.

Pola, María Jesús. 2002. *Feminicidio en República Dominicana.* Santo Domingo: Pro-Family.

Ramellini, Teresita, and Silvia Mesa. 2000. *La situación de la violencia de género contra las mujeres en Costa Rica.* San José: INAMU-UNDP.

Rivera, Jenny. 1995. Puerto Rico's Domestic Violence Prevention and Intervention Law and the United States Violence against Women Act of 1994: The limitations of legislative responses. *Columbia Journal of Gender and Law* 5 (1): 78–126.

Sagot, Montserrat. 2002. Los estudios feministas en Centroamérica: Contándonos a nosotras mismas desde la academia. In *Feminismos latinoamericanos: Retos y perspectivas,* ed. Gloria Careaga, 141–156. Mexico City: PUEG, UNAM.

———. 2004. *Resultados de la Encuesta Nacional de Violencia contra las Mujeres.* San José: Research Center for Women's Studies, University of Costa Rica.

Sagot, Montserrat, and Ana Carcedo. 2000. *Ruta crítica de las mujeres afectadas por la violencia intrafamiliar en América Latina.* San José: Pan American Health Organization.

Schild, Verónica. 1998. New subjects of rights? Women's movements and the construction of citizenship in the "new democracies." In *Cultures of politics / Politics of culture: Revisioning Latin American social movements,* ed. Sonia E. Alvarez, Evelina Dagnino, and Arturo Escobar, 93–117. Boulder, CO: Westview.

Sullivan, Donna J. 1994. Women's human rights and the 1993 World Conference on Human Rights. *American Journal of International Law* 88 (1): 152–167.

United Nations. 2000. *The world's women: Trends and statistics.* New York: United Nations.

Weldon, Laurel S. 2004. The dimensions and policy impact of feminist civil society. *International Feminist Journal of Politics* 6 (1): 1–28.

Young, Iris Marion. 2000. *La justicia y la política de la diferencia.* Valencia, Spain: Cátedra.

14

New Challenges in Feminist Practice

THE WOMEN'S INSTITUTES IN MEXICO

MARÍA LUISA TARRÉS

To say that institutional reforms alter behavior is a hypothesis, not an axiom.   —Robert D. Putnam

After thirty years of feminist mobilization and as a government with a conservative bent is adopting a gender discourse, it is well worthwhile to evaluate the results of women's collective action aimed at influencing the sexual dimensions of power and politics. Although by their nature government agendas tend to neutralize the subversive charge present in the proposals of any social movement, the history of the feminist movement in Mexico has been shaped by a changing context that has actually integrated a gender perspective into the political culture of a nascent democracy (Fraser 1991; Tarrow 1994). Between 1970 and 2000, the country went through great sociopolitical changes brought about by the adoption of a neoliberal model, the reform of the remaining institutions of the Mexican Revolution, and the long struggle to democratize the single-party system that had dominated the country for more than seventy years. Long-standing and stormy divisions among the traditional political elite, which led to the political reforms of 1997, compounded those structural changes. This reform, negotiated over a twenty-year period by a variety of social and party-political actors, successfully created pluralism in the party system and set out electoral regulations to ensure free and fair elections and the take-off of democracy.

In 2000 feminist and women's mobilization was faced with an unforeseen turn of events. Vicente Fox, of the Partido de Acción Nacional (PAN; National Action Party) assumed the presidency of Mexico's first democratically elected government. PAN is a party of Catholic origin with little prior political experience at the national level. Its leaders were relatively young, attended mostly church schools, and had their roots primarily in the private sector. Ideologically, this party spanned the political spectrum, from the most conservative fringes to the new middle-class business sectors, which, although they had benefited from the old redistributive economic policies of the Partido Revolucionario Institucional (PRI; Institutional Revolutionary Party) began to seek out connections with big business both domestically and internationally. PAN went on the offensive against the authoritarian government of the historically dominant PRI and took power in 2000.

By contrast, the history and experiences of the many and varied actors that make up the women's movement were quite different. Whereas the majority of the so-called old-school feminists came from the educated middle classes, from the 1970s onward they reached out to a variety of leftist groups and political parties, first to the Comunidades Eclesiásticas de Base (CEBs; Ecclesiastical Base Communities) inspired by Liberation Theology and later to low-income urban and peasant grassroots women's movements (Tarrés 2001). In the 1990s the women's movement built new alliances, this time with women civil servants, elected representatives, and party activists. However, when the moment came in 2001 to mainstream a gender perspective within government bureaucracy, the women's movement saw a decline in its ability to shape state policy. Members of the movement had fought for years for a democracy that respected gender differences, but their political allies lost the presidential elections, even though parties linked to the women's movement did manage to win some seats in the national legislature, as well as in the governorship of various states and the Federal District (Mexico City). Paradoxically, the state-level Institutos de Mujeres (Women's Institutes), which were meant to deliver gender mainstreaming, were created in a hostile political climate. What was the product, in some cases, of a life's work of intense debate and feminist activism, foundered and suffered considerable setbacks in a political context that did not offer many positive opportunities.

The Fourth United Nations World Conference on Women, in Beijing in 1995, generated the Plan Regional de Acción para Mujeres de América Latina y el Caribe (Regional Action Plan for the Women of Latin America and the Caribbean) (1995–2001), as a blueprint for the region's governments. Mexico had not abstained from this accord and, following some isolated local- and state-level initiatives to create programs and government offices to implement the Plan de Acción, it was included in the national agenda. PAN, which had just won the first truly competitive presidential elections in decades, thanks to resounding citizen support, set forth in its 2000–2006 National Development Plan its strategy to set up a Instituto Nacional de la Mujer (INMUJERES; National Women's Institute) and the Programa Nacional de Igualdad de Oportunidades y No Discriminación contra la Mujer (PROEQUIDAD; National Equal Opportunity and Nondiscrimination Program for Women).

The feminist and women's movements—which since the 1990s had fought hard for democracy and promoted such political ideals as equality in difference and as tolerance through visibility in public and institutional spaces—found themselves up against an unexpected situation. They had achieved one of their main goals, institutionalizing state gender mechanisms, but nonetheless lacked the political resources to determine the aims and objectives of these institutes. This was also complicated by the fact that their natural political allies, the Partido de la Revolución Democrática (PRD; Democratic Revolution Party) and other left-wing parties, had not won the political offices they had hoped for. Furthermore, the PRI, to which many long-time feminist politicians belonged, was left in total internal crisis by an electoral defeat that spelled the end of the party's political hegemony.

After the Beijing conference, the concept of gender, long accepted in Mexican society as a way of understanding women's subordination, was actually adopted by PAN as a political strategy. Now it was not just the secularist parties that espoused gender politics: PAN, which had hitherto rejected the concept, inserted in its 2000 electoral platform a notion of gender, developed by a group of women party activists. They redefined equality between the sexes by idealizing the traditional family and identifying women as the agents of biological and social reproduction. Although PAN had been incorporating new social groups and updating its discourse ever since elections had begun to be competitive, this redefinition of gender equality clearly demonstrated the extent to which the party's doctrine and actions were steeped in its historical links to the Catholic Church and to conservative sectors of Mexican society. For this reason, PAN's national-level control over institutions designed to promote gender-equity policies caused friction not only among its own party activists but also among feminists in the women's movement and in the ranks of the opposition parties. The former alleged that the party had abandoned its principles; the latter two groups accused PAN of selling out various feminist demands, such as free reproductive choice, freedom of sexual orientation, and women's emancipation.

Thus, the establishment of new institutions to include women as citizens within a development framework came up against various obstacles. These ranged from macrosocial factors that discriminated against or excluded women from culture, institutions, and economic activity, to political, class, ethnic, and religious differences. There was also disagreement about how to define a gender perspective among those involved in the institutionalization process, which became evident when the time came to set priorities for the government agenda

Despite these difficulties, one of the virtues of this process was to establish gender equality as the core value underpinning the structure, agenda, and activities of INMUJERES. Anne Phillips has shown that promoting equality, rather than valuing difference, can garner the widest support for overcoming women's subordination in a political system of historical divide-and-rule policies (1996, 7). Women's political campaigns against discrimination can use the principle of equality to override distinctions of class, ethnicity, or ideology. Gender equality, then, is politically profitable, because it promotes the creation of alliances, especially valuable in a highly heterogeneous country whose history has been marked by struggle against inequality.

Within this framework, the discourse of INMUJERES promised to transform government institutions and bring to public policies a gender perspective rooted in equality between the sexes, a position that could, in theory, speak to the ideologies of a diversity of actors on the national political scene. I say "in theory" because in practice, gender mainstreaming in a country where machismo is firmly rooted faces formidable challenges. The mission of INMUJERES was to alter not only the mechanisms of a government that regulates societal activities by maintaining inequalities in legal, bureaucratic, and administrative structures but also the symbolic universe in which society is constructed. Gender mainstreaming is a process that aspires to encompass all public policies and redefine values, practices, and administrative procedures.

Moreover, intersectoral public policies are shaped both by those who draft them and those who demand them. Institutionalization, in the end, depends on whether and how government workers and civil society take on a gender perspective and value the equality of women in society and in the political system. Therefore, the success of such public policies depends not only on decent institutional design but also on the social and political context in which the institutions operate (Putnam 1994). In practice, similar formal institutions function in distinct ways and obtain different results in different contexts. Good institutional engineering is not enough; the context and the gender culture of the actors also matter. The robustness of gender mainstreaming as a principle and as an organizational objective, as well as its influence on the behavior of civil servants and social actors, is largely defined by the long-term commitment of state and society to gender equality and equity. Therefore, gender-mainstreaming mechanisms need to invest extra energy in legitimizing their functions to carry out their agendas and activities.

This chapter outlines the development of the Institutos de Mujeres in Mexico's federal and state governments, the rhythm of their development, and the legal status they have acquired. Next, it explores certain conflicts arising from the insertion of the Institutos into different sociopolitical contexts, showing how the dynamic of similar institutions depends on the state in which they operate, despite similar objectives and a common national political environment. Finally, it identifies some of the difficulties faced by such institutions, which are dependent on legal and administrative factors in party politics and on different conceptions of gender. The latter derives principally from the political ideologies, either secular or religious, of the main political parties, which inevitably influence the heads of the Institutos. This is an exploration of some of the challenges prompted by the insertion of feminist demands into the sphere of government institutions.

INMUJERES and the State Institutos:
Between Autonomy and Dependence

Among gender-mainstreaming policies, the Institutos de Mujeres played a central role in designing an agenda for influencing public policy-making processes in the federal and state governments. Following several isolated attempts in different parts of the country to set up bodies to this end, INMUJERES was created by a presidential decree on January 12, 2001.[1] It was founded on the idea that women's exercise of their rights as citizens was a prerequisite for the democratization of Mexico, which was linked with the notion of gender equality and equal opportunities. Both values were shared by different women's groups, which in turn supported and contributed to the creation of this institution. Thus, INMUJERES, a federal-level organization, took on as a core task "the coordination of activities with state-level institutions, with the understanding that all of them share a gender perspective and the need to institutionalize it at the federal level" (INMUJERES 2001, 40).

In addition to the national institute, Institutos de Mujeres exist at the state level and even, in some cases, at the municipal level. By April 2005, when the state of Tamaulipas's Instituto came into being, thirty Mexican states had an Instituto. The existence of these bodies the length and breadth of Mexico made for very valuable capital to promote crosscutting gender issues and to create common public policies aimed at equality and equal opportunities on a national level.

The rate at which these bodies were set up was largely a function of the political opportunities that opened as a gender perspective was legitimized by the advent of a new democratic government and the publication of PAN's National Development Plan, which required new government gender-mainstreaming institutions and mechanisms. As table 14.1 shows, ten institutions were created before the year 2000, the rest after that date. All the same, despite the obvious achievement represented by the Institutos, they were hampered by being so new, by lacking material and professional resources, and by needing legitimacy in the eyes of society and government. A national program was difficult to consolidate, given that over time party-political conflicts generated frictions and stalled the coordination of joint projects.

Although there were basic, formal accords expressed in PROEQUIDAD, such agreements did not always work, because the directors of the state-level Institutos adapted goals depending on their relationships with local authorities, with other Institutos, and with other women's organizations. Access to funding and even individual interpretations of the goals of INMUJERES's agenda also affected the scope for coordination between the national and state offices. Therefore, the majority of the state Institutos did what they could with the human and material resources they could pull together and in regional contexts where women's rights were not always a priority of local authorities. Of course, these local authorities were obliged to consider gender, given the requirements imposed by international donors and the National Development Plan, yet they tended to see such requirements as just more paperwork when it came down to designing or implementing gender-aware public policies. The national distribution of Institutos is shown in table 14.1.

The administrative status of the state-level Institutos was not uniform across the country. In some states they were classified as either decentralized or deconcentrated public bodies, giving them greater status and autonomy within the state bureaucracy than those classified as programs or councils, as in Veracruz and Querétaro, respectively. Only in the state of Guerrero did the Instituto have the status of a Secretariat. Furthermore, some of the Institutos were created by decree, others by law, and some by simple accords or through the internal regulations of an existing public institution.

The origins of each Instituto determined its degree of stability over time. Institutos created by laws benefited from the approval of the legislative body, which gave them greater sustainability: to shut them down the laws creating the Institutos would have to be revoked and new ones passed. Those created by executive decree

Table 14.1   Creation of State Institutos de Mujeres

Federal Entity	Name	Legal status	Year founded	Governor's party in 2005	Director's party in 2005
Aguascalientes	Instituto Aguascalientes de las Mujeres (Aguascalientes Women's Institute)	Decree	2001	PAN	PAN
Baja California Norte	Instituto de la Mujer para el Estado de Baja California (Women's Institute for the State of Baja California)	Law	2001	PAN	PAN
Baja California Sur	Instituto Sudcaliforniano de la Mujer (South California Women's Institute)	Law	1999	PRD-Convergencia	PRD
Campeche	Instituto Estatal de la Mujer en Campeche (State Women's Institute in Campeche)	Accord	2000	PRI	PRI
Chiapas	Instituto de la Mujer de Chiapas (Women's Institute of Chiapas)	Accord	2000	PRI	PRI
Chihuahua	Instituto Chihuahuense de la Mujer (Chihuahua Women's Institute)	Decree	2002	PRI-PVEM	PRI
Coahuila	Instituto Coahuilense de las Mujeres (Coahuila Women's Institute)	Decree	2001	PAN-PRD	NGO*
Colima	Instituto Colimense de las Mujeres (Colima Women's Institute)	Decree	1998	PRI	PRI
Durango	Instituto de la Mujer Duranguense (Durango Women's Institute)	Decree	2000	PRI	PRI
Federal District	Instituto de las Mujeres del D.F. (Women's Institute of the F.D.)	Law	2002	PRD	PRD
Guanajuato	Instituto de la Mujer Guanajuatense (Guanajuato Women's Institute)	Decree	2001	PAN	PAN
Guerrero	Secretaría de la Mujer en Guerrero (Secretariat for Women in Guerrero)	Decree	1987	PRD-Convergencia-PRS	PRI
Hidalgo	Instituto Hidalguense de la Mujer (Hidalgo Women's Institute)	Decree	2002	PRI	PRI

(continued)

Table 14.1   Continued

Federal Entity	Name	Legal status	Year founded	Governor's party in 2005	Director's party in 2005
Jalisco	Instituto Jalisciense de las Mujeres (Jalisco Women's Institute)	Law	2002	PAN	PAN
México State	Instituto Mexiquense de la Mujer (Mexico State's Women's Institute)	Decree	2000	PRI	PRI
Michoacán	Instituto Michoacano de la Mujer (Michoacán Women's Institute)	Decree	1999	PRD	PRD
Morelos	Instituto Estatal de la Mujer en Morelos (State Women's Institute in Morelos)	Decree	2002	PAN	PAN
Nayarit	Instituto de la Mujer en Nayarit (Women's Institute in Nayarit)	Decree	2003	PRI	NGO*
Nuevo León	Instituto Estatal de las Mujeres en el Estado de Nuevo León (State Women's Institute in the State of Nuevo León)	Law	2003	PRI	PRI
Oaxaca	Instituto de la Mujer Oaxaqueña (Oaxaca Women's Institute)	Decree	2000	PRI	PRD
Puebla	Instituto Poblano de la Mujer (Puebla Women's Institute)	Decree	1999	PRI	PRI
Querétaro	Consejo Estatal de la Mujer en Querétaro (State Women's Council in Querétaro)	Decree	1997	PAN	PAN
Quintana Roo	Instituto Quintanarroense de la Mujer (Quintana Roo Women's Institute)	Decree	1998	PRI	PRI
San Luis Potosí	Instituto de las Mujeres del Estado de San Luis Potosí (Women's Institute of the State of San Luis Potosí)	Law	2002	PAN	PRI
Sinaloa	Instituto Sinaloense de la Mujer (Sinaloa Women's Institute)	Decree	2000	PRI	PRI

Table 14.1   Continued

Federal Entity	Name	Legal status	Year founded	Governor's party in 2005	Director's party in 2005
Sonora	Instituto Sonorense de la Mujer (Sonora Women's Institute)	Decree	1998	PRI	PRI
Tabasco	Instituto de Mujeres de Tabasco (Women's Institute of Tabasco)	Law	2001	PRI	PRI
Tamaulipas	Consejo para el Desarrollo Integral de la Mujer (Women's Comprehensive Development Council)	Decree	2000	PRI	PRI
Tlaxcala	Instituto Estatal de la Mujer en Tlaxcala (State Women's Institute in Tlaxcala)	Decree	2000	PAN-PT	PRD
Veracruz	Programa Estatal de la Mujer en Veracruz (State Women's Program in Veracruz)	Internal Regulation	1999	PRI	PRI
Yucatán	Instituto para la Equidad de Género en Yucatán (Institute for Gender Equity in Yucatán)	Decree	2002	PAN	NGO*
Zacatecas	Instituto para la Mujer Zacatecana (Institute for Zacatec Women)	Accord	1999	PRD	PRD

*NGO = Nongovernmental organization

would remain stable unless a new executive revoked the original decree. In the third case, those created by accord or internal regulation were hostage to the agreement between the executive branch and the head of the government agency on which the Instituto depended. Querétaro and Veracruz, two states that pioneered gender-policy mechanisms, had still not, by 2005, approved the transformation of their programs into Institutos. This was chiefly due to administrative sluggishness, as these programs' directors were nominated by governors who did not consider women's movement experience to be requirements for the position. These governors seemingly held a conservative view of the role of women, although they belonged to different parties (PAN, PRI). The same occurred in Tamaulipas, which until July 2005 had a Consejo para el Desarrollo Integral de la Mujer (Women's Comprehensive Development Council). It was then upgraded to an Instituto by the newly elected governor, who seemed to fall into the conservative pattern: his decision was not so much a recognition of the importance of the women's movement or gender mainstreaming but rather a reward for the women who had voted him in.

The location of the Institutos de Mujeres within the public administrative apparatus also varied. In some states the Institutos fell directly under the aegis of the Secretary General of Government. In others, they answered to the State Executive, Secretariat of Social Development, Planning and Development Secretariat, Subsecretariat of Citizen Affairs, Finance Secretariat, or the Health Secretariat. This meant that the platform for gender mainstreaming varied greatly from state to state in terms of recognition, ability to act and influence policy, and scope for institutional development. As the state Institutos were key to disseminating gender-aware public policies, how they were institutionalized would help or hinder them in obtaining human and material resources to consolidate themselves. Moreover, how the Institutos were created and where they were located in the governmental hierarchy affected their ability to promote public policies and coordinate joint actions with INMUJERES, other state-level Institutos, civic organizations, and the public administration of the states in which they were embedded.

Obstacles to the Coordination of a National Gender Perspective

The insertion of the Institutos in the public bureaucracy, their dependence on different branches of government, and the political context of each state all determined their capacity to develop coordinated and consensus-creating gender-mainstreaming actions. They all faced a series of obstacles to coordinated action:

1. Legal Obstacles

By law, the Institutos and other state institutions were reliant on the executive branch or on the state bureaucracy. They established relations only of coordination or communication with INMUJERES, which lacked the power to force compliance with its decisions about particular goals or how they should be reached. INMUJERES's official mission was to work with the state Institutos to carry out national projects, such as the generation of social indicators, studies on violence against women, the design of surveys on a range of issues, and the distribution of budget allocations to organize or strengthen women's programs in states or municipalities, among others. Although the states were interested in such projects, there were frictions because the state Institutos rarely participated in the design of the projects and felt that they did not reflect regional or state-level realities. INMUJERES did not consult with the state Institutos on matters such as time constraints and the local alliances that were needed to carry out the projects. Therefore, the Institutos viewed INMUJERES as little more than an instrument and an imposition of the federal government and saw its initiatives as limiting their input to only carrying out decisions and directives. This widespread reaction made the state-level officials uncomfortable and hostile to INMUJERES's activities.

2. Administrative Obstacles

Although the state Institutos shared a common name, and were regarded by INMUJERES as its counterparts, their political-administrative status was quite distinct in some states. As noted earlier, at one end of the spectrum, most Institutos were classified as decentralized public institutions and benefited from a similar status in the state-level government structures. At the other end were those that had not succeeded in consolidating themselves as Institutos, despite the existence of feminist groups and/or grassroots women's movements with long traditions. By 2005 the Institutos of Campeche, Chiapas, and Zacatecas had been weakened over time, as they had been created by local accords. Therefore, when the actors who made these pacts left the government or were unable to renew the agreements, their permanency was thrown into doubt. In other states, where the gender mechanisms were created before the 2001 law, their political-administrative status was different, as was the case with Guerrero's Secretariat. The differences between apparently similar institutions took on further dimensions when they were located at the state level, because their activity was autonomous from the federal level. The day-to-day success of coordination efforts then depended on the quality of relationships with the state governments.

3. Party Membership

The scope for putting together a common agenda through dialogue between the officers of the different state Institutos and also between the state officers and INMUJERES was reduced not only by federal-state administrative divisions but also by competition between political parties, a factor that varied according to state and local electoral junctures. As the last two columns of table 14-1 demonstrate, in a number of states, the governing parties were adversaries of the party of the federal government, as well as of the governing parties of other states. While this made it difficult for INMUJERES to work with some state Institutos on a common agenda or activities, INMUJERES was also guilty of withholding support for state-level initiatives or ignoring successful projects promoted by state Institutos run by directors linked to political parties other than PAN. Unfortunately, these political tussles were neither openly expressed nor debated, with the result that women's interests often ended up being subordinated to the party rivalries between the different Institutos.

The dependence of the Institutos on the state-level executive branch for the nomination of their directors actually helped their local activities, as they were able to build or strengthen relationships with political, governmental, and civil society actors. However, this same dependence hampered relations with INMUJERES, whose director was nominated by the country's president, and was therefore a representative of his party. Political preferences in the states simplified local efforts but complicated relations with INMUJERES. Thus, when INMUJERES encountered interparty conflict, its role was reduced to setting out general lines of work or requesting collaboration from the state Institutos to achieve common goals.

Table 14.2   Distribution of Federal Resources among the States by Political Party
in 2004

Party	Number of governors*	Percentage of allocated resources	Number of federally funded programs	Percentage of federally funded programs
PRI	16	50	4	25
PAN	8	27.8	8	100
PAN in alliances	2	3.5	1	50
PRD	6	18.7	3	50
Total	32	100	16	50

*Includes the thirty-one states and the government of the Federal District.

The responses of the states to INMUJERES's requests were indeed generally permeated by political party considerations, which generated a downward spiral in which the national body preferred to work with Institutos directed by members of PAN.

Two cases, perhaps a bit limited or anecdotal, illuminate these latent conflicts. In a survey conducted by INMUJERES in February 2003, intended to map out the institutional capacities of the state-level Institutos, directors belonging to the same party as INMUJERES's director gave full responses. However, those linked to a different party answered very few of the questions, or simply did not respond at all.

A similar issue arose with the creation of an informal network of state Instituto directors who belonged to opposition parties. Formed in 2004, the network's goal was to pressure the central government for resources for projects funded by international development agencies. This network had the advantage of connecting directors who had not met, allowing the sharing of individual state experiences, and promoting debate about the theory of gender mainstreaming. However, the network also came to act as a focal point for political party opposition, making dialogue with INMUJERES very difficult. That said, the reactions against INMUJERES were probably not without reason and may have been the result of situations created by INMUJERES itself, such as its policy of selective support for the state-level Institutos. Although hard to fully substantiate with detailed empirical evidence, data suggest that resources allocated by INMUJERES in 2004 to strengthen state programs tended to be distributed along party lines. The distribution of sixteen such projects is shown in table 14.2.

Although INMUJERES was able to finance only half of the states with this fund, and information on the funding of other projects is not available, the distribution criteria clearly followed party lines. Half the states were governed by the PRI, yet only 25 percent of their projects were approved by INMUJERES. Similarly, the PRD, which governed 18.7 percent of the states (including the Federal District), saw only half of its projects supported. By comparison, PAN ran 27.8 percent of the states, all of which received support. In the 3.5 percent of the states governed by alliances of PAN with other parties, only half received support.

4. Secular and Religious Ideologies

Although many government officials may hold personal religious convictions, the predominance of a particular religious outlook on the part of the officials of the national governing party produced conflicts. Generally buried beneath interparty divisions, these conflicts centered on the meaning of gender and around public gender-equity policies, separating PAN officials from those who were not religious or who practiced privately while espousing state secularism. The problem was not a minor one, not just because the majority of PAN's members were Catholics, but also because the struggle between Catholics and secularists for control of the state is deeply rooted in Mexico's history, lasting well into the twentieth century.[2]

While some female politicians and high-level government officers made great efforts to smooth things over, calling for *affidamento* (dialogue and trust among women on the basis of shared experience and interests), this did not work with the directors of some state Institutos, who held their posts through party links or membership of philanthropic or religious associations connected to PAN, rather than through a demonstrated commitment to gender equity or the women's movement. So, the picture was complex and, although the very creation of the Institutos allowed great strides, these difficulties remained real challenges to gender mainstreaming. This task demanded a shared vision, not least as the state institutions functioned in a sector-specific, centralized, and hierarchical way, and women's organizations and other actors do not constitute a homogeneous community.

5. The Institutos in the Context of the States

Matters looked rather different at the state level, as the experiences of the state Institutos reflected local or regional political contexts. Although it is beyond the scope of this chapter to present the wealth and heterogeneity of individual experiences, a few cases indicate the diversity of the Institutos, depending on where they operated. Institutos such as the Instituto de la Mujer Oaxaqueña (IMO; Oaxacan Women's Institute) turned their distance from INMUJERES to their political advantage, coordinating their projects autonomously in conjunction with the state administration. In just three years, the IMO managed to launch a program, unique in Mexico and in Latin America, that mainstreamed gender issues into state planning and budgeting processes (Tarrés 2006). The state of Oaxaca was governed by the PRI, and the IMO's director was from the PRD, but they collaborated because both parties were in opposition to that of the central government and shared a vision of a secular state. Had the presidency of the republic and INMUJERES not been controlled by PAN, a party linked to the Catholic Church since its inception, this relationship probably would not have been possible.

Another case in point is that of the Federal District under the 2000–2006 PRD government, when the same party also held a parliamentary majority. Here, instead of attempting to transform government institutions, the state Institutos tried to encourage equal opportunities and the exercise of women's rights through citizen participation in local social and economic arenas. The mayor and his team avoided confrontations with the Catholic Church by generating social development programs for lower-class groups, designed to counteract enormous socio-economic inequalities and to strengthen their electoral base. But while there was a significant representation of women in decision-making positions in the PRD government, gender mainstreaming was confused with social redistribution programs benefiting vulnerable groups of women. In the Federal District the Institutos (INMUJERES-DF) lacked the most basic resource, that is, the political support of the authorities to design a systematic plan to mainstream gender into public policies and the state apparatus. They were therefore forced to adapt their gender perspective to the programs of the Secretariat of Social Development of the Federal District, whose first priority was to benefit low-income sectors.

That adaptation consisted of conflating women's rights with social programs. The right to a decent standard of living was linked to programs for gender-violence prevention, and the right to work was promoted through job-creation programs, credit unions, and training for women entrepreneurs. INMUJERES-DF also developed important programs to promote the right to health among women and encouraged active citizenship by strengthening women's leadership in social organizations within the Federal District. Those programs were made possible by a network of local branches in each of the sixteen administrative zones of Mexico City. They established a common policy and connected their institutional work with local women's organizations and civil society involved in the social programs.

By prioritizing social programs at a local level to promote equal opportunities, participation, full citizenship, and an end to discrimination, the INMUJERES-DF deployed a strategy similar to that of other governmental institutions in the Federal District and distinct from that of other state-level institutes. In Oaxaca, the IMO targeted the decision-making level of public administration, where social policies were designed and rolled out. What is interesting about these two cases is not what they did, but rather how context and the political will of government leaders shaped the way in which gender mainstreaming was taken up by the Institutos.

Both Institutos were embedded in areas of government run by opposition parties, but their relations with the Catholic Church varied, even as they introduced a gender perspective into each government's modus operandi and priorities. In Oaxaca, gender policy developed around a secular mindset and was worked into a system of decentralized and deconcentrated public administration. Although a secular orientation also predominated in the Federal District, a strategy aimed at avoiding conflicts with the church authorities' undermined gender as a primary focus in public policy. In the end, a less modern way of thinking about gender relations seemed to prevail in INMUJERES-DF under the 2000–2006 administration, compared to Oaxaca's Instituto during the same period. It is a paradox of political life, considering that scientists and analysts make claims about the postmodernity of Mexico City, and Oaxaca is seen as a less developed state.

6. Different Ideas about Gender and Gender Mainstreaming

This recent gender mainstreaming has shaped the understandings of gender that underpin the design of new institutions, laws, regulations, and resources aimed at improving women's lives. It is a process subject to, and conditioned by, the internal logic of political systems, the acceptance of pluralism, and the cultural value assigned to equality. In general, the dominant economic model has impacted negatively on the real scope for including women's interests in state policies (UNRISD 2006). Nonetheless, the presence of women's movements and feminists within the state means that the meanings assigned to gender were questioned and evaluated, which can have positive influences on the institutionalization process.

While there is agreement at the international, national, and local level about the importance of gender mainstreaming, there are still heated debates about differing conceptions of gender and gender mainstreaming. Among the great range of proposals generated by the different streams of feminism, the most controversial is the idea that the private is public, and the personal is political. Such controversies arise because they question not only the institutional order that subordinates and disciplines women in public spaces but also the cultural models of sexuality and family that define and fix relations between human beings, universally subordinating women and stigmatizing any digression from those relations. The feminist attempt to redefine the codes and organization of relations between the sexes questions the very core of traditionalist discourse and creates disagreements that are often masked by modernization policies and sometimes express themselves through violence.

Such conflicts are neither clearly expressed in national debate nor apparent at first glance. There are indicators, such as the political conflicts mentioned earlier or the withdrawal of numerous feminist groups and poor women's organizations from state institutions. There are also differences in academia between those who offer their technical and educational talents to the Institutos and other public institutions and those who conceive of academic work as a critical practice. This all indicates implicit problems that have not been brought into the open, probably in the interest of avoiding antagonizing politicians and public officials who, for better or worse, are doing something for women. Nonetheless, the project of ending women's subordination, despite acquiring a neutral and technocratic tone upon entering the state apparatus, touches on personal matters of identity and gender relations, causing reactions that are visible only in certain moments. What then underpins the contrary worldview that opposes a gender perspective?

Ultraconservative sectors and groups were known to be secretly and openly pressuring or working within PAN.[3] These groups, which were attempting to impose on secular society a vision of sexuality, family, and the role of women inspired in Catholic doctrine, have grown in institutional relevance since the victory of the new government in 2000. Although these groups had a long history, their contemporary interest stems from the fact that, when the first feminist demands appeared in the 1970s, they created associations to mount a countermovement to feminism (Tarrés 1987, 22–52). Among the various groups that became visible since

PAN's election, two had a primary mission to fight feminism, communism, and atheism and to draw in women with discourses focused on preserving traditional culture, national values, and the family. These associations actively participated in the debates over birth control, the legalization of abortion, and free sexual orientation. With the recent approval of the morning-after pill as part of the standard line of medications, they sought to stop the legal process by which this policy would become law, alleging that it destroyed human life. The secretary of government, a well-known Catholic activist, headed the support for the church leadership in opposing this measure. This climate led members of PAN, with well-known links to conservative organizations, to form a commission to define the party's position on the morning-after pill, common-law marriages, medical cloning, euthanasia, and a general policy on birth control.

What was new about this initiative was that it took place within the heart of government. Since the 1980s there had been an increase in so-called PAN intermediate groups. These were sectorial organizations of citizens whose objective was to recruit members, especially women, who made up their support base. The Asociación Nacional Cívica Femenina (ANCIFEM; National Female Civic Association) and the Comité Nacional ProVida (PROVIDA; National Committee for Life) were perhaps the organizations that mustered the greatest persistence and fury to rally women around the defense of the family and the principle that considered life as starting from the moment of conception, demonstrating the cultural upheaval feminism has inflicted on conservative ideology.

Although some of these organizations and PAN had always actively propounded a conservative discourse about gender, two different kinds of events forced them to refresh and adapt that discourse to new circumstances. The first was the clearly changing role of women in society, brought about by their entry into the paid labor force, birth control, and formal education. The second was the transformation of the political landscape due to increased electoral competition, which saw parties compete for the female vote. Both shifts obliged them to expand their definition of women as the natural guardians of the family to include the task of being responsible citizens in political life. Thus, in 1981 PAN changed its existing women's section into a Secretaría de Promoción Femenina (Secretariat for Promoting Women), stating that "the idea of a section belongs to the time when women were not citizens," which is somewhat ironic, considering that Mexican women have had the right to vote since 1953 (Hidalgo 2000, 285). Thereafter, ANCIFEM and other such associations made similar changes in their principles and internal structures.

However, it was in the heat of various midterm elections and the preparations for the fourth Beijing conference, in which PAN members participated, that its women's Secretariat incorporated some of the proposals of that conference and made significant gains for women in the party. They achieved a greater presence not only in the party's internal structures but also in elected legislative posts, with women winning 30 percent of the party's seats in the Chamber of Deputies. Thus, in the discourse of PAN, its proxy organizations, and its associates, the role of women was modernized when they recognized that to advance equality women needed to exercise full citizenship rights. That said, the role of women continued to appear in the party's documents as "moral educator, mother of the home from which women and men emerge to make up the social fabric and contribute to the common good" (Hidalgo 2000, 306).

Curiously, in their discourses and different proposals justifying women's access to power, the members of PAN's Women's Secretariat set themselves apart from feminism, defining themselves as "postfeminists," claiming to base their ideas on a new concept of love, friendship, family, justice, society, state, and party. In their version of postfeminism, they "work together with men, without competition, and moreover, defend as a doctrinal principle the human right to life from the moment of conception to the moment of death" (Hidalgo 2000, 287, 356). That the party and its close affiliates felt the need to differentiate themselves from feminist politics, as well as to adjust their politics in the face of a secularizing society, shows the difficulties they faced in mainstreaming gender awareness in the party.

Gender mainstreaming is a complex process that provokes resistance both in a party with religious foundations and in many social groups, as it seeks to change the established norms of behavior in everyday life, as well as the symbolic universe on which the state institutional order is grounded. Institutional orders (such as the market, the family, or religion) consist of both a symbolic system and one of actual material practices. In consequence, reforms aimed at establishing gender equity are a more complicated matter than simply changing procedures or redefining certain organizational rules. Rather, they also form a part of a symbolic process, since such changes create a parallel culture that challenges the hegemonic order so that human beings may be recognized and valued regardless of their sex. Without a doubt, this generates conflicts and political struggles to control the meanings and definitions of sexual difference and gender relations. In the end, gender mainstreaming faces huge sociopolitical and cultural obstacles that resist the naturalization of gender equity as a legitimate value of contemporary democratic life.

Concluding Remarks

In this chapter I have explored the efforts to mainstream gender in a political system that is moving along a winding road toward constructing a democratic culture. The creation of the federal- and state-level Institutos de Mujeres from 2001 onward constitute an achievement for the feminist and women's movements, as well as for the government in enacting the pledges made in international and national agreements over a period of thirty years. The Institutos became a platform for an agenda that recognizes women as citizens deserving of special attention by virtue of the subordination they experience. Despite the justice inherent in these agreements, actually implementing decisions designed to realize the goals of such accords faces a series of obstacles, derived as much from the structure of the Institutos themselves as from the sociopolitical operating environment of the reforms intended to transform traditional conceptions of public policy.

This analysis shows that the Institutos operated within a complex logic, one that surpassed bureaucratic rationality, because there were many obstacles to achieving a national project. Beyond the structural conditions of inequality induced by a neoliberal model that reduces the scope for a gender-equity program, obstacles were also generated by the very structure of the Institutos and the identity of the actors responsible for setting them up. These include problems of an administrative nature and of party and religious affiliation, issues related to the centralization of decision making within the federal government, and the struggle for state autonomy. These factors indicate that the underlying logic of public administration is determined by the sociopolitical environment. In Mexico, this is of central importance, given the competition between parties that have different and often opposing ideas about gender and gender relations, as well as about secularism in political and social life.

This dynamic undoubtedly had significant but not necessarily visible effects on the relationships between officials and politicians associated with the projects and programs of the Institutos de Mujeres. It created tough challenges in a context where conservative groups had only recently gained access to political power and government office. Although there is now pluralism in contemporary Mexico's political life, and society is secularizing with giant strides, conservative groups retain a great deal of influence when it comes to ending women's subordination, even when public policies privilege equality over more apparently subversive aspects of feminist discourse. Ironically, the very conservative sectors that fought against authoritarianism and for democracy over many years reacted aggressively when it came to gender-mainstreaming proposals in the areas of sexuality, reproductive health, family, and marriage, even questioning basic institutional and administrative arrangements to combat those proposals. Their stubbornness in opposing a project intended to liberate women is not isolated: it is echoed in international circles, especially by the U.S. government and the Vatican, whose support spurs on the radicalism of these sectors.

In such a situation, the feminist and women's movements find themselves disorientated, probably because the role of the Institutos remains uncertain. In the beginning, feminist reactions to the governor's nominations of the directors were negative in practically all of the states, but such reactions gradually calmed down. Most local civic associations and women's organizations assumed that, as they had actively campaigned to establish these mechanisms, they would be given priority to administer them. They did not imagine that, after Beijing, the gender agenda would enter the political system and would be taken up by quite unexpected (in the eyes of the movement) actors. The establishment of a government-level agenda has left feminists and the women's movement facing new challenges, given that they do not control the direction of the policies developed in the Institutos and therefore need to come up with new strategies to influence decision making.

Some have gotten involved, investing in the consolidation of institutions where they might be able to lay the foundations to generate policies favorable to women or programs that would maintain relationships with civic organizations. These groups have defined what is and is not negotiable within the ethical boundaries of feminism. Other groups have distanced themselves from the state institutions, declaring their autonomy and right to engage in cultural critiques. Academic research teams have conducted studies of parallel social processes beyond the Institutos around the construction of practical citizenship, the ramifications of migration, poverty, violence, and the emergence of collective projects, among others. The reactions of different members of the women's movement are distinct, yet all of them maintain a common front when faced with conservative attacks. Beyond ideological or partisan differences, which have been further accentuated by extensive conservative-sector activism, a collective political effort aimed at strengthening the Institutos as key bodies in the structure of state and federal governments is essential. The Institutos could thus become a public, universal resource above party politics and be consolidated and recognized as institutions dedicated to effective gender-mainstreaming policies across the country.

ACKNOWLEDGMENTS
Translated by Daniel Russell.

NOTES

1. INMUJERES is an autonomous, decentralized public institution within the Federal Public Administration, with independent legal status and autonomy over its budget, spending, operation, and management.

2. Mexico underwent a violent separation of church and state in the nineteenth century. The church revived in opposition to the revolution in 1913–1924, culminating in the so-called Cristero War (Guerra Cristera) of 1927–1929. Later, the Cristeros dispersed into various civil organizations, one of which entered the political fray as PAN (Bailey, 1974). As a result of this war, the Mexican government prohibits to this day religious instruction in public and private schools. Only recently did Carlos Salinas de Gortari's administration (1988–1994) reestablish relations with the Vatican.

3. González Ruiz identified more than a hundred conservative lobbies, connected to the Catholic Church, which have gained power thanks to their links with PAN and federal, state, and municipal government institutions (1994, 2).

REFERENCES

Bailey, David. 1974. *Viva Cristo Rey! The Cristero Rebellion and the church-state conflict in Mexico.* Austin: University of Texas.

Fraser, Nancy. 1991. La lucha por las necesidades: Esbozo de una teoría crítica, socialista, feminista del capitalismo tardío. *Debate Feminista* 3:3–40.

González Ruiz, Edgar. 1994. *Conservadurismo y sexualidad: Como propagar el SIDA.* Mexico City: Rayuela.

Hidalgo, Antonieta G. 2000. *Las mujeres en Acción Nacional: 60 años de trabajo y consolidación política.* Mexico City: Epessa.

INMUJERES. 2001. *Primer informe de labores.* Mexico City: INMUJERES.

Loaeza, Soledad. 2003. Prologue to *Los panistas,* ed. Mireya Cuéllar. Mexico City: Editorial La Jornada.

Phillips, Anne. 1996. *Género y teoría democrática.* Mexico City: PUEG, UNAM.

Putnam, Robert. D. 1994. *Para hacer que la democracia funcione.* Caracas, Venezuela: Galac.

Tarrés, María Luisa. 1987. *Campos de acción y formas de participación de las mujeres de clase media*. Informe de Investigación. Mexico City: PIEM, CES, COLMEX.

———. 2001. Las organizaciones del movimiento de mujeres en la reforma política. In *La sociedad civil: De la teoría a la realidad*, ed. Olvera Alberto, 217–257. Mexico City: COLMEX.

———. 2006. *Equidad de género y presupuesto público: La experiencia innovadora de Oaxaca*. Serie Buenas Prácticas 371. Oaxaca: Instituto de la Mujer Oaxaqueña.

Tarrow, Sydney. 1994. *El poder en movimiento: Los movimientos sociales, la acción colectiva y la política*. Madrid: Alianza.

UNRISD. 2006. *Igualdad de género: La lucha por la justicia en un mundo desigual; Sinopsis*. Geneva: UNRISD.

15

Women's Struggles
for Rights in Venezuela

OPPORTUNITIES AND CHALLENGES

CATHY A. RAKOWSKI

GIOCONDA ESPINA

Since 1958, when the current period of democratic rule began, and until 1992, when there were two attempted coups, Venezuela was considered a model of democratic consolidation. Leaders used oil revenues and international loans to advance a program of national economic development and a social democracy based on political pacts. In particular, leaders invested in public services (such as education and health) and in public works. This system led to the rapid expansion of an urban middle class; great demand for educated women workers (especially in the public sector starting in the sixties); and improvements in national productivity, per capita incomes, and educational and employment levels. Civil society groups organized, encouraged by the state, into neighborhood and other civic associations, cooperatives, and unions.[1]

This Venezuela seemed to be a model of rapid economic development, coordinated by an investor state. However, given the volatility of international prices, high petroleum revenues could not be sustained and the first in a series of economic crises was declared in 1983. Citizen groups, primarily middle class, also demanded state reform with greater citizen control and a more accountable and responsive state. Over a period of several years, reform committee members held meetings with almost all social sectors to get input for reform, and in 1989 Venezuela began to implement political, administrative, and fiscal decentralization.[2]

The nineties witnessed new economic and political crises. The process of decentralization was slow and piecemeal and faced many barriers—in part due to the continued implementation of austerity policies identified with the International Monetary Fund. There were protests, military repression, two attempted coups (February and November 1992), removal of an elected president for corruption, conflict over proposed privatization of state industries, deterioration of public services and infrastructure, increasing poverty and insecurity, and loss of confidence in traditional political parties. New political movements arrived on the scene, along with nontraditional candidates—including a former military officer/coup leader and a former Miss Universe/popular mayor.

In 1998 Lieutenant Colonel Hugo Rafael Chávez Frías, leader of the attempted coups, won the presidential election and set about creating a Fifth Republic. He convoked a constituent assembly and, after the new Constitution was passed by national referendum in 1999 and he was reelected in 2000, set about implementing a process known first as a "peaceful Bolivarian Revolution" and later as "twenty-first-century socialism."[3] The result has been a polarization of citizens into *chavistas* and *anti-chavistas*. Following his reelection in 2006, in 2007 he attempted unsuccessfully to push through a reform of the 1999 Constitution that would have eliminated presidential term limits and consolidated power in the national Executive.

What about Women?

Since at least 1936, primarily educated and politically active women have organized to promote women's rights and to struggle against repressive governments. Despite their importance to the overthrow of dictator Marcos Pérez Jiménez in 1958, under democratic rule women encountered little political support for advancing women's rights (see Friedman 2000b). Although the Constitution of 1961 prohibited sex discrimination, most laws continued to relegate women to second-class citizenship and gave fathers and husbands almost complete control over women. Nonetheless, professional women, political party militants, and community activists from poor neighborhoods fought for social change and class equality. In the sixties the first feminist and women's support groups emerged in universities and low-income neighborhoods. Since 1974 there also have been diverse women's state entities: advisory committees, ministerial offices, a women's council, and since 2000 a national institute.[4]

Beginning in the mid-1970s and lasting for most of the eighties, women of civil society formed coalitions among themselves and with politicians and "femocrats" to advance women's rights.[5] They referred to their coalition building as "unity in diversity" (Castañeda 1998). This pattern of collaboration among women has had ups and downs because it is difficult to sustain high levels of interest and activism or to achieve consensus on strategies and priorities over the long term. Economic and political crises led many women to shift energies to work and to family and community problems. In the 1990s leadership in women's rights was institutionalized by a Consejo Nacional de la Mujer (CONAMU; National Women's Council) and through women holding seats in Congress. Since 1998 the situation has been complicated through the Bolivarian Revolution and political polarization. Coalition building is sporadic and often contentious, and efforts, objectives, and ideologies among organized women of all classes and political affiliations are more fragmented (see, for example, De Vincenzo 2002). What follows is a brief overview of women's coalition building, the institutionalization of women's rights, and differences that divide women's rights advocates today.

Two Decades of Growing Cooperation and Solidarity

During the fifties many women participated in the clandestine struggle against the dictatorship and, post-1958, in the growth of political parties and the new democracy. In the mid-sixties and during the seventies, new feminist and activist groups joined women's professional associations, middle- and working-class women's community service and religious groups (e.g., Círculos Femeninos Populares [CFP; Popular Women's Circles], originally a Christian base organization), and women's offices or secretariats in labor unions and political parties. Previously, there were few, if any, experiences of collaboration among women of different classes or political tendencies, apart from during the clandestine struggle against Pérez Jiménez. The first broad coalition of women was an equal rights campaign from 1979 to 1982, and the second was networks of women's nongovernmental organizations that were most active between 1985 and 1990.

The coalition of 1979–1982 worked to reform the civil code to establish the legal basis for women's rights as citizens and for democracy within the family.[6] Its leaders—lawyers and judges from the Federación Venezolana de Abogadas (FEVA; Venezuelan Federation of Women Lawyers)—took advantage of a campaign promise to support the reform that was made by new president, Luis Herrera Campins, a Christian Democrat. After taking office, he created the first ministerial-level position dedicated to women's rights and problems—the minister for the integration of women in development—and named a woman who was a university professor, sociologist, political activist (also Christian Democrat), and nonfeminist to the position. She agreed to be the political *madrina* (godmother) of the reform—funding campaign events and creating publicity—and became the public face of the campaign.

At the time, the coalition to reform the civil code was the largest experience of unity in diversity for women of different social strata and political tendencies (see Castañeda 1998; Espina 1994; Espina and Rakowski 2002; Friedman 2000b; Rakowski 1998).[7] Supporters included congresswomen, homemakers, women from NGOs and all political parties, feminists, academics, labor unionists, neighborhood activists, and professionals such as doctors, filmmakers, and journalists. Once the reform passed in July 1982, the coalition disappeared. However, its success led to subsequent coalitions for other goals.

Several patterns were established during the civil code campaign that characterized subsequent collaborations. The coalitions formed later were opportunistic; women took advantage of them to create new political opportunities or to mobilize to confront a perceived threat. Participation in these coalitions was voluntary and decision making was based on consensus. Legal reform and influencing public policy have been the main focus in Venezuela. Coalitions often used international accords to pressure lawmakers and sometimes received funding from international agencies.

The Rise of Civil Society Women

Following reform of the civil code, some civil society women's groups, academics, and other feminists continued to work with politicians on new legal projects. Other activities also proliferated: cultural events, feminist magazines, nontraditional articles about women in major newspapers, university courses and lectures on women's issues, and women's neighborhood organizations. NGOs working for women's rights and academic feminists joined together to prepare a document for the NGO forum at the Third United Nations World Conference on Women, held in Nairobi in 1985. In addition, the minister of youth (later, of the family) and her team in the ministry's Office of Women's Affairs (which replaced earlier women's offices and committees) asked these civil society women to also help prepare the official country report that Venezuela presented during the United Nations conference in Nairobi. They accepted (needless to say the two documents were very similar). This event marked another change in women's organizing.

After the conference in Nairobi, the minister of youth/family institutionalized consultations with women of civil society through a series of committees set up to study women's issues and to propose policy; each committee specialized on a different issue (e.g., sexism in textbooks, violence, sexuality and health, employment, poverty, the media). Estimates vary, but probably close to a hundred women from diverse political and social sectors served at one time or another on those committees. Until then, women's rights initiatives had originated among women of civil society, who then called on politicians and femocrats to join and support them. As consultations became institutionalized from above, femocrats and politicians led initiatives, calling on civil society women to support official projects (Espina and Rakowski 2002).

Initially, civil society women welcomed these new opportunities to advance women's rights. New women's NGOs and networks appeared, eager to influence policy. The largest and most active network was the Coordinadora de Organizaciones No Gubernamentales de Mujeres (CONG; Coordinating Committee of Women's Nongovernmental Organizations). It was founded in 1985 with twenty-six member organizations; at its peak, approximately fifty-five groups were active (Espina 1994; Friedman 2000b). The most active members were academic feminists, women from leftist parties and the labor movement, members of three professional associations (FEVA lawyers, doctors, journalists), and representatives of the national network of CFP (women from working-class and poor barrios).

CONG leaders cultivated strategic relations with women in the major political parties, elected officials, and femocrats in state agencies. Examples of activities include generating media campaigns to free a young mother from jail and protesting the death of a pregnant employee and the lack of protection for working mothers. CONG members rallied against the exploitation of women's bodies. They also made videos of aging women leaders (for example, the first Afro-Venezuelan and feminist to head a major political party) (Espina 1994; Espina and Rakowski 2002). In 1990 two CONG groups (FEVA and CFP) introduced an unsuccessful petition to Congress with some thirty thousand signatures to propose a law against domestic violence. The last major activity of the CONG as a network was its work on Title 6 of the Organic Labor Law (approved in 1990). In the early 1990s the CONG dwindled to a few individuals, who occasionally spoke to the media in representation of a "women's movement" as late as 1997 (Castañeda 1998). These individuals helped write Venezuela's official report for the Fourth United Nations World Conference on Women in Beijing in 1995 (see Friedman 1999).

There are several hypotheses regarding the CONG's decline. Some relate to the pressures of economic and political crises demanding women's attention. Some women had mobilized to achieve specific goals; once achieved, they became inactive. Some members left in protest because the new labor law did not improve rights of domestic workers. Some autonomous feminists left because they believed that some members used the CONG to promote their political or consulting careers. There also were disagreements over who could legitimately call themselves feminists and over controversial topics such as abortion and sexuality.

The Rise of Femocrats and Politicians

During the eighties and nineties, women in political parties also advanced their interests. They organized a network of Mujeres Dirigentes Unidas (United Women Leaders) in 1987 to confront sex discrimination in political parties. In 1990 they created a new congressional standing committee, the Comité Bicameral de los Derechos de la Mujer (Bichamber Committee for Women's Rights), that included all women in Congress. They received strong public support for these initiatives from members of the CONG.

Also in 1990 newly elected president Carlos Andrés Pérez from the Partido Acción Democrática (Democratic Action Party) created another temporary ministerial position—minister for the promotion of women—and named a party militant (Social Democrat), sociologist, feminist, and university professor to the post. She established a new Comisión Femenina Asesora de la Presidencia (Women's Presidential Advisory Committee) with women from all political parties and civil society, particularly academics. She promoted women's offices and centers in state and municipal governments and created a national coordinating network, calling a series of meetings with women from all sectors of society to promote the idea of institutionalizing women's struggles. She encouraged academics to create women's studies centers in their universities and a few did. By this time, many civil society women were convinced of the need for a permanent agency that would defend women's rights and that, unlike temporary ministerial appointments, would be permanent and have its own budget (García Prince 2003). So when Pérez announced in 1991 that he would eliminate the ministerial position, women's rights advocates and women politicians responded with an intense political and media campaign for the creation of a permanent agency. In 1992 the president created CONAMU and its Fundación de la Mujer (Women's Foundation) (to obtain and administer private and international funds). By law, CONAMU's board of directors included members of women's NGOs and a new practice appeared—civil society women and NGOs were contracted by femocrats as consultants, service providers, and gender experts.[8] Relations between Venezuelan and international femocrats also strengthened through funding and consulting, thereby solidifying leadership roles for politicians and femocrats, who displaced civil society feminists and led women's rights organizing throughout the nineties.

With public support from civil society groups, politicians promoted a Law of Equal Opportunities (passed in 1993 but not implemented) and achieved Venezuela's ratification of the international antiviolence agreement known as the Convention of Belém do Pará (1994) and the Law against Violence against Women and the Family (introduced in 1996 and passed in 1998). They achieved partial reform of the Suffrage Law to permit electoral quotas of 30 percent women candidates on party lists (1997) and approval of the first National Plan for Women (prepared by CONAMU with civil society consultants and approved by presidential decree in 1997).

In summary, during the seventies and eighties, feminists and women's rights groups claimed leadership of the women's rights struggle, built networks, and formed coalitions to influence femocrats and politicians. In the nineties, leadership passed to women in Congress who continued to partner with some civil society groups, ranging from lawyers at FEVA to academic feminists to leaders of the CFP. With the leadership of CONAMU and the Bichamber Committee in Congress, the women's rights struggle was institutionalized.

During the rest of the nineties, academic feminists, women's NGOs, and grassroots activists built up educational and service programs, and research on women increased. For many women, it was important to maintain a feminist consciousness (based on the common goal of gender equality) and open lines of communication. Friendships had been established from working together, and criticisms of each other and of politicians and femocrats were kept "in house" in the interest of putting rights advances first.[9] Even women from competing parties refused to attack those of other parties, often marching together to protest sex discrimination in politics and introducing legislative projects together.

From 1998 to 2007: Discord and Parallel Organizations

Before assuming the presidency for the first time in 1998, Hugo Chávez Frías established a new political movement—the Movimiento Quinta República (MVR; Fifth Republic Movement)—that became a political party and formed coalitions with the Partido Comunista (Communist Party), Patria para Todos (PPT; Fatherland for Everyone), Podemos, por la Democracia Social (We Can, for Social Democracy), and many other small parties that supported his political project.[10] At first, Chávez enjoyed the support of popular classes, the middle class, and the business sector. Most Venezuelans saw in him a genuine opportunity to achieve fundamental changes in the state, improve democracy with more direct citizen participation, and end the reign of corrupt political parties. Once elected, Chávez convoked an Asamblea Nacional Constituyente (ANC; National Constituent Assembly). Following approval of the new Constitution in 1999, he was reelected in 2000. Surviving a coup in April 2002, he then faced crippling national strikes in December 2003 and January 2004. He won a recall election in August 2004 and was reelected again in December 2006. During his terms, his supporters have won most of the seats in the new, single-chamber National Assembly, state legislatures, and city councils; most opposition parties abstained from these elections.

But the details of his proposal for a "peaceful Bolivarian socialist revolution" surprised many, especially in the business sector and the middle classes, and led to growing opposition and violent clashes between Chávez supporters and members of the opposition. The opposition blamed him for shortages of consumer goods and food staples, deteriorating public services and infrastructure, invasions of private property, business failures, inflation, and rising crime rates. They also rejected his close relations with Fidel Castro and the militarization and Cubanization of the public sector. Chávez, on the other hand, accused the opposition of savage capitalism, enrichment through exploitation of the poor, and being "lackeys" of George W. Bush and *"el imperio"* (the empire of the United States).

Following Chávez's reelection in 2006, he almost single-handedly drafted an extensive reform of the 1999 Constitution that included mechanisms to consolidate his power and to remain in power indefinitely. Following many student-led demonstrations demanding that he take the reforms to a vote (as required by law), elections were held in December 2007 and—to the surprise of Chávez and the opposition alike—the proposed reforms failed by a small margin.[11]

Political polarization has affected women's rights organizing as well. Initially, the combination of new political opportunities or possible reversals in rights that a Chávez presidency offered contributed to renewed, widespread mobilizing by women politicians, femocrats, civil society groups, and feminists. Over time, however, new class divisions and the politicization of the national women's agency have made it difficult to mobilize coalitions across classes and political parties in support of women's rights. Most mobilizing has been to support a political project—for or against the Bolivarian Revolution. Following is a summary of the ups and downs of women's organizing since 1998 and a brief explanation of some major divisions among groups identified with women's organizing and activism.

The Changing Place of Women in the Bolivarian Revolution

Although women today play key roles in revolutionary social change, in 1998 this was not the case. Chávez named no new women to his first cabinet (although one from the preceding administration continued as minister of finance for a time) or to high-ranking positions. His language was sexist (i.e., off-color jokes in public) and his actions paternalistic; he spoke to and about women only as self-sacrificing mothers and victims of poverty and racism. Then it was revealed that CONAMU's budget would be cut by 80 percent, and rumors circulated that Chávez planned to name the wife of a military officer as its director. Among the persons he hand-picked for the constituent assembly, there were few women (less than 5 percent). Faced with these threats to women's hard-won rights and representation in politics and public administration, politicians, femocrats, and civil society groups mobilized (see Castañeda and del Mar 2000; Vera 2000).

First, some women of the MVR and a few others who supported him as early as the 1992 coups focused on raising Chávez's consciousness. They educated him on the significance of gender, the history of women's struggle for rights, the achievements of Venezuelan women, and the importance of using a language that was inclusive and nonsexist. They presented him with lists of women fully qualified to hold important public positions. This was an important transformative process for Chávez. Initially, his speeches had emphasized race and class justice. He now added gender justice. He appointed women to his cabinet and to high-level positions. He began to reach out to women as actors, urging them to organize as "revolutionary mothers" who will "give birth to a new Venezuela."

Second, women's rights activists mobilized to defend CONAMU and to propose candidates for the constituent assembly. Over one hundred women attended an emergency meeting in Caracas in 1998, convoked by the Centro de Estudios de la Mujer de la Universidad Central de Venezuela (CEM-UCV; Women's Studies Center of the Central University of Venezuela) and by women in Congress; a smaller group met later in a law office. Those at the meetings drafted strategies to defend rights already achieved, and two letters were delivered to Chávez. The letters—signed by well-known academics, representatives of NGOs and professional associations, and several former ministers—explained the importance of CONAMU to gender justice. One letter proposed María León of the Communist Party, long-time Chávez supporter and cofounder of the CONG, as director. Chávez agreed.

At the same time, women from diverse political parties and labor unions, femocrats, and civil society groups organized intensive campaigns to guarantee that gender equity would be consecrated in the new Constitution. Their motto was "not one step back" on rights. They took advantage of the fact that members of the constituent assembly were obliged to consult with all sectors of civil society and receive proposals for constitutional change. Several coalitions appeared, such as Mujeres por la Democracia (Women for Democracy) and Frente Femenino por la Asamblea Constituyente (Women's Front for the Constituent Assembly). Women of the MVR, the Polo Patriótico (Patriotic Pole), and CONAMU organized strategy-building meetings across the country (see Castillo and de Salvatierra 2000). Dozens of workshops and conferences were organized, some with financial support and participation of international networks and agencies.

Among the more successful proposals that were included in the new Constitution is the following:

> use of nonsexist language; principles of equality and equity; recognition of women's rights as human rights that are universal, indivisible, inalienable, inviolate and protected by the State; nondiscrimination based on gender, age, sex, sexual orientation, creed, or social condition; the right to a life without violence; the right to eligibility and exercise of power and decision making; sexual and reproductive rights; recognition of the economic value of housework and equal pay for work of equal value; an obligation to respect and implement validly entered-into international treaties, pacts, accords and conventions signed by representatives of the Republic. (García and Jiménez 2000, 106–107)

In the ANC, five women from the MVR played a critical role in drafting a nonsexist Constitution. They garnered support for almost all the demands that women's rights advocates had proposed during three decades, with the exception of the decriminalization of abortion. Some academic feminists and former congresswomen helped behind the scenes to prepare the final text.

After the Constitution was approved by popular vote and new elections were held, Chávez, now fully aware of women's political importance and strongly advised to do so by María León, established the Instituto Nacional de la Mujer (INAMUJER; National Institute for Women)—contemplated in the earlier Law of Equal Opportunities—with León as its president. He also created the office of the Defensoría de la Mujer (Defender of Women) within INAMUJER and named an academic from the CEM-UCV to the position. In 2001 he created the Banco de Desarrollo de la Mujer (Women's Development Bank) to offer micro loans and to provide training in socialist ideology and gender awareness. He named another academic, a feminist economist from the CEM-UCV, as its president. A new phenomenon emerged: the widespread mobilization of working-class and poor women as part of the Bolivarian Revolution.[12]

INAMUJER and Popular Feminism

Once Chávez realized women's importance as voters and their organizational capacity, he charged María León with organizing them politically. This charge politicized INAMUJER and conflicted with its original mandate to work with and on behalf of all sectors of women.[13]

Subsequently, teams from INAMUJER and the Women's Bank have offered both practical training and socialist and gender education to large numbers of women from poor communities. INAMUJER's Web site announced in November 2004 that "the revolution has woken women up." The site emphasized the goals of "achieving women's full political participation and implementation of the Constitution, preventing and eliminating violence against women and the family, promoting the integrationist thinking of the liberator, Simón Bolívar, and promoting networks among popular sector women's organizations." Increasingly, the Web site and the documents published by INAMUJER emphasize goals that reflect "President Chávez's political platform" (2003) and claim Chávez as the liberator of women. "If the president decides that women's movements should unite, be dignified, and converge in a single organization, it is because he is the one who can convoke women . . . uniting women is a task of President Hugo Chávez . . . I am convinced that above our President in this country there is no one, only God, and God is with Chávez" (María León, quoted in Lolita 2005).

To work more effectively with popular feminists and to connect with their communities, INAMUJER has developed the mode of *puntos de encuentro* (encounter points).[14] They function as a means of "linking women in every community with the State." Points are groups of five or more women and INAMUJER estimates that almost two hundred thousand women have been organized in this way nationally.[15] INAMUJER estimates the number of women who attend national events (i.e., to celebrate International Women's Day or march in support of the president) varies from five thousand to ten thousand.

INAMUJER no longer partners with or provides support to women's rights advocates or their NGOs and no NGOs are on its board of directors; most contact is limited to hiring NGOs and individual feminists as paid gender consultants. Most long-active NGOs and feminists attribute the advances in women's rights to women's organizing, not to President Chávez; many express concern over women's exploitation as volunteer labor in state-directed community programs and over a political rhetoric that divides women into antagonistic classes.

Opposition Feminism

Self-denominated "opposition women" first took to the streets to oppose the state order to apply a Bolivarian academic agenda to teach socialism in private schools. Some began to refer to themselves as "new feminists." They blamed Hugo Chávez (a "charismatic caudillo"), his government ("undemocratic"), and state policies (that "ignore the middle class") for the country's problems. They rejected the official feminism represented by INAMUJER, accusing it of being co-opted by "the enemy state," and proposed to rescue the women's rights agenda from radical feminists and the state, by opposing abortion and quotas. They appropriated the banner of feminism for interviews and press releases before and just after the recall referendum. Their leaders made clear that their objectives were a conservative defense of "family and morality," human rights, and "middle-class values." They berated as "uncouth" the public behavior of pro-Chávez activists. Nonetheless, this movement was short-lived and involved only a small group out of the many women who were opposition activists.

For the public and those in government, this handful of opposition militants—professional women and middle-class homemakers, most with no previous political or feminist experience—were the face of the opposition. They included the wives of deposed military officers jailed following the coup of April 2002, mothers of children in private schools, and activists from human rights movements. They organized in groups such as Mujeres por la Libertad (Women for Liberty), Vigilantes de la Democracia (Democracy Vigilantes), and Mujeres de Rosado (Women in Pink). After international observers ratified Chávez's victory in the referendum, most disappeared. None ever participated in meetings organized by women's rights advocates.

Nevertheless, there were other militants in the opposition with a long history of feminist and political struggle. They could be called the "historical feminists of the opposition." Some served in Congress or as former ministers, some were militants in traditional political parties and labor unions, and some were academic feminists. All have promoted women's rights and many were former members of the CONG. They maintained a low profile relative to the "new feminists," preferring to work behind the scenes on political proposals and strategies. Just before the referendum, in the name of a Frente Nacional de Mujeres (National Women's Front), they publicly presented "feminist proposals" to confront the conservative political platform developed by male opposition leaders. They promised to defend the 1999 Constitution with its gender perspective and demanded that, if the opposition were to win the referendum, existing women's rights legislation must be implemented. Some participated in feminist initiatives to promote women's rights.

Efforts to Organize a Broad-Based Women's Movement

Shortly after elections were held in 2000 under the new Constitution, a core group of women in the new National Assembly (with help from a core group of academic feminists, lawyers, and international advisers) returned to work on the legislative agenda for women's rights. Their initiatives included several unsuccessful proposals to decriminalize abortion by reforming the penal code—with texts provided by civil society feminists—and an unsuccessful project in 2001 to extend social security to housewives. They also sponsored an unpassed 50-50 initiative, with INAMUJER support, to demand parity for women as electoral candidates and in public administration. INAMUJER successfully introduced a National Plan of Equal Opportunities that included an unsuccessful proposal for a National Women's Union, under the direction of INAMUJER, that would coordinate *all* women's NGOs and civil society groups (INAMUJER 2003).

As 2003 neared its end, something unexpected occurred that provoked a new, brief coalition of women across party lines. The attorney general introduced a motion in the Supreme Court, requesting the cancellation of Articles 3 and 39 (the so-called precautionary measures, or *medidas cautelares*) from the 1998 Law against Violence against Women and the Family. He found them to be unconstitutional because they advocated arresting the accused for seventy-two hours to remove him from the home. Women from diverse social sectors and political affiliations mobilized immediately to protest the motion and demand its withdrawal. The most visible leaders were academics from the CEM-UCV and other universities, women from NGOs working on issues of violence, and FEVA lawyers and judges. They were joined later by INAMUJER. INAMUJER and women of civil society prepared parallel, but separate, legal arguments defending the precautionary measures. They shared notes and held strategy meetings. The arguments prepared by civil society women were submitted to the Supreme Court, in the name of a Venezuelan Movimiento Amplio de Mujeres (MAM; Broad-based Women's Movement). INAMUJER delivered its legal arguments separately, representing the "Bolivarian women's movement." Women from both groups participated in demonstrations held at the Supreme Court, but ultimately the court struck down the measures.

In September 2004, after the failed recall referendum, the CEM-UCV and some civil society groups called a series of meetings to convoke an Asamblea de Mujeres (Women's Assembly), where all women could participate regardless of political affiliation or lack thereof. Some fifty women attended the first meeting, described as "broad-based and united," where they discussed shared strategies and a plan to include women's NGOs, government agencies, and international agencies. Leaders organized demonstrations at the National Assembly and the Supreme Court, calling for greater rights for women and a new antiviolence law to replace the existing 1998 law, after its precautionary measures were declared unconstitutional. The idea was to reestablish civil society leadership for rights initiatives, although politicians and INAMUJER staff were still invited to participate. This move directly contradicted the plan for a national women's union under INAMUJER's direction.

This initiative was a result of concerns that first arose before Chávez became president and that intensified during his presidencies. Many politically autonomous feminists—including academics and women in NGOs—had never been comfortable with the transfer of initiatives from civil society to femocrats and politicians and did not trust the patriarchal state to defend women's rights. The politicization of INAMUJER and the mobilizing of popular women in the service of a political project, rather than for their rights as women, intensified their antipathy. When three rights issues emerged before and after the 2004 referendum—the precautionary measures discussed earlier, the case of Linda Loaiza López, and new efforts to decriminalize abortion—some longtime activists and academics sought a return to "unity in diversity."

Linda Loaiza, eighteen years old, was discovered near death on July 19, 2001, in the apartment of a man whose family had powerful political connections. She had been tortured and raped during four months of imprisonment. Despite her obvious permanent physical damage and dozens of surgeries, her alleged abuser was not brought to trial. After the 2004 referendum, Linda began a hunger strike at the Supreme Court. The case of Linda Loaiza was important for several reasons. For one, it coincided with the struggle to retain the precautionary measures. Second, she became an icon in the public eye—she put a (much-damaged) face on the issue of violence against women and generated widespread sympathy and outrage. Her case was a symbol of the failure of the justice system to defend the rights of women and the poor.

At first, there was total silence from femocrats and politicians, not even a word from the office of the Defensoría de la Mujer. Some "new feminists" of the opposition tried to capitalize on her case as an opportunity to criticize Chávez. At the first meeting of the Women's Assembly, a measure to support "Justice for Linda" (the motto of the campaign) passed unanimously. Those present declared, "We all are Linda Loaiza" (a motto disseminated through bumper stickers, posters, and T-shirts) and incorporated her case into their campaign to defend the precautionary measures. Following many public demonstrations and widespread media coverage, her abuser was put on trial. The judge who declared him not guilty was removed from her position; the National Assembly repudiated the verdict and demanded a new trial. (The perpetrator was found guilty at a second trial.) Efforts shifted from reinstating the precautionary measures to passing a new, more effective antiviolence law.

For much of 2005 and 2006, civil society women and the Comité sobre Familia, Mujer y Juventud (CFWY; Committee on Family, Women, and Youth) focused on the decriminalization of abortion (unsuccessful), the passage of laws to protect paternity and maternity rights and to promote breastfeeding (passed), and a new antiviolence law (passed in November 2006), which, among other provisions, criminalized rape and established special domestic violence courts. However, most members of the National Assembly showed no interest in discussing abortion, both for electoral reasons and as a matter of "conscience" or religion.

Levels of organizing varied in 2005 and all but died out in 2006. The few recent collaborations have tended to be opportunistic, focused on specific goals or issues, and have involved only a handful of women. For example, in the name of a "broad-based women's movement," a list of demands were circulated during the 2006 election campaigns through meetings with the press and candidates, but had no discernible impact.

A new group appeared in February 2007, called "el grupo ese." Members referred to themselves as "feminists and *sexodivers@s*" (persons of various sexual orientations and identities). Their goal was to prepare and present a list of demands for Chávez's planned extensive reform of the 1999 Constitution and for a related Ley Habilitante (Special Powers Law) that would allow the president to legislate without the approval of the National Assembly. Several high-ranking government officials—including members of INAMUJER's board of directors and of the Defensor del Pueblo (People's Defender), along with the National Assembly deputy heading up the presidential reform committee—met with the group and seemed encouraging. But none of their proposals (e.g., explicit constitutional rights for gays, lesbians, and transgendered people; decriminalization of abortion; implementation of social security for homemakers, etc.) were included in the final version of the ultimately unsuccessful reforms.[16] Once the objectives of constructing and delivering demands for reform were achieved, the group ceased meeting.

Challenges for the Future

At the beginning of 2009, there continued to be no detectable mobilizing on the part of women's rights activists, and even the extensive e-mail networks showed little activity. For femocrats and politicians and President Chávez, much of 2008 was consumed by efforts to overcome the failure of the proposed constitutional reforms. With his advisers and supporters in the National Assembly behind him, Chávez considered other options for future reforms and advanced plans for a socialist Venezuela. Among the strategies used were the passage and implementation of new laws and tightened control over the judicial branch to avoid confronting issues of unconstitutionality. In February 2009 another special election successfully overturned presidential term limits established by the Constitution, leaving Chávez free to be reelected indefinitely.

The opposition was unusually quiet during most of 2008, focused on preparations for regional and local elections in November, where its candidates won governorships in the five most populous states and in major municipalities, including the capital of Caracas. In 2009 the opposition has rallied following Chávez's removal of authority over education, health, and police services and the denial of federal budget outlays to those governors' and mayors' offices. These political crises were added to a deepening economic crisis that began in 2008, brought on by the sudden and sustained decline in oil income. Deep cuts in the federal budget have led to widespread unrest in diverse social classes.

The 2006 antiviolence law was partially implemented in 2008. After some ten years of discussion over a proposed Organic Law of Gender Equity and Equality, the project entered into discussion in the National Assembly in 2009. However, feminist critics have pointed out that agreed-on articles on the decriminalization of abortion and the legalization of civil unions for same sex partners disappeared from the text of the project prior to discussion, removed by the chair of the CFWY. The project also fails to include instructions to implement existing legislation on pensions for homemakers or fifty-fifty parity in electoral candidates and civil service appointments; without such instructions, the laws will not be implemented. As of July 2009 and following several years of minimal activity, a few feminist and gay rights activists were again using blogs and e-mail lists in an attempt to garner support to exert pressure on members of the CFWY to strengthen the law and include abortion and civil unions. The Catholic Church, however, was working equally hard to assure failure of the law in the National Assembly.

Whether or not there will be new coalitions to advance women's rights depends on many factors, including political opportunities and challenges to women's demands, such as the right to abortion and homemakers' pensions and whether key divisive issues, such as the politicization of INAMUJER, can be overcome.

A main dynamic is the rupture and growing hostility between INAMUJER and non-chavista civil society groups. Many civil society rights advocates express regret and anger over the institutionalization of women's rights, particularly in light of an INAMUJER considered by autonomous feminists to be so politicized that there is no hope the agency will work with a broad range of women's groups and on a broad range of issues. Criticisms of INAMUJER and María León, once kept in-house, are increasingly aired in public arenas such as in consulting reports, opinion pieces, interviews, and blogs. Some long-active civil organizations such as FEVA have ceased activities or no longer collaborate on legal projects. Others limit their involvement to accepting paid contracts to provide services or research or to giving occasional feedback on documents circulated on e-mail networks.[17]

A second factor is an increasing tension between civil society feminists and women of the National Assembly's CFWY. The defeat of so many legal initiatives and the failure to implement laws already passed have led to criticism by feminists that women of the CFWY are unwilling to confront resistance and force implementation. Another conflict is over the recent laws to protect the family, maternity, and paternity and to promote and protect breastfeeding. Former feminist advisers dismiss the laws as poorly conceptualized and potentially harmful to women (i.e., for pressuring women to breastfeed for a prolonged period).

A third factor is the general confusion and disagreements surrounding claims to "feminism" as an ideological project and to women's rights as a political project. Brief appropriation by the "new feminists" of the opposition had little effect on organizing, but appropriation by María León and INAMUJER is widely debated. Autonomous feminists in general and academic feminists in particular reject claims that Chávez is a "women's leader" and their liberator or that INAMUJER's training in socialist ideology and gender awareness has led to greater consciousness and activism on the part of the popular women identified by León as practicing a nonelite feminism (Lolita 2005). Research conducted in poorer neighborhoods provide rich data on how popular women focus on educational, health, and income issues that affect them and their families and on their dedication as volunteers in the service of their communities and in support of President Chávez. But researchers working with working-class and poor women challenge the notion that they embrace and understand concepts like gender and feminism or that a significant number place women's rights high on their list of priorities.

A fourth factor relates to some of the recent issues prioritized by feminist activists and "el grupo ese." Many are considered controversial even by some women's rights advocates and by many politicians and popular women. They include rights for homosexuals (civil unions, adoption, inheritance), the decriminalization of abortion, mandated imprisonment for batterers, and 50 percent parity quota in public employment and elections. Sexual rights and abortion have generated absolute silence on the part of both the president, opposition leaders, and even the National Assembly deputies who initially supported discussion of these rights. These obstacles to future collaboration among different groups of women for the shared goal of advancing women's rights cannot be dismissed. But are they insurmountable? Following are a few bright spots on the horizon.

First, organized women—including professionals, academics, activists, politicians, and femocrats—share a long history of working together. Many remain committed to goals of justice and equity that, in the past, have transcended political differences. If they could set aside political, ideological, and class differences in the past, both openly or working behind the scenes, why not again? There are feminists who continue to keep alive the goals and discourse of feminism, just as their counterparts used to do (Espina and Rakowski 2002). In particular, e-mail networks with as many as three thousand members facilitate easy communication for future mobilizations. Given the right opportunity or threat, the potential exists.

Second, the proposed Ministerio del Poder Popular para la Mujer y la Igualdad de Género (MEAMUJER; Ministry of Popular Power for Women and Gender Equality) exists in name only and INAMUJER continues to be the official state agency for women. Its director, María León, is officially the minister for women and gender equality and both names appear on the banner on INAMUJER's Web site. If INAMUJER were to be elevated to a ministry, then it might become a future ally for women's rights organizing because of the consequent increase in power and funding. But as of July 2009 criticisms of INAMUJER's shortcomings remain valid; León has met privately with some feminist critics to discuss their concerns. If the agency returns to a focus on women's organizing (softening the idea of Chávez as women's liberator) and community work, INAMUJER could potentially once again become an ally for civil society organizing for women's rights and for sexuality rights, a new issue on the legislative agenda. León and her staff have significant credibility with international agencies and other branches of government because of their implementation of antiviolence programs in the past, their ability to organize popular women, and their support from Chávez. Great challenges remain, including a propensity for secrecy on the "encounter points," politically charged discourse and idealization of Chávez, and a failure to facilitate communication and contact between popular women and other organized women, including feminists.

Third, young feminists and young community leaders are emerging in the national spotlight and behind the scenes. Many of the feminists are from universities but some come from NGOs, prodemocracy political activist groups, and community activism. Some community leaders, both women and men, show keen awareness of gender issues as critical to social justice. This new generation appears to have considerable ideological clarity regarding women's rights and politics and, unlike their foremothers, many do not fear being labeled feminists. They include lesbians and heterosexual women, and gay and heterosexual men. Some young feminists attended women's coalition meetings in 2005 and participated in public demonstrations. Some have published Internet essays and scholarly commentaries on feminism and socialism, and some have worked closely with members of the contemporary core group or as part of "el grupo ese."[18] One INAMUJER staff member discussed some young community activists who are preparing themselves for leadership roles in local and national politics and many who share specific concerns over violence against women and women's poverty (interview, Masaya Llavaneras, July 23, 2007, Caracas).

In addition to the three main factors, some other bright spots exist. During the prodemocracy and proconstitutional reform student movements of 2007, new compellingly articulate student leaders emerged on both sides. They have remobilized in 2009 to demand respect for democracy and to debate the constitutionality of censorship and attempts to remove some legally elected mayors and governors of opposition parties. Hundreds of thousands of poor women have benefited from mission programs, the social programs that target the poorest families and communities. Women are the volunteers, paid staff, and organizers of many mission programs and a majority of those enrolled in educational programs and receiving financial subsidies (Espina and Rakowski 2007). Their grassroots volunteerism and political activities may prepare them for other gender-specific organizing both in and beyond their communities.

No one can predict Venezuela's future with any degree of confidence, even in the short term. The surprising results of the unsuccessful constitutional reform elections and the publicly aired internal struggles in the Partido Socialista Unido de Venezuela (PSUV; United Venezuelan Socialist Party) may indicate that new surprises are to come. The creation of a new ministry, MEAMUJER, has not led to significant changes for women's rights, organizing, or women's role in the revolution. Fiscal problems related to declining oil revenues and tension over unconstitutional policies and state corruption are divisive factors. Given both the obstacles and the bright spots, we await the next chapter in the saga of Venezuelan women's struggle for rights.

NOTES

1. Although mandated by law to be democratic, some of these civil society groups were "colonized" by political parties.

2. February 1989 also saw the *caracazo*—the first mass demonstration opposing the implementation of austerity measures. Many political observers consider this the beginning of the end of the Punto Fijo system based on party pacts (known today as the Fourth Republic). The Fourth Republic is a term applied to the period of representative democracy through party politics from 1958 to 1998. The Fifth Republic refers to the period beginning in 1998 that shifted to participatory democracy and then to socialism. Party pacts are a common practice where political parties agree to collaborate in the interest of promoting democracy.

3. The Bolivarian Revolution is named after "El Libertador" Simón Bolívar, a hero in the South American struggle for independence.

4. See Friedman (2000a) for a history of women's agencies.

5. Femocrats are feminists who hold elected office or work in state or international agencies.

6. In spite of a Constitution that prohibited sex discrimination, the civil code gave the male head of household absolute control over the family and his spouse. The wife was a legal minor under his tutelage. Women in nonlegal unions had no rights, and children born outside of marriage did not share the same rights as "legitimate" children.

7. The coalition to reform the civil code was also the first time that a legal project was introduced to Congress through a petition signed by more than thirty thousand citizens.

8. The phenomena of NGOization and gender specialists have been analyzed for other countries (see Alvarez 1999).

9. Consultants and femocrats were accused of political co-optation, politicians of being self-serving, and CONAMU of giving too much decision-making power to international feminists.

10. In 2006 Chávez disbanded the MVR and attempted unsuccessfully to consolidate its previous members and other independent parties that supported him into the PSUV. Some parties followed suit, but several have remained independent.

11. Election analyses point to high abstention in neighborhoods of heavy support for Chávez in the 2006 elections as the major factor.

12. Some groups were also organized around issues of racism to raise consciousness regarding the structural and cultural links between class and race. Over time, the emphasis on class and poverty has increased while that on race has decreased.

13. In March 2008 Chávez announced that a new ministerial office, MEAMUJER, would replace INAMUJER. However, INAMUJER continues to be the state agency for women

14. We use the concept of "popular feminism" here because it is widely applied to women in diverse Latin American countries who are involved in communal and human rights struggles, especially poor women and workers (Alvarez 2000). It is not limited to economic status but includes demographics.

15. In July 2007 an INAMUJER staff person who works with these groups informed us that many community activists are older women with a long track record of community activism under prior administrations. Although a few women may take gender issues to heart, most work as volunteers in service programs in poor neighborhoods and are committed to fighting poverty and/or political activism in their communities.

16. The president proposed thirty-three articles and the National Assembly thirty-six more for the proposed constitutional reform.

17. The two NGOs that are called on occasionally by INAMUJER and women in the National Assembly are Asociación Civil de Planificación Familiar (Plafam; Civil Association for Family Planning) and Asociación Venezolana para una Educación Sexual Alternativa (AVESA; Venezuelan Association for an Alternative Sex Education).

18. Older feminists refer to the younger women as the long-awaited replacement generation (*generación de relevo*).

REFERENCES

Alvarez, Sonia. 1999. Advocating feminism: The Latin American feminist NGO "boom." *International Feminist Journal of Politics* 12:81–204.

———. 2000. Translating the global: Effects of transnational organizing on local feminist discourses and practices in Latin America. Diálogo Solidaridad GLOBAL. www.antenna.nl/~waterman/alvarez.html. Subsequently published in *Cadernos de Pesquisa*, October 22, 2000. www.sociologia.ufsc.br/cadernos/Cadernos%20PPGSP%2022.pdf (accessed July 2009).

Castañeda, Nora. 1998. Las políticas públicas y la dimensión equidad de género en Venezuela 1990–1997. *Revista Venezolana de Estudios de la Mujer* 3 (1): 32–49.

Castañeda, Nora, and María del Mar. 2000. Proceso constituyente: Propuestas para la Constitución de la República de Venezuela desde la mirada de las mujeres. *Revista Venezolana de Estudios de la Mujer* 5 (14): 147–154.

Castillo, Adicea, and Isolde de Salvatierra. 2000. Las mujeres y el proceso constituyente venezolano. *Revista Venezolana de Estudios de la Mujer* 5 (14): 37–88.

De Vincenzo, Teresa. 2002. Las mujeres que marchan. *El Universal*. September 22, sec. 1, p. 9.

Espina, Gioconda. 1994. Entre sacudones, golpes y amenazas: Las venezolanas organizadas y las otras. In *Mujeres y participación política: Avances y desafíos en América Latina*, ed. Magdalena León, 167–181. Bogota: T/M.

Espina, Gioconda, and Cathy A. Rakowski. 2002. Movimiento de mujeres o mujeres en movimiento: El caso Venezuela. *Cuadernos del CENDES* 49:31–48.

———. 2007. Chávez, populismo y las venezolanas. Paper presented at the Twenty-seventh International Congress of the Latin American Studies Association, Montreal, Canada, September 5–8.

Friedman, Elisabeth. 1998. Paradoxes of gendered political opportunity in the Venezuelan transition to democracy. *Latin American Research Review* 33:87–136.

———. 1999. The effects of transnationalism reversed in Venezuela: Assessing the impact of UN global conferences on the women's movement. *International Feminist Journal of Politics* 13:357–381.

———. 2000a. State-based advocacy for gender equality in the developing world: Assessing the Venezuelan national women's agency. *Women and Politics* 21 (2): 47–80.

———. 2000b. *Unfinished transitions: Women and the gendered development of democracy in Venezuela, 1936–1996.* University Park: Pennsylvania State University Press.

García, Carmen Teresa, and Morelba Jiménez. 2000. Proceso constituyente, identidad femenina y ciudadanía. *Revista Venezolana de Estudios de la Mujer* 5 (14): 89–122.

García Prince, Evangelina. 2003. Hacia la institucionalización del enfoque de género en políticas públicas. January. Unpublished document prepared for the Friedrich Ebert Foundation, Caracas.

INAMUJER. 2003. *Plan Nacional de Igualdad de Oportunidades para las Mujeres.* Caracas: Ministry of Health and Social Development. www.inamujer.gob.ve.

Lolita. [Edith Franco]. 2005. María León: El socialismo del siglo XXI es el comunismo. Interview. *Joven Guardia*, September 5. www.jotaceve.org (accessed March 15, 2007).

Rakowski, Cathy A. 1998. Unity in diversity and adversity: Venezuelan women's struggle for human rights. *INSTRAW News* 28:26–33.

———. 2003. Women's coalitions as a strategy at the intersection of economic and political change in Venezuela. *International Journal of Politics, Culture, and Society* 16 (3): 387–405.

Vera, Esperanza. 2000. La agenda está integrada a un proceso. *Revista Venezolana de Estudios de la Mujer* 5 (14): 17–36.

16

Trickling Up, Down, and Sideways

GENDER POLICY AND POLITICAL OPPORTUNITY IN BRAZIL

FIONA MACAULAY

This chapter examines how, since the early 1980s, the Brazilian women's movement has navigated political and institutional terrains in pursuit of new state mechanisms for promoting gender equity and equality policies.[1] It begins by tracing the ups and down of the Conselho Nacional dos Direitos da Mulher (CNDM; National Council for Women's Rights), now the Secretaria Especial de Políticas para as Mulheres (SPM; Special Secretariat for Policies on Women). The fortunes of the CNDM—one of the earliest national governmental units for women in the region—illustrate how features of the political and institutional environment can constitute both obstacle and opportunity. The CNDM highlights the need for institutionalization in the face of a weak and often opportunistic party system, but also the potential to advance gender policy through the multiple, parallel entry points afforded by a federal system of government. Ironically, systematic undermining and neglect of the CNDM by successive central administrations in the 1990s contributed to the emergence of horizontal and vertical networks composed of women's grassroots groups, nongovernmental organizations (NGOs), and state- and municipal-level government units, as the women's movement regrouped to compensate for the vacuum created at the center. The second section of this chapter examines the role of these networks inside and outside the state, and below the level of central government, looking specifically at the state and municipal women's councils, the women's caucus in Congress, and the networks and hubs of women's groups and NGOs. The chapter concludes by evaluating the overall impact on state-level gender policy making of over two decades of activism by a diverse feminist policy community.

The Peaks and Troughs of the CNDM/SPM

In 1936 feminist pioneer Bertha Lutz made the first attempt to set up a national unit dedicated to the promotion of women's rights in Brazil.[2] She proposed a National Women's Bureau to deal with female workers rights, public assistance to women, social security, and issues related to the household, maternity, and children (Saffioti 1978, 207–209) and argued that it should have executive functions, unlike the advisory U.S. Department of Labor's Women's Bureau on which it was modeled. However, the installation of the authoritarian rule of President Getúlio Vargas in the Estado Novo (New State) period (1937–1945) rendered the discussion moot. Some four decades later, as the military regime of 1964–1985 was easing, a well-organized women's movement seized the opportunity offered by the return to democracy. Female federal deputies in the official opposition party, the Movimento Democrático Brasileiro (Brazilian Democratic Movement) proposed a Ministry for Children and the Family (Tabak 1989, 95), to which the president-elect Tancredo Neves agreed in 1984. The Partido do Movimento Democrático Brasileiro (PMDB; Party of the Brazilian Democratic Movement), as it became known after the reorganization of the party system in 1979, was eager to establish its progressive credentials in its newly won state governments. The women's movement thus managed to convert the political capital it had accumulated by opposing military rule and organizing for the campaign for direct presidential elections into a number of additional gender policies, such as pioneering women-only police stations to deal with domestic and sexual violence, an integrated women's health care program, and advisory councils on women's rights, attached to the state administrations.[3]

Even though Vice President Sarney, who took on the presidency after Neves's premature death, had few dealings with the opposition or social movements, the CNDM initially prospered under his government (1985–1989). Although it was constituted as a consultative body, it enjoyed political space that gave it considerable de facto executive and deliberative powers.[4] The CNDM possessed administrative and financial autonomy, a ring-fenced budget of three million U.S. dollars allocated by Congress, a technical support staff, and an executive-secretariat to carry out tasks mandated by the board.[5] Its wide-ranging mission statement to work for national policies against the discrimination of women was based on the Convention on the Elimination of All Forms of Discrimination against Women (CEDAW).

The CNDM seized another institutional opportunity when it put forward more than a hundred proposals to congressional committees during the Constitutional Assembly (1987–1988). The skillful orchestration of the joint action of sympathetic female legislators, councils, and independent women's groups enabled the women's movement to get over 80 percent of its demands incorporated into the final text of the 1988 Constitution. The CNDM also worked on many operational policy issues and conducted regular cross-sectoral meetings with ministry representatives. It collaborated with the Ministry of Education on nonsexist schoolbooks, and with the Ministry of Health to promote information on reproduction and contraception, implement the Programa de Assistência Integral à Saúde da Mulher (PAISM; Comprehensive Women's Health Care Program) and ensure provision of legal abortions.[6] It set up a Committee for Black Women, urged the Federal Supreme Court to rule against the use of the "honor defense" by men who murdered their spouses or partners, instituted sanctions against businesses that contravened labor laws, extended employment benefits to female domestic and rural workers, and established women's right to hold land titles (Pitanguy 2002). It was staffed by

experienced feminist activists skilled in public policy formulation and political lobbying, who benefited from high credibility with the movement and good currency
with the party of government.

However, the PMDB's support for the CNDM turned out to be highly contingent on individuals in the government, principally the president and minister of
justice. By the late 1980s the party had lost its foundational raison d'être as the chief
opponent to military rule and mutated into a classic catch-all party, losing its more
principled social democratic members to the PSDB in 1988 and acquiring new ideologically ill-defined fellow travelers from the Right. As this occurred, feminists
lost their influence within the party and started to migrate to other options on the
Center-Left, such as the Partido dos Trabalhadores (PT; Workers' Party). By the
end of the Sarney government and throughout the Collor/Franco government
(1990–1994), successive ministers of justice regarded the CNDM as simply another
locus for patronage and oversaw its dramatic deinstitutionalization, replacing its
chief executive and board with individuals who had no women's movement connections. A 1990 decree removed the CNDM's administrative and financial autonomy, and it was reduced to two rooms in the annex, after having occupied two
floors in the main Ministry of Justice building. Its staff of 150 people was cut back to
the chief executive, one employee, and a secretary by 1992. Although the CNDM's
consultative functions and board structure remained intact, for the next decade it
lacked any executive capacity to design or promote cross-sectoral gender policies.

Women activists' hopes in President Fernando Henrique Cardoso, a progressive sociologist and founder of the Partido da Social Democracia Brasileira (PSDB;
Party of Brazilian Social Democracy), were soon dashed. He reneged on a manifesto pledge to evaluate and redefine the role of the CNDM, flatly refused demands
to upgrade it to a ministerial-rank secretariat, and failed to restore it to its former
status. In part, this was due to the fiscal concerns of a government whose credibility was staked on the control of inflation and public spending. However, the PSDB
was also impermeable to the claims of any other social movement. A classic caucus
party born of an elite-level schism, it had no mass membership in the manner of its
European social democratic counterparts. As a party it never developed any policy
on gender issues, and feminists within it tended to act individually, not collectively.
This essentially technocratic character afforded the women's movement no entry
point through which to influence the tightly knit clique of party leaders.

It was hardly a surprise, then, that Cardoso appointed as the new head of
CNDM a crony without strong movement support. With just one staff member,
the CNDM tried to carry out its limited Program of Action, based on the Beijing
Platform for Action, in partnership with other entities better endowed with
resources, such as the Secretaria Nacional de Direitos Humanos (Ministry of
Justice's Human Rights Secretariat), sector-specific ministries, and the Comunidade
Solidária (Community Solidarity) fund, headed by the president's wife, eminent
anthropologist Ruth Cardoso. It was only in the final months of Cardoso's eight-
year government that the Council regained its own executive staff, albeit still under
the aegis of the Secretaria Nacional de Direitos Humanos. In September 2002, he

used an executive decree to create the Secretaria de Estado dos Direitos da Mulher (National Secretariat for Women's Rights), which the incoming PT government immediately transformed into the SPM.

It is not clear why Cardoso took this unilateral step; perhaps he wanted to leave a better historical record on women's issues while bequeathing the financial implications to his successor. The PT, on the other hand, was fulfilling a commitment to the institutional reinvigoration of the CNDM that the party had been making in its election manifestos since 1994. It has been more responsive to women's movement demands and has run and elected more women for legislative office than any other party. The PT differed from its competitors in many ways, largely due to the special circumstances and character of its genesis in the late 1970s. It was founded on twin social pillars: first, the social movements closely linked to the progressive Catholic Church and focused on collective consumption in which women were key protagonists; and second, a radicalized trade union movement. The military regime's suppression of male labor militants led to the formation of the Movimento Feminino pela Anistia (Women's Amnesty Movement), which provided a ready-made network of women eager to help set up the new party.[7] Several features of the PT as a new left-wing party appealed to feminists, such as its emphasis on a discourse of ethics and a pluralist conception of citizenship that did not seem to privilege class as a political framework. As a result of two decades of activism by feminists within the party, both internally and within the PT's municipal and state administrations, the transition team appointed by the president-elect Luiz Inácio Lula da Silva included two feminists tasked with sensitizing the incoming cabinet to gender issues. He also appointed an unprecedented number of women to his cabinet, and in his first presidential message affirmed the new government's commitment to women's rights.

Under previous governments the CNDM had been attached to the Ministry of Justice, a logical institutional home that afforded it the opportunity to introduce significant legal changes and develop a rights-based discourse. However, this location was also to prove an obstacle to closing the implementation gap between the letter of the law and its application through concrete policies, as the ministry's head had historically acted chiefly as a "political fixer," mediating between the state governors and the president. On Lula's first day in office he signed an executive decree establishing the SPM within the President's Office. The SPM's secretary of state was accorded the status of minister and a seat in the cabinet. Smaller than the CNDM in its heyday, comprising a cabinet and three subdepartments (for institutional networking, monitoring of thematic programs, and gender planning), the SPM has a similar mission: to advise the president on the drafting, coordination, and implementation of gender policies, discrimination awareness campaigns, and gender-planning mechanisms for all government levels; to cooperate with national and international organizations; and to oversee the enforcement of agreements, conventions, and action plans on gender equality agreed on by the federal government.[8]

The Lula government also designated 2004 National Women's Year and launched a nation-wide consultation that culminated in the hundred-page *Plano*

Nacional de Políticas para Mulheres (National Plan on Policies for Women) (SPM 2006), the most comprehensive gender-equity and gender-equality blueprint yet produced in Brazil. Supported by an interministerial working group, the plan focuses on nonsexist education, women's health, gender violence, workplace discrimination, and mainstreaming strategies, with the last three selected as the SPM's initial priorities. Meanwhile both the upper and lower houses established special parliamentary committees to systematize the various gender-related bills and adapted the SPM's proposals to reflect the overall priorities of the Lula government, including social welfare, work, housing rights, prevention of violence, and social security, with each theme handled by a working group. In 2007 a Segunda Conferência Nacional de Políticas para as Mulheres (Second National Conference on Policies for Women) was held with 2,800 delegates, to evaluate and update the plan and determine priorities for the rest of Lula's second term. The revised plan again emphasized women's access to the labor market, antipoverty and inequality measures, pensions and social security reform, reproductive and sexual rights, and gender violence and, this time, included a specific chapter on black and indigenous women's issues and on lesbophobia, as a result of lobbying by the respective advocacy networks.

For such consultations between the state women's bureaucracy and the women's movement to be meaningful, they need to have a direct impact not just on policy but also on the implementation of that policy, which is totally reliant on national and state budgets. The consultation process in 2007 meant that the Second National Plan was not completed before governmental negotiations over the Multiyear Plan, which sets budgets for the period 2008–2011 (AMB 2007a). With the SPM's institutional structure restored, apparently stable and not subject to the political predations that its predecessors suffered, the women's movement has turned its attention to the impact of national spending on gender relations, that is, to the task of mainstreaming proper. The chief gripes concern firstly the SPM's low level of funding relative to the enormity of the task: in 2006 it was allocated twenty-four million *reais* (that is, 0.56 percent of the overall national budget). The women's movement has also been carefully tracking the government spending in all areas considered to have an impact on gender relations. However, just as the Cardoso government did, the Lula administration tends to underspend on the social welfare budget approved by Congress.[9] In the years 2005–2007, the government disbursed only 70 percent of the earmarked "women's budget," sequestering the remainder to shore up its balance of payments surplus. Of the money spent, 40 percent is accounted for in the programs in basic health care and the Family Grant, a nationwide conditional cash transfer. Participants in the second conference were also very critical of the government's macroeconomic policies, which had either impacted negatively or only slightly on the structural drivers of inequality and exclusion.

In summary, the impact of individual parties on the women's movement's opportunities to influence policy is evident. However, in a party system populated for the main part by nonideological, ill-disciplined parties with few organic roots in society and oriented around rent-seeking and clientelistic practices, the permeability and protean quality of the system and its component parties have been both blessing and curse. Women were not crowded out of the political arena by the consolidation of formal channels of democratic political participation, as occurred with the restoration of the political parties in the countries of the Southern Cone once the transitional moment had passed during which they could exert some leverage. Nonetheless, Brazilian parties remain important gatekeepers between the state and women's movement demands, due more to their internal culture and certain foundational and organizational characteristics, than to their ideological positioning.

Although the attitudes of these three parties to the feminist agenda have ranged from indifference, to co-option, to sympathy, no individual party in the Brazilian system could be deemed actively hostile. This may be attributed to the almost complete absence of cleavages based on the classic sociological dividing lines of race, class, religion, and gender; Brazil has never had a significant Christian Democratic or church-associated party. Through the 1980s and 1990s the rightward shift in the Vatican had comparatively little impact, as the National Council of Bishops and much of the flock remained committed to the social justice perspective that the Brazilian Catholic Church embraced in the 1970s, a posture that at the ballot box primarily benefited the PT, a secular, pluralist party. In consequence, the women's movement did not face much organized, value-based opposition around gender or "private" issues such as sexuality, family, and reproduction. During the 1993 constitutional revision process, an attitudinal survey of deputies and senators concluded that, while the Center-Left was predictably consistent in its support for extending women's rights, the Right was not necessarily hostile. The latter's priorities are centered on state power, not on morality, and it opposed gender legislation only when it required financial commitments by the state, such as for child care or pension provision (CFEMEA 1993).

Recent years have seen a surge in the membership of evangelical Christian churches, which are more socially conservative but whose members and representatives have been highly dispersed, with many in small, opportunistic parties, obviating any political focus for a fundamentalist, antisecular backlash. Indeed, in 2006 their numbers in Congress dropped due to implication of many in corruption scandals. The conservative wing of the Catholic Church has also enjoyed a resurgence, boosted by the visit of Pope Benedict XVI in 2007, who canonized Frei Galvão as the patron saint of pregnant women. Thus the feminist movement is faced not with concentrated political opposition in the shape of a specific party but rather by diffuse opposition exercised through the Catholic and Evangelical cross-bench groupings and the media, making entry points for influence more difficult to identify.

The Formation of a Feminist Policy Community

The process of generating legislation and lobbying politicians, the business sector, and the media was led until 1989 by the CNDM and taken up in the 1990s by a policy community composed of three different types of feminist networks. This decentered, plural gender-policy community differs territorially, ideologically, sectorally, and thematically. It stretches horizontally to encompass women's NGOs, advocacy groups, women legislators, and party feminists and reaches vertically down through subnational structures through a variety of state-sponsored spaces for gender-policy debates in local government. This community became denser with time, as the women's movement reacted to external catalyzing factors, such as the Constitutional Assembly, the Fourth United Nations World Conference on Women, held in Beijing in 1995, and periodic legislative moves to restrict reproductive rights.

State and Municipal Gender Policy

Federalism has provided the women's movement with multiple opportunities and instruments to engage the state. Following the closure of political space in central government, initiative on gender policy was taken up by the network of state and municipal councils on women's rights. Over two decades these multiplied and by 2002 totaled ninety-seven (nineteen state and seventy-eight municipal). For its part, the PT also began to experiment with new institutional formats to invite women's movement participation in policy making. It disliked the way opposition parties had tried to co-opt the women's movement during the transition to democracy through sponsoring women's federations and councils, and criticized the hybrid character of the women's councils, in which the functions of participation, representation, and decision making were blurred. The party began to set up executive-branch women's offices in many of its state and municipal administrations. These ranged from full-blown municipal departments (secretariats), with their own budget, staff, and powers to execute programs, to Coordenadorias Especiais da Mulher (Women's Coordinating Committees), attached to the mayor's or governor's office, with the responsibility to oversee gender-related work programs in other departments, to Assessorias dos Direitos da Mulher (Women's Advisory Units), often subordinated either to the mayor's office or to a social welfare or human rights department, government divisions with the lowest status and fewest resources and powers. Party feminists also recognized the need for both a foothold in the administrative apparatus through informal groupings of women bureaucrats and better means of engaging local women in policy debates. The latter they achieved through redesigned women's councils with a more genuinely representative role and intermediary function, combined with open-access, periodic women's forums. In some places, such as in São Paulo, Rio de Janeiro, and Londrina (one of the birthplaces of Brazilian feminism), well-organized local women's movements were able to press politicians for these state gender-policy structures. However, in other cases, such as in Santo André, a town in the industrial belt around São Paulo, there was no movement as such, and it was the local government that initially provided the institutional space in which women could meet and coalesce into a more durable independent movement.

Women activists have used these and other governance mechanisms, such as city planning tools, participatory budgeting, and state and municipal legislation, to secure local government commitment. As a result, many subnational constitutions detail state and municipal governments' responsibility for promoting gender justice through executive action on reproductive rights, domestic violence, and the labor market. Interestingly, the revival of the federal women's agency has not resulted in a displacement or a weakening of these initiatives, quite the opposite. There has been a surge in the number of local women's councils, secretariats, coordinating committees, and advisory units. Brazil's sixth periodic report under the CEDAW, submitted in 2005, states that there existed 23 state-level and 130 municipal-level councils (CEDAW 2005). The state of Rio Grande do Sul claimed in April 2008 to have 47 municipal coordinating committees, with more on the way.[10] This is the result of a synergy between the decentralized and participatory practices of the Brazilian women's movement and the PT's approach to local government. However, while they were pioneered and developed in the party's subnational administrations, their current number shows a contagion effect beyond party-political bounds, accelerated by central government support from the SPM, which hosts periodic conferences for these entities. This horizontal network was also useful to the consultation, conducted through municipal and state meetings and a national conference, on the two National Plans on Policies for Women, involving some 120,000 women for the first plan launched in 2005 and 200,000 for the second plan agreed on in 2007. However, some in the women's movement felt that such a highly participatory consultation process put a strain on the mobilizational capacity of the women's movement, particularly in locations where the women's coordinating committees were underfunded or there were still few municipal women's councils. This also points to the difficulty, identified in the second conference, of persuading municipal and state governments to move beyond a rhetorical commitment to gender equity to drawing up realizable plans of action. The minister of state for women had toured the country with the first plan to get it to "trickle down," by encouraging both state and municipal governments to commit formally to implementing it, just as the São Paulo state women's council had done with a local version of the CEDAW in the early 1990s, and as the Rio de Janeiro and Paraná councils did with the Beijing blueprint in the latter part of the decade. However, by 2007 it was clear that more mobilization and scrutiny by local women's networks was needed to overcome the obstacles of budget constraints and the lack of understanding of gender mainstreaming (AMB 2007b).

The Women's Caucus in Congress

The women's parliamentary caucus (bancada feminina) was first set up informally during the Constitutional Assembly, when a women's movement campaign elected an unprecedented number of feminists, including Benedita da Silva, the first black woman elected to the national parliament, with the aim of inscribing women's rights into the new Constitution.[11] Half a century earlier nine women, mostly members of the suffragist Federação Brasileira pelo Progresso Feminino (Brazilian Federation for Women's Progress), were elected in 1934 to state constitutional assemblies for a similar purpose (A. Costa 1998, 99; Schumaher and Brazil 2000). Led by the Center-Left, particularly the PT, the bancada's agenda has been guided by the CNDM and feminist NGOs such as the Centro Feminista de Estudos e Assessoria (CFEMEA; Feminist Research and Advisory Center). All female federal deputies and senators are members and most back it solidly. With most parties are indifferent on gender issues, bancada members have been successful at steering their party's votes on key bills, such as reforms to the civil and penal codes, maternity and paternity leave, rights of women prisoners, reproductive rights, antidiscrimination measures (race, HIV status, sexual orientation), gender violence, and the electoral gender quota.[12] For example, in 1995 the whips of nearly all the parties instructed their members to vote against a constitutional amendment to protect life "from conception," which runs contrary to the norm of a "free" vote on such controversial issues (Htun 2003, 161).

The internal cohesion and effectiveness of the caucus has been helped by the changing profile of female legislators. The proportion of women elected on the strength of a male relative's family name had decreased over two decades to just 10 percent by 2002, and this period has seen two significant intakes of feminists, in 1986 (mainly from PMDB) and in 2002 (one-third from the PT). After the mid-1990s, many of the new female legislators already had experience in women's issues, through either participation in the Beijing conference, membership of state or municipal women's councils, involvement in parliamentary inquiries into topics such as maternal mortality and sterilization, or legislative activity on gender policy. This partly explains why women politicians have tended to frame gender justice claims around ideas of equity, fairness, and rights rather than around women's allegedly essential "special" inherent qualities, such as nurturing, honesty, or pragmatism. Feminism is also not such a taboo word in Brazilian political discourse and is even appropriated by conservative politicians. This is due to multiple factors, including the racial and religious heterogeneity of Brazilian society and the relatively high tolerance for personal sexual choice.[13] In addition, the Catholic Church has had a relatively low capacity to frame public debates on issues of personal morality, and the military regime has been relatively indifferent to women as standard-bearers of traditional femininity and "Western Christian values."[14]

The success of the women's parliamentary caucus proves the point that the influence of women elected representatives can be attributed not so much to "critical mass" but rather to their activities as "critical actors" (Macaulay 2005a). Nonetheless, it may be that in the longer run, the continued leverage of the women's caucus will face an external constraint, which is the very low rate of increase in female representation in Congress, with Brazil now lagging behind regionally and globally.[15] The percentage of women elected to the Chamber of Deputies rose from 8.2 percent in 2002 to only 9.5 percent in the 2006 elections. Since 1998 Brazil has had statutory legislation obliging parties to run at least 30 percent women candidates on their lists. However, there is no enforcement mechanism for those parties that fail to meet the quota, and in an open-list, multiparty, proportional representation system there is no direct relationship between the proportion of women candidates and the proportion elected. In the absence of a clear demand for the women's movement for electoral and party-system reform—a topic that has ebbed and flowed among Brazilian politicians and academics for over a decade—the SPM and its allies have turned their attention to getting representation for existing women representatives on the governing bodies of the parties, the two legislative houses, and on key committees, to give them a higher *quality* of leverage.

Women's Movement Networks

One of the hubs of this policy community was CFEMEA, a highly effective feminist advocacy group founded in 1989 by four former CNDM staff members when the CNDM collapsed. They had been "loaned" to the CNDM from other government departments because of their expertise in gender issues. This mobility of women's movement personnel is visible in all these networks, as activists move from autonomous groups to NGOs, representative positions in the councils, executive positions, and elected office, often moving sideways as well as upward. This makes for a very cohesive policy community. CFEMEA has been pivotal in enabling the women's movement to plot a tactical course through a snowstorm of legislative activity.[16] In the last decade, over 150 bills affecting women's status have awaited consideration in Congress each year and, during the 1993 constitutional revision process alone, 17,246 proposals and 12,614 amendments were tabled, of which 956 concerned the chapter on social rights and would have affected women in the areas of work, health, family, and education. CFEMEA provided a platform through which a heterogeneous women's movement could share knowledge in a political system with multiple access points and formed a bridge between this movement and the political process by consulting thematic women's movement networks over specific policy proposals on the one hand and lobbying legislators on the other (Macaulay 2000). A few years later, the preparation and aftermath of the Beijing conference spawned a new national women's network, the Articulação de Mulheres Brasileiras (AMB; Network of Brazilian Women), representing some eight hundred women's groups in twenty-seven state-level women's forums. They mobilized around the twenty-five priority areas of the Platform of Action, translating them into Strategies for Equality, a template for secondary legislation for all three levels of government in the areas of women's health, reproductive rights, family and labor law, gender violence, and political rights.[17] Issue networks also emerged around the specific gender-policy areas, such as women's health, reproductive rights, violence, and race, that formed the core of the first National Plan on Policies for Women. Some populations, such as rural women, enjoyed the backing of related social movements, such as the Movimento dos Trabalhadores Rurais Sem Terra (Landless Rural Workers Movement), and of some legislators, which has enabled them to translate mobilization into policy victories, such as pensions and maternity benefits for rural women workers. Black women now have the institutional voice of the Secretaria Especial de Políticas de Promoção da Igualdade Racial (SEPPIR; Special Secretariat for the Promotion of Policies on Racial Equality), created at the same time as the SPM.[18] Since 2000 a coalition of trade union, working-class, and rural women workers has emerged, which stands somewhat outside the preexisting, often middle-class, feminist networks. The Marcha Mundial das Mulheres, inspired by the Montreal-based World March of Women and a chapter of a worldwide movement, has a socialist-feminist orientation and has spearheaded the criticisms of Brazil's neoliberal economic policies.

Policy Impact

The success of a network depends, however, on developing clear, shared goals. For example, the most consistent gender policies applied by local and national governments concern domestic violence, a politically uncontentious issue and a cornerstone of the feminist agenda. However, the issue network could not find a consensus beyond the need for service provision to victims. Meanwhile, without consultation with the women's movement, judicial reformers introduced institutional changes into the way that the criminal justice system handled domestic violence.[19] It was not until 2004 that the network managed, in conjunction with the SPM, to produce Brazil's first comprehensive and dedicated legislative bill on domestic violence, making it virtually the last in the region to do so (Macaulay 2005c).[20] That bill finally passed as the Maria da Penha law, which mandates the use of dedicated courts for family and domestic violence. By May 2008 twenty-one such specialized courts had been set up in twelve states and the Federal District, and thirty-two more were adapted to the purpose.

In the case of reproductive rights, the issue network has been more unified but faced stiffer cultural and political resistance. The 1980s saw the emergence of an array of women's health groups alongside a progressive movement for health reform. This alliance enabled the women's movement to shift the terms of the debate away from population control toward women's rights and to plot a course between two previously polarized camps—the neo-Malthusians, associated with authoritarian ideologies, and their opponents within the church and on the Left— both of which began to fragment. This feminist alliance with sympathetic professionals and politicians succeeded, in the first instance, in regulating the overuse of sterilization, making alternative forms of contraception more readily available, and creating the health care program PAISM. The 1990s saw the formation of a very effective issue network, the Rede Nacional Feminista de Saúde, Direitos Sexuais e Direitos Reprodutivos (Feminist Network on Health, Sexual Rights, and Reproductive Rights), known as RedeSaúde, which has kept reproductive rights on the agenda.[21] Although abortion restrictions resemble those in most of the rest of Latin America, the Brazilian movement advanced significantly in campaigning to make provision of legal abortions a responsibility of the state. One result was the proliferation, in the 1980s, of local ordinances in cities such as Campinas, São Paulo, and Rio de Janeiro, that obliged public hospitals to perform the procedure. This policy was later adopted by the Ministry of Health as a federal directive in 1998.

That said, what the SPM now terms "voluntary interruption of pregnancy" has remained a huge political stumbling block. No party has dared take up legalization of abortion as a policy commitment even though male and female legislators from several parties have worked with the issue network on terminations. However, the

PT in general, Lula himself prior to his election, and his health ministers have all insisted on framing abortion as a public health issue, rather than one of rights, so they could not be held hostage to a counterdiscourse of fetal rights by antiabortion campaigners.[22] The Lula government took the relatively bold step of constituting a special commission, composed of representatives of the executive, legislature, and civil society, to examine existing legislation. The minister in charge of the SPM, Nilcéa Freire, herself a doctor and academic, was given a mandate by the Primeira Conferência Nacional de Políticas para as Mulheres (First National Conference on Policies for Women) to present a bill legalizing abortion on demand up to three months, which she did in 2006. Nonetheless, the executive branch has been loath to back the decriminalization of abortion, leaving the women's policy community to push the boundaries of a public debate in which there is now a degree of organized backlash from religious groups. This reluctance is in part related to the legitimacy and strength of the Lula government, which spent the latter half of its first mandate fighting off corruption scandals, some linked to its attempts to hold together a governing coalition. This has eroded the PT's claim to the moral high ground in Brazilian politics, and the government is unwilling to expend its remaining political capital on an issue that would bring it no electoral rewards.[23] In addition, public opinion on the issue has oscillated but not shifted much further toward decriminalization, and the feminist policy community will have to find new ways of shifting the terms of the debate and breaking the political deadlock.

What lasting legacy, then, has all this activism over two decades left in broad terms and in specific policy areas? Brazil's national government unit for women has focused on different policy objectives during the distinct cycles of its institutional life. At the very beginning, it campaigned vigorously to put domestic violence into political and public debate, and CNDM's first director, Ruth Escobar, counts the installation of the women's police stations as its initial policy victory (Entrevista com Ruth Escobar 2005). Her successor, Jacqueline Pitanguy (1985–1989), sees the three years of work on drafting the national and state constitutions, together with their sectoral work, as having laid a long-lasting legacy that could not be eradicated by hostile or indifferent governments, as evidenced by the CNDM's reincarnation as the SPM (20 anos de CNDM 2005). After the paralysis of the Collor government, under Cardoso the CNDM concentrated its limited influence to persuade the government to allocate a budget specifically for domestic violence, amplifying and strengthening the network of referral centers and refuges and carrying out a critical evaluation of the women's police stations. The SPM departed from a substantial base of knowledge and experience, accumulated on the one hand through the CNDM's position within the federal bureaucracy and, on the other, through the PT's very localized work on gender policies. Its institutional revitalization has seen Brazil's gender unit return to a much wider mainstreaming mission.

Conclusion

The combination of a weak and permeable party system, variable state capacity, and a strongly federalized administration has resulted in a multidirectional diffusion and replication of gender policy. Sometimes it has trickled *upward*, when municipal initiatives prompted by women's activism at a very local level, such as ordinances promoting gender equality or gender equity, are adopted by sympathetic policy makers at the state or federal level. For example, in 1992 the Federal District copied São Paulo's municipal ordinance prohibiting businesses from demanding from female employees either a sterilization certificate or pregnancy test, and this became federal law in 1995. Even in the case of abortion this is visible. Sometimes gender policies trickle *sideways* when a practice promoted by a particular actor in government is copied by its rivals or counterparts. This would be the case with state and municipal women's councils, initially set up by the PMDB at the behest of their own feminist membership and then copied by other parties on the Center-Left. The variety of local state machineries for promoting women's rights—the coordinating committees, secretariats, and advisory units—developed by the PT is another case in point, their horizontal proliferation encouraged by the SPM. Another case of horizontal contagion is the spread of internal party quotas for women in leadership positions, pioneered by the PT in 1991 and subsequently adopted by several other Center-Left parties, again through the insistence of organized women's lobbies within each party.

In Brazil gender policy has, until recently, not automatically trickled *downward* as it does in countries with a more centralized political and administrative system, such as Chile or Costa Rica, where the national women's ministry is directly responsible for overseeing the application of centrally designed gender equity and equality plans at the provincial and municipal levels. In the first phase, the heyday of the CNDM, the women's movement focused its mobilization on helping a strong central agency establish the legal underpinnings of a new era of gender justice, by lobbying in support of the new Constitution and carrying its provisions over into state constitutions. The following stage saw a decentering of the movement, as feminists sought out opportunities with local political allies, most notably but not exclusively in the form of PT municipal governments, to start the process of devising practical public policies for gender equity. The most recent stage has seen a newly fortified women's ministry join forces with locally based women's groups to create a blueprint for gender policy. Its application at all three levels of government, that is, a new phase of trickle-down gender policy, clearly depends on pressure from above (the SPM) and from below, through a multinodal women's movement that extends through different levels of government and across party boundaries and administrative divisions and that encompasses a diverse membership. At its most effective, the movement has been able to capitalize on the propensity of certain parties to promote a gender agenda at a particular moment and then to institutionalize that goodwill. The Lula government's commitment to gender equality represents both the fruits of more than twenty years of feminist strategizing, networking, and mobilizing and an opportunity to push for wider and deeper gender-equity and gender-equality policies to make a real change to Brazilian women's lives. The CNDM and then the SPM, backed by women's movement networks, have very effectively undertaken the first two stages of legal reform and policy design for gender justice. However, both the femocrats strategically located in government posts at all levels and the women's movement are now having to tackle the third and most difficult stage, that of securing sufficient resources for implementation, mainstreaming gender thinking into all institutions and public policy.

NOTES

1. Material in this chapter draws on my book *Gender Politics in Brazil and Chile*, published by Palgrave Macmillan in 2006, and is reproduced here with the kind permission of the publisher.

2. Bertha Lutz was one of the first women elected to Parliament, serving as a stand-in from 1935 to 1937.

3. For a full account of the growth of the women's movement in the late 1970s and early 1980s, and the ways in which it found leverage with the PMDB, see Alvarez (1990).

4. Three main types of state-civil society councils advising on various social policy areas were established in the wake of the 1988 Constitution: statutory, for the oversight of social policies (health, education, children's welfare); ad hoc, to deliver special government policies such as school meals or employment opportunities; and thematic, founded often on local initiatives, addressing issues such as race (Tatagiba 2002, 49; Draibe 1998). The women's councils encompass both advisory and executive functions, whereas the other social sector councils tend toward either one or the other function (D. Costa 1997, 92).

5. The CNDM had a twenty-member unpaid advisory board appointed by the president, composed of one-third women's movement representatives and two-thirds government officials.

6. Abortion in Brazil is permitted in the case of rape or danger to the mother's life.

7. Like the wider pro-amnesty campaign, the Movimento Feminino pela Anistia demanded unrestricted amnesty for all those who had lost their political rights or been exiled by the military regime.

8. The CNDM has been retained as a collegiate body, with representation from both the state and civil society, with a remit to oversee the direction and implementation of gender equality policy in Brazil.

9. The Cardoso government had allocated the SPM 10.9 million *reais*, increased to 24 million at the beginning of 2003, but in a round of sweeping budget cuts designed to balance the books and placate international lenders, the budget was cut to just over 4 million *reais*.

10. While many of these state and municipal governmental units for women have been institutionally strengthened over the last two decades, they are not immune to the dangers of co-option by political parties and the neglect that had afflicted the CNDM.

11. The percentage of women in the Chamber of Deputies rose in the 1986 elections from 1.7 to 5.3 percent. Over 40 percent of these were elected for the PMDB.

12. All parties must now include at least 30 percent of either sex on their lists for city councillor and for state or federal deputy.

13. De facto marital unions have long been legally recognized in Brazil, and antidiscrimination clauses protecting sexual minorities are contained in dozens of state and municipal constitutions. This is not to ignore, of course, the homophobia and violence that still exists in a country that claims transsexuals and transvestites as national icons in specific circumstances, such as during the Carnival.

14. President Geisel (1974–1979), a Lutheran, even pushed through a divorce bill in an attempt to undermine the Catholic Church and alienate it from the prodivorce PMDB. He also supported women's right to noncoercive family planning and established the women's health program demanded by feminists (Htun 2003, 68, 94).

15. In 2009 the world average female representation in the lower or single house of national legislatures was 18.6 percent, while in Latin America it was 19.9 percent. Argentina had 40 percent and Costa Rica 36.8 percent while Brazil ranked in 104th place globally, with only Panama and Colombia having worse female representation in the region (Inter-Parliamentary Union 2009).

16. Since then, other feminist policy and lobbying groups have emerged, such as Ações em Gênero, Cidadania e Desenvolvimento (AGENDE), which focuses on monitoring the executive branch.

17. Secondary, or "enabling," legislation enables constitutional provisions to be put into effect.

18. The first head of SEPPIR, Matilde Ribeiro, was a black feminist whose activist background includes work in local PT administrations.

19. Previously, domestic violence cases were heard in the Juizados Especiais Criminais (criminal small claims courts), which were much criticized for adopting conciliation procedures ill-suited to the very specific characteristics of gender violence (see Macaulay 2005b and Campos and Carvalho 2006).

20. The consortium involved in drafting this legislation was formed by the NGOs CFEMEA; AGENDE; Advocacia Cidadã pelos Direitos Humanos (ADVOCACI); Cidadania, Estudo, Pesquisa, Informação e Ação (CEPIA); Instituto para la Promoción de la Equidad / Comitê Latino-americano e do Caribe para a Defesa dos Direitos da Mulher (IPÊ / CLADEM); and Themis.

21. RedeSaúde was founded in 1991 in ten states; by 2000 it had two hundred affiliates in twenty-one states. For more detail on women's rights in general, see Lebon (2003) and CEDAW (2003, 2005).

22. An estimated 1.1 million abortions are carried out in Brazil annually, requiring around two hundred thousand women to be hospitalized.

23. President Cardoso had also expressed himself supportive of greater liberalization of abortion before taking office and, indeed, his government was very progressive in tackling other sexually related issues such as AIDS. However, he also faced the problem of managing a multiparty, coalitional government and rationing his political capital.

REFERENCES

20 anos de CNDM. 2005. *Mulheres em Pauta*, June 16.

Alvarez, Sonia E. 1990. *Engendering democracy in Brazil: Women's movements in transition politics.* Princeton, NJ: Princeton University Press.

AMB. 2007a. Avaliando a política nacional para mulheres e sua implementação através dos planos de políticas para mulheres. *Articulando a luta feminista nas políticas públicas.* www .articulacaodemulheres.org.br / (accessed June 12, 2008).

———. 2007b. Comparando conferências para avançar na implantação da política nacional para mulheres. *Articulando a luta feminista nas políticas públicas.* www.articulacaodemulheres .org.br / (accessed June 12, 2008).

Campos, Carmen Hein de, and Salo de Carvalho. 2006. Violência doméstica e Juizados Especiais Criminais: Análise a partir do feminismo e do garantismo. *Revista de Estudos Feministas* 14 (2): 409–422.

CEDAW. 2003. *Combined initial, second, third, fourth and fifth periodic reports of States parties: Brazil.* UN Document no. CEDAW / C / Bra / 1–5.

———. 2005. *Sixth periodic report of States parties: Brazil.* UN Document no. CEDAW / C / Bra / 6.

CFEMEA. 1993. *Direitos da mulher: O que pensam os parlamentares.* Brasília: CFEMEA.

Costa, Ana Alice Alcântara. 1998. *As donas no poder: Mulher e política na Bahia.* Salvador: Núcleo de Estudos Interdisciplinares sobre a Mulher, FFCH, UFBA.

Costa, Delaine Martins, ed. 1997. *Democratização dos poderes municipais e a questão de gênero*. Serie Experiências Inovadoras 7. Rio de Janeiro: Instituto Brasileiro de Administração Municipal / Fundação Ford.

Draibe, Sônia Miriam. 1998. *A nova institucionalidade do sistema brasileiro de políticas sociais: Os conselhos nacionais de políticas sectoriais*. Caderno de Pesquisa, no. 35. Campinas: UNICAMP.

Entrevista com Ruth Escobar. 2005. *Mulheres em Pauta*, May 30.

Htun, Mala. 2003. *Abortion, divorce and the family under Latin American dictatorships and democracies*. Cambridge: Cambridge University Press.

Inter-Parliamentary Union. 2009. Women in national parliaments. www.ipu.org/wmn-e/classif.htm (accessed August 17, 2009).

Lebon, Nathalie. 2003. Brazil. In *Women's issues in Central and South America*, ed. Amy Lind. Encyclopedia of Women's Issues Worldwide. CA: Greenwood.

Macaulay, Fiona. 2000. Getting gender on the policy agenda: A study of a Brazilian feminist lobby group. In *The hidden histories of gender and the state in Latin America*, ed. Elizabeth Dore and Maxine Molyneux, 346–367. Durham, NC: Duke University Press.

———. 2005a. Cross-party alliances around gender agendas: Critical mass, critical actors, critical structures or critical junctures? Paper prepared for the United Nations Expert Group Meeting on Equal Participation of Women and Men in Decision-Making Processes, with Particular Emphasis on Political Participation and Leadership, Addis Ababa, Ethiopia, October 24–27. UN Document no. EGM/EPWD/2005/EP.12.

———. 2005b. *Gender politics in Brazil and Chile: The role of political parties in local and national policy-making*. Basingstoke, UK: Palgrave Macmillan.

———. 2005c. Private conflicts, public powers: Domestic violence in the courts in Latin America. In *The judicialization of politics in Latin America*, ed. Alan Angell, Rachel Sieder, and Line Schjolden, 211–230. London: Palgrave Macmillan / Institute for the Study of the Americas.

Pitanguy, Jacqueline. 2002. Movimento de mulheres e políticas de gênero no Brasil. www.eclac.org/mujer/proyectos/gobernabilidad/documentos/jpitanguy.pdf (accessed August 19, 2009).

Saffioti, Heleieth I. B. 1978. *Women in class society*. New York: Monthly Review.

Schumaher, Schuma, and Erico Vital Brazil. 2000. *Dicionário mulheres do Brasil de 1500 até a atualidade*. Rio de Janeiro: Jorge Zahar.

SPM. 2006. *Plano nacional de políticas para mulheres*. Brasília: Presidência da República / Secretaria Especial de Políticas para Mulheres.

Tabak, Fanny. 1989. *A mulher brasileira no congresso nacional*. Brasília: Câmara dos Deputados.

Tatagiba, Luciana. 2002. Os conselhos gestores e a democratização das políticas públicas no Brasil. In *Sociedade civil e espaços públicos no Brasil*, ed. Evelina Dagnino, 47–105. São Paulo: Paz e Terra.

PART VI

THE POLITICS OF SCALE
*Local, Regional, and Global
Feminist Agency*

17

From Insurgency
to Feminist Struggle

THE SEARCH FOR SOCIAL JUSTICE,
DEMOCRACY, AND EQUALITY BETWEEN
WOMEN AND MEN

MORENA HERRERA

Looking back to the past means acknowledging one's own wounds: both the visible ones and the hidden ones on the inside, those that cure more slowly and sometimes are never completely healed. To do so is to confront two types of contradictions: those that life serves us and those that we ourselves embrace. It also involves challenging the lack of recognition of women's participation in social processes, in spite of our undeniable presence, and as such realizing our dreams for a more just life. These next few pages are a reflection about women's sociopolitical participation in El Salvador, from the armed conflict to the present.[1] I first discuss key characteristics of gender relations under the extreme conditions of war and then look at the Peace Accords in El Salvador and their failure to address women's rights and gender equity. In addition, I examine the birth of the Asociación de Mujeres por la Dignidad y la Vida (Las Dignas; Women's Association for Dignity and Life), one of the feminist organizations that for more than fifteen years has been working to eradicate the subordination of women. Lastly, I provide an initial reflection on the newly formed Colectiva Feminista para el Desarrollo Local (Women's Collective for Local Development) and its efforts to link local women's organizations with representatives of municipal governments, as part of a pluralist strategy to influence both public policy and the construction of a contemporary women's movement.

Gender Relations and the Participation
of Women in the Armed Conflict

The question of whether the war was worth so much sacrifice has always made me uncomfortable, perhaps because a negative answer would be too painful, given the persisting social inequality, but also because it is illusionary to suggest that we could have chosen another path. At that time we were convinced that the armed struggle was the only path capable of generating the social changes necessary.

Analyses of women's participation in any given scenario generally tend to look at women as a homogenous group. In reality we represent a diversity of identities, desires, roles, and responsibilities. To deny this multiplicity at the moment when peace strategies were being designed would have limited us to the roles of either victims or revolutionary heroines whose only desire was the triumph of the cause. I remember some of the most famous images from the armed conflicts in Central America: that of a young woman, an armed combatant, carrying her child, and another, that of a refugee woman breast-feeding her child. These images erase the complexity of roles, realities, and positions in which we found ourselves. And the expectations of the majority of women, who do not identify with either one of these stereotypes, would have largely not been met.

Even though many women participated in armed conflicts moved by their traditional roles as mothers and caregivers, their contributions engaged a diversity of roles and responsibilities. For example, while some of us participated directly in the military, others were in charge of finding safe-houses for refuge, and yet others were involved in the political direction of the movement. In addition, some women worked within organizations that promoted solidarity, and others attended the creation of logistical networks. We were active protagonists of this process, even though this has gone mostly unrecognized by our male *compañeros*, the Peace Accords themselves, and even in the documents that recount the official version of history.

The difficulties in visualizing ourselves as protagonists derive from our socialization, for example, our being educated for "unlimited service," living for others, and giving everything without expecting anything in return. As a first step toward being valued, it is essential that, as women, we demand recognition for our efforts. Neither the Peace Accords nor the reconstruction processes of the postwar period incorporated women's perspectives, nor did they take into consideration the material and emotional repercussions that participation in the armed conflict had on women.

I have often been asked about how our participation in the insurgency impacted our lives as women. I must admit that at the beginning of 1981, when the first guerrilla camps were organized in rural areas and governmental repression and terror were widespread in the cities, being a woman seemed of little relevance to me. As time went by, experience taught me that to be a man or to be a woman had different connotations. It has been a slow and painful learning process through twelve years of civil war and thirteen of postwar, which is not the same as peace. These experiences have left their mark on the memories of those who directly participated in the process.

The women and men of the guerrilla shared ideals, dreams for a more just and democratic world, and the conviction that the armed struggle could achieve desired changes. However, our experiences were marked by gender. These invisible dynamics were present each time jobs were assigned and recognition bestowed; they all represent the ways in which power and authority are exercised during times of war. Assigning spaces and roles in function of the sexualized body were decisions that had a profound impact on the lives of women but, nevertheless, went unquestioned. These decisions involved discriminatory and marginalizing practices against women but unfortunately, at the time, we did not realize it nor denounce it. This is the essence of the reflections collected in the work authored by

Las Dignas, "Women as Mountains," which analyzes the position of female and male leaders at the war fronts. "Even those willing to put their lives on the line . . . did not believe in the possibility of change in gender relations. Perhaps they considered that these changes were such a remote possibility that they were unwilling to question the sexualized material and symbolic divisions which marginalized more than half of the population" (Vázquez et al. 1996, 75).

These forms of subordination and domination came along with other teachings. We were told to not question authority, nor express our feelings, because to do so reflected weakness. Ensconced in our illusion of building a guerrilla army as an instrument for national liberation, we ended up contributing to the construction of a hierarchical body, intrinsically patriarchal in its relationships, in which it was ever more difficult to deconstruct the elements of feminine oppression, and where the word feminism was prohibited. It was considered to be a petite bourgeoisie distraction from the central causes for which we were fighting.

Women's Experiences of Sexual Violence within the Context of War

Following the first years of war, the General Command of the Frente de Liberación Nacional Farabundo Martí (FMLN; Farabundo Martí National Liberation Front) established a series of norms known as the Revolutionary Law. These norms applied to all the members of the five organizations of the FMLN. One of these norms established the death penalty in the case of rape, whether the victim be a civilian or a member of the guerrilla army. The enforcement of this law was not always easy or consistent. I remember a case, at the end of 1984, on the Guazapa Front, where I had spent the first four years of the war and had later returned.[2]

In their account of the events that took place during my absence, the comrades told me proudly that they had resolved an issue that had generated a great deal of tension and had also made them think a lot. Three combatants had raped a woman who served as a camp cook. According to the established norms, they had to be shot. But they were three combatants! A jury was instituted, the issue was widely debated, and finally, they agreed on sanctions. They decided to carry out a symbolic firing squad with fake bullets. When the three men discovered that the bullets had not harmed them, one of the commanders proceeded to explain to them that the revolution was generous and thus they had been granted the opportunity to be reborn and behave in accord with the revolutionary principles. The sanction appeared as truly generous and sensible in such circumstances. However, the two other disciplinary measures reprimanded the victim for being flirtatious and provocative! The four individuals were sentenced to visit various guerrilla camps in the area, hold meetings, and share their experiences recognizing their errors, the men as the rapists and the victim as the provocative flirt! The third measure consisted in sentencing the four comrades to build a tunnel going through a small mountain called El Perical. The tunnel would be used as an air raid shelter and as a teaching tool for future generations. During the construction, the woman was to remain with the three combatants, who were required to be unarmed for several months, as long as there were no confrontations with the government's army.

The comrades were proud of their decision. When I told them the sanction received by the woman did not appear fair, they responded that I was not assigned to that region and hence did not have the right to an opinion.

While this case exemplifies the search for a new framework of justice by those in command, it also demonstrates the absence of reflection and clarity on gender power dynamics and the major impact these dynamics have in the multiple manifestations of sexual violence against women. Also, the process of revictimization to which the woman comrade was submitted goes without acknowledgment.

Sexual violence was also used as a weapon of war and terror by the government's army. Such cases were not always denounced as crimes of war, possibly due to the idea that this crime belonged to the private sphere. Yet in the eyes of some women ex-combatants, rape and sexual harassment are even more painful when perpetuated by trusted compañeros. These abuses were often not denounced, and the majority of the victims still live silently with their memories. Very few women received the support to work through their sexual harassment experiences. Remaining silent has been a frequent practice.

In 1995 Las Dignas carried out a study on how the war had impacted maternal and sexual conceptions and practices. The testimonies gathered during this research are very revealing: "I felt very pressured and desperate. It was then when a fellow compañero took advantage of me. He told me that unless he accompanied me, I was at risk of being assaulted by other men. Since he was the leader of the encampment, he said that if he stayed by my side the others would respect me. One day he came into my tent and forced me. At that point, he said that if I remained alone after having slept with him, everyone else would want to abuse me because they would know that I slept with anyone who came into my tent" (Silvia, quoted in Vázquez et al. 1996, 181).

As with other groups, the sexual harassment acts perpetuated against the women in the guerrilla camps were expressions of the (mis)use of masculine power and authority in the pursuit of sexual encounters. These incidents were even more dramatic among women members of the urban commandos. Under these commandos, members were required to remain in clandestinity and maintain discretion. These conditions increased women's vulnerability toward sexual harassment. The majority of these cases were not denounced and, unfortunately, the few that were made public did not generate any type of response or corrective action among those in charge of the revolutionary forces.

The Sexual Division of Labor on the War Front

When the war began we were more antimilitarist. We came from a tradition that repudiated the armed forces, a repressive apparatus that was the most emblematic representation of that government. Little by little we began to adopt the military behavior that we had previously rejected. Not only did we dress in olive green, but we also started internalizing a new hierarchical and authoritarian order. With limited room for deliberation and critical thinking, we had to resist as well as develop our own military strategies.

Those of us living in the small pockets of territory controlled by the insurgency began to build an army. And with the distribution of responsibilities in the guerrilla began the reproduction of gender roles. Men for the most part occupied the highest ranks, while women made up the majority of the civilian population responsible for protecting the children and the elderly. It was also women who, for the most part, fulfilled the supportive roles of feeding, hiding, and caring for wounded combatants.

As a member of the guerrilla and command structure, these differences and inequalities were often not evident to me. Nonetheless, I remember feeling bothered by the lack of recognition accorded the civilian populations—which back then we called "the masses"—and their contributions. It was during this period that we came up with the slogan: "Masses and military: All one army." Behind it was a demand to value the support tasks carried out primarily by women. It is within this context that in 1982 the Asociación de Mujeres Lil Milagro Ramirez (Women's Association Lil Milagro Ramirez) was born as a mechanism to incorporate women into the support tasks of the guerilla struggle.[3] We organized to provide better care for the wounded, prepare meals, and organize more secure areas of refuge and routes of retreat in the face of advances gained by the government's forces.

The majority of women who participated in the support activities for the guerrilla saw themselves essentially as mothers and caregivers and simply extended those roles to include all *the boys*, as they fondly called the guerrilla soldiers. Motivated by the maternal logic of devotion, they became a nurturing force that cared for the insurgency. At the end of the war, when we began to analyze the role of women, we discovered that this nurturing force—so fundamental to the revolutionary strategy—indeed had gender characteristics, having been composed mostly of women. Unfortunately, even with this revelation women were not granted significant recognition for their contributions during the postwar period.

It is also important to point out that the war brought changes in the lives of many women who assumed responsibilities unimaginable in other contexts. In some cases, the long-established sexual division of labor was broken as women began to take on tasks traditionally assigned to men, while in other circumstances women only had to adjust their traditional functions. Thus, while men continued to occupy the positions of command, women made up the majority of the health care personnel, radio operators, cooks, and logistical providers for the guerilla army.

Despite the fact that maternity and paternity were not topics addressed in the reflections of the guerrilla movement, they too underwent notable changes. Such changes took place, above all, among women, given that men, in their unaltered masculine prototype, continued to "leave children in the care of women." For women, especially for those in the guerrilla, the traditional implications that sexuality stamped on becoming pregnant, giving birth, and caring for children, were dramatically altered by revolutionary participation. This generally resulted in high emotional costs for women who had to leave their children in the care of others while fighting.

When analyzing the emotional effects of maternity during wartime, we found heartrending and contradictory testimonies. The notion that to fulfill our role as women we had to be mothers was never questioned by the leaders or by the grass-roots female or male activists. Nevertheless, the exercise of maternity did undergo significant changes. As the war intensified, it became more and more difficult to care for our children while, at the same time, carrying out revolutionary tasks. Finally, it became impossible. The separation from and abandonment of their sons and daughters to the care of family members and, in some cases, of humanitarian organizations, has left deep wounds on both mothers and children. And those who chose to stay, or had no other alternative but to care for their children, found their ability to play a more active role in the revolutionary process limited.

The identification of women with motherhood went unquestioned during the war. At times, motherhood was used to justify measures that under different circumstances were prohibited within the guerrilla. In some cases motherhood, as a justification, mediated desire. During a workshop we organized to reflect on motherhood, a woman who had her first child at age fifteen told us: "My first pregnancy was planned. I was in a guerrilla front and wanted to get out, but I wasn't allowed to leave. A compañera told me that the only way to be granted permission to leave by the leadership was to get pregnant. So I purposely got pregnant by the leader of my unit."

Compelled by their environments, many women also modified their conceptions regarding intimacy and sexuality. Some learned about contraceptives and discovered that pregnancy was not the inevitable result of a sexual encounter. Unfortunately, there was a lack of gender analysis in the majority of these cases, which were conceived as the product of exceptional circumstances. In this sense, both men and women lost the opportunity to generate more profound and liberating social and personal transformations.

The signing of the Peace Accords in 1992 established the conditions that ended the armed conflict and gave us an opportunity to implement a survey on the participation and contributions of women in the armed conflict. Usually, women evaluated their participation in the FMLN according to the circumstances under which they joined. Those who joined the guerrilla and urban commandos voluntarily, as a result of consciousness raising and personal commitment to the revolutionary causes, were generally more positive—despite having faced difficulties—than women who were forced to join either because their families were involved or because they lived in a war zone.

This study also demonstrated that "the only favorable conclusion reached as a result of the participation of women in the war was the symbolic and practical questioning of the most conservative frameworks that established what was and was not permissible for women. The war demonstrated—both to women themselves and to the rest of society—that women can fight, conspire . . . and be efficient in tasks previously considered to be exclusive to men. It was also clear that if women did not reach the highest levels of leadership within the military and party structures, it was not because they were not capable of leading, but because within the FMLN sexist prejudices predominate" (Vázquez et al. 1996, 230).

Gender Equity and Women's Rights within the Peace Accords

It was the night of New Year's Eve when we received the news about the Peace Accords.[4] We all experienced ambiguous feelings. We felt joyful about the revolutionary gains but were also aware of the process's contradictions. The Peace Accords did not convey all the transformations that we had dreamed of and for which we had fought. Nonetheless, the end of the armed conflict appeared to open new venues through which new social and political trends could be initiated.

The Peace Accords ignored women as political subjects, protagonists, survivors, and beneficiaries of the war. Neither in the content nor in the ideals promoted by the Peace Accords were there any references to women, the need to recognize their rights, or any specific means to foment changes in gender relations. For this reason, various women's organizations came together to carry out a collective review of the accords, and represented our conclusions on an empty page, which we also published in the national media.[5]

Centered on the processes leading to the political transformation of the government, as well as the demobilization, disarmament, and dismembering of the military apparatus, the accords aimed to establish conditions that would generate a democratic government. However, by ignoring the power inequalities that exist between women and men, the accords missed the opportunity to question the cultural and social foundations on which the authoritarian and exclusionary aspects of Salvadoran society are based.

The Peace Accords are celebrated as a watershed moment in history and recognized for their "founding character" with respect to Salvadorian democracy. Unfortunately, fundamental issues have been ignored in these agreements, with multiple repercussions. Perhaps one of the most far-reaching effects, in terms of achieving real democracy, has been the absence of methods to eliminate the marginalization of half of the population. In other words, measures that promote the full participation of women in political affairs, establish paternal responsibility, and redistribute domestic and child care chores were missing. Furthermore, the accords could have contributed to eradicating the invisibility of women in the peasant economy, as well as promoted the elimination of gender violence and targeted the discrimination against women in labor and educational arenas, among others.

Despite the fact that women made up 30 percent of the FMLN's demobilized forces and more than 60 percent of the social base that sustained and supported the guerrilla forces, during the reinsertion process into civil society, the accords failed to contemplate the particular needs of women. In the face of social pressure, many women returned to traditional roles. Hence, wartime experiences did not necessarily lead to more equitable postwar gender relations. Instead, the lack of women's inclusion and recognition had very tangible costs. Ex–guerrilla women combatants and female FMLN collaborators had to struggle to be included in the initial lists of beneficiaries of the Programa de Transferencia de Tierra (PTT; Land Transfer Program), even though many had spent years cultivating the land all by themselves, in the absence of their male partners.

Even though the Comisión de la Verdad (Truth Commission) recommended concrete steps toward granting emotional reparations and economic compensation for survivors who had lost sons, daughters, fathers, or mothers during combat, the implementation of the Peace Accords was not very promising, neither in the arena of justice nor in the process of reinstating the social relationships ruptured by the war. Due to a lack of political commitment on the part of the government as well as by the FMLN, women have faced numerous difficulties in obtaining their indemnification allowances, leaving pending an agenda against impunity.

More than a decade later, women's organizations continue to be dissatisfied with the achievements of the Peace Accords. This sentiment has been caused by the absence of concrete transformative measures, a lack of compliance on the part of the government, and the limitations in the process of democratization.

Development of Autonomous Women's Organizations: The Experience of Las Dignas

Las Dignas is a feminist nongovernmental organization that has transitioned through various stages. Even though we started working since March, the organization was officially founded in July 1990. These were the final years of the war, and a time of change for the country. National and international events signaled a decline in support for armed confrontations and, to a certain extent, pushed toward the negotiation process. At the time we believed that a democracy was being founded.

A critical reflection of our participation in the armed conflict established the basis for the creation of Las Dignas. We did not want to repeat the same history of having our interests, problems, and demands as women considered secondary. We did not want to edit the sectarian practices that separated us for belonging to different organization. We wanted to affirm ourselves, women, as political subjects and from this position convince ourselves and the world that no cause justifies postponing women's rights. Indeed, we believed that no struggle was truly revolutionary if it did not include changes that eliminated discrimination against women.

The birth of Las Dignas was marked by the confluence of two processes. On the one hand, there was the creation of a women's guild by the Resistencia Nacional (RN; National Resistance), which brought the FMLN's female constituency together.[6] As part of this collective, women voiced RN's revolutionary proposals and served as instruments to secure international funds. On the other hand, there were the actions and reflections of our group, a collective of women—also affiliated to RN—who wanted to create a space in which women would no longer have to postpone their needs and rights. Even though we all shared a long trajectory of participation in the revolution, we came from diverse locations. While some of us took part in the urban guerrilla, others belonged to the rural forces as well as to some grassroots organizations.

Being accepted as an autonomous organization with a name of our own was one of our first challenges. Our vision to become independent and protagonist political subjects faced great opposition. The name Las Dignas arose in response to the incomprehension encountered among our comrades, who did not understand why we demanded autonomy and who also ridiculed us for wanting greater dignity for women, along with more rights. Also questioned were our gender demands, as well as the possibility of building women's alliances capable of transcending class differences. But our growing understanding of how women's shared subordination was independent of one's individual situation helped us see the urgency in building women's coalitions. In this sense, calling ourselves Las Dignas represented a collective demand for and an affirmation of autonomy.

Fifteen years have passed since we learned that to be autonomous does not mean to be isolated or to cut off relations with other political and social actors. Instead, it implies taking on the challenge of building an organization without the support of a political party: "Our internal cohesion was, to a great extent, the result of the antagonism suffered at the hands of the party from which we were born. The struggle to win spaces of autonomy within the party marked our internal development" (Las Dignas 2000, 12). We understood that to gain strength as a women's movement, it was essential to define our own identities and objectives. We learned that personal autonomy implies questioning the very conceptions on which our identity as women was erected.

Our first years as an organization were marked by a great deal of changes and discoveries. Learning about feminism enabled us to name the common ills derived from our subordination and discrimination, moving us from a stage of denouncing to articulating a more proactive discourse and generating our own perspective, which constitutes the basis for political and ideological autonomy.

By the end of 1993, it was evident that the efforts invested in promoting small productive projects had not generated the expected results in terms of empowering women. Of those early projects, only a bakery and a few small stores belonging to women in rural communities remain. Along with a critical evaluation of these strategies, we embarked on a project to honor our then unacknowledged war losses. Out of this venture emerged the idea to build a monument to pay tribute to the civilian victims of the armed conflict. The Monument to Memory and Truth, built in collaboration with other organizations, stands today in Cuscatlán Park.

This was also a time in which we experienced various tensions within the group, derived mainly from our diverse views concerning strategy. On the one hand, we worked with rural women on small local projects, and on the other, we targeted women's rights and feminist activism more broadly defined. Moreover, we also recognized that despite breaking most ties with the Partido Revolucionario (Revolutionary Party), its opinion still bore weight on us, influencing our decisions. This confirmed that, to some extent, we were still a feminine branch of the party. This was the context in which we decided to reaffirm ourselves as a political feminist organization dedicated to the creation of an organized women's force. We sought to promote social, political, cultural, and economic transformations in which eradicating women's subordination would become an essential component of social justice and democracy.

We strongly denounced gender injustices and, in conjunction with other women's organizations, we called attention to the need of implementing public policies oriented toward resolving women's issues and transforming gender relationships, for we believed these were the basis for any egalitarian and inclusive society. We drew our strength from knowing that we were part of a broader women's movement that transcended national boundaries, as well as from our multiple ties with urban and rural women. Together we learned that having control over our own bodies and sexualities is a political but often unspoken issue. It is through our bodies that we, as women, first exercise power, but as an ordinary daily practice, this power often becomes invisible.

Based on these convictions, we joined the commission that organized the Cuarto Encuentro Feminista de América Latina y el Caribe (Fourth Latin American and Caribbean Feminist Encuentro). During this event, we built coalitions with other Latin American women's groups. Sharing our experiences inspired us to launch the Plataforma Mujeres 1994 (Women 1994 Platform), our first Salvadoran autonomous political program. The platform allowed us to move from simply making demands to formulating proposals. It also served as a guide during our negotiations regarding gender-specific policy with the central government. During those years, we also promoted the elaboration of women's platforms in various municipalities, to be presented in the 1994 elections and, in this sense, broadening the capacity of women to make proposals at the local level.

Thanks to the reflection on our war experiences, our growth as an institution, and access to international support, by the mid-1990s Las Dignas was well on its way toward becoming an NGO with a feminist approach. Building the institution meant deepening our analysis of issues related to women's subordination, which little by little also began to change those who worked for Las Dignas. The organization, initially based on an assembly model, was professionalized through the creation of expert teams that combined tasks of investigation, project formulation, training, political advocacy, and service provision around their particular issues. We also differentiated the coordinating body from institutional leadership. Currently, our organization is divided into four institutional programs in charge of developing women's training initiatives, research, and political advocacy with regard to women in the economy, nonsexist education, sexual and reproductive rights, and violence prevention. In addition, we provide special services in legal counseling and attention to victims of violence and women's labor rights, among other types of assistance.

A Few Notes on Achievements and Challenges

One of the main challenges for Salvadoran feminists in recent years has been to find viable paths to forge basic social consensus affirming the existence of a secular state that guarantees the application and integrity of human rights for all, especially sexual and reproductive rights. In 1997 a constitutional counterreform was ratified, establishing in Article 1 of the Constitution that the concept of personhood is determined at the moment of conception, thus blocking any possibility of legislative amendment. This reform eliminated the three forms of legal abortion in place since the 1950s.

Later, ultraconservative groups were also able to impede the development of a sex education program for youth. In practice, this program represented the only official initiative to fulfill state commitments from the Cairo conference in the areas of teen-pregnancy prevention and paternal responsibility, both prevailing issues in the country. Latin American feminists often denounce the repercussions that these conservative policies have in the lives of thousands of women and their families: high teen-pregnancy rates, clandestine abortions, repression, illegality, unsanitary health practices, imprisonment, and female mortality due to "unknown" causes. To confront these realities with creativity and motivation constitutes a challenge not only for Las Dignas but also for all feminist organizations in the country.

Another important battle is the prevention of violence against women. In present times and globalized contexts, such as that of Central America, societies are inundated by weapons and general violence is on the rise. Age-old forms of violence against women related to women's otherness also assume new manifestations, such as the practice of femicide, the most brutal form of violence against women.

The increasing social recognition of women's discrimination is one of the most significant achievements gained by the feminist movement. This recognition constitutes an important instrument for denouncing acts of discrimination, as well as for establishing institutions and organizations centered on these issues. Unfortunately, along the way we lost our impetus in condemning and analyzing the foundational causes of gender discrimination, tending to disregard the intrinsic political nature of gender oppression.

The implications of depoliticizing the concept of gender are very serious. Due to our fear of seeming confrontational or conflictive, oftentimes we allow "gender diagnoses" to become long lists of sex disaggregated data. These lists omit the breadth of gender inequalities present in most social contexts, as well as ignore the root causes of the power hierarchies between men and women. Nonetheless, today thousands of women can now recognize the problem of inequality, are made uncomfortable by it, and see the necessity to change this reality.

I believe that in this terrain we must take on the challenges that come with our victories but still maintain a critical eye to engage in deep analysis and be less tolerant with those who think that they have taken the step toward liberation but who are blind to the link between female discrimination and the more complex components of gender inequality. It is important to keep in mind the fact that women are diverse; every woman experiences a different reality and has specific demands that we must address. But we should remember that regardless of a woman's particular social location, we all are victims of gender oppression, which is a universal phenomenon. Hence, feminist demands convey a political and revolutionary significance.

We have also made every effort to reform and institute laws that address women's individual needs. I am referring to the various international conventions and resolutions and to the body of laws that target women in all areas of life. Even though these measures have been useful to some degree, their capacity to question and transform the hierarchical character of gender relations is still limited. We must keep working on these issues, expanding our understandings of woman's oppression and being aware of the fact that most women's emancipatory policies continue to be peripheral measures with only partial and superficial applications. Unfortunately, our governments lack the political will to make women's needs a top priority. Nonetheless, these laws and measures are conquests that we should not abandon. To make them useful means turning them into instruments for consciousness raising, to make visible our problems and our points of view. Above all, we should use them as tools that can serve as a guide for the creation of a new institutional framework that will provide coherence to the exercise of governance.

The Political Participation of Women: Requalifying Democracy

Feminist proposals for deepening democracy imply a real presence of women in decision-making spaces as well as the application of this democratic model to people's daily life. This implies questioning the rigid division between public and private spheres that still prevails in society. Some laws have already been changed and gender-specific policies on behalf of women have been instituted at the national and municipal levels. Nonetheless, inequalities and injustices persist: violence against women continues to be unacknowledged as a public safety problem, men still constitute 90 percent of the body of elected officials, and women often earn much less than men for equal work and are the majority within the informal sector, often working under the most precarious conditions. Moreover, the notion that women's place is in the home still prevails.

The widespread crisis of the nation, along with a lack of response to women's demands on the part of national institutions, led many organizations to turn their eyes toward their municipalities for solutions. These relatively fragile public entities operate at the local level but are the closest governmental bodies available to the population. In addition, they appear more open to implementing innovative measures with the potential of transforming the population's everyday lives.

In this context, we believe that any action that promotes the decentralization of the state while furthering local and municipal development takes on vital importance. From a perspective that includes both local and global platforms, we should ask whether the redistribution of power across territorial units—from the national capital city to more local units—is or could serve as an opportunity to bring about changes in gender power relations; in other words, whether or not citizen participation and local democracy represent opportunities to democratize relations between men and women.

The demand for women's participation in decision-making spaces has taken a new course. Nevertheless, we should not forget that one of the areas of greatest tension within the feminist movement has been feminist involvement in institutional politics. Beyond our disagreements about particular leaders or specific contexts, we still need to reflect more thoroughly about the meaning of this debate. The complexity of this issue is linked to the following elements:

- Difficulty exists in conceiving the public sphere as realizing full human potential, when women are excluded only because of their gender. I do not use the word "public" to refer only to state institutions but in the sense of public dialogue and debate over common issues of society, defining the path of our communities and municipalities.
- Many times, our feminist critiques regarding the patriarchal character of these spaces makes us deny the importance of taking part in them and thus, we return to "the home." We renounce the forum that since the time of the Greeks has been a privileged space for those who possess the necessary qualifications to make decisions that affect all of us, men and women alike.
- We have settled for a weak commitment to parity, perhaps forced by a realistic reading of the political context. Hence, our proposals, such as quotas of political participation, are restricted to those that can be easily justified within the context of a conservative society like El Salvador. The problem is that along the way we forget that we are really fighting to overcome the exclusion that we have been subjected to as women, which denies us our full human condition.
- Another difficulty is the set of limitations that women who assume public office face. Their minority status, having a voice that must be ratified by men, and their constant need to learn and create more inclusive regulatory approaches influence most women who assume public office. Even if initially they intended to work for women, they end up assimilating into the dominant masculine model. This disillusions those who supported them, bringing them to question such strategy. It is important to keep in mind that, in the collective imaginary, women are interchangeable not only as partners but also as politicians. Hence the combustibility of female political power: either they "burn-out" on their own or we "burn them out" more quickly and frequently. To overcome this reality we must build feminine genealogies; in other words, we must grant each other mutual recognition, learn from one another's achievements and mistakes, and reference women as our models.

There are many challenges we must confront to achieve greater presence and competence in decision-making arenas. We must understand that, as women, we need to take different routes to obtain political power. As long as we continue working from the margins, unable to form a critical mass, we will remain a minority, used either to fulfill the diversity quotas or to serve as decorative objects.

The challenge is to transform the marginality surrounding women's participation and replace it with a critical and creative public political agency. This requires understanding that simply being a participant does not grant access to the center of power. We also need to be aware of the fact that even though we lack the ability to endow other women with power and authority, our work, even from the margins, can significantly strengthen other women. But only by reinforcing preexisting connections and building new alliances between women can we become politically stronger. Rather than being merely tolerant of differences, we need to really appreciate the richness of the differences among us.

Returning to Our Beginnings: The Feminist Collective's Strategies for Local Development

The emergence of the Colectiva Feminista para el Desarrollo Local has its origins in a long search for feminist strategies with which to build and strengthen the women's movement as a political actor in El Salvador. This effort began with the Programa de Participación Política y Desarrollo Local (PPDL; Program for Political Participation and Local Development), founded by Las Dignas. Over the last five years, this program combined the consolidation of local women's organizations, promotion of their agency, support for their autonomy and political impact, and the development of pluralist alliances with female town and city council members. This has been negotiated directly with the local groups, as well as through the Asociación Nacional de Regidoras, Síndicas y Alcaldesas Salvadoreñas (ANDRYSAS; National Association of Women City Council Members, Prosecutors, and Mayors). Together with local governments, the Colectiva has advocated for, advised, and comanaged the formulation and application of gender policies and affirmative action in support of women.

After lengthy considerations, in December 2003 Las Dignas recognized that within the institutional matrix various kinds of programmatic work had not always achieved the desired collaboration. Given PPDL's proposal to develop a broad entity capable of articulating women's groups and organizations, Las Dignas decided to make the program autonomous. They established a new kind of relationship with local organizations, themselves associated with women council members and ANDRYSAS. This new path solidified Las Dignas's founding vocation of promoting new organizational expressions in the women's movement. It also guaranteed the strategic vision of the PPDL, now renamed the Colectiva Feminista para el Desarrollo Local, of strengthening alliances between female public servants in charge of municipalities and local women's associations. These partnerships have fostered women's empowerment, increasing their political participation and transforming their organizations from voices of victimization to pressure groups.

Through the permanent questioning of hierarchy, we aim to contribute to the eradication of women's subordination. Our main goal is to fashion the women's movement into a political actor, starting off locally with concrete challenges women face on a daily basis, while being mindful of their needs, problems, and potentialities. This strategy we put into effect by creating ties between local women's organizations and municipal governments. We promote women's leadership and bring together various groups so that they can strengthen their capacity to negotiate at the local and national levels. In addition, we foster discussions, forums, analyses, training workshops, and the emergence of new understandings that can lead the way to a more democratic and egalitarian society.

Concerning the issues of poverty and unemployment, it is important to strengthen our support for women's economic and productive opportunities geared toward income generation or subsistence efforts. We are revaluing communitarian exchanges and proposing small-scale initiatives, linked to productive chains that promote reciprocal marketing and information-sharing webs. All of these factors should support women's efforts to become primary economic actors. At times we ask ourselves whether we are repeating the same history of the small projects of the 1980s and 1990s. However, today we do not expect these projects to organize women. The associations and their networks already have many ties in this respect. The fusion of some of the new initiatives with existing dynamics that promote local economic development assures our new projects' basic economic independence and links them to municipal investing and promoting strategies. Moreover, they help us learn about and critique market dynamics that exclude women as productive actors.

The Colectiva Feminista is an entity that supports the autonomy of each and every one of the women's organizations involved and also promotes local initiatives carried out by the women's movement. It promotes empowerment, hoping that women's experiences will provide new avenues to transform women's oppressive social, economic, political, and cultural realities. In addition, we advocate for the establishment of social spaces where men and women can embrace relationships based on respect, justice, and equality.

We believe that local development should be a pathway for the creation of alternative social initiatives that include women as active political actors and decision makers rather than simply as beneficiaries. We promote the development of a feminist movement that embraces women's diverse realities and is based on political, social, ethnic, sexual, and cultural pluralism. We want to build a women's movement capable of forming alliances with other feminist organizations and social institutions that also work in favor of democracy, justice, and equality. We hope that democracy stops being just a formal discourse and becomes an effective model equally implemented both by grassroots organizations and national political entities.

In conclusion, going back to our beginnings does not mean to return to the same place where we started. Instead, it implies taking on the challenge of broadening and strengthening the women's movement, embracing the experiences and knowledge gained through our participation in the social transformation of El Salvador. We need to solidify the gains achieved over the years but also accept the challenges of new political scenarios in which to conceive pluralism as collective enrichment. In our quest, we must also include women with whom we do not share a common history, either because they did not participate in the war or because they come from different backgrounds. Our struggle should also involve the inclusion of men in the construction of equitable relationships. Lastly, we must be the most diligent about promoting our cause among *all* people and not just preach to the choir. We need to be just like salt, which, to release its power, has to melt away.

ACKNOWLEDGMENTS
Translated by Christine H. Damon, reviewed by Blanca Torres.

NOTES

1. The civil war in El Salvador lasted mainly from 1980 to 1992, when Peace Accords were signed. About seventy-five thousand people were killed.

2. The Guazapa Front, located on the mountain of the same name, near the capital city of San Salvador, was one of the zones of the most intense combat throughout the entire war.

3. Lil Milagro Ramirez was a student, poet, revolutionary leader, and member of RN, who disappeared in 1976.

4. The signing of the Peace Accords took place during an official ceremony on January 16, 1992, in Chapultepec, Mexico. It followed a series of negotiations mediated by representatives from various Latin American countries and under the sponsorship of the United Nations.

5. In February 1992, the Primer Encuentro Nacional de Mujeres (First National Encuentro of Women) was held. The blank page was published in *La Prensa Grafica*.

6. RN was one of the five political forces that made up the FMLN.

REFERENCES

Las Dignas. 2000. *Una década construyendo feminismo*. San Salvador: Las Dignas.

Elo Mayo. 2004. Ninguna causa es tan importante como para postergar los derechos y demandas de las mujeres. Interview with Morena Herrera. *La Fogata Digital*. www.lafogata.org/04latino/latino6/sal_mujer.htm.

FUNDE. 2005. Notes from a workshop organized in collaboration with the women from the Social and Economic Micro-Region (MES) in the municipality of Tecoluca and facilitated by the Local Economic Development Program, Tecoluca, El Salvador, May.

MES. 2005. Notes from workshop facilitated by the Local Economic Development Program (FUNDE), Tecoluca, El Salvador, May.

Murguialday, Clara. 1995. *Las mujeres antes, con, contra, desde, sin, tras . . . el poder político*. San Salvador: Las Dignas.

Vázquez, Norma, Cristina Ibáñez, and Clara Murguialday. 1996. *Mujeres montaña, vivencias de guerrilleras y colaboradoras del FMLN*. Madrid: Horas y horas. En el marco de las becas del Programa de Investigaciones sobre Derechos Reproductivos (PRODIR II), Fundación Carlos Chagas, Brazil.

18   The Latin American Network of Católicas por el Derecho a Decidir

MARYSA NAVARRO

MARÍA CONSUELO MEJÍA

What Is Católicas por el Derecho a Decidir?

Católicas por el Derecho a Decidir in Latin America (CDD en América Latina; Catholics for the Right to Decide) is a network composed of organizations and persons who define themselves as Catholics committed to social justice and to changing existing cultural and religious patterns that oppress women. It is part of the Latin American and Caribbean feminist movement and thus promotes women's rights, especially sexual and reproductive rights, and seeks to attain equity in gender relations and to advance women's citizenship in society and the churches.

Founded in 1994, in Uruguay's Fortín de Santa Rosa, CDD en América Latina is a heterogeneous organization composed of various autonomous groups. Its most active members are in Brazil and Mexico. Its most recent are in Bolivia (La Paz and Santa Cruz), Colombia, Argentina (Córdoba and Buenos Aires), Chile, Paraguay, and Nicaragua; there are also Catholic voices that support CDD's message in El Salvador, Panama, and Peru. It also includes a group of Spanish Catholic feminists, who agree with the stance and activities of the network. It is coordinated by a collective composed of representatives from Brazil, Argentina, and Colombia, and its mandate is to maintain and foster the unity of the network through communication, joint activities, and training programs. To that end, it raises funds and maintains contact with other regional and international networks.

A central activity of the collective is *Conciencia Latinoamericana*, a quarterly publication that seeks to develop Catholic feminist thinking from a Latin American perspective. The first issue appeared in 1989. The magazine is distributed free of charge to approximately ten thousand individuals and institutions, and it covers a variety of topics. For example, in 2004 an entire issue was devoted to HIV/AIDS and included such articles as "La Feligresía Católica, la Conciencia y el Uso de Condones" (Catholics, Conscience, and the Use of Condoms), by Anthony Padovano; "Mulheres, AIDS y Religião" (Women, AIDS, and Religion), by Yury Puello Orozco; and "Desigualdad Social y SIDA: El Contexto Neoliberal de la Epidemia" (Social Inequality and AIDS: The Neoliberal Context of the Epidemic), by Bernardo Useche and Amalia Cabezas. The network has also published a series of booklets under the title *Hablando Nos Entendemos* (We Understand Each Other Talking) on abortion, sexuality, motherhood, and violence against women.

Among the numerous feminist networks that have emerged in Latin America and the Caribbean during the last twenty-five years, CDD is the only network with a Catholic feminist perspective. Its origin goes back to 1988, when a small group of Latin American feminists discovered Catholics for a Free Choice (CFFC), a U.S. Catholic feminist NGO committed to political action and reflection in support of women's reproductive rights.

Catholics for a Free Choice

Catholics for a Free Choice (since March 2007, Catholics for Choice, CFC) was founded in 1973 by Joan Harriman, Patricia Fogarty McQuillan, and Meta Mulcahy, the same year the Supreme Court issued its landmark decision known as *Roe v. Wade*. Before this case, the U.S. Catholic hierarchy had repeatedly voiced its opposition to a woman's right to choose. After the decision, this church joined other groups determined to overturn the decision, an endeavor that continues to this day. The founders of CFFC recognized the danger posed by the opposition organized by the hierarchy. They were also convinced that the stance of U.S. bishops regarding women's reproductive rights, including the right to have an abortion, did not represent the practice of Catholics. They knew that both Catholic and non-Catholic women sought abortions and that men and women who claimed to be Catholic supported the decriminalization of abortion. As feminists, they also criticized the subordination of women within the structure of the Catholic Church— their lack of power and visibility in the highest spheres of power, especially in those where fundamental decisions are made. These positions would soon receive crucial help from a new generation of women theologians.

CFFC was undoubtedly a product both of the feminist movement as it developed in the United States and of the changes in the Catholic Church brought about by the Second Ecumenical Vatican Council, which began to meet in October 1962. The *Declaration on Religious Freedom: Dignitatis Humanae*, promulgated by Pope Paul VI in 1965, is an essential document to understand the ideas of the CFFC leaders. This declaration reaffirmed the separation of church and state, pluralism, and the primacy of conscience. Under the leadership of Frances Kissling, who was its president from 1982 to 2007, CFFC has been a voice for Catholics who believe that the Catholic tradition includes a woman's moral and legal rights in matters of sexual and reproductive rights. It has participated in numerous United Nations conferences and forums, working with Catholic, feminist, and reproductive health organizations both in the United States and in Europe. In support of its commitment to social justice and human rights in the Catholic Church and in society, it produces numerous publications, including the magazine *Conscience*, and has become a rich source of information and theological knowledge on all these issues. It is located in Washington, DC, and since March 2007 it has been headed by Jon O'Brien.

In the heated U.S. debate on abortion, CFFC has played a special role that has gained the respect of the feminist movement. It has defined abortion as a moral issue and not only as a question related to women's rights or a religious or legal issue. In the words of Frances Kissling, "We have supported free choice by acknowledging that when we talk about abortion, we talk about values" (1988, 24). At a time when feminism was gaining legitimacy in Latin America, this message found an echo in many women who were distancing themselves from the Catholic Church. They were concerned about the impact of unsafe abortion on women's lives, especially on poor women, and rejected the sexual repression and the symbolic weight of the prevalent conservative ideology regarding these questions. They had also begun to publish works that reflected their new concerns, including Mariví Arregui's *Las Hijas Invisibles Cuestionan la Iglesia* (The Invisible Daughters Question the Church, 1987); Adriana Novello and Isabel Molina's *El Aborto en México* (Abortion in Mexico, 1976); Olga Rivera and Victoria Reyes's *Presencia y Ausencia de la Mujer en la Iglesia del Perú* (Presence and Absence of Women in the Peruvian Church, 1982) and Rosa Dominga Trapaso's *Iglesia, Mujer y Feminismo* (Church, Women, and Feminism, 1987).

Católicas por el Derecho a Decidir

The first contact between Latin American women and CFFC took place when the U.S. theologian Mary Hunt, a member of the CFFC board, traveled to Buenos Aires. During her visit, she met the anthropologist Safina Newbery and gave her Spanish translations of a few CFFC publications. Jorge Villareal Mejía, a Colombian physician who for many years had worked to reduce unwanted pregnancies and unsafe abortions, had persuaded CFFC to translate into Spanish two booklets he considered crucial for women: Jane Hurst's *The History of Abortion in the Catholic Church: The Untold Story* (1984) and Marjorie Reiley and Daniel C. Macguire's *Abortion: A Guide to Making Ethical Decisions* (1987).

Two other Latin American women had access to those publications: Sylvia Marcos, a Mexican psychotherapist, and the Brazilian writer, Rose Marie Muraro, who worked at Vozes, a Rio de Janeiro Catholic publishing house. They met for the first time during the Quinta Reunión Internacional de Mujer y Salud (Fifth International Meeting on Women and Health), held in 1987 in Costa Rica. Other participants were the Argentinean anthropologist Safina Newbery, the Uruguayan physician and sexologist Cristina Grela, the Colombian educator Rocío Laverde, the Peruvian journalist Ana María Portugal, and the Chilean activist Amparo Claro. Marcos and Newbery took part in a panel called The Right to Choose. This debate and their meeting with Frances Kissling, who also attended the meeting, was a revelation for many of them. As Cristina Grela remarked recently, after having heard Kissling, they realized immediately that they could be feminists and Catholics and still work to improve women's health and lives. They also realized that it was possible to talk about free and responsible sexuality from a Catholic perspective. In a recent interview, Cristina Grela recalled, "When I met Frances, I realized there was an answer to my concerns as a gynecologist deeply worried about maternal deaths from unsafe abortions" (interview, July 28, 2005, Montevideo, Uruguay). Full of enthusiasm after their meeting with Kissling, they proposed to bring CFFC's ideas to Latin America and create local groups. With CFFC's support, in 1989 they opened a regional office in Montevideo, Uruguay. Thus began an intense and complex collaboration between CFFC and CDD América Latina. CFFC has supported and provided the technical assistance that CDD has requested and has organized and sponsored workshops and trainings in theology, advocacy, strategic planning, fundraising, and relations with the media. Additionally, CFFC has provided financial support for other activities designed by CDD.

Grela became the coordinator of the group that met with Kissling in Costa Rica. They decided to call themselves Católicas por el Derecho a Decidir to reflect both their agreement with CFFC and also the Latin American character of their new organization. They rejected a literal translation because the word "choice" in Spanish is *elección* and that word in Latin America lacks the political weight, the historical background, and the resonance it had acquired in the United States.

One of the first public activities of the new organization was to publish in 1989 the book *Mujeres e Iglesia, Sexualidad y Aborto en América Latina* (Women and Church, Sexuality, and Abortion in Latin America). It was edited by Ana María Portugal and funded by CFFC. In it, the founding members of CDD questioned for the first time the conservative Catholic position concerning women, their sexuality, motherhood, their rights, and their agency in decision making.

In 1989 and 1990 Grela traveled throughout Latin America to promote and present the book at various meetings organized by other feminist groups. She actively looked for women willing to accept the challenge of becoming the public voices of CDD. And every time she found them, she encouraged and supported them. In Brazil, Grela met the theologian Ivonne Gebara, a nun who had discovered feminism and believed that with the inclusion of rights specific to women, liberation theology acquired a necessary dimension overlooked by male theologians. Thus began a relationship between Gebara and CDD en América Latina that has had a profound impact on the network. Gebara also met María José Rosaldo (Zeca), a former nun who defines herself as "a sociologist by profession, a feminist by conviction, and a Catholic for the right to decide by indignation." In 1993, encouraged by Grela, she created a feminist group composed not exclusively of Catholics that eventually became Católicas pelo Direito de Decidir (Catholics for the Right to Decide) in São Paulo, Brazil. Zeca became its first coordinator.

The founding members looked for the best ways to disseminate CDD's ideas in their respective countries. In Mexico, Sylvia Marcos distributed CDD publications and tried to identify women interested in joining the new movement. In 1993 CFFC decided to send the theologian Sarita Hudson to Mexico to establish a chapter of CDD. Hudson knocked on doors, established contacts, and found enough supporters to eventually found CDD Mexico in compliance with all the legal and administrative requirements established by Mexican laws. In 1994, after a search, María Consuelo Mejía was hired as director. For Mejía, becoming the Director of CDD Mexico has meant the recovery of her Catholic identity and the possibility of integrating activism with professional work.

That same year, Cristina Grela from the Montevideo regional office organized a meeting with the participation of Frances Kissling, other members of CFFC, some twenty persons representing organizations, and individuals who identified with CDD's ideas. Several activities were organized, including a workshop led by Ivonne Gebara titled "Reconceptualizing the Concept of God." The Red Latinoamericana de Católicas por el Derecho a Decidir (Latin American Network of Catholics for the Right to Decide) was created at that meeting. The existing groups became part of it, and at a later stage they were joined by groups in La Paz, Bolivia, and Valparaíso, Chile.

Two years later, in December 1996, the network met in Caxambu, Brazil. The Declaration of Principles adopted at that meeting is its founding charter, its political platform, and the conceptual framework accepted by all the organizations that are presently part of the Latin American network and that identify themselves as Catholics for the Right to Decide (see appendix A).

When Cristina Grela stepped down in 1998, the network decided to name a coordinating team composed of representatives from Brazil, Argentina, and Mexico, with the regional office in Córdoba. In 2002 the network chose a new collective with representatives from Colombia, Argentina, and Brazil, and since January 2007 this collective is formed by representatives from Argentina (Córdoba), Bolivia, and Mexico. Thanks to the Internet there is no longer need for a regional office and the appropriate division of tasks among the three coordinators has reduced the meetings to one a year.

Achievements

In the past fifteen years, CDD has become a significant presence wherever NGOs discuss strategies and seek to influence national, regional, and international public policies affecting human rights and women's lives, their health, and especially their sexual and reproductive rights. It maintains a close relationship with other Latin American networks that work for women's rights, including the Red por la Salud de las Mujeres en América Latina y el Caribe (Latin American and Caribbean Women's Health Network), the Comité Latinoamericano para la Defensa de los Derechos de la Mujer (Latin American and Caribbean Committee for the Defense of Women's Rights), and the Red Latinoamericana y Caribeña de Jóvenes por los Derechos Sexuales y Reproductivos (Latin American and Caribbean Youth Network for Sexual and Reproductive Rights). They have participated actively in the organization of campaigns throughout the continent, for example, the Campaña 28 de Septiembre por la Despenalización del Aborto (September 28 Campaign for the Decriminalization of Abortion), the Campaña por la Convención Interamericana por los Derechos Sexuales y Reproductivos (Campaign for an Inter-American Convention for Sexual and Reproductive Rights), and the Campaña contra los Fundamentalismos (Campaign against Fundamentalisms). Additionally, CDD network members coordinate activities with other networks on March 8 (International Women's Day), November 25 (International Day against Violence against Women), and December 1 (World AIDS Day).

CDD also participates in CFFC's worldwide campaigns. These include See Change (2000), which questioned the status of the Vatican at the United Nations; Call to Accountability (2001), launched after Maura O'Donohue denounced the rape of nuns by priests in twenty-three countries; and Condoms4Life (2001), which urged, with some success, Catholic bishops not to forbid the use of condoms to prevent the spread of AIDS. Furthermore, CDD has coordinated activities against the cover-up by U.S. church authorities of the sexual abuse of young Catholic men by priests.

CDD en América Latina has publicly supported initiatives launched by other networks. On December 3, 2003, for example, as part of the World AIDS Day activities, it issued a statement protesting the Vatican's position on HIV and AIDS. On December 4, 2004, it published another statement confirming its commitment to the Action Program adopted at the Cairo International Conference on Population and Development. It also expressed its sadness and indignation at the letter issued by the Congregation for the Doctrine of the Faith—the successor of the Inquisition, presided by the then cardinal Ratzinger—on the collaboration of men and women in the church and in the world. Finally, after the death of Pope John Paul II and the election of Benedict XVI, it reminded the public in still another statement that, as a cardinal, Ratzinger, the new pope, had "silenced progressive and dissident voices, closed spaces to discussion, and proclaimed his truth to be the only possible way of living within the Church" (Católicas por el Derecho a Decidir México 2005a).

CDD is frequently and actively present in regional feminist conferences, where its participation is highly valued because it speaks with a feminist Catholic voice that offers an alternative to the conservative and sexist discourse of church leaders. The network has played a significant role at the international United Nations conferences in the 1990s, especially the International Conference on Population and Development, held in Cairo in 1994, and the World Conference on Women, held in Beijing in 1995. It has actively participated in the review of all regional and global processes of these conferences and in the conventions for the elimination of violence against women in Latin America. CDD was also present at the Economic Commission for Latin America and the Caribbean (ECLAC) meeting held in Santiago de Chile in 2004, to evaluate progress and reaffirm the commitment of the region to the Cairo Program of Action. It presented the results of a survey of relations between church and state in Bolivia, Colombia, and Mexico and of sexual morality and abortion among Catholics in those countries (Belden Rusonello and Stewart 2003). The survey revealed the widening gap between what the Catholic hierarchy states and dictates and the actual practices of the Catholic population.

At international conferences, CDD and other Latin American NGOs have provided an important dissenting voice, thus demonstrating that the church does not speak with one voice or that the Vatican is the only authority in the Catholic Church. At the last international conference, Beijing +10, held in New York in March 2005, three members of CDD América Latina were part of the official delegations representing Argentina, Brazil, and Bolivia at the United Nations General Assembly. At this conference, CDD issued a statement titled "Catholic women urge the governments of the world to defend the consensus of the Beijing's Platform for Action," which was highly publicized by the media. The statement protested the U.S. delegation's attempts to coerce the poorer countries to withdraw their support of the Platform for Action.

At every international meeting, CDD presents solid arguments, grounded on Catholic doctrine, that reaffirm the moral authority of Catholics, their freedom of conscience, and their right to dissent from the church's moral teachings that ignore the needs and wishes of Catholic women. Additionally, it documents the contradictions of the Catholic hierarchy, which denies church members (priests, nuns, and believers) the possibility of experiencing sexual pleasure while covering up sexual abuse by priests, hence allowing them to have sexual relations for the sake of pleasure even when these acts violate the most basic human rights.

In a continent where the ideological and cultural weight of the Catholic Church has been and continues to be fundamental, the influence of its ideas on sexuality and reproduction has strongly shaped the limits of women's autonomy and their agency in making serious and responsible decisions. CDD is the only regional network that speaks of "the right to decide," using Catholic arguments that strengthen the moral agency of all persons, especially women, because it considers them capable of making decisions about their lives, particularly concerning their sexuality and reproduction. It is also the only network that defends the primacy of conscience and the right to dissent from the Catholic teachings that have not been declared infallible.

CDD has emerged during a process of democratization in most countries of the region that has made possible the discussion of important issues for Latin American Catholic women. However, as legislative and cultural changes have multiplied, producing a positive impact on women's autonomy and rights, the most conservative sectors of society, supported by the Catholic hierarchy, have been quick to counterattack. The Catholic hierarchy has embarked on a crusade against the exercise of sexual and reproductive rights by Catholics and non-Catholics and has led various groups to actively oppose all public policies that may facilitate the exercise of those rights. A coalition of diverse types of fundamentalism is committed to hinder, hold back, repress, and smother expressions of cultural, religious, and sexual diversity, in particular women's sexuality.

CDD continues to respond to the campaign of the Catholic hierarchy despite frequent attacks and threats of excommunication by Episcopal conferences in the countries where the network operates. On June 30, 2005, in São Paulo, Brazil, Regina Soares Jurkewicz, a teacher for eight years at the Institute of Theology of the Santo André Diocese and a member of Católicas pelo Direito de Decidir, was fired. She was informed that the Institute did not agree with or accept her ideas published in the magazine *Época* of Brazil from her recently published doctoral dissertation. In her thesis Soares analyzes the evasive responses of the Brazilian Catholic Church to complaints of violence and sexual abuse. Her documentation reveals that the Catholic hierarchy, fearing scandal and attempting to preserve the good image of the church, covered up cases of abuse and violence by transferring the accused priests to other parishes.

The effectiveness of CDD's discourse and agency to counteract the conservative Catholic arguments helped contribute to the successful campaign for the decriminalization of abortion in Mexico City—led by the National Alliance for the Right to Decide, a coalition of five organizations including Equidad de Género, Ciudadanía, Trabajo y Familia (Gender Equity, Citizenship, Work, and Family); Grupo de Información en Reproducción Elegida (Information Group on Reproductive Choice); Ipas Mexico; Population Council Mexico; and Católicas por el Derecho a Decidir—notwithstanding the opposition of the Catholic Church. On April 24, 2007, Mexico City's legislative assembly adopted a law that legalizes abortion during the first twelve weeks of gestation and lowers sanctions for women who seek an abortion after that period. The measure won by a two-thirds majority and had the support of five political parties. The new law also requires the Mexico City Ministry of Health to provide abortion services, free of charge to any woman living in Mexico City (even if she is covered by other public or private insurance) and at a moderate rate for women from other states of the country and for foreigners. Furthermore, it includes provisions for sexual education and campaigns in support of reproductive and sexual rights and for the availability of contraceptive methods and counseling for all women considering an abortion. The bill put Mexico City at the forefront of abortion liberalization in Latin America and the Caribbean, placing it on equal footing only with Cuba, Guyana, and Puerto Rico; it represents a comprehensive approach for the prevention of unwanted pregnancies, while at the same time respecting women's right to decide.

This decision of Mexico City's Legislative Assembly was the result of a combination of social and political factors aligned at the right time and in the right place: a dominant left-wing party in the Mexico City legislature in an environment of political polarization between the left and the right, an international human rights framework in favor of abortion rights, and above all more than thirty-five years of a determined struggle by the feminist movement, the women's movement, and its allies in civil society to maintain abortion rights on the public agenda. Over the years, a broad range of perspectives on public health, bioethics, philosophy, human rights, social justice, secular, and Catholic prochoice arguments in support of safe and legal abortion helped prochoice advocates to educate the public, the media, legislators, the health sector, and the judicial branch about the complexity of the issue.

Other critical factors were the long-established separation of church and state in Mexico and the scandals surrounding pedophile priests, which weakened the Catholic Church and negatively affected its public image in the months prior to the presentation of the bill. During the debate, the church hierarchy denounced the law. Its discourse became increasingly aggressive, especially toward legislators who were threatened with excommunication if they voted in favor of it. The hierarchy retracted these threats when CDD revealed through a public advertisement that the canon law code establishes mitigating factors for women who have an abortion and states that a person may not be punished for what he or she thinks. Many Mexicans saw these desperate efforts by the church as bullying and highly disrespectful, particularly in the context of the church's poor track record on standing up for the human rights of those abused by its own priests.

On April 27, 2007, three days after the adoption of the law, legal abortion services were already in place at fourteen public hospitals run by the Mexico City Ministry of Health. One year later, more than 19,000 women had access to information and counseling and approximately 8,000 women chose to terminate a pregnancy, exercising their right to decide according to their freedom of conscience. According to Ministry of Health statistics, 85 percent of these women were Catholic, 26 percent were students, 29 percent were employed, and 38 percent were exclusively housewives. Significantly, only 6.2 percent were under eighteen (Pineda 2008). These figures, which have been published in national newspapers, are helping to debunk myths about women who have abortions and ultimately destigmatize this issue.

The most recent data (August 2009) confirms the tendency observed since April 2007. According to the Mexico City attorney general Leticia Bonifaz, masses of women are not running to the public hospitals of Mexico City to ask for the termination of their pregnancies; on the contrary, out of 50,963 women who have asked for information about legal abortion services, only 29,212 have actually terminated their pregnancies, of which 1,647 are minors. These statistics reveal that women are able to make informed decisions about their pregnancies.

During the public debate that preceded the adoption of the law, CDD Mexico was very active in providing prochoice Catholic arguments in different forums, as well as in demanding respect for the secular state, denouncing the cover-up of pedophiles by the conservative hierarchy, and demanding accountability and respect for children's rights. When the legislative discussions began, CDD developed an advocacy strategy together with the coalition Alianza Nacional por el Derecho a Decidir, agreeing upon a division of labor and a multistrategic approach to change the discourse on abortion, frame sexual and reproductive rights—including abortion rights—as human rights, position these issues on the public agenda, gain public opinion in favor of women's right to choose, and widen the social base of support for abortion rights. As the debate proceeded, CDD continued to provide prochoice Catholic arguments with timely advertisements, participate in the public discussions sponsored by the legislative assembly, and distribute publications used widely by many legislators to inform their votes in support of the bill.

Prior to the success of decriminalizing abortion in Mexico City, the actions of the Catholic hierarchy and its fundamentalist allies had been so worrisome for Latin American feminists that in April 2004 several women's groups gathered in Córdoba, Argentina, to launch the Declaración de Córdoba, Estrategias y Acciones Proactivas frente a los Fundamentalismos en la Región (Córdoba Declaration, Proactive Strategies and Actions against the Region's Fundamentalisms). In their final statement, the groups asked for a true separation between church and state, "where churches do not limit the state's public policies or interfere with the state's compliance with international commitments regarding women's rights, specifically sexual and reproductive rights. We understand that states legislate for all citizens, regardless of their religious beliefs, while preserving individual plurality and self-determination" (see appendix B).

The challenge of being a public dissenting voice within the Catholic Church requires a solid commitment and a vocation in the defense of justice. Fortunately, most of the members of CDD en América Latina have been advocates all their lives and have widely demonstrated their will, persistence, and commitment to achieve justice and equality for women within society and the church.

APPENDIX A: DECLARATION OF PRINCIPLES OF THE NETWORK CATÓLICAS POR EL DERECHO A DECIDIR EN AMÉRICA LATINA

We are an autonomous movement of Catholics committed to social justice and the transformation of the existing cultural and religious parameters of our societies.

We promote women's rights, especially sexual and reproductive rights.

We seek to achieve equity in gender relations and women's citizenship in society and in churches.

We are in a process of collective construction, working in a democratic and participatory manner.

We affirm

1. The right of women to have autonomy to control their own bodies and the pleasurable enjoyment of their sexuality, regardless of class, race/ethnicity, creed, age, and sexual orientation.
2. The moral agency of women and men to make responsible decisions about their lives, particularly about their sexuality and reproduction.
3. A theological thought that acknowledges the moral value of women's reproductive decisions without assigning blame to them, even in the case of abortion.
4. Respect for plurality, diversity, and difference, as essential factors in achieving freedom and justice.

We propose to

1. Create ecumenical spaces for ethical and religious reflection to promote public dialogues on sexuality, religion, and human reproduction, in societies and churches.
2. Debate on voluntary pregnancy termination, broadening the ethical, medical, and legal aspects of the discussion.
3. Exert influence on society so as to give women the right to free, voluntary motherhood and to decrease the number of abortions, as well as maternal mortality.
4. Continue our efforts to decriminalize abortion.
5. Involve and sensitize civil society, especially legislators and the groups working in reproductive and sexual health, education services, human rights, and communications, about the need to change the cultural patterns of our society.

We demand that the state

1. Comply with the commitments made at the United Nations conferences in Cairo (1994) and Beijing (1995).
2. Implement sex education programs with a sexual and reproductive rights perspective.
3. Implement legislation, public policies, and affordable health services of high quality so as to ensure access to all women, especially poor women, to fully enjoy their sexual and reproductive health.

Caxambu, Brazil, December 10–15, 1996.

APPENDIX B: INTERNATIONAL SEMINAR, THE CÓRDOBA
DECLARATION. *Proactive Strategies and Actions against the
Region's Fundamentalisms*, APRIL 9–10, 2004, CÓRDOBA,
ARGENTINA

We, the feminist organizations and networks of Latin America gathered in Córdoba, declare,

The feminist movement and women's organizations have achieved great progress in the last twenty years: national laws and international agreements that recognize our rights, our political protagonism, and our growing leadership.

Despite our progress, religious fundamentalisms serving world domination projects—political, economic, cultural, and bellicose in nature—fostered by the U.S. government, have undertaken actions against the exercise of sexual and reproductive rights in Latin America, threatening freedom of conscience, freedom of thought, and freedom of assembly and expression and disregarding the pluralism that characterizes a democratic and secular society.

We declare our support of true democratic, sovereign, and lay states, where the separation of church and state is real and where churches do not limit the state's public policies or interfere with the state's compliance with international commitments regarding women's rights, specifically sexual and reproductive rights. We understand that states legislate for all citizens, regardless of their religious beliefs, while preserving individual plurality and self-determination.

We wish to live in a democracy that provides equal opportunities, where sexual and reproductive rights are viewed as human rights.

We believe it is essential to broaden the public debate on these issues to include the different social and human rights movements.

Our actions seek not only to create lay states but also to incorporate into the political arena the ethics and values promoted by feminist movements as a contribution to democracy, peace, and justice.

For all of these reasons, we, the networks attending this seminar, commit to launch a Latin American campaign for effective lay states in our countries. The campaign will incorporate the issue into existing networks and campaigns and will promote actions in favor of the lay state among our own organizations.

Córdoba, Argentina, on April, 10, 2004, as part of the international seminar "Proactive Strategies and Actions against the Region's Fundamentalisms."

Católicas por el Derecho a Decidir en América Latina
Comité Latinoamericano para la Defensa de los Derechos de la Mujer (Regional)
Campaña contra los Fundamentalismos
Campaña 28 de Septiembre por la Despenalización del Aborto
Red por la Salud de las Mujeres en América Latina y El Caribe
Red Mujer y Hábitat Latinoamericana
Campaña por la Convención Interamericana por los Derechos Sexuales y Reproductivos

REFERENCES

Arregui, Mariví. 1987. *Las hijas invisibles cuestionan la iglesia.* Santo Domingo: CEDEE.

Belden Rusonello, Nancy, and Kate Stewart. 2003. *Actitudes de los Católicos sobre derechos reproductivos, iglesia, estado y temas relacionados: Tres encuestas nacionales en Bolivia, Colombia y
México.* Washington, DC: CFFC.

Católicas por el Derecho a Decidir México. 1996. *Somos iglesia.* Mexico City: CDD.

———. 2004a. *Conciencia Latinoamericana* 13, no. 10.

————. 2004b. Declaración de Córdoba, Estrategias y Acciones Proactivas frente a los Fundamentalismo en la Región, 9 y 10 de abril del 2004, Córdoba, Argentina. www .catolicasporelderechoadecidir.org/declaraciones-1.php (accessed March 6, 2006).

————. 2005a. Declaración de la Red Latinoamericana de Católicas por el Derecho a Decidir: Ante la elección del nuevo papa. www.catolicasporelderechoadecidir.org/declaraciones-7 .php (accessed April 20, 2005).

————. 2005b. Declaración de la Red Latinoamericana de Católicas por el Derecho a Decidir: Las mujeres católicas exhortamos a los gobiernos del mundo a que defiendan el consenso logrado en la Plataforma de Acción de Beijing. www.catolicasporelderechoadecidir.org/ declaraciones-5.php (accessed March 3, 2005).

Gebara, Ivonne. 1994. *El rostro nuevo de Dios: La reconstrucción de los significados trinitarios y la celebración de la vida.* Mexico City: DABAR.

————. 1995. *Teología a ritmo de mujer.* Mexico City: DABAR.

Hurst, Jane. 1984. *La historia de las ideas sobre el aborto en la Iglesia Católica: Lo que no fue contado.* Mexico City: CFFC.

La Jornada. 2009. Amenazada, legislación del aborto en el DF: Instituto de las Mujeres. August 28, Sociedad y Justicia section, 13.

Jurkewicz, Regina Soares. 2005. Entienista de Eliane Brum: O Pecado do Silêncio. *Revista Época,* June 20.

Kissling, Frances. 1988. A church lost in the Pelvic Zone. *Guardian Magazine,* March 29.

Macguire, Marjorie Reiley, and Daniel C. Macguire. 1987. *Aborto: Una guía para tomar decisiones éticas.* Washington, DC: CFFC.

Novello, Adriana, and Isabel Molina. 1976. *El aborto en México.* Mexico City: FCE.

Pineda, Georgina. 2008. There are more than 8 thousand legal abortions. *Milenio.* July 3, City and Estate sec., 27.

Pope Paul VI. 1965. *Declaración sobre la Libertad Religiosa: Dignitatis Humanae.* www.vatican.va/ archive/hist_councils/ii_vatican_council/documents/vat-ii_decl_19651207_dignitatis -humanae_sp.html (accessed March 5, 2006).

Portugal, Ana María, ed. 1989. *Mujeres e iglesia: Sexualidad y aborto en América Latina.* Mexico City: Fontamara S. A.

Rivera, Olga, and Victoria Reyes. 1982. *Presencia y ausencia de la mujer en la Iglesia del Perú.* Puno, Peru: Instituto de Estudios Aymaras.

Soto Campos, Francisco, ed. 2000. *Concilio Ecuménico Vaticano II. Constituciones, Decretos, Declaraciones.* Mexico City: Dabar.

Trapasso, Rosa Dominga. 1982. *Iglesia, mujer y feminismo.* Lima: Creatividad y Cambio.

19

Constructing New Democratic Paradigms for Global Democracy

THE CONTRIBUTION OF FEMINISMS

VIRGINIA VARGAS

Social movements—and feminisms as an expression and part of them—are not unfamiliar with eras of transformation or their contradictions, limitations, and sensitivities. In this most recent period, social movements' modes of operating have changed in response to the challenges raised by the cultural, political, social, and economic climate of the new millennium. The conditions and impetus for the rise of the second wave of Latin American feminisms were dramatically different from those prevalent today. Feminist politics emerged in Latin America early on in the struggle against dictatorships, authoritarian governments, and seemingly democratic governments, against which confrontation and deep mistrust had been growing. Perhaps for this reason the strategies of second-wave feminisms, in the early stages, focused more on civil society itself rather than interact with, much less negotiate with, states and governments. It was within civil society that feminisms flourished, creating a multiplicity of groups, networks, gatherings, feminist calendars, symbols, and subjectivities. This consolidation produced a series of epistemological ruptures that gave way to new interpretative models of reality. By "politicizing" private life, feminists took on "women's discontent" (Tamayo 1997), generating new categories of analysis, new visibilities, and even a new language to name that which previously had no name; domestic violence, sexual harassment, marital rape, and the feminization of poverty are some of the new meanings that feminism placed at the center of democratic debates. Throughout this process, Encuentros Feministas de América Latina y el Caribe (Latin American and Caribbean Feminist Encuentros)—held from 1981 to the present—have been crucial in reactivating the historically internationalist character of feminisms, connecting experiences and strategies, and expressing the progress, tensions, and conflicts that result from the great variety of feminist explorations throughout the region.

The transition from the eighties to the nineties was accompanied by new political, ideological, economic, and cultural scenarios that influenced feminism and social movements in general. New political arenas opened up during the nineties, with the spread of democracy as a form of government. There was a newfound validity for the discourse of rights, and emphasis was placed on the expansion of citizenship by civil society and social movements, as well as by states. However, they had different perspectives (or at least they attempted to, without always succeeding). Civil society and especially feminist focus on rights appeared as a rebellious and conflictive terrain of dispute, producing permanent "wars of interpretation" (Slater 1998) and promoting alternative meanings to state hegemonic discourses that were partial and exclusionary. Feminisms sought not only access to equality but also recognition of diversity and difference, access not only to existing rights but also to the process of discovering and permanently expanding rights, thus creating new social meaning. The struggle for the recognition of sexual and reproductive rights, as not only women's rights but also as a constitutive part of the construction of citizenship, is an example of this process.

The transformations of the nineties significantly influenced the dynamics and forms of social movements and, among them, feminism: the neoliberal logic impacted not only the economy but also the social and cultural spheres. Neoliberalism accentuated the trend from a movement-based logic to a more institutional logic, as well as the tendency in society toward the privatization of social behavior and a growing fragmentation and individuation of movements' collective action, generating a "me culture," as Norbert Lechner states, "reluctant to become involved in collective commitments" (2007, 311). Economic, political, and sociocultural globalization opened new fields of action for social movements, including feminisms, and new landscapes of struggle for citizen rights in a globalized world. The dramatic levels of exclusion in each country, together with changes in the nature of the nation-state and its increasing inability to respond to citizens' needs, gave rise to new struggles and areas of advocacy, regionally and globally. Substantial impetus was provided at an international level through the United Nations, which developed new global agendas throughout the 1990s in its summits and world conferences on topics relevant to contemporary democratic life. A significant sector of feminist organizations was active in disputing meanings and perspectives at each one of these international conferences. Thus feminists became fundamental actors in the construction of democracy in regional and global civil societies, broadening the spaces of proposition and confrontations.

Undoubtedly the multiplication of feminist struggles and the emergence of other processes and social actors brought about changes in how feminist (understood in a plural and diverse sense) proposals were applied. Strategies became more diverse, both concretely and symbolically, operating on multiple scales. As Sonia Alvarez states, feminism expanded into "a broad, heterogeneous, polycentric, multifaceted and polyphonic field of discourse and action. The spaces multiplied where women who call themselves feminists acted or could act . . . caught up not only in classically political struggles . . . but also simultaneously involved in disputes over meanings, definitions, in discursive struggles, and in essentially cultural battles" (1998, 295). Feminisms were thus in transition toward new forms of expression, at a time when the paradigms and certainties that had accompanied them until then were no longer present. Uncertainty permeated the movement. But, as Boaventura de Souza Santos states, this could be an advantage, because it forced feminists to think more creatively about the future (2002).

Latin American Feminisms in the New Millennium

These tendencies and new scenarios are manifested more clearly in the new millennium, revealing that we are not only experiencing an era of intense change but are also facing a "change of era" (Human Development Report, Chile 2000). We could compare this to how it must have been after the discovery of the wheel or after the Industrial Revolution. In such times of profound change, identities and subjectivities are also transformed. This crisis of identities is so strong that, as Heriberto Cairo Carou states, "some discourses are re-signified while others, in different ways and with different objectives, emerge in opposition to dominant discourses, and new discourses are created on the basis of old narratives." In a nutshell, "the previous order is shaken up" (2000, 110). In the dialectics between action and knowledge in this new disorder, there is a permanent dose of uncertainty and ambiguity.

However, as De Souza Santos predicted, instead of being a limitation, uncertainty has become a powerful impetus for these explorations, at a time when previous paradigms no longer suffice and new paradigms are still in the process of construction (2002). Various feminist writers have contributed to understanding these new challenges. Diana Maffia talks of the urgent need to invent new interdisciplinary arrangements for constructing, what she calls, "impertinent knowledge" that delegitimizes traditional discourse (2001).

Also pertinent to this new scenario is what Julieta Kirkwood called at the start of second-wave feminism the "license to speak," referring to a sort of irreverence toward the scientific paradigm and its concepts, impertinently mixing up everything and thus producing a declassification of codes and an inversion in the significance of what is important (1986). Other authors note that this process of disputing significance and creating new meanings is particularly relevant at this historic juncture. The new historical context, according to Peter Waterman, has not only brought about neoliberal hegemony, it has also been accompanied by the relative disintegration of the old political left and its replacement by a more plural and diverse left, through progressive civil society actors who are becoming increasingly radicalized (2004). As Waterman notes, emancipation has been proposed not from the state and capital, nationally and globally, but from ideologically archaic schemes of interpretation. For this concert of uncertainties and discomfort to be recognized, new ways of understanding the political sphere, as well as the new meanings and directions, are required.

Contingent to this new political culture and theory is the understanding that transformation of reality presupposes a "changing perspective" (Beck 2004). For Ulrich Beck, this new perspective also implies a shift of imagination, from one centered only on the nation-state toward a cosmopolitan imagination that, at the same time, sheds light on the local.[1] The cosmopolitan identity, says Beck, does not betray the national identity. They are complementary viewpoints that allow the "fiction" of each to dissolve, but it is the cosmopolitan viewpoint that is closest to today's reality, because it opens up possibilities for action that the national viewpoint, on its own, forecloses. From the perspective of social movements, the cosmopolitan or global solidarity viewpoint (Waterman 2004) is fundamental for understanding the new dynamics that they have introduced into their local-global interactions, expressing a plurality of emancipatory struggles and discourses. Beck expresses this plurality well, emphasizing its incidence on global-local scales: "The conflicts based on gender, class, ethnicity, and homosexuality certainly have their origins in national frameworks, but they haven't been at that level for a long time; rather, they are overlapping and interconnecting globally. The growing cosmopolitanism of social movements is also evident, as well as the fact that they have become transmitters of global ideas, values, conflicts, vindications, rights, and responsibilities" (2004, 90).

New Directions

The new dynamics, collective actors, and scenarios of globalization have also brought about, as noted earlier, the obsolescence of old paradigms and uncertainty about how and with what to replace them. Maintaining their local and regional impact, feminisms have gone global, affirming new viewpoints and paths from which they can foster new paradigms, broaden and extend feminist goals, and, from a perspective of radical democracy, generate a culture of resistance and alternatives to neoliberal globalization and current capitalist development.

These processes change the scenarios for social movements and actors, developing what Elizabeth Jelin calls "new interpretive frameworks for action."[2] These new interpretive frameworks carry ideas, cultural traditions, values, beliefs, perceptions, and cognitive elements of social action. This is the basis on which political opportunities are taken advantage of and constructed. The development of social action, takes us, for example, from an interpretive framework based on the idea of luck or destiny, to another that recognizes injustice and the human capacity to influence history. Or, movements with specific demands gain new meaning when they are framed within broader movements, and new alliances expand their referential horizons to include demands for local democracy or to incorporate other proposals, such as the right to equity in daily life proposed by feminists: "In any of these cases, the change of framework implies the broadening of the subject of action, of the referent 'us' and of the movement's field of action" (Jelin 2003, 42).

Returning to Beck and his "change of perspective": until recently the dominant interpretive framework for collective actors has been the nation-state (Jelin 2003), weakened by the effects of globalization (porous borders, explosion of nationalities, lack of correspondence between territory and nation, etc.). New interpretive frameworks are taking shape, decentering previous understandings. In this process, which is neither linear nor direct, the actions of social movements intensify and influence different scales of social action, from the most local to the global. These scales superimpose and penetrate each other, interacting and generating a multiplicity of meanings for action itself. This diversity of levels or scales (Jelin calls it a map of scales), shares a central axis, an axis of meaning, which is the backbone of the "interpretive framework." Particular interpretations of the framework depend on where the accent is placed on this axis of meaning (Jelin 2003, 51).

In the new millennium, feminisms' interpretive frameworks begin to reveal some central pathways. One of them deals with reclaiming and enriching the human rights paradigm, negotiating universality with specificity and paradigmatic cohesion with radical flexibility, to incorporate emerging rights corresponding to new risks, or new actors making visible their existence and proposals. Other dimensions also exist that have in many ways been subjectively conquered but still require formal recognition (Vargas and Celiberti 2005a). Sexual and reproductive rights are in that category, including sexual diversity and abortion, which are most resisted today. Other contemporary feminist concerns include efforts to intersect gender, class, and race as constitutive elements of a system of domination, thus enabling us to overcome the fragmentation of feminist struggles and construct more solid and diverse foundations for a new democracy.

Absences and Emergences: The Body as an Emerging Political Site

Resistance to the forces of globalization and the elaboration of new pathways and perspectives are informed by a novel conceptualization of the body, one that identifies it as a political site affected by those very global forces. Proof is in the stigmas the body endures and the rights it struggles to attain.

One idea that brings me closer to understanding the interrelated dimensions of movements is that reality cannot be reduced to what exists but that it also includes what is suppressed, what exists as residual or is confined to a single dimension. To highlight and mainstream the change of perspective, one needs an "epistemological operation," which De Souza Santos calls the "sociology of absences and the sociology of emergence." The aim of the sociology of absences is to identify and value available social experiences in the world, even if they are declared as nonexistent by hegemonic reason and knowledge. The sociology of emergence seeks to identify the signs of possible future experiences, which are actively ignored by hegemonic reason and knowledge (De Souza Santos 2002). The sociology of emergence analyzes these tendencies or latent possibilities with those who are constructing new interpretive frameworks for action.

And it is the body as a political site that can be seen as an actively emerging absence, having failed to be recognized in previous interpretive frameworks, in spite of the numerous signs of its existence. As Claudia Bonan (2001) notes, a new interpretive perspective has emerged for reading the body. Contrasted with biomedical, religious, and state theoretical frameworks, an emancipatory theoretical framework is emerging that positions the body as one of the integral elements of these new political perspectives, not only referring to its pertinence in the private sphere or its relation to the individual but also fully associating with the public sphere (Harcourt and Escobar 2003). The body has become a field "steeped in citizenship," through a series of "available social experiences," which facilitate interconnections (Avila 2001).

This new interconnectivity brings feminism(s) into contact with many other areas of women's and men's lives, generating social struggles that bring to light new and old dynamics of power, discipline, and control, while creating emancipatory alternatives to them. Undoubtedly, one expression of disciplining the body is the denial of people's sexual and reproductive rights. As such, in the new millennium, feminisms have led the struggle for the recuperation of the right to choose, positing the value of intimacy as a substantial part of democratic life and of the meaning of citizenship, and thus radicalizing the significance of the right to liberty and autonomy, while separating the traditional association between sexuality and reproduction. They also emphasize the right to pleasure and a life without violence in the private and intimate sphere, while seeking to express these rights in the public arena. As such, they incorporate this dimension of freedom into the very nucleus of citizenship. The decriminalization of abortion is emblematic in this search for autonomy and freedom, and so is the struggle for sexual diversity, especially by transsexuals, transvestites, and intersex people striving for formal recognition of their rights. As visible and political actors, they radicalize the public sphere with their demands for the right to difference. It is also expressed in the fight against AIDS, as can be seen by the enormous resistance of ecclesiastic hierarchies of all stripes and even of democratic governments, as well as by their unwillingness to confront the monopoly of transnational companies over drug patents.

Representations of the political body are multifold. Disciplining the female body through terror and militarization is expressed with unimaginable crudeness in armed conflicts and wars, where, for all sides, women's bodies are assumed to be part of the spoils. The devaluation of the body is also reinforced by racial discrimination that exacerbates social, cultural, economic, and emotional exclusion, which in the case of women has a particular impact on their sexual bodies.[3]

The impact of social exclusion on the political body is increasingly compounded by neoliberal economic policies, deepening poverty and hunger and reducing the capabilities of the bodies of new generations. In the name of a market supremacy that disregards citizens, this model affects women's capabilities even more, by not recognizing the economy of human reproduction and nurture inherent in unpaid domestic labor.

This political body is present in all private and public spaces and interactions. All its dimensions currently inform local and global struggles. However, the body is not recognized as pertaining to the political arena, and as such does not exist. But that which does not exist, notes De Souza Santos, referring to the sociology of absences, is actively constructed to not exist. Having a new perspective implies transforming both theoretically and politically the impossible into possible, and absence into presence (2002). For that reason, changing the conditions of nonexistence goes beyond the politics of naming or specific contextual proposals. Other democratic changes are necessary for the legitimacy and recognition of the body as political and should have an impact on that which acts to deny its existence, recuperating it actively in their forms of emergence, in the ways it expresses itself, in the conflicts it generates, and in that which limits its expansion. And here, a robust theoretical and practical agenda has appeared that sheds light on these new dimensions in which new rights are produced, while reaffirming that without advances at other levels of democracy it is not possible to transform a political culture to recognize the body as the bearer of citizenship.

It is this field of multiplicity and multidirectionality that energizes the interpretative frameworks of feminist struggles in the new twenty-first century. To place the political body into dispute is a way of making it visible. This visibility allows for building alliances with other movements, thus broadening one's own perspectives through interaction with others, while simultaneously informing the vision of other movements. Thus the body, in its political expression, can potentially bring together multiple emancipatory interests and visions. The radical and countercultural transformations that feminisms aspire to are more viable when connected with other democratic struggles in the building of a democratic alternative whose objective is the intersection of multiple and different struggles against various kinds of oppression (Mouffe 1996).

These processes of dispute, connection, and recognition and the broadening of interpretive frameworks are taking place today in global arenas, such as the World Social Forum and its regional and local forums. It has not been an easy process but rather one of dispute, which permanently expands the margins of debate and leads to new perspectives and new questions. The ability to question reality from the viewpoint of all social actors is the key to visualizing the absences and making them present.

The World Social Forum as a Space of Democratic Confluence and Dispute

> [The World Social Forum] is a space where protests unite in hope, and despair turns to the construction of alternatives; where the landless and the homeless, and the indigenous and afro-descendent movements meet with the youth, economists, transsexuals, feminists, those who have political messages, academics, those who struggle against genetically modified products and the transgendered. Hindus, Muslims, Jews, Catholics come together with trade unionists and those who promote Esperanto as a universal language. (Garrido 2002, 602)

The World Social Forum (WSF), initiated in 2001 in Porto Alegre, Brazil, is now set on the horizon and in the strategies for the changes in networks and social movements, contributing to fostering a global perspective.[4] "Another world is possible" and "no to unilinear thinking" are the two powerful and mobilizing slogans of the forum that express the orientation of another globalization, whose strength is the ethical and utopian conviction that alternatives can be built by democratic and emancipatory world forces. There are neither recipes to achieve this, nor hegemonic subjects of transformation, but rather a multiplicity of social actors contributing diverse forms of resistance and ways of building democracy with social justice and equity.

The Charter of Principles of the World Social Forum, approved in 2001, has been the instrument of cohesion for these multiple perspectives and strategies. Designating it as meeting place for social movements in favor of democratic civil society, the charter has established the autonomy of the forum as a plural, noncon-fessional, nongovernmental, and nonparty space. It also solicits respect for and active affirmation of existing differences among movements and forces for change: respect for that plurality, along with its contributions and strategies, should consti-tute the very building blocs of the forum as a meeting place and a process rather than a momentary consideration. The forum therefore does not attempt to reach conclusions or to generate public declarations in its name, since this would under-mine the foundations of the enormous plurality that the different networks, organ-izations, and movements bring, and lead them in one way or another to feel obliged to assume a unified position. The Charter of Principles establishes the rules of engagement in this global space.

The WSF is also a space for the affirmation, expansion, and construction of rights, now on a planetary level. For this reason, it is a meeting place for broaden-ing subjective and symbolic democratic horizons: the interaction between these multiple experiences, social movements, networks, and diverse forms of recuperat-ing utopian perspectives and proposing a different world is empowering. Nobody leaves this interaction indifferent; rather, one leaves impressed in many ways, with new questions, with the recognition of new presences, and with the possibility of generating new political cultures that inspire one's democratic imagination. This is the most important contribution of the WSF.

The WSF has created a fascinating multiplicity of dynamics that express the ways in which a global perspective is being built through diversity. It has also had the capacity to reflect about itself and continue modifying its own dynamics to seek greater democratization and expansion.[5] Undoubtedly a space-process of such mag-nitude would be unthinkable—except ideally—without tensions, different aims, anxieties, and power dynamics. There are tensions arising from its very growth that generate ambivalence between old and new subjectivities and that are an expres-sion of the difficult process of generating both new forms of political debate and new contents for democratic political cultures. In sum, the WSF is both a space and a global way of thinking, with a plural and radically democratic content.

Feminist Disputes in the World Social Forum

"Another world is possible," is the slogan of the World Social Forum. Looking at it from a feminist perspective the task is much greater than it seems. Without doubt, we are unsettling the dominant mode of unilinear thinking. But is our own machismo, racism, and other forms of intolerance also unsettling to us? The specificity of the World Social Forum is to establish dialogue among diverse groups. This gives the forum originality and strength in building a global citizenship on Planet Earth. But the road is long and full of obstacles. I hope that women will radicalize us, by acting as they have until now: chal-lenging us and making us uncomfortable. (Grzybowsky 2002)

Feminisms have penetrated these global spaces, fostering this alternative glob-alization with their proposals and bringing to the process their multiple experiences and connections. With a rich practice of international solidarity, progressively expressed in the Encuentros, and with their insertion in regional and global thematic and identity-based networks that took off during the United Nations conferences, feminisms have constantly expanded global networking. As Waterman notes, there is no doubt about the contribution of feminist thinkers of the seventies and eighties to what is considered today the movement for global justice, because much of this reflection on the new moment can be traced back to their previous international feminist practices (2002).

The feminisms that come together in the WSF are multiple and reflect diverse dynamics that represent innumerable nuances, strategies, and tendencies for confronting neoliberal globalization. With different ways of insertion and expression in the distinct forums held to date, feminists have participated in the organization of workshops, the presentation of panels, exchanges and alliances with other movements, and the development of global campaigns. They have also held leadership positions in distinct areas of the forum, such as in the International Council.[6] Regional and global networks also connect with other movements, promoting important global campaigns in each of the forums. One example is the campaign for the Global Charter for Women, from the World March of Women. Another is the Campaign against Fundamentalisms, People Are Fundamental, introduced by the Articulación Feminista Marcosur (AFM; Marcosur Feminist Organization), which broadens the analysis of fundamentalist practices and concepts to include "all the religious, economic, scientific or cultural expressions that attempt to deny the diversity of humanity, legitimizing violent methods of subjection of one group over another, and of one person over another" (AFM 2002).[7] Panels included Abortion into the Democratic Agenda, The Effects of Neoliberalism on the Lives of Women, and, to introduce a feminist perspective on growing militarization, Women against the War, the War against Women. The initiative of the Dialogue between Movements panels also deserves special mention. They were organized by a collection of networks from different regions of the world.[8] The panels began in Mumbai in 2004 and were repeated in Porto Alegre in 2005, bringing together trade unionists, dalits (known as "untouchables"), peasants, homosexuals, lesbians, and transsexuals in an open discussion of their diversity and differences as a point of departure for forging a common ground of emancipation.[9]

What is the feminist contribution toward radicalizing the forum, as Cándido Grzybowsky wishes? The WSF is home to a multiplicity of movements whose common ground is the struggle against the catastrophic consequences of neoliberalism. However, differences in ideas about how to proceed and from where to act create additional strife. A singular vision of the impact of neoliberalism and the dynamics of social change can result in the exclusion of other struggles, oriented through cultural meaning and other subversive ways in which democratic change is developed at local and global levels. For this reason, feminisms consider the WSF a place to make connections as well as a terrain of democratic dispute, where unilinear thinking and hegemonic inequalities and exclusions, that are also present in the forces and dynamics of change, can be confronted.

Feminists in the forum share an agenda with other social actors and movements, but due to their particular social positioning, other facets of their agenda are not easily espoused by these actors, making it necessary for feminists to explicitly state their case. Even in terms of their common goals against neoliberalism and militarism, the specific methods of action and aspects preferred also depend on the social position of the actor.[10]

However, there is another phenomena contingent to neoliberal globalization that particularly impacts women's lives and bodies. Fundamentalisms are today an axis of inequality and exclusion for women as people and citizens, shaping their body as a political site. They also stamp inequality and exclusion on the movements for sexual diversity and impact the struggle for sexual and reproductive rights, dimensions that are fundamental for the creation of "other possible worlds." However, the effects of fundamentalisms go beyond their impact on women. They also foster unilinear thinking and exclusionary, antidemocratic ways of dealing with difference and viewing the world. However, this corporal dimension, which highlights the embodied diversity of life experiences and subjectivities, is not yet considered a fundamental part of the transformative proposals in the WSF. And that is one of the feminist disputes within the WSF.

It has not been easy. Brother Betto, the prestigious liberation theologian, stated in one of the panels of the fifth forum that feminisms had been born and had disappeared in the twentieth century and therefore were not committed to the transformations proposed by the anti-neoliberal struggle. An open letter from Brazilian feminists circulated at the forum states that his words threw a vibrant and actively present movement into invisibility and nonexistence. "To make a political subject nonexistent is a grave sign of enormous arbitrariness and is contrary to the democratic practices of social struggles" (Open letter to Brother Betto 2005).

Viewpoints that ignore the presence of movements such as feminism feed on the idea that some political actors are more important than others. Such a vision of emancipation is simply based on nonemancipatory practices. The feminist fight against these exclusionary dynamics within the forum and the International Committee has been fierce. They aim to increase their visibility and democratize participation in panels and activities so that the concepts of "gender" and "diversity" are mainstreamed into the themes of the forum, and the struggle for "a better world" in the singular is broadened to "better worlds," thus expressing the diversity of emancipatory perspectives and proposals of liberation.[11]

Feminists, as well as other actors, have confronted these restricted viewpoints. This was evident in the most recent tensions in the WSF in 2005, when the Youth Camp confronted the forum organizers and the International Council for not including their interpretations and perspectives in the dynamics of the forum or its coordinating bodies.[12]

Nonetheless, being a space of dispute is one of the most valuable contributions of the WSF. The tensions and contradictions and their different levels of expression manifest a diversity of sensitivities and questioning that have emerged from the new scenarios of globalization. The conflicts are also raw material for the elaboration of more audacious proposals that broaden and link visions. These disputes have informed a new way of understanding democracy. Teivo Teivainen talks of the idea of demodiversity as a useful antidote against rigid and singular conceptions of democracy. He defines this demodiversity as the "peaceful or conflictive existence of different models and practices of democracy in a given social field" (2006, 63).

To influence this new construction of democracy, it is necessary to raise the profile of one's own contribution. This is the basis of the multiple strategies of feminists who come together at the forum, contributing and committing themselves to the struggles of other social movements, giving impetus to the forum, incorporating the politicized vision of democracy and change that feminism espouses, and promoting dialogue with other movements on the most sensitive dimensions of difference and the challenges of finding common ground. This is also a struggle for recognition. To achieve it, feminists have to politicize the differences, as Marta Rosemberg notes, celebrating the awareness of equality as a vehicle for justice and protecting the expressions of difference as an act of freedom (2002).

Difference as an act of freedom led to the inclusion of the Campaign against Fundamentalisms, with the feminist intention of making it a central theme of refection. This was evident in the press release that the AFM presented on the last day of the 2005 WSF, in the Women's Ship:

> The struggle for sexual freedom and abortion is one of the most extensive forms of opposition to fundamentalisms in the framework of the WSF. . . . To date equity in the forum has not been achieved. Main activities carried out by well-known male leaders reveal the need for the forum to be more democratic. . . . The AFM wants the WSF to be a radical, democratic experience, with equality among diverse people.[13] (AFM 2005)

This is also the proposal of feminists participating in the International Council of the WSF.

WSF Feminist Dialogues: Recognizing Difference

> As feminists we are aware that our bodies are imbued with cultural and social meanings, and our experience is also that women's bodies are key sites where many political and moral battles are fought. It is through women's bodies that the community, the state, the family, fundamentalist forces (state and non-state), religion and the market attempt to define themselves. These forces and institutions, through the plethora of patriarchal controls, transform women's bodies into expressions of power relations. Women's bodies, therefore, are at the heart of authoritarian and democratic proposals. (AFM 2005, 77)

The WSF has also been a learning experience for the group, offering methodological and political lessons, as well as the discovery of other viewpoints, knowledge, forms of questioning reality, and the possibility of achieving different results with the same strategies. It is enriching to know that the common causes of justice

Box 19.1

A collection of networks and organizations fomented a space at the WSF for dialogue among feminists from all over the world. Initiated in 2003, in Porto Alegre, Brazil, this first attempt led to the creation of the Feminist Dialogues in Mumbai, India, in 2004; Porto Alegre, in 2005; and Nairobi, Kenya, in 2007. A total of 180 women came together in Mumbai, 260 in Porto Alegre, and 200 in Nairobi, despite infrequent direct communication for many or prior participation in a global feminist dialogue, although they did have other forms of connectivity. The Feminist Dialogues sought to link feminist contributions to the main themes of the Forum (neoliberalism, militarism, etc.), adding the theme of fundamentalisms and placing the "body" at the center of a radical democracy.

and liberty do not necessarily require the same strategies or yield the same results, because this extends the limits of what is possible. A particularly significant example is the emphasis on abortion in India and Latin America. While for Latin American feminisms the struggle for abortion is a visible part of their political agenda, Indian feminists who have achieved its decriminalization are raising other questions. In their case, this expansion of freedom for women has turned against them, since the majority of women are aborting female embryos on a massive scale. This does not invalidate the struggle but it complicates feminist ventures. Every culture offers other resources and presents other challenges, and common issues can mean different risks and different solutions. All this raises doubts once again about universal solutions and unilinear thinking, while it enriches our horizons by posing new questions.

Conclusion

In the new millennium feminists are calling for the development of new paradigms, combining local, national, and global levels; the interconnection of multiple agendas; and the opportunity to introduce a deeper comprehension of justice that includes economic, social, cultural, and symbolic considerations. They also discuss the political contents and methods of social movements in global spaces such as the World Social Forum. They propose an integrated vision of the human condition and of possible transformations as part of a new cultural politics of social movements. This vision contributes to the deconstruction of the dichotomy between primary and secondary struggles and the consequent separation of the economic, the political, the cultural, the social, and the subjective. In this way, sexuality and equity become an integral part of movements for economic justice and the deepening of democracy. The recognition of these differences and the inclusion of these dimensions in building a new paradigm of emancipation are fundamental for achieving "other worlds" and stand out as one of the most significant contributions of feminisms to their construction.

NOTES

1. Beck employs a historical definition of the cosmopolitan being: he or she who lives in a double country and maintains a double loyalty, as a citizen of the "cosmos" and as a citizen of the "polis" (2004, 70).

2. Frameworks, states Jelin, denote schemes of interpretation that allow individuals to locate, perceive, identify, and label—that is to say, understand and apprehend—events in their daily life and in the wider world. Frameworks organize experience and guide individual and collective action, helping to evaluate events. These frameworks are neither consensual nor singular. There can be different interpretive frameworks in a historical moment, competing or in conflict with each other, challenging hegemonic frameworks and suggesting alternative courses of action (2003, 41). It is an active process of cultural construction.

3. It was demonstrated in the Report of the Truth Commission of Peru how women's bodies were also an unrecognized, naturalized battlefield of war (Comisión de la Verdad y la Reconciliación 2003). One dramatic example of racial discrimination is that most women who were raped in Peru's civil war were Quechua-speaking Indians or of Indian descent, and also the majority of the victims were from the indigenous Andean regions, which are the poorest in the nation. This brutal story has also been confirmed in Guatemala, the ex-Yugoslavia, and many other places.

4. An antecedent of the new dynamics of global mobilization is undoubtedly Mexico's Zapatista Movement of 1994. However, the WSF should be considered the main facilitator of the major global mobilizations that began in Seattle (1999) at the end of the twentieth century and are continuing in many other points around the globe.

5. The WSF's capacity to reflect on itself, centering on the exclusions and tensions present in the use of power, has resulted in a permanent process of transformation. One of the most significant changes has been the radical modification of the forum's methodology, taking away decision-making power from the International Council and committing to strengthening a facilitating process, basically self-managed, with consultation and dialogue among the different actors. Another substantial modification has been brought about by the internationalization of the WSF beginning in 2004, with its relocation from Brazil to Mumbai, India, and the organization of three polycentric World Social Forums in January of 2006 (in Venezuela for Latin America, Pakistan for Asia, and Mali for Africa). In 2007 the WSF took place in Nairobi, Africa, and returned to Brazil in 2008.

6. It is interesting to note that in the International Council there is an active presence of a small number of feminist networks that make a substantial contribution to the ongoing democratization of the WSF. They include the AFM from Latin America; the World March of Women, worldwide; the Red de Mujeres Transformando la Economía (Network of Women Transforming the Economy) from Latin America; African Women's Development and Communication Network (FEMNET) from Africa; Development Alternatives with Women for a New Era (DAWN), worldwide; the Red de Educación Popular entre Mujeres (Network of Popular Education among Women) from Latin America; the Ashkara Network from India; the LGBT South-South Network, worldwide; among others.

7. Launched at the WSF in 2002 by the AFM of Latin America, the Campaign against Fundamentalisms is now a global campaign.

8. The organizations and networks that initiated these panels are Ashkara, Women's International Coalition for Economic Justice, AFM, FEMNET, DAWN, and Inform from Sri Lanka.

9. This experience, initiated in the Mumbai Forum in 2004 and repeated in the forum in 2005, is in keeping with the forum's new methodology, which seeks to bring together and promote dialogue between different networks and movements interested in achieving an exchange of strategies and proposals.

10. In the case of militarism, aside from confronting a violent culture that privileges war, feminists focus on the implications of war for women's bodies. Neoliberalism not only makes

work flexible, it also allocates to the private sphere social welfare obligations that should be provided by the state. This increases women's workload and responsibilities, as they are expected to be the guardians of the family, health, and so on.

11. This dispute has been evident since the first WSF, where the presence of women was greater numerically than that of men, but their participation in the public panels was little more than 10 percent. In the second WSF a few feminists managed to organize some panels, but the responsibility for organizing the central themes (each of them bringing together six or seven large-scale panels) remained in the hands of men. In the third WSF, two of the five themes of the forum were organized by two feminist networks and movements: the AFM and the World March of Women.

12. The Youth Camp has existed since the first forum. It is autonomous in many ways, based on an ecological mode of organization and principles of economic solidarity (Teivainen 2006). In the 2005 WSF, one of the global networks organized a panel in the Youth Camp as a dialogue between them and members of the International Council. The criticisms raised by the Youth movement were harsh: lack of transparency, weakening of the principles of economic solidarity and the ecological premise, and failing to provide a "friendly space" in terms of spatial organization. A case of rape in the Youth Camp was also reported.

13. The Ship was organized by the Campaign against Fundamentalisms, providing a space for diverse activists, workshops, debates, and exhibitions on a wide range of themes, such as water as a scarce resource, and even debates led by and with some transvestites and transsexuals.

REFERENCES

AFM. 2002. Campaign against Fundamentalisms, People are Fundamental Declaration. www .mujeresdelsur-afm.org.uy/index_i.htm.

————. 2005. Forummmentalisms: The contradiction of the World Social Forum 2005. http:// mujeresdelsur-afm.org.uy/index_i.htm.

Alvarez, Sonia. 1998. Latin American feminisms go global: Trend of the 1990s and challenges for the new millennium. In *Cultures of politics/politics of cultures: Re-visioning Latin American social movements*, ed. Sonia Alvarez, Evelina Dagñino, and Arturo Escobar, 293–324. Boulder, CO: Westview.

Articulación Feminista Brasilera. 2005. Open letter to Brother Betto/Carta abierta a Frei Betto. Letter circulated at the World Social Forum 2005. Porto Alegre, Brazil.

Ávila, María Betania, ed. 2001. Feminismo, ciudadanía e transformação social. In *Textos e imagens do feminismo: Mulheres construindo a igualdade*, ed. María Betania Ávila. Recife, Brazil: SOS Corpo.

Beck, Ulrich. 2004. *Poder y contrapoder en la era global: La nueva economía política mundial.* Barcelona: Paidós.

Belluci, Mabel, and Flavio Raspisardi. 1999. Alrededor de la identidad: Las luchas políticas del presente. *Revista Nueva Sociedad*, no. 162:41–53.

Bonan, Claudia. 2001. Política y conocimiento del cuerpo y la estructuración moderna del sistema género. Rio de Janeiro: Universidad Federal de Rio de Janeiro. www.ufrj.br/.

Cairo Carou, Heriberto. 2000. Jano desorientado: Identidades político-territoriales en América Latina. *Leviatán*, no. 79:107–111.

Castells, Manuel. 1999. Los efectos de la globalización en América Latina por el autor de "La era de la información." *Insomnia: Separata Cultural*, June 29.

Celiberti, Lilian. 2001. Retos para una nueva cultura política. *Lola Press*, no. 15. www.lolapress .org/iv/lo15.htm.

Comisión de la Verdad y la Reconciliación. 2003. Informe final 2003. Lima, Peru. www.cverdad .org.pe/ifinal/index.php.

Concept Note of the Feminist Dialogues. Feminist visions and strategies. *Feminist dialogues 2005 report*, app. 2, 77–78. Porto Alegra, Brazil. http://feministdialogue.isiswomen.org/index.php?option=comcontent&view=article&id=27&Itemid=124.

Correa, Sonia. 2002. Globalización y fundamentalismo: Un paisaje de género. In *Alternativas de desarrollo con mujeres para una nueva era*, 1–3. Abordando el Foro Social Mundial. Suplemento Red DAWN, Porto Alegre, Brazil. www.dawnnet.org.

De Souza Santos, Boaventura. 2002. In search of a global citizenship: Interview with Boaventura de Souza Santos. *Lola Press* 18 (November). www.lolapress.org/index/lastissue.htm.

Fraser, Nancy. 1997. *Justitia interrupta: Reflexiones críticas desde la posición "postsocialista."* Bogotá: Siglo del Hombre Editores, Facultad de Derecho, Universidad de los Andes.

Garrido, Lucy. 2002. ¿Quién quiere tener género cuando puede tener sexo? *Revista Estudos Feministas* 11 (2): 599–607. Universidade Federal do Rio de Janeiro.

Grzybowsky, Cándido. 2002. ¿Es posible un mundo más femenino? *Foro Social Mundial*, January 31–February 5. www.forosocialmundial.org.

Harcourt, Wendy, and Arturo Escobar. 2007. Las practicas de la diferencia. Introduction to *Las mujeres y las políticas de lugar*, 11–26. Mexico City: PUEG, UNAM.

Hardt, Michael. 2002. Soberanía nacional y militancias en red. *Clarín* (Argentina), March 23.

Human Development Report, Chile. 2000. Towards a stronger society to govern the future: Social capital and citizenship UNDP. Santiago, Chile. www.hdr.undp.org/nationalreports/chile.

Jelin, Elizabeth. 2003. La escala de la acción de los movimientos sociales. In *Mas allá de la nación: Las escalas múltiples de los movimientos sociales*, ed. Omar Arach, Máximo Badaró, Karina Bidaseca, and Elizabeth Jelin. Buenos Aires: Libros del Zorzal.

Kirkwood, Julieta. 1986. *Ser política en Chile: Las feministas y los partidos*. Santiago: Latin American Faculty of Social Science.

Lechner, Norbert. 2007. La (problemática) invocación de la sociedad civil. In *Norbert Lechner obras escogidas*, 305–317. Vol. 2 of *Colección pensadores latinoamericanos*. Santiago, Chile: LOM.

Maffia, Diana. 2001. Ciudadanía sexual: Aspectos legales y políticos de los derechos reproductivos como derechos humanos. *Feminaria* 14 (26): 27–28.

Melucci, Alberto. 2001. *Vivencia y convivencia: Teoría social para una era de la información*. Madrid: Trotta.

Mouffe, Chantal. 1996. Feminismo, ciudadanía y política democrática radical. In *Las ciudadanas y lo político*, ed. Elena Beltrán and Cristina Sánchez, 1–20. Madrid: Woman's Studies Institute, Autonomous University of Madrid.

PNUD. 2004. Informe sobre democracia en América Latina. www.undp.org/spanish/informeProddal.html.

Rosemberg, Marta. 2002. Struggling for sexual and reproductive rights: The case of the Second World Social Forum, Porto Alegre 2002. Transnational Alternativas. www.tni.org/tat.

Sanchís, Norma. 2004. Fundamentalismo económico, fundamentalismo del mercado. Foro Social de las Américas. Articulación Feminista Marcosur. www.mujeresdelsur-afm.org.uy/fsm/2004/f_ame_ns.htm.

Slater, David. 1998. Rethinking the spatialities of social movements: Questions of (b)orders, culture, and politics in global times. In *Cultures of politics/politics of cultures: Re-visioning Latin American social movements*, ed. Sonia Alvarez, Evelina Dagnino, and Arturo Escobar, 380–401. Boulder, CO: Westview.

Tamayo, Giulia. 1997. La "cuestión de la ciudadanía" y la experiencia de paridad. Centro Flora Tristán, Lima, Peru. Documento inédito.

Teivainen, Teivo. 2003. Pedagogía del poder mundial: Relaciones internacionales y lecciones del desarrollo en América Latina. Manuscript. Programa Democracia y Transformación Global, Universidad Nacional Mayor de San Marcos, Lima, Peru.

————. 2006. *Global civil society in action: Dilemmas of democratization in the World Social Forum.* London: Routledge.

Vargas, Virginia, and Lilian Celiberti. 2005a. Los nuevos escenarios: Los nuevos/viejos sujetos y los nuevos paradigmas de los feminismos globales. Articulación Feminista Marcosur. www.mujeresdelsur.org/publicaciones.

————. 2005b. La tensión entre universalidad y particularidad. Articulación Feminista Marcosur. www.mujeresdelsur.org-afm.org.uy/publicaciones.

Waterman, Peter. 2002. What's Left internationally and what is to be done about it? www .labournet.de/diskussion/wipo/seattle/whatsLeft.html.

————. 2004. The global justice and solidarity movement and the ESF: A backgrounder. In *Challenging empires: World Social Forum,* ed. Jai Sen, Anita Anand, Arturo Escobar, and Peter Waterman, 55–66. New Delhi: Viveka Foundation.

PART VII

CONCLUDING CONSIDERATIONS

20

Concluding Reflections

RENEGOTIATING GENDER IN LATIN
AMERICA AND THE CARIBBEAN

ELIZABETH MAIER

Context, Identities, and Strategies

Four decades is just a historical wink of the eye, and yet in Latin America and the Caribbean women's lives have changed significantly. Presently, women are almost 40 percent of the workforce. They make up approximately 28 percent of regional emigration. The mother/child ratio has been reduced by half over the past thirty years, now at 2.6 children per woman. Women marry later, have their first child later, and 80 percent use some method of family planning. Girls are on relatively equal educational footing with boys in primary and secondary levels, and in some countries even surpass male participation in careers requiring a university degree.[1] Though still in striking disadvantage in most national political arenas, female political representation has grown notably during these last decades, doubling from only 8 percent in 1990 to 16 percent in 2005 (ECLAC 2006). While many of these changes are anchored in women's national and global agency in favor of gender-equitable societies, the impact of hegemonic free-market economic policies has also brought major changes for women.

The time frame of this book functions as both a real and symbolic reference for analyzing gender relations and sexual politics in the region. It celebrates the beginnings of second-wave feminism in many Latin America and Caribbean countries in the 1970s, as the impetus of a new civilizatory discourse that has progressively permeated the collective cultural imaginary of the area. It underlines the importance of the United Nations–sponsored World Conference on Women, held in Mexico City (1975); the first international Women's Year (1975–1976); and the Women's Decade (1975–1985) as watershed events that institutionalized the development of globally recognized instruments to address women's inequality, while propelling sexual politics into the regional cultural conversation. This eventually led to what we could call Latin American and Caribbean third-wave feminism—or complex identity feminism—beginning in the eighties with the lesbian movement, popular feminism, and the Afro-Latin and Afro-Caribbean women's movements and continuing in the nineties with indigenous women's movements. This time span coincides with the neoliberal economic experiment, initiated with the Chilean military coup of 1973, a model that has since dominated much of the economic activity and mind-set in the region, causing radical social reorganization and informing the reconfiguration of family, gender roles, and gender relations.

Thus, women's increasing public, economic, and political presence in Latin American and Caribbean societies—and their growing awareness and resistance to their traditional, subaltern social position—corresponds to the dynamics of particular historical, political, developmental, and cultural circumstances that have fashioned identity politics, informed strategies, resignified representations of femininity, and contributed to the gradual democratization of families and nations. Whether immersed in the local tensions of the geopolitical dynamics of the cold war paradigm, linked to the cultural evolution of a minority—but increasingly consolidated—middle class, or embedded in the profound economic, political, and technological transformations of late modernity, the range of women's agency reflects the economic, social, cultural and political diversity that is the upshot of the region's complex history. Although class, race, sexual orientation, and ethnicity have undoubtedly tattooed disparate needs and priorities onto women's lives and struggles over these decades, the presence and extension of democracy on the national scene has also been a key factor in forging differential experiences of womanhood, shaping new female representations in some cases and resignifying traditional gender roles with a more public and valued meaning in others.

Feminist movements irrupted onto the sociopolitical scene of the seventies in formally democratic countries such as Mexico, Venezuela, and Costa Rica, demanding the denaturalization of gender inequality, the unbinding of social and cultural controls that repressed the female body, and the politicization of issues considered to belong to the private realm.[2] Southern Cone dictatorships of the same period unintentionally spawned iconoclastic representations of political motherhood, as Mothers and Grandmothers redefined maternity as a collective, public, and militant activity in defense of their disappeared children (Di Marco, chs. 5, 9; Maier, both in this volume). During the same period, repressive Central American regimes gave rise to women's growing activism in grassroots, opposition support networks, while female guerrillas and commanders forged new representations of fearless women in positions of authority, risking their lives for their vision of a more equitable society.

These novel representations of womanhood have played an important role in remaking cultural sense of gender in the region. They have disputed traditional gender beliefs of feminine fragility, public incapacity, dependency, and powerlessness and, together with progressively increasing educational and economic participation, have influenced the profile of gender mandates in Latin American and Caribbean societies (Herrera; Di Marco, ch. 5; Kampwirth; Maier, all in this volume).[3] These political contexts should be viewed as prime incubators of the female social actors who have *resituated women's place in society* and contributed in representational and discursive terms to advancing gender equity in the region, but electoral democracy is the political regime in which gender-based, autonomous women's movements emerged and flourished.[4] Increased women's agency has been situated within the extensive transformations experienced by Latin American and Caribbean societies over the past four decades, and that very agency has impelled even more changes, thus highlighting the intimate dialectic tension among context, identity, and strategy in the constitution and consolidation of social actors (Alvarez et al. 1998) and in the revision of gender patterns.

With proxy wars—secret and declared—playing out cold war scenarios in many Latin American countries, the emergent vigor of global capitalism and its growing hegemony on the world horizon, together with the sudden demise of the world socialist order, deeply influenced the recent course of regional history. Some of these unanticipated circumstances contributed to the consolidation of electoral democracy in South America, while others accelerated the peace processes of the Central American civil wars and imposed a radical restructuring of national economies, which posited differential opportunities and challenges for women according to their social and cultural positioning. The revised international division of labor has reorganized social relations in the region over the last decades, resulting in mounting disparity between an enriched, privileged, and globalized minority and an increasingly impoverished, vulnerable, and excluded majority, ever more dependent on a combination of women's paid and unpaid labor for its daily and generational reproduction. Finally, advances in communications technology have also been crucial in promoting feminist agendas and equity strategies, facilitating global, regional, national, and local interconnection among feminist organizations, women's movements, and international institutions and playing a central role in extending and consolidating the influence of this first globalized, sociocultural movement of late modernity.

These profound political, economic, social, and technological transformations have fashioned the conditions in which women's socioeconomic, political, and cultural contributions to local and national development have been progressively recognized and valued, as their workload has increased. Gender roles are gradually being interrogated and revised through a range of overlapping processes, which include women's agency in all areas, gender-oriented public policy, and neoliberal economic restructuring (Macaulay; Tarrés; Colón and Poggio, all in this volume). However, contrary to these notable changes in women's public roles, Pierre Bourdieu's notion of *habitus* (1996, 16) still explains intimate and familial relationships between men and women as marked by voluntary and reflective resistance by both men and women to reorganizing traditional power structures in more equitable terms (Herrera; Núñez, both in this volume).[5] This is exemplified by the consensual reproduction of traditional masculine symbolic capital within the Cuban family, in spite of women's growing economic and professional power in the public sphere and the existence of comprehensive, legal guarantees for full gender equity (Núñez, this volume).[6]

Globalization and Women's Work:
Reconsidering the Gender Division of Labor

Economic restructuring, inherent to neoliberal globalization, has reframed the gender division of labor, becoming progressively more dependent on women's undervalued workforce to generate extraordinary corporative profits through direct means—and indirectly from domestic and family work—and also through the downward pressuring of the general value of the workforce (Hite and Viterna 2005, quoted in Safa, this volume). In Latin America and the Caribbean, these last three decades have witnessed a radical, shock-doctrine (Klein 2007) transition from protectionist, internal market economies to free-market, privatized, state-trimmed systems, whose main comparative advantage has been cheap labor, both as a domestic and export commodity (Safa; Colón and Poggio, both in this volume). Women have been essential in cementing this mammoth transition. Although their economic participation is not homogenous, and an increase in female employment has been registered in white-collar service and professional slots as well as unskilled labor, undoubtedly the majority of women are situated in the least protected, most unstable, and worst-paid occupations of the global economy. They are particularly prominent in the precarious zones of the maquiladora industry; the flexible, temporary work arrangements in the formal sector; industrialized agriculture; domestic employment; and the variety of informal occupations of self-employment that Latin American and Caribbean women invent everyday as part of their multifaceted survival strategies (Colón and Poggio, this volume).

Growing economic participation has had positive and negative effects on women's lives. For some, it has made them less dependent on men, offering more relative autonomy, self-esteem, and a growing sense of entitlement. This is especially—but not exclusively—true among educated, professional women, who have accrued greater social and personal capital with which to renegotiate conditions and power within gender relations and family. However, considering that individual income for the vast majority of the population does not guarantee self-sufficiency, but rather is only a part of collective, household survival strategies that depend on multiple incomes, minimum-wage salaries in Latin America and the Caribbean do not offer the same freedom and autonomy for working-class women. While paid work resignifies women socially as productive agents and boosts gender value in general terms, the ambivalent effects of bottom-rung, precarious employment have demonstrated in the Caribbean and other female-centered labor markets, for example, that fragile working conditions, inadequate salaries, lack of labor and human rights guarantees, and absence of government support systems all impact family cohesion, marriage, and household organization (Safa, this volume).

Although women in Latin American and Caribbean societies have increasingly entered traditional male domains of paid labor, they have not yet broken the glass ceilings of management and leadership in most walks of life. Equally, men have not yet assumed a comparative share of women's traditional responsibilities with housework, child care, family nurturing, and household administration (Colón and Poggio; Herrera; Núñez; Safa, all in this volume). For working women this has meant bearing the brunt of double and triple workdays and compounding roles and tasks within and outside the home, as well as assuming the main responsibility for most facets of everyday family reproduction, including constant participation in the increasingly complex web of public and private institutions devoted to family welfare. Some scholars have suggested that the shift to neoliberal globalization in Latin America and the Caribbean has been contingent on women's extended and intensified workdays, with serious costs for their physical and mental health (Maier 2006, 411; Colón and Poggio, this volume).

This has been especially evident in local assembly economies, like the maquiladora zones of northern Mexico, Puerto Rico, the Dominican Republic, and El Salvador, where the lack of demand for male workers has undermined their traditional gender role as providers, often resulting in the fragmentation and reorganization of nuclear or extended families; fostering male absence through migration, separation, divorce, abandonment, or substance abuse; and exacerbating violent behavior toward women and children. As such, the new global modality of capitalist reproduction seems to suggest a tendency in developing economies toward the disintegration of the nuclear, working-class family and the rise of a new extended family structure, with resignified gender roles, as well as single-parent families.

While volatile transnational capital easily uproots itself and migrates to more investment-attractive parts of the world, continuing trends in female-oriented employment in the global workforce press Latin American and Caribbean women to immigrate to more dynamic international labor markets. Women's migration has also had profound implications for family and gender relations. In the Dominican Republic, for example, the tendency to substitute marriage and patriarchal family models for collective, matrifocal family arrangements and the feminization of working-class, family, and child-care support networks is the apparent upshot of world economic reorganization (Safa, this volume). On the other hand, immigrating female workers are positioned in the lowest echelons of the receiving societies, providing support systems for middle- and upper-class families, while contributing with substandard salaries and lack of benefits to reducing the production costs of industrialized agriculture and to maintaining competitive advantages of national industries that otherwise would be unable to contend with low-cost production in developing countries (Colón and Poggio, this volume).

Contrasted with their agency to secure better living conditions for their families and themselves, the extreme vulnerability of undocumented female immigrants is emblematic of the plight of the so-called losers of this modern-day, metaphoric game of musical chairs that our precarious era of "liquid modernity" (Bauman 2006) has staked out for the poorest of the global economy. This marginalized social positioning leaves these transnational workers with notoriously less freedom of choice, opportunities, and benefits than enjoyed by those at higher ranks of the pyramid of power (12–13). This fragility is compounded for women in transterritorial situations, as exemplified by myriad victims of "migrant-rape" during this modern-day Middle Passage or by the terrifying web of the transnational sex trade, which has enslaved tens of thousands of unwitting women and has flourished in the shade of global economics (Colón and Poggio, this volume).

Thus, paradoxically, while the past four decades have witnessed advances in the discourses on women's political citizenship globally and nationally, Latin American and Caribbean countries have also registered notorious declines in key aspects of social citizenship, with growing poverty, lack of state-sponsored social services, overwork, diminishing labor rights, treacherous transits to international labor markets, and the economic and political disenfranchisement of undocumented workers (Merlet; Colón and Poggio, both in this volume). The discord between political and social citizenship hampers the effective exercise of citizenship for the great majority of women. At the same time, these disparities show how the intersection of gender and class inscribes distinct discursive texts on women's bodies and lives, ultimately fashioning differential needs, interests, opportunities, and choices.

Focusing exclusively on gender equity without also attending to the intersection of gender, class, ethnicity, and race within the global structure cannot achieve gender equality. Rather, official strategies need to take account of the gender consequences of economic restructuring and offer support programs for women that ease the burden of multiple workloads and intersected role demands; job (re)training programs for unemployed men that include components of gender sensitivity that explore masculine dissatisfaction created by contemporary changes in gender relations; and, above all, permanent educational campaigns and programs highlighting gender-equity values and strategies. At the same time, new definitions of family and family relations are required in national legislations, so as to protect the diversity of family models that coexist in contemporary societies and to guarantee equitable relationships among their members (Safa, this volume).

Similarity and Difference: The Political
Challenges of Complex Identities

Our era of uncertainty and mobility has also repositioned and resignified cultural identity in Latin America and the Caribbean, defining "who we are, and who I am" in the tension between local roots and traditions and the broader, more complex frontiers of transnational scenarios and interconnectivity. Local identities have been strengthened by collective awareness, mounting self-esteem, and agency that have given rise to powerful female multidimensional sociopolitical actors. In many instances, they have been decisive in channeling national politics toward new appreciations of equality and justice, by redressing traditional ethnic, racial, and class positions with a gender perspective while injecting the specificities of ethnicity and race into national feminist and women's agendas (Prieto et al.; Di Marco, ch. 9; Caldwell; Lebon, all in this volume). Equally, dissident sexual identities have emerged from the social shadows of modernity to interrogate hegemonic discourses of homogenous heterosexuality (Mogrovejo, this volume).

Indigenous women, Afro-Latinas, lesbians, and working-class women have had to juggle more than one dimension of social subordination in naming their needs, defining their priorities, designing their strategies, and identifying their allies. As such, their political action invokes a complicated process of recognizing the mechanics of overlapping and compounded dimensions of exclusion, domination, and power in specific Latin American and Caribbean contexts (Caldwell; Lebon, both in this volume). Their agency has forged new discourses of human rights and citizenship that underscore diversity as the emblematic value of late modernity and situate similarity and difference among women as a tensioned dialectic in constant dispute and negotiation.[7]

Certainly, the region's periodical feminist Encuentros have been emblematic laboratories for disputing and defining the margins and bridges between difference and sameness. Since the Cuarto Encuentro Feminista de América Latina y el Caribe (Fourth Latin American and Caribbean Feminist Encuentro) in Taxco, Mexico, in 1987, the relatively homogeneous composition of Latin American and Caribbean feminisms has been interrogated by women who were not sure that they were feminists but were certain of their right to be included in the regional puzzle that explored and defined women's needs, opinions, and desires. Since then, the explicit contrasting of identities, perspectives, goals, and strategies has tended to be more effective in reconfirming particular perspectives of specific female sectors than it has been in building consensus among the diversity of women. Nevertheless, the very circulation of distinct discourses of womanhood and the contact among diverse groups of women, as tenuous as that may be in some cases (Prieto et al.; Carrillo and Chinchilla, both in this volume), has generated awareness of each other's positions (Carrillo and Chinchilla; Di Marco, ch. 9; Kampwirth, all in this volume).

This tension between diversity and similarity has both characterized and challenged women's sociopolitical participation. Diversity brought conflict to the region's feminist movement, questioning the utopian idea of sisterhood and confronting priorities, objectives, and perspectives. Nonetheless, this multiplicity of female actors contesting and negotiating common ground and, in the best of cases, mutually sensitizing each other to disparate positions should be considered the women's movement's greatest attribute and most significant contribution to the international feminist movement (Vargas and Wieringa 1998, 178).

While difference among women has been addressed in all United Nations conventions and conferences since the first one on women in 1975, it was at the International Conference on Women, in Beijing in 1995, that the strategy of mainstreaming was institutionalized as a methodology for dealing with it in public policy. With increasing contemporary recognition of the complexities of identity and new multidimensional collective actors emerging onto the Latin American and Caribbean political scene, difference has become a constant presence in the debates of the region's women's movement. Nonetheless, recognition of diversity has not yet translated into effective mechanisms for collaborative dialogue, leaving difference to trump sisterhood in determining priorities, strategies, and allies (Carrillo and Chinchilla 2006; Prieto et al., this volume; Rakowski and Espina, this volume).

Particularly challenging for feminists are divergent positions related to reproductive and sexual rights, given their recognition of how the female body is disciplined into being a political body by patriarchal power shaping its sexuality and reproductive capacity (Vargas, this volume), and the inalienable bond between those rights and feminist agendas (Carrillo and Chinchilla, this volume). That these rights are at the core of the contemporary dispute for cultural meaning between feminisms and fundamentalisms also makes this issue especially difficult

(Maier 2006, 419). However, this only indicates the need to prioritize the promotion of inclusive spaces of dialogue among the distinct expressions of the Latin American and Caribbean women's movements, so as to better understand each other and identify points of convergence and divergence in the elaboration of shared strategies among women.

The Dialectics of National, Regional, and International Agency

Feminisms have exhibited a singular capacity to foster synergy between women's rights activists, feminist theoreticians, and international functionaries in the promotion of a global agenda of gender equity. United Nations conferences centering on women's rights and other major themes of late modernity, such as population, development, human rights, racial and ethnic diversity, and the environment, exemplify the efficacy of *transversal* proposals in the advancement of gender equality, while being instrumental in developing a framework of premises, rights, and obligations for a progressively more democratic and sustainable global culture. For Latin American and Caribbean countries, United Nations conferences, conventions, and action plans have been pivotal in promoting women's organizing, disseminating gender consciousness, championing equity-oriented public policy, and stimulating regional thematic networks that have assured greater interconnectivity, specialization, and political effectiveness in deconstructing gender inequality (Herrera; Macaulay; Kampwirth; Vargas, all in this volume).

Regional involvement in this exercise of global citizenship has reverberated on various levels: (1) it has symbolically represented Latin American and Caribbean women as major players on national and international scenes, (2) it has effectively promoted gender policies linked to the needs and interests of women of the region, and (3) it has served as a training ground for local civil society representatives to accrue political know-how and clout, forging capable political operators committed to promoting gender-sensitive national policies and legislation (Herrera; Macaulay; Kampwirth; Vargas, all in this volume).

Both regional women's interests and lessons learned through local activism have equally informed an increasing global gender agenda, contributing culture-specific context and content to the building of universal instruments of gender equality. The regional contribution toward understanding the effects of war on advancing women's empowerment and gender equity has been noteworthy, pitting the symbolic importance of resignifying female representations against postponing gender-centered demands and movements, reproducing hierarchical gender relations, and generally returning women to their traditional roles once the crisis is over (Herrera; Kampwirth, both in this volume). Understanding the gender causes of violence against women and its insertion as an international human rights issue has also been particularly significant (Sagot, this volume). Similarly, Latin American and Caribbean women's movements have been decisive in exposing the effects of neoliberal globalization on women (Colón and Poggio; Vargas, both in this volume), detailing the influence of the Catholic Church on reproductive and sexual rights (Navarro and Mejía, this volume), and recognizing the intersecting nature of economic, religious, and moral fundamentalisms (Vargas, this volume).

The Convention on the Elimination of All Forms of Discrimination against Women (CEDAW), considered the foundational, global constitution of women's rights, has been a fundamental framework for all levels of women's agency in the region. The United Nations International Conference on Population and Development, held in Cairo in 1994, provided a new and integral discourse on reproductive rights, in a geographic area of overwhelming Catholic hegemony, assigning sexuality relative autonomy from reproduction and orienting national population policies toward offering necessary information and services for women to decide if, when, and with what frequency to have children (Kampwirth, this volume). The United Nations World Conference on Human Rights, held in Vienna in 1993, democratized the paradigm itself, recognizing women's rights as human rights and incorporating the personal and intimate spheres as geographies of rights violations. For this part of the world that midwifed human rights militancy by documenting the atrocities of the dictatorships of the seventies and eighties, this expansion of the human rights perspective allowed many of these very actors to come to terms with the rights violations silenced or rendered invisible in their own lives (Di Marco, chs. 5, 9; Herrera; Maier, all in this volume). The regional norm prohibiting violence toward women, as expressed in the Organization of American States' Inter-American Convention on the Prevention, Punishment, and Eradication of Violence against Women (1994), has been imperative in bringing about national laws in most countries of the area, with more severe consequences for perpetrators specified in Costa Rican legislation, where unyielding feminist agency finally achieved fuller criminalization of gender violence in 2007 (Sagot, this volume). Finally, gender mainstreaming, one of the pillars of the 1995 Plan of Action, from the Fourth United Nations World Conference on Women, has been central to constituting women's secretariats and institutes in all Latin America and Caribbean nations and in propelling gender equity into the pulse of national agendas.

Gender Agency: Autonomy and Mainstreaming

During the first decades of second-wave feminisms, autonomy was the pivotal premise of the Latin American and Caribbean movements: autonomy from the state, from political parties and other sociopolitical organizations, and from ubiquitous gender hierarchies that permeate all social institutions in the region.[8] Women's consciousness-raising groups provided sheltered environments for individual and collective rediscovery, offering secure frameworks in which to share and analyze individual life experience within the context of the cultural reproduction of gender inequality (Maier, this volume).

The new global and regional conditions of the nineties favored the promotion of mainstreaming gender equity into public policy. Mainstreaming is a strategy that assures that concerns for gender equity inform the design, implementation, monitoring, and evaluation of all public policy (United Nations 2001, 7). This new premise implied a sweeping change of strategic course for regional feminisms, repositioning the geography of transformation from individual women or small groups to the domains of political negotiations, thematic specialization, and the formulation of public policy.[9] While promising to broaden the influence of feminist agency by embedding a gendered vision into national and local laws and policies, it also threatened to dilute the more radical feminist initiative of gender transformation, given the political negotiations and consensus implicit in mainstreaming. Furthermore, it foresaw a deeper segmentation of the region's women's movement, by benefiting an already privileged sector of educated advisers and top-echelon functionaries. The dispute between feminists on different sides of this strategic divide has deeply marked regional feminism and personal relationships among women activists over the past fifteen years. While the majority of feminists fully favors entering the public policy arena, the *autonomous* feminist tendency has maintained its opposition, highlighting concerns about goals, ethics, orientation, and the very essence of the movement (Mogrovejo, this volume).

However, rather than conceiving them as competing proposals, the chapters in this book emphasize a double-pronged strategy that complements mainstreaming agency with organizational methodologies that allow women to caucus and deliberate autonomously within—and outside of—mixed contexts.[10] As such, Latin American and Caribbean feminists have been able to rely on the virtues of autonomy without the risks of social isolation, while extending their range of action to a broader spectrum of the population. In some instances, this has meant coordinating among women's groups, legislators, and functionaries (Herrera; Macaulay; Rakowski and Espina, all in this volume). In others, it has signified articulating gender policies in multiple government dependencies (Macaulay; Tarrés, both in this volume). Yet in others, it has resulted in the demand for specific policies that respond to the needs of women who have overlapping dimensions of social exclusion (Caldwell; Di Marco, ch. 9; Prieto et al.; Rakowski and Espina, all in this volume). In counties such as Brazil, a flexible combination of all of these strategies has resulted in a multifaceted "trickling up, down, and sideways" offer of political opportunity for gender agency (Macaulay, this volume).[11]

Nonetheless, institutionalizing gender equity has also proven to be risky. Partisan politics and political dependency hamper the authenticity and effectiveness of gender politics, interrogating the scope and scale of autonomy with which women's institutional machinery operates (Kampwirth; Rakowski and Espina; Tarrés, all in this volume). In Mexico, for example, political affiliation shapes women's institutes, programs, and policies with differential gender ideologies (Tarrés, this volume). Some have fully assimilated the "gender perspective," in accordance with the range of objectives of United Nations conventions and accords, while others subtly promote the "family perspective," based on traditional gender relations and values, but skillfully employ gender-equity discourses to suggest international compliance. This dispute for control of women's bureaucracies and gender politics highlights the centrality of human reproduction and sexuality in the contemporary ideological contest, while illustrating the sociocultural process of transforming women's biology into a political tug-of-war between differing ideologies.

The meaning and implications of autonomy have also been up for debate in countries based on corporatist state models, where the amalgamation of state apparatuses, government functions, mass social organizations, and a dominant political party determines the orientation and priorities of all public policy. Doubts about the role of populist tactics and the subordination of gender to class identity and other political interests, along with the growing lack of autonomy, have been expressed by some feminists in Venezuela, for example (Rakowski and Espina, this volume). However, tensions between feminist perspectives and government gender policy in both Sandinista Nicaragua in the late 1980s and Venezuela's present-day Bolivarian Revolution do not seem to invalidate patent advances toward more gender-equitable societies in these very countries (Kampwirth; Rakowski and Espina, both in this volume). This is particularly evident in Venezuela today, where even opposition feminists have insisted on preserving all the gender-policy achievements of the Chavez government in the event of a change in political administration (Rakowski and Espina, this volume). However, government focus on the needs of the vast majority of poorer women and the synergy created in defense of the regime only underscores the importance of other identity dimensions in fashioning political loyalties and programmatic priorities and in identifying allies for women (Maier 2006, 418).

The Cuban experience seems to reconfirm the efficiency of a statist model in putting into place full legal guarantees for gender equity, while also demonstrating the limitations of legal machinery alone in transforming the habitus embedded in the depths of individual and collective psyches (Núñez, this volume). An effective strategy must have at least two major components: (1) the revision of laws and public policy to guarantee formal gender equity, and (2) continuous educational campaigns in formal and informal environments, constant media reinforcement, and other sensitizing efforts that reinform the collective imaginary by demonstrating the benefits for women and men of modifying discriminatory and prejudicial perceptions, thoughts, feelings, and actions.

Autonomy was an excellent mode for sensitizing women to the inner workings of gender during the first few decades of second-wave feminism and has weathered the strategic shifts in the region's feminist and women's movements, continuing to be a valued strategy for women's deliberations in collective contexts. For the Latin American and Caribbean lesbian movement, for example, autonomy from gay men and feminist *others* has been central to establishing a proper identity profile as lesbian feminists. That identity interrogates the very category of gender, by crossing the boundaries that produce and reproduce heterosexual hegemony and shape dissident sexualities into peripheral and marginalized ones (Mogrovejo, this volume). It also infuses the notion of political body with a more complex and enriched proposal of citizenship.

For indigenous, Afro-Latin, and working-class women, autonomous practices based on the intersection of ethnicity or race, class, and gender also provide epistemic privilege for understanding the interrelationship and mutual reinforcement of these dimensions of exclusion in forging life experiences and reproducing the matrix of social power that consolidates national and local societies (Moya, quoted in Caldwell, this volume). As such, the Afro-Brazilian women's movement illustrates a double or triple militancy that addresses compounded life experiences of multiple subordinations and interrogates and informs monodimensional discourses of social oppression, singularly based on race, class, or gender (Caldwell, this volume). On the other hand, within the Ecuadorian indigenous movement, women's intersected dimensions of autonomous practice mediate multiple gender discourses that circulate at distinct cultural levels. A revised origin mythology of male-female complementarities is a central discourse at present that promotes ethnic unity and positions indigenous men as privileged allies, however not without an emerging awareness on the part of women of the need for more gender justice and equity within the confines of the ethnic community (Prieto et al., this volume). In Argentina, in autonomous women's caucuses linked to the diverse, class-oriented social movements that emerged from the chaotic conditions of the neoliberal experiment, working-class women deliberate their gender specificities and needs in a new version of popular feminism that promises to secure a far greater dose of gender consciousness and feminist resolve than its precursors of the 1980s (Di Marco, this volume, ch. 9).

Finally, in the midst of the multiple discursive perspectives attempting to forge a new paradigmatic alternative to neoliberal globalization, Latin America feminists share autonomous spaces with feminists from all over the world, negotiating premises, practices, and proposals for inclusion—not without dispute—in the general declarations of the alter-globalization movement. Although striving to surpass binary visions and insert gender parity into the very fabric of social justice, radical democracy, and freedom, as Chantal Mouffe (1999) suggests, the inner functioning of the political process—even a progressive one like the alter-globalization experience—seems to still depend on identity politics as a preferential method for communicating, negotiating, and building sociopolitical alternatives (Vargas, this volume).

Backlash: The Mark of Misogyny

Reaction to women's changing condition and feminism's proposals and progress has also been varied in expression, intention, and intensity. On the one hand, impulsive, unconsciously rooted and intensified, violent urges of misogyny threaten to discipline women's bodies, their use of public space, and their daily lives through extreme expressions of gender-based violence. New forms of ferociousness toward women have emerged over these last decades, together with an expansion in the more traditional modes of gender violence that historically have contributed to validating sexual hierarchies in family and intimate relationships. The feminist naming of gender-rooted female assassination as "femicide" references a practice that renders visible an exercise of social power that, in the last decades in Latin America, has taken on new characteristics and dimensions. Grotesque examples of misogyny have come to light, including severe sexual torture and the physical mutilation of thousands of young women in different geographic locations.

While Juarez, Mexico, has become internationally emblematic for this kind of gender brutality, El Salvador and Guatemala, among others, also report alarming statistics of female carnage (Carrillo and Chinchilla, this volume; Herrera, this volume). Although there appears to be an important link to the perversion of patriarchal patterns of organized crime consortiums that have become an integral part of the globalized economy, copycat femicide seems to speak to another substratum of gender dynamics. Gruesome levels of gender sadism are ritualized in anomic social behavior that is officially ignored or tolerated. Together with the increase in domestic violence in most Latin American and Caribbean societies, seemingly related to male frustration with limited economic opportunities, reconfigured gender roles, and renegotiated power (Safa; Colón and Poggio, both in this volume), this extreme form of gender brutality can be seen as a collateral backlash to the changing gender order.

On the other hand, multidimensional, technologically interconnected, internationally coordinated strategies based on religious beliefs now aim to revert or resignify gender advances by reconfirming traditional gender roles and values. Since the emergence of the second wave in the late sixties, the progressive honing of an essentialist counterdiscourse has consolidated an ideological backlash that stakes out the female body as one of its primary battlegrounds. Such was the case of the raped Nicaraguan girl, whose body became a disputed territory between feminists defending her right to a legal abortion for ethical, physical, and mental health reasons and embryonists, who reduced her being to a corporal vessel obliged to engender life, in spite of the brutal origin of that conception (Kampwirth, this volume).

This backlash reached its peak in the twenty-first century, with the rise to power of political projects linked to religious fundamentalism and conservative missions in various countries of this geopolitical region.[12] The elaboration of an integrated, interfaith, global oppositional strategy is particularly significant. Its sui generis discourse of human rights prioritizes the embryo's right to life above that of the woman's and places control of women's bodies, lives, health, and choices, together with human sexuality, at the center of one of the most fervent ideological confrontations of this century (Maier 2006, 419; Navarro and Mejía, this volume). The interconnectivity of cybertechnology facilitates regional and global networks that energize international organizations dedicated to disseminate a fundamentalist interpretation of the family, promote a traditional view of reproduction and marriage, and defend the exclusivity of heterosexuality. These organizations and networks have been particularly active in Latin America and the Caribbean.

The Vatican, its national functionaries and representatives, allied associations, and a slice of its faithful are leading the counteroffensive, together with some, but not all, of the evangelical religious expressions that have gained ground within the region's religious camp (Bourdieu 2006) during the past thirty years. They have been the primary organized opposition to the legalization of abortion in places such as Mexico City in 2007 (Navarro and Mejía, this volume), as well as vehemently vociferous actors in the public debates against reproductive rights. In countries such as Argentina, they have positioned themselves in national women's

Encuentros (Di Marco, this volume, ch. 9) and have lobbied, together with other stripes of religious fundamentalism, in United Nations conferences and committees, in favor of the traditional nuclear family perspective (Vargas, this volume). In contrast, as feminist Catholics, Catholics for the Right to Decide in Latin America has been in the forefront of some of the most confrontational reproductive rights debates in the region, demonstrating that diversity is also emblematic of the Catholic faith today, while embodying the tension between the paradigms that are fiercely competing today for the privilege of making sociocultural sense of contemporary reality.

Future Challenges

This anthology resumes five primary immediate challenges for advancing gender consciousness and equality in Latin America and the Caribbean: (1) the need for precise and extensive gender analysis as to the effects of globalization of women's and men's lives and the implications of those effects on gender and family relations; (2) the urgency to construct mediations and mechanisms that facilitate a renewed and respectful dialogue among women of different classes, ethnicities, races, and sexual orientation, to mention only some of the most significant dimensions of difference; (3) the development of new strategies for more active male participation in the discourses and practices of gender-inequity deconstruction; (4) protection and promotion of the international accords that have articulated a new gender paradigm; and (5) vigorous defense of the separation of church and state. These five aspects constitute a roadmap for promoting gender democracy in Latin American and Caribbean societies. Democratizing the sexual and emotional spheres of life, together with formal politics and economics, and promoting a horizontal rather than hierarchical notion of relations between men and women will "democratize democracy" (Giddens 2003, 76) and extend and enrich the idea of citizenship.

NOTES

1. In Cuba, for example, women constitute 75 percent of all enrolled university students studying for careers that require a degree (Núñez, this volume).

2. Authoritarian democracies produced a diversity of new female actors and representations, including feminists and Mothers' committees for the disappeared, among others.

3. Interestingly, there seems to be a contradiction between the real levels of gender discrimination that women experienced in armed movements and the impact of these new representations in bolstering women's self-esteem; interrogating the traditional, collective imaginary; and ultimately reshaping gender (Herrera, this volume).

4. See Di Marco (ch. 9), Macaulay, Rakowski and Espina, Herrera, Kampwirth, and Carrillo and Chinchilla, all in this volume.

5. The category of habitus refers to the psychocultural process that incorporates a binary gender system of perceptions, thoughts, emotions, and actions into the depths of individual psychological structures and the collective imaginary and somatizes it into corporal gestures and reflexes. This dual process of internalization and somatization guarantees the reproduction of an apparently natural and immutable gender division of life.

6. Although Cuba is a unique example of national development in Latin America and the Caribbean because of its socialist model, the reproduction of traditional gender power relations within the family, while women are fully integrated into the labor force and public life, is

indicative of the challenges facing the achievement of gender equity in traditionally *machista* cultures.

7. See Caldwell, Di Marco (ch. 9), Mogrovejo, Prieto et al., and Vargas, all in this volume.

8. Parts of this section are based on my article "A Modo de Conclusión: Reflexionando lo Aprendido" in Maier (2006).

9. See Herrera, Kampwirth, Macaulay, Maier, Tarrés, and Vargas, all in this volume.

10. See Carrillo and Chinchilla, Di Marco (ch. 9), Herrera, Lebon, Macaulay, and Rakowski and Espina, all in this volume.

11. It should be stressed, as Kampwirth (this volume) states, that not all women politicians and functionaries in Latin American and Caribbean counties have a gender perspective. On the other hand, growing numbers of men do. It may be time to institute a three-pronged strategy of interrelated and synergetic tactics and actors: feminist women's autonomy; gender mainstreaming; and autonomous, feminist, mixed groups of men and women, committed to developing gender-equitable societies.

12. In the United States, for example, the Bush administration's infusion of religion into the veins of the lay state favored fundamentalist policies that severely restrict reproductive and sexual rights and the availability of international funding for reproductive policies. Due to the influence of geopolitics in the region, reproductive and demographic programs have born the weight of these policy changes, frequently having to disband programs and moderate reproductive health discourses.

REFERENCES

Alvarez, Sonia, Evelina Dagnino, and Arturo Escobar. 1998. The cultural and the political in Latin American social movements. In *Cultures of politics/politics of cultures: Revisioning Latin American social movements*, ed. Sonia Alvarez, Evelina Dagnino, and Arturo Escobar, 1–32. Boulder, CO: Westview.

Bauman, Zygmunt. 2006. *Vida líquida*. Barcelona: Paidós.

Bourdieu, Pierre. 1996. La dominación masculina. *La Ventana*, no. 3:7–95.

———. 2006. Génesis y estructura del campo religioso. *Relaciones* 27 (108): 7–95.

Carrillo, Lorena, and Norma Stoltz Chinchilla. 2006. De femina sapiens a Kaqla: Treinta años de feminismo(s) en Guatemala. In *De lo privado a lo público: 30 años de lucha ciudadana de mujeres en América Latina*, ed. Nathalie Lebon and Elizabeth Maier, 221–235. Mexico City: Siglo Veintiuno.

ECLAC. 2006. *Statistical yearbook: Sixth reunion*. Santiago: ECLAC.

Giddens, Anthony. 2003. *Runaway world: How globalization is reshaping our lives*. New York: Routledge.

Hite, Amy Bellone, and Jocelyn S. Viterna. 2005. Gendering class in Latin America: How women effect and experience change in the class structure. *Latin American Research Review* 40 (2): 50–82.

Klein, Naomy. 2007. *The shock doctrine: The rise of disaster capitalism*. New York: Metropolitan Books.

Maier, Elizabeth. 2006. A modo de conclusión: Reflexionando lo aprendido. In *De lo privado a lo público: 30 años de lucha ciudadana de las mujeres en América Latina*, ed. Nathalie Lebon and Elizabeth Maier, 409–421. Mexico City: Siglo Veintiuno / UNIFEM / LASA.

Mouffe, Chantal. 1999. *El retorno de lo político*. Barcelona: Paidós.

Vargas, Virginia, and Saskia Wieringa. 1998. The triangle of empowerment: Processes and actors in the making of public policy for women. In *Women's movements and public policy in Europe, Latin America, and the Caribbean*, ed. Geertje Nijeholt, 3–23. New York: Garland.

United Nations. 2001. *From Beijing to Beijing +5*. New York: United Nations.

Notes on Contributors

NATHALIE LEBON (COEDITOR) is an anthropologist and an assistant professor in the Women, Gender, and Sexuality Studies Program and affiliated with the Latin American Studies Program at Gettysburg College, Pennsylvania, United States. Her work on Brazilian women's movements, and in particular on the process of professionalization, has been published in journals such as *Organization* and *Estudos Feministas*. Most recently, she has published "Beyond Confronting the Myth of Racial Democracy: The Role of Afro-Brazilian Women Scholars and Activists" in *Latin American Perspectives* in 2007. She is coeditor (with Elizabeth Maier) of *De lo Privado a lo Público: 30 Años de Lucha Ciudadana de las Mujeres en América Latina* (Siglo Veintiuno, 2006). Her current research focuses on the consolidation of popular and black feminisms in Brazil and the role played by professionalization and institutionalization in this process.

ELIZABETH MAIER (COEDITOR) is a sociologiest with a PhD in Latin American studies and works as a professor and researcher at the Colegio de la Frontera Norte (College of the Northern Border), Baja California, Mexico. She is a member of the Sistema Nacional de Investigadores (National System of Researchers); ex-cochair of the Gender and Feminist Studies Section of the Latin American Studies Association (2003–2005); author of multiple journal articles, book chapters, and books, including *Las Madres de los Desparecidos: ¿Un Nuevo Mito en América Latina?* (Jornada, 2001), *Género, Pobreza Rural y Cultura Ecológica* (Portrerillos, 1998), *Las Sandinistas* (Cultura Popular, 1986), and *Nicaragua: La Mujer en la Revolución* (Cultura Popular, 1980); and coeditor (with Nathalie Lebon) of *De lo Privado a lo Púbico: 30 Años de Lucha Cuiudadana de las Mujeres en América Latina* (Siglo Veintiuno, 2006). She is presently researching the twenty-first century's dispute for cultural meaning between feminisms and fundamentalisms and gender politics and policies at the local level.

SONIA E. ALVAREZ is the Leonard J. Horwitz professor of Latin American politics and society and the director of the Center for Latin American, Caribbean, and Latino Studies at the University of Massachusetts, Amherst, United States. She has written extensively about social movements, feminisms, NGOs, and transnational organizing and has been active in feminist, antiracist, and alter-globalization movements.

KIA LILLY CALDWELL is an anthropologist and teaches in the Department of African and Afro-American Studies at the University of North Carolina, Chapel Hill, United States. Her work has been published in journals in the United States and Brazil, and she is the author of *Negras in Brazil: Re-envisioning Black Women, Citizenship, and the Politics of Identity* (Rutgers University Press, 2007).

ANA LORENA CARRILLO works as a historian, professor, and researcher at the Instituto de Ciencias Sociales y Humanidades of the Universidad Autónoma de Puebla (Institute for Social Science and Humanities at the Autonomous University of Puebla), Mexico. She is a member of the Sistema Nacional de Investigadores (National System of Researchers) and author of *Las Luchas de las Guatemaltecas del Siglo XX: Mirada al Trabajo y la Participación Políticas de las Mujeres* (Ediciones del Pensamiento, 2004) and *Árbol de Historias: Historia y Literatura en Severo Martínez y Luis Cardoza y Aragón* (forthcoming).

NORMA STOLTZ CHINCHILLA is a professor of sociology and women's studies at California State University, Long Beach, United States. She is the author of *Nuestras Utopías: Mujeres Guatemaltecas de Siglo XX* (Terra Magma / Agrupación de Mujeres Tierra Viva, 1998), along with a number of articles on feminism and women's movements in Latin America. She is the coauthor (with Nora Hamilton) of *Seeking Community in a Global City: Guatemalans and Salvadorans in Los Angeles* (Temple University Press, 2001).

ALICE COLÓN is a researcher at the Centro de Investigaciones Sociales de la Universidad de Puerto Rico (Social Science Research Center at the University of Puerto Rico), Río Piedras. She is the author of books and articles on topics such as Puerto Rican and Caribbean women's participation in social processes, women's regional participation in labor markets, and reproductive rights. She is an ex-cochair of the Gender and Feminist Studies Section of the Latin American Studies Association (2004–2006) and a member of various feminist organizations.

CLORINDA COMINAO is an anthropologist, with a master's degree in social sciences at the Faculdad Latinoamericana de Ciencias Sociales (Latin American School of Social Science), Ecuador; and an honorable mention in ethnic studies. She specializes in themes such as urban indigenous (Mapuche) organizations, indigenous education, intercultural health, and Mapuche identity.

GRACIELA DI MARCO is a professor at Universidad Nacional de San Martín (National University of San Martin), Argentina, and the director of the Programa de Democratización de las Relaciones Sociales y el Centro de Derechos Humanos (Program for the Democratization of Social Relations and the Center of Human Rights). Her research addresses democratization, citizenship, women's rights, and social movements. She is the author of numerous books and articles, including, more recently, *Reflexiones sobre los Movimientos Sociales en Argentina* (Baudino, 2004) and *Democratización de las Familias* (UNICEF, 2005).

GIOCONDA ESPINA is a psychoanalyst and professor of feminist theory in women's studies at the Facultad de Ciencias Económicas y Sociales de la Universidad Central de Venezuela (Faculty of Economic and Social Sciences at the Central University of Venezuela). She was the coordinator of the master's program in women's studies and is the author of *Psicoanálisis y Mujeres en Movimiento* (Universidad Central de Venezuela, 1997), among other works.

ALEJANDRA FLORES is a professor of Spanish, with a master's degree in social sciences at Facultad Latinoamericana de Ciencias Sociales (Latin American Faculty of Social Sciences), Ecuador, and an honorable mention in ethnic studies. She is a Ford Foundation scholar and the coauthor of *Chacha Warami: Relaciones de Género en el Mundo Andino* and *Somos el Pueblo Aymará*.

MORENA HERRERA was a member of the Frente de Liberación Nacional Farabundo Martí (FMLN; Farabundo Martí National Liberation Front) during the 1980s and is the founder and ex-director of the women's NGO Las Dignas. She is also the founder of the Asociación Nacional de Regidoras, Síndicas y Alcaldesas Salvadoreñas (ANDRYSAS; National Association of Women City Council Members, Prosecutors, and Mayors), the Feminist Collective for Local Development, and the Union of Local Women's Organizations of El Salvador. Her research includes women's political participation and women's movements in El Salvador, and she is a consultant on gender equality for municipal and national public policy.

KAREN KAMPWIRTH is a professor of political science and the chair of the Latin American studies program at Knox College, Illinois, United States. She is the author, most recently, of *Feminism and the Legacy of Revolution: Nicaragua, El Salvador, Chiapas* (Ohio University Press, 2004) and *Mujeres y Movimientos Guerrilleros: Nicaragua, El Salvador, Chiapas y Cuba* (Plaza y Valdés, 2007) and the editor of *Gender and Populism in Latin America: Passionate Politics* (Penn State University Press, 2009).

FIONA MACAULAY is a political scientist and associate professor of development studies in the Department of Peace Studies, University of Bradford, United Kingdom. Her books and articles, including *Gender Politics in Brazil and Chile: The Role of Political Parties in Local and National Policy-Making* (Palgrave Macmillan, 2006), focus on gender rights, political representation, the impact of political parties on gender politics and women's machineries, access to justice, and domestic violence.

GINA MALDONADO has a master's degree in social sciences at the Facultad Latinoamericana de Ciencias Sociales (Latin American Faculty of Social Sciences), Ecuador, with an honorable mention in indigenous studies. She is the author of *Comerciantes y Viajeros: De la Imagen Etno-arqueológica de "lo Indígena" al Imaginario del Kichiwa Otavalo "Universal"* (FLACSO, 2004).

MARÍA CONSUELO MEJÍA is an anthropologist, with a master's degree and doctoral studies in Latin American studies. She has been the executive director of Catholics for the Right to Decide, Mexico, from 1994 to the present; a researcher at the Universidad Nacional Autónoma de México (National Autonomous University of Mexico) during fifteen years; and the senior program officer at the International Planned Parenthood Federation, Western Hemisphere Region, 2004. In 1998 she won the Amnesty International USA award for her work in defense of women's human rights.

MYRIAM MERLET was a researcher, with a master's degree in economics. She was the author of numerous articles on the status of women, a long-time feminist activist, and a member of the coordinating committee of the Organisation de défense des droits des femmes (Organization for the Defense of Women's Rights). Since 2006 she had been the chief of staff to the secretary of the Department for the Status of Women and Women's Rights, Haiti. Her death in the earthquake of January 2010 was a great loss for the women of Haiti and Haitian democracy.

NORMA MOGROVEJO is a professor and researcher at the Universidad Nacional Autónoma de México (National Autonomous University of Mexico) and a member of the Sistema Nacional de Investigadores (National System of Researchers). She is a lawyer, has a master's degree in sociology and a PhD in Latin American studies, and is the author of several books, articles, essays, and chapters about the Latin American lesbian movement, sexuality, and dissident identities.

MARYSA NAVARRO is the Charles Collins professor of history at Dartmouth College, New Hampshire, United States, where she has taught Latin American history since 1968. She is the founder of Dartmouth's women's studies program and Latin American studies program, ex-president of the Latin American Studies Association, president of the board of directors of Catholics for Choice, and member of the board of the Católicas por el Derecho a Decidir (Catholics for Choice), Mexico.

MARTA NÚÑEZ SARMIENTO is a professor at the Center for Studies of International Migrations at the Universidad de Habana (University of Havana), Cuba, with a PhD in economics and a master's degree in sociology; her research deals with gender topics in Cuba. She has been an adviser on gender for United Nations agencies, the Association of Caribbean States, and various NGOs. She has also worked as a diplomat for Cuba.

ANDREA PEQUEÑO has a master's degree in social sciences at the Facultad Latinoamericana de Ciencias Sociales (Latin American Faculty of Social Sciences), Ecuador, with an honorable mention in gender and development studies. She specializes in issues related to national, gender, and ethnic-racial identities and has recently published *Imágenes en Disputa: Representaciones de Mujeres Indígenas Ecuatorianas* (Abya-Yala, 2007).

SARA POGGIO is an associate professor of Spanish and social sciences at the University of Maryland, Baltimore County, United States; and an ex-cochair of the Gender and Feminist Studies Section of the Latin American Studies Association. Her research interests include transnational families and remittances, Latino immigrant children and school performance, Latin American women and politics, and immigration policy and cultural diversity.

MERCEDES PRIETO has a PhD in anthropology and is a professor in the Programa Estudios de Género de la Facultad Latinoamericana de Ciencias Sociales (Gender Studies Program at the Latin American Faculty of Social Sciences), Ecuador. Her current research interests center on gender relations and ethnicity and on the construction of national identity. She is cochair of the Gender and Feminist Studies Section of the Latin American Studies Association and coordinator of graduate studies at Facultad Latinoamericana de Ciencias Sociales, Ecuador.

CATHY A. RAKOWSKI is an associate professor of rural sociology and women's studies at Ohio State University, United States. She has conducted research in Venezuela since 1979 and her work focuses on processes of social change. Recent publications focus on gender, politics, organizing, and populism in contemporary Venezuela. She is working on a book on gender and decentralization in a planned industrial city.

HELEN SAFA is a professor emerita of anthropology and Latin American studies at the University of Florida, United States. She was the director of the Center for Latin American Studies at the University of Florida from 1980–1985 and president of the Latin American Studies Association from 1983 to 1985. In 2007 she received the Kalman Silvert prize, a lifetime achievement award, from the Latin American Studies Association. Her research has focused on gender, development, and race, particularly in the Caribbean.

MONTSERRAT SAGOT is a professor of sociology and women's studies at the Universidad de Costa Rica (University of Costa Rica) and a founding member of the anti–violence against women movement in Central America. She was a facilitator for some of the first support groups for abused women created in Costa Rica in the 1980s. She is the author of *The Critical Path of Women Affected by Family Violence in Latin America: Case Studies from 10 Countries* (Pan American Health Organization, 2000) and coauthor of *Femicidio en Costa Rica: 1990–1999* (Pan American Health Organization / INAMU, 2001).

MARÍA LUISA TARRÉS has a PhD in sociology and is a professor and researcher at the Centro de Estudios Sociológicos del Colegio de México (Center of Sociological Studies at the College of Mexico) and a member of the Sistema Nacional de Investigadores (National System of Researchers), Mexico. She has written several books, including, most recently, *Equidad de Género y Presupuesto Público: La Experiencia Innovadora de Oaxaca* (Instituto de la Mujer de Oaxaca, 2007) as well as a wide variety of journal and anthology articles on social movements, democratization, and citizenship among different group actors, especially women's groups.

VIRGINIA VARGAS is a sociologist, activist, and feminist theorist active in Peru, in Latin America, and in global spaces. She is a founding member of the Flora Tristán Center, Peru; a member of the Articulación Feminista Marcosur (MarcoSur Feminist Organization) in Latin America; and a globally active participant in the World Social Forum. She is a visiting professor at the Universidad Nacional Mayor of San Marcos (Major National University of San Marcos), Peru, and at other universities in Latin America and Europe.

Index

CPSIA information can be obtained at www.ICGtesting.com
Printed in the USA
BVOW011832241012

303789BV00003B/5/P